HEGEL'S LAWS

Jurists: Profiles in Legal History

William Twining, General Editor

Hegel's Laws

THE LEGITIMACY OF A MODERN LEGAL ORDER

William E. Conklin

STANFORD LAW BOOKS

An imprint of Stanford University Press

Stanford, California 2008

Stanford University Press
Stanford, California
© 2008 by the Board of Trustees of the Leland Stanford Junior
University. All rights reserved.

Library of Congress Cataloging-in-Publication Data

Conklin, William E.
   Hegel's laws : the legitimacy of a modern legal order / William E.
Conklin.
      p. cm. — (Jurists: profiles in legal history)
   Includes bibliographical references and index.
   ISBN 978-0-8047-5030-1 (cloth : alk. paper)
   1. Hegel, Georg Wilhelm Friedrich, 1770-1831.   2. Law—
Philosophy   I. Title.

K457.H43C66 2008

340'.1-dc22

                                                   2007040292

Printed in the United States of America
on acid-free, archival-quality paper

Typeset by Thompson Type in 10/13 Galliard

For Sabine

audentes Fortuna iuvat
—Vergil, *Aeneid,* X.284

Contents

Acknowledgments

This effort is an opportunity to look back on my own times when I was reading Hegel's works and reflecting about their relation to contemporary Anglo-American legal education, private law, constitutionalism, and international law. My experiences as a law student and law teacher ignited an interest in the possibility that there was more to the nature and identity of law than the analysis of rules immunized from the ethicality presupposed in the content of the rules. After teaching law for some years, I leapt back into the prelegal world of nineteenth- and twentieth-century phenomenology in the form of a PhD under the guidance of H. S. Harris, Millie Bakan, and Barbara Godard. Immersed in a teaching culture that warrants little interest or value in *Vernunft,* I am especially grateful to the following scholars who read at least one chapter and who offered detailed feedback from which the book was greatly improved: Douglas Moggach, Graeme Nicholson, Debra Cook, Robert Pinto, Roger Cotterrell, Walter Skakoon, Jonathan Lavery, Jeff Noonon, Henry Pietersma, John Russen, Kostas Calfas, and John Lunstroth. Numerous participants of my conference papers have helped to spot the need for clarification. An anonymous referee at an early stage, Alan Brudner and two later referees aided the effort in important respects as did Michael Salter and David Gray Carlson, both of whom offered important suggestions.

William Twining read the whole of an early draft and responded with detailed comments about style, structure, and argument. William's encouragement, since my early years of law teaching, remains especially appreciated. I have also greatly benefited from deep and heated discussions with my daughter, Annalijn, about Hegel's attitude toward women. Although she may still find my reading of Hegel's attitude toward women unsatisfactory, I hope that she and other women will find Hegel's perspective more difficult to address because of my response to Annalijn's vibrant input. The lady to whom I have dedicated this book, Sabine Grebe, continually egged me on with my German, German history, and Latin. Finally, I have been greatly helped by Randy Stevens, Margaret Pinette, Kate Wahl, and Amanda Moran, all of whom have been associated with Stanford University Press. All errors and errors of interpretation are my own.

William E. Conklin,
Law Faculty,
University of Windsor,
January 16, 2008

Key to Abbreviations

A: means an Addition (*Zusatz*) to *Philosophy of Right* by Hegel after the text was published and as incorporated by his student, Eduard Gans from Gans's Notes of Hegel's lectures.

CG: "The Constitution of Germany" [1798-1802] in Hegel, *Political Writings,* H. B. Nisbet trans.; Laurence Dickey and H. B. Nisbet, ed. (Cambridge: Cambridge University Press, 1999), 6-101. Cited by page number.

EL: G.W.F. Hegel: *Encyclopaedia of Logic* [*Lesser Logic*] (Part One of the *Encyclopaedia of Philosophical Sciences* with the *Zusätze*) [1817, 1826, 1830], trans. by T. F. Geraets, W. A. Suchting, and H. S. Harris (Indianapolis, IN: Hackett Publishing Co., 1991). Cited by paragraph number.

NL: *Natural Law* [1802-03], trans. by T. M. Knox with Introduction by H. B. Acton (Philadelphia: University of Pennsylvania Press, 1975). Cited by page number.

PH: G.W.F. Hegel, *Lectures on the Philosophy of World History: Introduction* [1822 & 1828, 1830], trans. by N. B. Nisbet with an Introduction by Duncan Forbes (Cambridge: Cambridge University Press, 1975). Cited by page number.

PM: *Hegel's Philosophy of Mind* (Part Three of *Encyclopaedia of the Philosophical Sciences* 1845, 1930] with the *Zusätze* in Boumann's Text (1845), trans. by William Wallace and A. V. Miller, with Foreword by J. N. Findlay (Oxford: Oxford University Press, 1971). Cited by paragraph number.

PR: G.W.F. Hegel, *Elements of the Philosophy of Right* [1821], ed. by
   Allen W. Wood & trans. by H. B. Nisbet (Cambridge: Cambridge
   University Press, 1991). Cited by paragraph number Remarks (R) by
   Hegel and Additions (A) as compiled by Gans. Translation is from
   Hegel *Vorlesungen über Rechtsphilosophie,* ed. K.-H. Ilting (Stuttgart:
   Frommann Verlag, 1974).

   W: G.W.F. Hegel, *Philosophy of Right,* trans. by Alan White
   (Newburyport, MA: Focus Philosophical Library, 2002).

   Knox: *Hegel's Philosophy of Right,* trans. with Notes by T. M. Knox
   (Oxford: Oxford University Press, 1942). References are cited as Knox.

   Dyde: G.W.F. Hegel, *Philosophy of Right,* trans. by S. W. Dyde in
   1896 and reprinted Amherst, NY: Prometheus, 1996. References are
   cited as Dyde.

PS: *Phenomenology of Spirit* [1807], trans. by A. V. Miller (Oxford: Oxford
   University Press, 1977). Cited by paragraph number.

R: means a remark or elucidation by Hegel. Hegel described the remarks
   as *Ammerkingen*

SL: *Hegel's Science of Logic* [1812-16], trans. by A. V. Miller (London:
   Humanities Press, 1969). Cited by page number.

1817/18: Lectures delivered in that year at Heidelberg and now translated
   in G.W.F. Hegel, *Lectures on Natural Right and Political Science,* trans.
   by J. Michael Stewart and Peter C. Hodgson (Berkeley: University of
   California Press, 1995). Cited by paragraph and line numbers.

1818/19: Lectures delivered in that year at Berlin University and included
   as an Appendix to Stewart and Hodgson above.

1819/20: Lectures delivered in that year and included in part as
   Supplements in White. References are to page numbers in White
   translation and based on students' transcriptions by Gans.

1822/23: Lectures delivered in that year and included in part as
   Supplements in White. References are to page numbers in White
   translation and are based on students' transcriptions by Gans. Wood
   also offers some translations of these lectures as an Appendix to PR
   cited above.

1824/25: Lectures delivered in that year and included in part as
   Supplements in White. References are to page numbers in White
   translation and based on students' transcriptions by Gans.

HEGEL'S LAWS

Introduction: Hegel's Crises

> As far as the individual is concerned, each individual
> is in any case a *child of his time*; thus philosophy, too,
> is *its own time comprehended in thoughts*. (PR 21)

The legal philosophy of Georg W. F. Hegel (1770–1831) responds to a formidable question, "why is a legal unit binding in a culture which ascribes to
the autonomy of a thinking being?" Conflicting interpretations of Hegel's
response have filled the academic journals and publishers' lists of many
languages. The responses to this question, though, have been generally
implicit. Apparently, grander issues have been at stake. Not least, in Anglo-
American commentaries, Hegel's legal philosophy has been held out as a
political apology for the repression by the Prussian state subsequent to the
publication of Hegel's *Philosophy of Right* in 1821.[1] Indeed, Hegel's *Philosophy
of Right* has been said to set the stage for the authoritarian and imperial-
ist National Socialist state.[2] Hegel's philosophy has also been offered as
the justification for war.[3] It has even been claimed as the philosophy for
the "total state which no longer knows anything absolutely nonpolitical,"[4]
a state which dominates all intermediate social organizations[5] and which
stands "qualitatively distinct from society and higher than it."[6] More recently, Hegel scholars have associated Hegel's philosophy with the liberal
freedoms of expression, the press, trial by jury, and legal equality.[7] And still
more recently, his *Philosophy of Right* has been said to explain, if not justify,
a philosophy of social freedom.[8] I shall take a different tack than the above
interpretations. Instead of concentrating upon the relationship of the individual vis-a-vis the state, I shall directly address Hegel's philosophy about
the nature and identity of law.

And here, Joseph Raz (1939–) and Carl Schmitt (1888–1985) aid us by
clarifying two very different projects for legal philosophy.[9] First, "what factors are incorporated into legal reasoning?" Today, this question addresses

whether legal reasoning works with rules, policy, principles, constitutional values, or other standards. This question concerns the identity of "what is a legal unit?" A great deal of Anglo-American jurisprudence discontinues any further inquiry. The second question addresses the nature of binding laws. Political philosophers and increasingly constitutional scholars have phrased this question in terms of "legitimacy" instead of authority. The legitimacy question asks, "why is a norm legally binding?" Contemporary Anglo-American general jurisprudence has frequently kept these two questions separate. Indeed, it is often accepted that the legal philosopher can respond to the first issue without having to be concerned with the second.[10] Hegel excoriates his contemporaries (philosophers, politicians, legal scholars, and judges), however, for believing that legality can be addressed without considering the legitimacy of a legal order. The nature of law is especially important because the Enlightenment had, in place of tradition, ushered forth the autonomy of the thinking being. Unless the philosopher or the jurist examined why laws were binding, legal formalism, and worse, political terror would result. The appeal to tradition, a priori duties, the original intent of the Founding Fathers of the state and a social contract neither explained nor justified nor obligated the individual to act. Such foundations of legitimacy were presupposed externalities to human experience. Legal obligation had to be located internal to the individual's act of thinking. The appeal to externalities to such consciousness avoided any such inquiry into the act of thinking that preceded the presupposed externalities. Hegel holds out that the legitimacy of an institutional order depends upon the extent to which an autonomous (*auto* signifying "self" and *nomos* signifying "legislating") individual bonds with such an order.

Legitimacy is not an academic issue for Hegel. For the Holy Roman Empire was dissolving before his eyes as Napoleon marched through his adopted town, Jena, in 1806, and when Napoleon then proceeded to displace the Empire with a very different form of legality (*Reichputation-shauptschluss*). This new sense of "what is a legal unit?"—accepted at the time in Spain, France, and England—was identified with the sovereign state. The state became the sole legal person in public international law. Although this state-centric international law was generated many centuries earlier in the city-state system of Renaissance Italy, this system had been recognized by the territories of Hegel's Europe with the signing of the Treaty of Westphalia, 1648. The state claimed the ultimate title to all territory which it physically possessed, a plenary legitimacy to posit laws prescribing and proscribing conduct for all inhabitants, a monopoly of force, a freedom of noninterference into its own domestic affairs, and a *domaine reservée* which included the authority (that is, legitimacy) to confer legal standing only to some inhabitants and not to others. This emerging state-centric European legal structure was not without its tensions with the Enlightenment conception of an autonomous subject. The state-centric structure also opened dreaded terror when romanticism and transcendental morality legitimized state action.

Hegel had to contend with the need to legitimize state-posited laws in a culture where the individual was autonomous of the state. Two responses addressed this issue in his day. The first one, a product of the Enlightenment, considered morality as generated from the rational will that was purged of all historically contingent content. Although posited laws were immersed in a phenomenal world, the legitimacy of posited laws was rooted in a priori concepts of morality external to human experience. The second tradition accepted the emotive values of conscience or of the *Volk* as the identity of a legal unit. The *Volk* also functioned as the source of legitimacy for the unit. The *Volk* was grounded in the customs of German principalities or even in the historical genesis of Germanic customs in Roman law. Hegel found both traditions one-sided. He feared that the ramification of the one-sidedness was state terror exemplified by the terror after the French Revolution. Hegel's response was to locate legitimacy in experiences and to reconcile the objectivity of institutions and posited laws with such experiences, by which he meant the self-consciousness of the autonomous subject.

Such an inquiry into legitimacy might well appear to the reader as impractical or even utopian. After all, laws are laws. Our time and energy ought to be focused upon the intricate network of rules in the vast subjects of "the Law." However, Hegel lived through trying personal and public crises when the legitimacy of legal structures was challenged and unclear. State violence dwelled around the corner of every individual action. Indeed, a study of Hegel's legal philosophy would be misdirected and shallow if Hegel's concern for the legitimacy of a legal order were pictured as one more exercise of an ivory tower intellectual aloof from the social and political crises of his day. To this end, I shall, in this Introduction, briefly outline several important personal and external influences that played important roles in the maturation of Hegel's legal philosophy. I shall especially focus upon Hegel's early life and education, his depressive personality, the political crises through which he lived, and the influence of the Enlightenment culture as represented by Immanuel Kant (1724–1804).

Hegel speaks to his time as well as to our own. As with the individual today, Hegel daily experienced the social and political crises which tested the legitimacy of customary norms and coded rules. His personal friends, his philosophical peers, his students, his adversaries, the traditions in which he was immersed, and his very personality were impacting upon traditional explanations as to why laws were binding upon inhabitants. His immediate environment was also bringing into question "what is the identity of a legal unit?" For, until the Enlightenment, the legal unit had invariably been considered the product of tradition.

Hegel's legal philosophy also speaks to our own times. Important elements of his philosophy in this respect are his exclusion of indigenous legal orders from the proper study of legal philosophy; his philosophic method; the nature of legal personhood; the doctrines of property, contract, crime, and family law; the role of the state; legal education; and public international law. Hegel's legal philosophy has implicitly, and perhaps unknowingly, influenced wave after wave of contemporary legal theory through such themes as law and morality, law and society, critical legal thought, semiotics of law, feminist legal thought, aboriginal law, critical race theory, and on it goes. Hegel's legal philosophy also speaks to our times because he challenges what contemporary legal philosophers, legal scholars, and judges often take for granted, particularly the binding character of a statutory provision or a judicial precedent. Hegel also speaks to our own time because his philosophic originality went hand in hand with personal hardship and a lack of professional recognition. Hegel's contemporaries only recognized his effort when at the age of forty-seven, despite sustained efforts beforehand, he received his first salaried position at a university. Hegel warrants recognition by Anglo-American philosophers and legal scholars today, however. His contribution to an understanding of the identity and nature of law is sometimes oversimplified, often rejected from fear of the unknown, and more often unknown. My effort aims to explicate why Hegel deserves such recognition in the contemporary Anglo-American world of legal philosophy and legal pedagogy.

I. HEGEL'S EARLY LIFE

Hegel was born in Stuttgart in the principality of Württemberg on August 27, 1770, and he died in November 1831. His father was a legally trained civil servant (secretary to the revenue office at the court). Although successful financially, as a bourgeois family, Hegel's parents remained socially and politically excluded from the local elite of nobles, the clergy, important rural magistrates, and local political leaders. His early life is fundamentally important in understanding his mature legal philosophy. Two elements are particularly relevant: his education and his university friends.

a) Hegel's Education

Hegel's early education was formidable. His mother taught him Latin at an early age and, more generally, inculcated the value of education, widely understood. His parents also paid for private mathematics lessons from a local teacher. He became immersed in the classical languages and literature while at the *Gymnasium Illustre*.[11] From 1788–93, he attended the theological seminary or *Stift* at Tübingen where his readings influenced his later development of an original legal philosophy. His teachers introduced him to the major figures of the French, English, and Scottish Enlightenment. From his study of Greek and Roman classics, Hegel came to appreciate the importance of the ethos in understanding why laws are binding. Taking a concept from Plato's *Laws*,[12] Hegel believed that the tribal member and the citizen of the polis felt so immediate with their customs and institutions that the customs and institutions seemed like "a second nature" (PR 151). It helped that Fate (*Moira*) protected the *nomoi* of the tribe. When the polis displaced the tribe as the form of social organization, city gods guided and protected the polis.[13] Aside from Greek and Roman classics, important Enlightenment readings also heavily influenced Hegel's mature legal philosophy. Hegel was initially exhilarated when, after reading Jean-Jacques Rousseau (1712–78), he believed that a community could be constituted from autonomous citizens. Johann Christoph Friedrich von Schiller (1759–1805) and Friedrich Heinrich Jacobi (1743–1819) were other Enlightenment influences. Baron de Montesquieu (1689–1755) greatly influenced Hegel's understanding of modern constitutional law. Most importantly, Hegel read and interpreted the works of Kant.

b) Influence of His University Friends

While at the *Stift*, Hegel teamed up with two fellow students: Frederich Hölderlin (1770–1843) and Friedrich Wilhelm Joseph Schelling (1775–1854). Their friendship figured in an important way in Hegel's eventual understanding of the possibility of friendship writ large in a community where each community member recognizes oneself through the other and vice versa. Hölderlin and Schelling also impacted Hegel's intellectual outlook. Perhaps most importantly, the threesome became alienated from the traditions and formalism of the *Stift*. Their teachers assumed and reinforced the validity of the values of tradition and hierarchy, both of which were rapidly changing and being destabilized by the Enlightenment. The teachers accepted nepotism, rather than merit, as the natural basis of reward in academia as well as in society generally.[14] H. S. Harris reports that, upon graduation from the *Stift*, Hegel concluded that he had wasted his time there.[15] His two friends, without a doubt though, were a source of intellectual stimulation. In particular, Schelling urged Hegel to read Kant's works. And Hölderlin, destined to become the famous poet, persuaded Hegel that something presubjective and preobjective drives a human being to recognize a stranger as a friend.

Hölderlin's influence on Hegel, as Hegel exemplified in his description of "the Beautiful Soul" in *Phenomenology of Spirit* (1806), was "immense."[16] The "something" that preceded the separation of a subject from objectivity was twofold: logic and, more deeply I shall argue, love.[17] As in the case of Diotima's description of eros in Plato's *Symposium*, love reconciled the body with the mind. With this insight in hand, Hegel displaced his own depression at the *Stift* by an enthusiasm for life.[18] At a philosophical level, Hegel explains in his works on logic as well as on law that legitimacy rests in the reciprocal recognition of one human being with a stranger. This reciprocal recognition raises the possibility of ethicality in an ethos, a possibility that I shall address in Chapter 6.

2. HEGEL'S IMMEDIATE LIFE

What drove Hegel to gain an extraordinary breadth of reading about the development of the human subject in Western culture? His depressive personality certainly played a part.[19] On leaving the *Stift*, Hegel had gained employment as a private tutor for a family in Berne (1793–96) and again in Frankfurt (1797–1800). On both occasions he soon became melancholic. From Hegel's viewpoint, the Berne family epitomized the social shallowness of the upper classes. While at Frankfurt, Hegel begged his friend Schelling to help him find a job elsewhere. By 1800, Hegel was thirty years old, unpublished, unemployed in academia, financially stressed (except for a small inheritance from his father), and denied any recognition as a philosopher. Pinkard suggests that Hegel came to realize by 1800 that he had been living in a daydream.[20] Schelling responded to Hegel's plea with the invitation for Hegel to be Schelling's *Privatdozent* at Jena (1801–07). To gain a license to teach, Hegel had to write an *Habilitation* (1800), and this he did on the subject of "On the Orbit of the Planets." Par for his career, the grant of Hegel's *Habilitation* involved him in a political struggle at the university. Hegel thereupon became an unsalaried "Extraordinary Lecturer" (he received no salary although he did receive compensation based on the number of students who attended his lectures). When the University of Jena collapsed with Napoleon's march into Jena in 1806, Hegel's friends also left the city. Loneliness overtook his day-to-day life. And once again depression set in. Although several factors no doubt led to his depressive condition during his early life in Jena, it did not help that he remained professionally unrecognized, socially isolated from university life, psychologically deprived of the friendship with his friend Hölderlin—who was deteriorating into madness—imbued with self-doubt about his own intellectual capacities, conscious of his finiteness, and weighed down with jealousy towards his old school friend Schelling who—five years his junior—had been recognized as the leading intellectual during the 1790s.[21] In 1805, to add salt to the wound, Hegel lost the one university position that opened for competition in his field. In late 1807 Hegel departed from Jena to become a newspaper editor at Bamberg and then, from 1808–16, to be headmaster of the leading German gymnasium at Nürnberg. Once again, depression overtook his life.

Hegel's mature legal philosophy, crystallizing in *Philosophy of Right* (1821), was, however, more than the outcome of the influence of two friends and a depressive personality. Indeed, Hegel later described his move to Jena in 1801, the center of German cultural life and, in particular, of German romanticism, as the "turning-point" of his intellectual development.[22] Once in Jena, Hegel published his first book, *The Difference between Fichte's and Schelling's Systems of Philosophy* (1801).[23] Although Hegel found it necessary to address Schelling's privileging of nature as the foundation of the legitimacy of a legal order, Hölderlin's preoccupation with love also found its place in Hegel's early theological writings and in his "Natural Law" essay of 1802–03.[24] Until Napoleon disrupted their lives in 1806, Hegel regularly met and talked with Johann Wolfgang von Goethe (1749–1832), Johann von Herder (1744–1803), Schelling, Frederich Schlegel (1772–1829), Friedrich Schleiermacher (1768–1834), and Christoph Wieland (1733–1813). As an example of the influence of the Jena milieu, Schelling and Hegel edited a journal, the *Critical Journal of Philosophy*, from 1801 until 1803. Goethe, the Schlegel brothers, and Novalis (1772–1801) especially influenced Hegel's ideas during the first two years in Jena (1801–03). And Herder, a former student of Kant, added to the intellectual stimulation.

Surrounded in Jena by the leaders of German romanticism, Hegel soon became aware that, despite the autonomy of the Enlightenment subject, human beings were alienated from their institutions and laws. This brought his views into conflict with Johann Gottlieb Fichte (1743–1819) whose focus on rights helped to instill legal formalism. Hegel's concern with social alienation also set him against Schelling's reliance on nature as the ultimate source of legitimacy because nature, like rights, was external to human experience. Fichte's and Schelling's approaches to the philosophy of law were equally one-sided. Both associated the legitimacy of law in an external presupposition separate from human consciousness. When Hegel turned to the possibility of legitimacy in the human conscience of subjectivity, best represented by the historical school of law and founded by Gustav Hugo (1764–1844) during Hegel's Jena period, one-sidedness again characterized the discipline of legal philosophy. In this case, though, legitimacy was tilted towards the arbitrary and nonsystematic posit of the content of customary norms. The spirit of the *Volk* displaced Fate as the determinant of human action.[25] But the *Volk* lacked coherency with the Enlightenment's notion of a self-determining individual. Jacob Friedrich Fries (1773–1843) simplified the ad hoc and arbitrary romanticism of subjectivity.

In sum, Hegel's contemporaries either favored formalism to the exclusion of social relationships, as in the case of Kant and Fichte, or formalism to the exclusion of self-reflection, as in the case of Fries and the historical school of the *Volk*. Hegel's dissatisfaction with the dominant intellectual (and political) views of the state is reflected in his early essays such as "The German Constitution" (1798–1802).[26] The engine for his critique of contemporary political-legal thought was the need for philosophers to address the social-cultural context in which state officials and the individual subject were situated and to do so by observing whether and the extent to which the individual recognized a stranger as self-determining. At a macro level, this reciprocal recognition was manifested by the extent to which subject and stranger shared state-centric institutions and laws as their own. In *Philosophy of Right* many years later, Hegel called this reciprocal recognition between subject and stranger "ethicality" or "ethical life."

The notion of ethicality generated Hegel's reappraisal of Kant's separation of phenomena from a *noumenal* realm, Fichte's rights thesis, Schelling's association of legitimacy with nature, the historical school's acceptance of unsystematic customs, and Fries' romantic appeal to the *Volk*. Each approach grounded legitimacy in a presupposition external to human consciousness.[27] With the notion of ethicality in hand, Hegel proceeded to examine how individuals recognized each other through the mediation of shared institutions and posited laws. Neither a priori reasoning nor rights nor nature nor customs nor the people nor the state nor even God could legitimize a state-centric legality because each approach presupposed a source of legitimacy external to a reflective human consciousness.[28] Instead, Hegel's legal philosophy remained in social phenomena. Hegel argued that the legal scholar and philosopher should observe how individuals share universals in such phenomena. At the same time, though, Hegel realized that the philosopher could not know a particular experience without thinking about concepts that mediated between the particular immediacy of the experience and the objective world of institutions and laws.

Hegel's own immediacy with the objective world was influenced by his professional university experiences, which were no less vicious to an aspiring intellectual than they often are today in the legal academe. Foremost in Hegel's professional experience was Fries' effort to undermine Hegel's academic career. In 1805, Hegel had hoped to gain a university professorship at Heidelberg University since he was the oldest *Privatdozent* at the University of Jena. He wrote to many friends and contacts, including Goethe who was very influential in higher education in Jena and, apparently, in Heidelberg.[29] Fries obtained the position to Hegel's bitterness. Fries thereupon proceeded to obstruct Hegel's professional advancement for fifteen years until Hegel finally received a professorship at Heidelberg (ironically replacing Fries who had moved on to Jena) in 1817.[30] Their extraordinary contempt for each other worked its way into print. In his *Science of Logic*, Hegel described Fries' *System of Logic* as "insignificant," resting upon "anthropological foundations" and the "superficiality of the notion" (*Vorstellung Oberflächlichkeitder*).[31] In an 1811 letter to Friedrich Immanuel Niethammer (1766–1848), his friend from the *Stift* and his loyal patron (as well as a leading student of theology and another former resident of Jena), Hegel expressed utter disdain for Fries' effort to be a philosopher.[32] Fries, in turn, worked to prevent any philosopher from reviewing Hegel's *Logic* (1812, vol. 1) and, ultimately, Fries himself delivered a negative review of the text two years after it had been published.

Against the background of the rare congregation of leading intellectuals in Jena, Hegel surprisingly became deeply distressed once more.[33] He was so desperate, when he lost out to Fries for the Heidelberg chair in 1805, that he pressed the polymathic Goethe, then the minister of education for the region, that Heidelberg needed a speculative philosopher of nature to replace a departing botanist. Hegel would lecture about the philosophy of nature and, in addition, would maintain the botanical gardens. To no avail.[34] His inability to gain the Heidelberg chair joined with the exodus of his friends from Jena following the Battle of Jena in 1806, as noted above, to drive him into another depression. Hegel was left socially isolated once again from intellectual life. His financial situation now became critical.[35] He literally begged for money from Niethammer.[36] Terry Pinkard suggests that by 1806 a less ambitious academic might easily have resigned himself to being what I privately consider a part-time full-timer. But, withdrawn, passive and self-absorbed, Hegel immersed himself in writing *Phenomenology of Spirit* (1807). Hegel rushed the second half of his classic to the publisher so that he could receive an advance on the sales upon completion of the book.[37] Hegel's book, though, went largely unnoticed. More, Schelling, his school friend and mentor when he was a *Privatdozent*, interpreted the classic as a personal attack against himself.[38] Their friendship dissolved. To add to all the professional and financial disappointments, Hegel had had a liaison with his maid, Christina Charlotte Johnson Burckhardt, who, in turn, produced a son (Ludwig Fischer) on February 5, 1807, two weeks after Hegel had completed *Phenomenology*.[39] Hegel initially felt obligated to the (now familiar term today) "that woman" as he was later to call her just before his marriage to Marie von Tucker.[40] Harris reports, however, that Hegel saw no problem with this illegitimate offspring.[41]

Once again, to escape from depression (and financial desperation) in 1807, Hegel moved to Bamberg where, with the aid of his patron Niethammer once again, he became the town's newspaper editor from March 1807 until December 1808. His editorials emphasized his early interest as to why feudal customs or enactments posited by legislatures would be binding upon autonomous citizens. He also expressed how social recognition could anchor such a binding character to laws. Social bonding with institutions generated legal legitimacy. Unhappy as an editor, Hegel moved to Nürnberg in 1808 where, once again with Niethammer's help (this time as the central commissioner for Education and Consistory in Munich), Hegel was appointed the rector (headmaster) of the leading Gymnasium of Bavaria (1808–1816). Here, Hegel institutionalized a classical and philosophical education at the secondary school level, teaching philosophy himself.[42] As headmaster, Hegel wrote and published *Science of Logic* (1812–14). Even his marriage in 1811 to Marie von Tucker, the daughter of a local merchant and twenty years his junior, did not end his bouts of depression. He confided in correspondence with his future wife in the summer of 1811 that happiness in life would invariably include some melancholy.[43] His tenure as headmaster eventually led, once again, to depression.

The exiled scholar continually applied for academic appointments. Only in 1817, at the age of forty-seven, did Hegel receive his first salaried professorship. The call came from Heidelberg University. His lectures on the philosophy of law, parts of which are now translated into English and which I incorporate into this work, urged that the philosopher retrieve how the individual's consciousness recognizes strangers through the shared mediating institutions that his contemporaries had heretofore externalized from human consciousness.[44] In addition to his lectures, beginning in 1817, Hegel expounds his philosophy of law in two sets of texts: first, *Science of Logic*, published in three volumes between 1812 and 1816[45] supplemented in the more accessible *Encyclopaedia Logic* or *Lesser Logic,* which was first published in 1817 with new editions in 1827 and 1830;[46] second, *Philosophy of Right*, which was published in 1821.[47] The *Science of Logic* and the *Philosophy of Mind* (section two of part III of the *Encyclopaedia Logic*) concentrate upon the logic of freedom in an individual's consciousness. Hegel calls this subjective freedom. Subjective freedom concerns how the thinking subject recognizes her- or himself as free through self-consciousness. The *Philosophy of Right* concerns objective freedom. By objective freedom, Hegel examines how the thinking subject recognizes her- or himself through institutional universals shared with strangers. Such universals include statutes, customs, institutional practices, religious practices, personal and collectively shared values, and cultural assumptions and expectations. Objective freedom raises the issue of the legitimacy of institutions and their laws in a culture of the autonomous thinking individual.

In 1818, shortly after being appointed to Heidelberg University, Hegel was invited to Berlin to take the most prestigious philosophy chair in the German principalities of the day. When Hegel refused the call, the minister (von Alterstein) offered to supplement Hegel's income. One "carrot" was for Hegel to become the examiner for the state's Examination Board. Another carrot involved extra travel grants (including one to a spa). Hegel accepted the offer. His Berlin *Inaugural Lecture* of 1818, three years before the publication of *Philosophy of Right*, introduced his mature legal philosophy.[48] Here, Hegel openly contrasted his own "philosophical jurisprudence" with the empty legal formalism of Kant and Fichte, the nonreflective historicism of Friedrich Karl Savigny (1779–1861), and the arbitrary subjectivism of Fries. The *Inaugural Address* exclaimed how "the urgency of the times" had regrettably conferred "great importance on the *petty* interests of everyday life" to the exclusion of the "*political totality of national life and of the state,*" which lay behind "the *high interests* of actuality."[49] The traditional legal philosophies had concentrated upon the identity of law rather than upon the implied legitimacy of a modern state-centric legal order. Each traditional approach had appealed to an external presupposition—nature, the good will, the *Volk*, and conscience—as the legitimating source of legality. Legality implied legitimacy, and legitimacy begged the philosopher to ask how freedom was manifested through shared institutions.

3. THE ENLIGHTENMENT

Hegel's early education, his peers, and his bouts of depression had left an indelible mark upon the young Hegel. But he was also a child of his times. Kant and Rousseau became his antagonists as he worked out a legal philosophy. Kant represented the Enlightenment. The Enlightenment functioned as background to his critique of romanticism. The French Revolution, in turn, profoundly impacted upon his belief in freedom. The French Terror, which he attributed to Rousseau, raised his fears of subjective arbitrariness behind legal formalism. Napoleonic generated reforms in his province of Württemberg and in Prussia raised his hopes that a legal order could reconcile subjectivity with the institutions of the state.

(a) The Enlightenment

The Enlightenment had opened all ideas and all social assumptions to rational criticism. These assumptions protected feudalism, the church, specific customs, the divine right of kings, and tradition more generally. Rational criticism took two forms. The first form critiqued the laws of nature, such as the law of gravity and the divine right of kings, as external standards to evaluate the content of human laws. It was not easy, for example, to evaluate the laws of nature since they transcended human action (PR Pref. 13A). The second questioned the deeply felt beliefs nested in tradition and feudalism.[50] The Enlightenment now considered the individual as the author of her or his own beliefs. The rational critique of tradition opened the possibility that the individual could control her or his own future. But if the individual could determine her or his own future, the individual could be free.

The problem with such Enlightenment thinking was that one's thinking invariably assimilated bodily passions, inclinations, preferences and the like. Immanuel Kant entered the Enlightenment at this point. One could be morally free, according to Kant, if reason were cleansed of all such bodily inclinations. Moral persons were equal because they lacked a personal biography or context-specific experiences. But because humans invariably bring bodily inclinations into moral actions, the universal laws could, at best, be duties that the moral person *ought* to perform.

The consequence was important for the relationship between laws and morality. Both were the objects of human action. The moral laws were possible reasons for action, although individuals do not know why they act the way they do. Laws were posited by institutions: such institutions had to replicate the idealized Idea of a moral order. Since the empirical content of such moral laws was immaterial, the content of legally binding laws was also immaterial. As Hegel quotes from Kant, since this reasoning "involves abstracting from the whole content of knowledge (although truth is concerned with precisely this content), it is quite impossible and absurd to ask for a test of the truth of the content" (NL 123). The institutional rules had to cohere with the Idea of the moral order. Thus, the inclinations, being externalized from moral maxims of a rational person, were immaterial in an authoritative legal order. A rule would be binding despite the inclinations of the individual. Indeed, the separation of legitimacy from the bodily inclinations of phenomena risked that institutional laws would become dead. Another implication, though, was that legal reasoning was instrumental vis-à-vis the Idea from the *noumenal* realm of an ideal moral and legal order. The binding character of a posited rule lay beyond the control of institutional actors. The appeal to the *noumenal* source of legitimacy in Kantian philosophy had to be reconciled with the phenomenal contingency of legality. Legal reasoning became a matter of skills training and the intellectual differentiation of concepts. Hegel describes this, as I shall elaborate in Chapters 3 and 8, as *Verstand*. The externality of legitimacy in the externality of a noumenal realm fomented a problematic education that I shall address in Chapter 9.

b) French Revolution and Terror

Hegel's childhood was experienced during the upheaval of two revolutions, the American in 1776 and the French in 1789. The French Revolution profoundly impacted upon Hegel (and his friends) at Tübingen (1788–93).[51] Shortly after the Revolution, Hegel and his friends believed that the Revolution would restore the peaceful (or what he describes in *Phenomenology of Spirit* as) beautiful life of the *bon sauvage* of Periclean Athens. The Revolution had broken down the old feudal hierarchy that had deferred to the divine authority of a monarch. Feudal principalities had dissolved into the state of "France" where the former serf had become a "Frenchman." The Frenchman was free and equal with other Frenchmen. The prospect of freedom, held out by the French Revolution, remained with Hegel throughout his writings about law. How could the thinking individual be free if the sovereign state claimed a plenary of legal authority, title to all territory within its jurisdiction, a monopoly of force, and an arbitrary will as the sole source of legality? How could the thinking individual be free if the state were considered external to human consciousness?

The French Revolution left its mark upon Hegel's legal philosophy in three ways. First, the Revolution demonstrated that objectivity could evolve into an empty shell as did the feudal legal structure. Second, for a legal order to remain legitimate, the individual had to recognize her- or himself in others and others in her- or himself. In this way, the shared institutions and posited laws would mediate social relationships and yet, be the consequence of the self-determination of the individual. Third, the role of an institution had to be situated in the structure of consciousness that individuals presupposed.

Against the background of these three factors, the philosopher's role was retrospectively to retrieve the boundaries of structures of consciousness. What was a vibrant structure in one era might become a mere shell in a later one. As Hegel writes about his own epoch in his Preface to *Philosophy of Right*, "the culture [*Bildung*] of the present age has taken a new direction, and thought has adopted a leading role in the formation of values . . . Correct thinking is knowing [*das Kennen*] and recognizing the thing, and our cognition should therefore be scientific" (PR Pref. 14). An implied structure of consciousness was deep and vibrant because of its immanence through human experience. Accordingly, it was absurd for political leaders to cleanse a society of all its institutions and then to claim to have founded "the constitution" as did the American and French revolutionary rulers: "no state or constitution had ever previously existed or were in existence today, but that we had *now* (and this 'now' is of indefinite duration) to start right from the beginning, and that the ethical world had been waiting for such intellectual constructions, discoveries, and proofs as are *now* available" (PR Pref. 12).

A presupposed structure of legal consciousness was located in the socially and historically contingent circumstances of an ethos. The philosopher's consciousness of time exposed the extent to which new structures of consciousness emerged from the shapes of old ones. How an observed individual recognized a stranger was also situated in such time-consciousness. Statutes, customs, judicial precedents, religious practices, traditions, rituals and the like manifested the extent of the reciprocal recognition between thinking subject and stranger.

The French Revolution impacted upon Hegel's legal philosophy for another set of reasons: the Terror. Hegel's personal memory of the Terror remained with him throughout his life. When Hegel interpreted the works of Savigny, best known today as the representative of the historical school of jurisprudence,[52] Hegel envisioned another self-styled philosopher who was contemptuous of the lessons of the Terror. Similarly, when Hegel read Fries' efforts at philosophy, Hegel found a polemical forensic rhetoric which raised the prospect of arbitrariness and, indeed, terror. When Hegel considered Fichte's rights thesis, Hegel remembered how the social-cultural practices of everyday life were alienated from the universal claims of the Revolution. More generally, a legal order based upon the idea of a social contract, so endearing to the French Revolution, lacked any legitimacy as a structure greater than the sum of particular arbitrary wills. A contract was a mere shell that institutionalized the self-interests of monadic individuals. Hegel went so far as to suggest in his mature legal philosophy that Rousseau's social contract played a role in fomenting the Terror, in Hegel's view (PR 258A).[53] Hegel desired to explicate a legal philosophy where individuals inwardly desired to recognize strangers so that a community, a "we," would exist.

Napoleon raised the possibility and the prospect of legal formalism. Hegel had been initially excited about Napoleon's liberation of the German populace from the social and economic constraints of feudalism and from the chaos of disparate semisovereign principalities. He described Napoleon at one point as "the great professor of constitutional law."[54] Napoleon codified laws and, more generally, he held out the possibility that Germans could rationally control their destiny as a nation. Hegel hoped that Prussia would emulate Napoleon's centralizing reforms, including a public service which served the shared interests of each and all and which was employed on the basis of merit, public deliberation, the rule of law, and the rational codification of laws. With Napoleon's victory over the German principalities, Hegel wrote in a letter dated January 27, 1807, "there can be nothing more convincing than this history to show that education triumphs over rudeness, and spirit over spiritless understanding and mere cleverness [i.e., *Verstand*]. Science [i.e., *Vernunft*] alone is the [true] theodicy, and she will just as much keep us from . . . making the fate of empires depend on the occupation or non-occupation of a hill."[55] Philosophy could become socially "actual" (a special term that I explain in the next chapter) by concentrating upon the act of thinking.

4. LOCAL POLITICS

The background of the Enlightenment, the French Revolution, and Napoleon offered a momentary space of optimism for freedom. Hegel frequently reminds us, citing Grotius (1583–1645), that Germany could become a state in the interstate system of equal sovereign states.[56] If only Germany became a state like France, Spain, and England after the Treaty of Westphalia in 1648, Germany would be free vis-à-vis other states. The governments of Württemberg and of Prussia, however, exhibited corruption, nepotism, social hierarchy, and provincialism. Instead of a unified, self-determining state, Germany was governed by many principalities whose rulers accepted the suzereignty of the Austro-Hungarian emperor as the agent of God. The Holy Roman Empire ruled the territory of "Germany" through the local nobles. The Empire claimed title to lands, obedience by the inhabitants, and a monopoly of violence even though the Empire lacked legitimacy (GC 14, 35–40). To be sure, the political and religious principalities at the end of the eighteenth century were, in a sense, "states": the kingdoms of Württemberg, Bavaria, and Prussia were examples. Trade barriers, however, obstructed the travel and commerce between them. Each principality had its own local customs. The Holy Roman Empire collapsed when Napoleon dissolved the religious principalities in 1806 and assigned title to all lands to the secular principalities. Some new secular principalities had few inhabitants. The Duchy of Liechtenstein, for example, had only 5,000 inhabitants.[57] Similarly, in the early nineteenth century, the Duchy of Nassau was composed of twenty-three previously independent entities.[58] In 1813, a federation, the Rheinbund, had thirty-nine states within its territory. A customs union, *Deutscher Zollverein*, was established in 1830. In 1866 Austria succumbed to Bismarck's Prussia. The idea of a unified sovereign state of Germany was hardly imaginable in the late eighteenth century.

The consequence was that, unlike England, France, Spain, and the Netherlands, the principalities remained excluded from the international (or better described as the *ius publicum Europaeum*) legal order. Hegel feared that the inhabitants of the principalities would remain forever stateless.[59] Two of Hegel's early essays—"On the Recent Internal Affairs of Württemberg, in particular the inadequacies of the municipal constitution" (1798)[60] and "The German Constitution" (1798–1802)[61]—reflect Hegel's utter exasperation with the stateless condition of Württemberg. Hegel condemned the retention of feudal forms because they were so estranged from the beliefs, feelings, and autonomy of the serf. Hegel was puzzled as to why a thinking being would be bound to the edicts of a principality which, in turn, was a mere formal shell and a shell at that for a foreign empire.

Both the Enlightenment and romanticism destabilized the legitimacy of the Holy Roman Empire. The key to the legitimacy of law, according to Hegel, lay in the subjective experiences of the inhabitants. Philosophers had failed to recognize this newly emerging sense of legitimacy. They had been content with presuppositions, external to the reflective subject of the Enlightenment, such as the objectivity of a priori concepts (Kant and Fichte), the historical customs of the *Volk* (Savigny), and the arbitrary will of conscience (Fries). As long as an institutional structure and its posited laws remained external to the individual's experience, the individual would not be free. So too, as long as subjectivity grounded legitimacy, there would remain the risk that terror would displace freedom.

The kernel of Hegel's puzzle, then, lay in the contradiction between the externality of the formal "state" and its posited laws on the one hand and the subjectivism of the Enlightenment and French Revolution on the other. This contradiction would remain as long as philosophers were unconcerned with social relationships as represented through shared universals manifested in institutions, statutes, customs, and religious practices. The "state of nature" tradition of Hobbes, Locke, and Rousseau confounded the contradiction of objectivity with subjectivity because the state of nature presupposed beings that were abstracted from their individual biographies, language, intersubjective social relations and an ethos. A focus upon such abstract persons avoided the social dynamics nested in the legitimacy of a modern legal order. Hegel's insight was to undermine the contradiction by incorporating the objectivity of institutions and their laws into the consciousness of the individual and to do so in the context of an historically contingent ethos. The private realm would thereby become public. The individual would be at home in the reflective ethos which displaced the arbitrary will of the individual. Although the arbitrary will would have its day in what Hegel called "civil society," the reflective ethos was an organic legal order. An organic legal order would have a public character which would be greater than the sum of private interests (GC 77). As I shall explain in Chapter 4, when the individual acts against the shared norms of the public, she or he challenges the very legitimacy of the objectivity constructed by human consciousness.

The separation of subjectivity from objectivity destabilized what philosophers had heretofore assumed to explain the legitimacy of an institutional legal order. The most important essays in this respect were "The German Constitution" (1798–1802) and "Natural Law" (1802–03). Chapters V and VI of *Phenomenology of Spirit* (1806), however, offered profound insights into the legitimacy of ancient tribal, Greek, Roman, and contemporary European legal structures of consciousness. His studies of logic set the groundwork for his critique and departure from the traditional approaches to legal philosophy. In particular, in section two of part three (*Philosophy of Mind*, 1817) of his *Encyclopaedia*, Hegel shifted his logic from the intersubjective relations within the consciousness of individuality to the relation of such an individual to the institutional structure and the posited laws of a modern state. In the 1817–18 academic year at Heidelberg, Hegel began to lecture about the philosophy of law. He also embarked upon writing *Philosophy of Right* in that year, submitted the manuscript to the printer in 1819, withdrew it, wrote a Preface in 1820, and had the book published in 1821. Hegel continued lecturing about the philosophy of law at Berlin.[62] His eight sets of lectures, his early essays, his works on logic, and *Philosophy of Right* are seeped with insights about how the legality issue merges into the legitimacy issue. As examples of his analysis, Hegel demonstrates an extraordinary breadth of awareness about Roman law and contemporary English constitutional law as well as the legal systems of other territories of the world.

Hegel had a model constitutional regime from which to draw for his effort to break from the traditional legal philosophies of his day. In 1807, Baron Heinrich Karl vom Stein (1757–1831) became the chief minister of Prussia, although he was dismissed after only fourteen months in office. In his short time in office, Stein abolished serfdom. In particular, he abrogated the feudal land tenure system and all land distinctions throughout Prussia. He also worked to ameliorate class distinctions, to institutionalize merit in the military, to strengthen cabinet government, to constitutionalize liberal rights (including the protection of Jews), and to repeal tariffs. However, when Napoleon intercepted a letter where Stein predicted a nationalist uprising, Napoleon declared him an enemy of the French state. Stein resigned in November 1808 and journeyed to Russia in January 1809 where he served the Czar for many years.

Stein's short-lived liberal regime did not end the story. From 1810 until 1822, Karl August von Hardenberg (1750–1822) became prime minister (*Staatskanzler*) of Prussia. Hardenberg continued Stein's domestic reforms. Further, after the wave of nationalism and xenophobia against the French in 1813–15, the king of Württemberg, Friedrich II (1754–1816), attempted to institute constitutional reforms again. Friedrich II wished to constitutionalize legal equality, repeal restrictions against Catholics, and open opportunities for Jewish peoples to participate in government. The king, without consulting the Diet, posited a new liberal Constitution in 1815, expecting the Diet to approve it. The Diet, dominated by the estates (an institution I shall describe in Chapters 8 and 9) and the Protestant Church, rejected the Constitution. The "old" Constitution was consolidated. Friedrich died on 30th October 1816. Famine spread in 1817. The newly appointed King

Wilhelm I declared another new Constitution in 1817. He liberalized freedom of the press and aimed to create a new sovereign state of Württemberg against the objections of the old landed estates. These efforts to legitimize a liberal legal order lay in the background to Hegel's legal philosophy.[63]

In reaction to Napoleon's military conquests over Germanic principalities, anti-French nationalist sentiment erupted in Germany during 1813–15. When the Congress of Vienna proposed a German confederation in 1815, nationalism and anti-Semitism exploded among the student fraternities of the Protestant German universities (*Burschenschaften*), which had always excluded Jewish and foreign students. By this time, Hegel's old rival, Fries, had become the leader of the new romanticist political movement.[64] In 1816 Fries had published an anti-Semitic pamphlet where he had attacked "Jewishness" because, he alleged, Jewishness formed a state within a state.[65] On October 17–19, 1817, the anniversary of Luther's translation of the Bible into German, students and some professors met at the Wartburg Castle. Patriotic speeches were the name of the day. The *Code Napoleon*, the *German Police Laws*, and "un-German" books such as those of Karl Ludwig von Haller were burnt. The fraternities demanded a flag of black, red, and gold to stand for the unity of the German Reich. Fries inflamed the participants by appealing to the emotional and nationalistic life of the German *Volk*. The *Volk* alone, he claimed, provided the legitimacy for all German laws.[66] One of Fries' students advocated the "noble deed" of assassination in a "theory of individual terror." Some months later (March 23, 1819), a Burschenschaftern, Karl Ludwig Sand, a playwright, murdered August Kotzebue, who was suspected of being a Russian spy.[67] When stabbing Kotzebue, Sand, a student of Fries, exclaimed "[h]ere, you traitor of the fatherland." Karl von Ibell, an official of the *Lander*, was also murdered. In reaction to this political instability, the Austro-Hungarian Alliance and Austria, led by Metternich, announced the Karlsbad Decrees, 1819. The Decrees authorized the dismissal of any university professor who was believed to have "an influence on the minds of the young through the propagation of corrupt doctrines, hostile to public order and peace or subversive of the principles of the existing political institutions."[68] The state authorities categorized Fries as subversive. He was, accordingly, dismissed from the University of Jena in 1820 (though reinstated in 1824). In addition, the Decrees repressed legal and political rights, including freedom of the press and the denial of due process to detained students. Metternich instilled an atmosphere of fear not unlike we sometimes experience of our Western political leaders today.

One of the detained students, Gustav Asverus (1798–1843), was imprisoned for over seven years.[69] Hegel was particularly concerned that another of his students, Friedrich Wilhelm Carové (1789–1852), whom Hegel wished to be his *Privatdozent* at Berlin, was imprisoned for speaking out against xenophobia and anti-Jewish speeches at the Wartburg Festival in 1817.[70] Hegel's new faculty at Berlin University withheld the appointment of Carové because of his alleged political activity.[71] Hegel then succeeded in gaining the appointment of von Henning, also from Heidelberg, only for the latter to be imprisoned the following year. Hegel appears to have consistently supported all his imprisoned students, Jews and non-Jews.[72] Hegel's position was that his students were morally "innocent" bystanders and that only the fanatical students should be punished. In the Preface to the *Philosophy of Right*, Hegel dissociated himself from the student movement and the Wartburg riots.[73] Despite Hegel's facetious condemnation of Fries in the Preface, however, Hegel ironically shared several of Fries' beliefs, particularly the role of an historically instilled ethos and the association of legitimacy "from below" (Fries).[74] Hegel prudently withdrew his book from the publisher in 1919 for fear that it would be censored as a consequence of the Karlsbad Decrees. He then wrote the Preface. The Preface has been taken as an endorsement of the Prussian state even though Prussia did not author the Karlsbad Decrees. Further, Hegel was arguably endorsing the "enlightened" liberal leadership of von Hardenberg and von Altenstein.[75]

5. THE ROLE OF THE PREFACE

We are finally ready to explore Hegel's mature legal philosophy by turning to the famous Preface of *Philosophy of Right*. On the one hand, Hegel experiences contempt in the Preface for the romantic appeal to ad hoc feelings, conscience, and heart as the grounding of legitimacy. The Enlightenment had too much of a hold on Hegel for him to accept conscience as the legitimate source of binding rules. So too, Hegel rejects tradition as the legitimizing factor of state-centric posited laws because of its externality to consciousness. On the other hand, Hegel challenges Kant and Fichte because of their trivialization of the experiential subject. The subject constructs concepts from experience, not from some rational maxims in a noumenal realm of knowledge. Experience struggles internal to human consciousness. And the legitimacy of posited laws and institutions depend upon the reciprocal recognition of strangers as manifested in the content of laws. Hegel locates legitimacy in this reciprocal recognition. The latter, being the product of the act of thinking, logically precedes any external presupposition such as nature, tradition, the noumena, or conscience.[76]

The Preface to *Philosophy of Right* hints at Hegel's incisive criticisms of the traditional philosophies of law in his day. With respect to Schelling's and Kant's philosophies of law, Hegel argues, no empirical legal order resembled the empty alienated forms of nature and a priori concepts of legitimacy. Even Plato's *Republic*, Hegel suggests, was not about "an *empty ideal*" as is still often assumed today. Plato's republic was a socially contingent polis (PR Pref. 20). More generally, a norm or particular action is not binding if it counters the accepted contingent ethos of the day. As Hegel puts the point more generally in the Preface, "however exalted, however divine this right [the legitimate legal order] may be, it is nevertheless transformed into wrong if the only criterion of thought and the only way in which thought can know itself to be free is the extent to which it *diverges from what is universally acknowledged and valid* and manages to invent something *particular* for itself" (PR Pref. 12). Indeed, this inevitably happens because formal right cannot be accessed without the infusion of subjectivity. Without such an infusion, truth attaches to a priori forms of the noumenal realm. But such a pursuit for truth is a "futile endeavour" without a connection of an alleged truth to human consciousness. One can only access knowledge in the phenomenal world. Since Hegel associates phenomena with consciousness, the quest for truth in Kantian legal philosophy is "nothing but a problem" (PR Pref. 14).

With respect to Fries' and Savigny's appeals to conscience, Hegel expresses nothing but "contempt" for their works. Although romanticists claimed to know objects, they arbitrarily posited conscience as the source of legal legitimacy. What we had, as a consequence, was a "self-styled philosophy" which expressly claims "that *truth itself cannot be known* [erkannt], but that truth consists in what *wells up from each individual's heart, emotion, and enthusiasm* in relation to ethical subjects, particularly in relation to the state, government, and constitution" (PR Pref. 15). Such a subjectivism offended the very idea of philosophy: "this arbitrary sophistry has usurped the name of *philosophy* and persuaded a wide public that such activities are philosophy" (PR Pref. 17). Such sophistry demonstrated "the utmost selfishness of empty arrogance" and confused the public by appealing to words such as *"life," "enliven,"* and the *"people."* Hegel described the philosophy of conscience in this way: "[t]he *law* is therefore . . . the chief shibboleth by which the false brethren and friends of the so-called 'people' give themselves away" (PR Pref. 17). Sophistry, though, was "spiritless." Indeed, with "this superficial philosophy," the coded words were recirculated year after year, and rigorous thinking was amiss (PR Pref. 16). Professorial popularity won the day: "[w]hat has not been said in this connection to flatter the young in particular?" (PR Pref. 15). This subjectivist philosophy was *"dead, cold letter* and a *shackle"* (PR Pref. 17).

Hegel's animosity toward Fries colors every effort on Hegel's part to introduce philosophical jurisprudence. Hegel refers to Fries as "Herr Fries" (not Dr Fries nor Professor Fries nor Professor Dr Fries). He describes Fries as the "leader of this superficial brigade of so-called philosophers." Fries had exhibited "the temerity, at a solemn public occasion which has since become notorious" (that is, the Wartburg Festival of October 1817) and had proclaimed that public affairs should "gain its *life from below, from the people itself*" in the form of *"living* societies steadfastly united *by the sacred bond of friendship"* (PR Pref. 15). Further, Fries followed a shallow, formalistic differentiation of concepts instead of a deeper inquiry into the relation of concepts with social phenomena. In Chapter 3, I shall elaborate on how these different approaches to legal reasoning and philosophic method differ. The point to appreciate at this stage is that by alluding to Fries as the enemy of philosophy, Hegel hoped to pass the censor's stamp of approval in the newly emerging context of the European state authoritarianism against intellectuals. As Hegel expresses in the Preface, academics, such as Fries, had broken the trust by inflaming the student unrest at the Wartburg Festival. Philosophers had breached their trust to the public by succumbing to sophistry: "it has almost become dishonourable to continue to speak philosophically about the nature of the state" (PR Pref. 17). So much so that "right-minded men cannot be blamed if they grow impatient as soon as they hear talk of a philosophical science of the state." Even more understandable, Hegel continues, the breach of trust had led to the prospect that governments should question (such as presumably represented by the Karlsbad Decrees) what was being taught as philosophy. University teaching was no longer practiced, as in Greece, as a private art. Rather, the primary, secondary, and university education possessed "a public existence [*Existenz*], impinging upon the public, especially—or solely—in the service of the state." Indeed, Hegel advocated that, due to indifference towards philosophy, governments had authorized teaching posts in philosophy "only for reasons of tradition" in contrast with France where "to the best of my knowledge, chairs of metaphysics at least have been allowed to lapse" because no meritorious individuals could be found to fill the chairs (PR Pref. 17). Philosophers had breached their duty to the state by succumbing to rhetoric and the subjective conscience of the philosopher. Governments, for their part, had been indifferent to the quality of education with the consequence of a "resultant decay of thorough knowledge [*Erkenntnis*]."

6. HEGEL AND THE CRISES OF HIS TIMES

We can appreciate at this point that Hegel did not write his classic, *Philosophy of Right*, out of the blue nor did he intend to describe the philosophic issues of his day. That said, he combined the contemporary philosophic vocabulary with themes presented by his contemporaries: Schelling's never-ending quest for objectivity in nature, Hölderlin's primacy of love, Kant's dichotomy between noumena and phenomena, and the two general approaches to legal philosophy in Hegel's day (and in ours)—transcendentalism and subjectivism.

Against this background, Hegel constructed an original philosophy of the identity and nature of law. His philosophy of law drew from a special sense of reason (*Vernunft*), on which I shall elaborate in Chapter 3, along with a preoccupation with the ethicality of an ethos, which I shall outline in Chapter 6.[77] Hegel broke from the uncontrollable and uncontrolled Fate of Greek tribes, the gods which guarded the polis, the legal formalism of Roman law, the subjectivity of historicism and romanticism, and the legal formalism of Kant and Fichte. The constitutional reform movement in Prussia from 1807 until 1810 and of Württemberg between 1815 and 1819 served to offer a model for Hegel's effort to reconcile state institutions with subjectivity. France, Spain, and England served as models for a sovereign state that Hegel longed would institutionalize freedom in Germany.

Hegel's personal relationships with Schelling and Hölderlin as well as the influences of his peers in Jena set the framework for Hegel's later contribution to legal philosophy. The role of his two friends in the formation of his legal philosophy, however, came at some cost. For, as noted earlier, Hegel had lost the friendship of Schelling with the publication of the *Phenomenology*. Hegel also lost his friend, Hölderlin, only in this case to madness. Intellectually and professionally alone in a disruptive and explosive world and personally alienated from objectivity represented by corrupt and arbitrary institutions where nepotism still dominated, Hegel experienced continued financial insecurity, repeated failures to gain a salaried professorship, the sustained personal enmity of Fries from the days in Jena and of Savigny in later years, sustained bouts of depression, and all this at a time when his philosophy of law was unpopular amongst professional philosophers.

Hegel's legal philosophy is infused with his own self-identity as much as with his originality as a legal philosopher. He continually contrasts his own self-image as a speculative philosopher of human experience with the "self-styled philosophers" who presupposed conscience as the legitimizing source of binding laws. Further, he urges the philosopher to pry behind posited rules and institutional practices to understand the relationships between the individual and strangers. Laws must be known for the individual to feel bound to them. Codification aids in this enterprise. Institutional reforms are needed to open possibilities of a role for individuals in the enactment and decision making of state institutions so that legality will no longer seem external to the individual. The individual could then take responsibility for her or his future. *Actuality*, a term examined in Chapter 1 by which Hegel meant the presupposed structure of self-consciousness of an individual, was the object of speculative philosophy (PR 270, 216A). The individual could be free. This freedom was generated from a structure of legal consciousness shared in an ethos.

To appreciate the originality of Hegel's effort, one needs to understand what he considered the critical problematic of modernity. I address this in Chapter 2. Hegel situates the problematic in the contrast between a tribal legal culture and a "civilized" one. Thinking characterizes the latter. Legal thinking reaches its pinnacle with the establishment of a state. Hegel's argument posits an individual who slowly emerges from a stateless society to one where she or he increasingly becomes conscious of her or his autonomy from the objectivity represented by courts, legislatures, monarchs, and other institutions of the state. Hegel asks himself "why would a thinking being be obligated to obey the laws of a state-centric legal order?" Before we can grasp this problem, though, we need to gain a sense of Hegel's vocabulary. I address his vocabulary in Chapter 1. With his vocabulary and his problematic before us, Chapter 3 retrieves Hegel's theory of legal reasoning if freedom is to be institutionalized. Chapters 4 to 10 will discuss how the philosopher retrospectively retrieves the boundaries of legal consciousness for the thinking subject to gain a knowledge of legal objectivity.

In particular, I proceed in Chapter 4 to explicate why Hegel believed that a thinking individual would recognize the concepts of personhood, property, contract, and crime when the individual sought to possess external things of nature. Hegel's argument rests from his critique of the formalism that characterized traditional approaches to legitimacy. I retrieve Hegel's exposure of such formalism in Chapter 5. At this point, I identify and explicate an original element of Hegel's legal philosophy: the notion of ethicality. I explain in Chapter 6 that ethicality is hardly what we take today in Anglo-American legal philosophy as the morality of individual rights and duties. Rather, ethicality addresses how the individual recognizes strangers through social relationships in an ethos. Such relationships are represented by shared universals such as statutes, precedents, and customs. So too are universals manifested in religious practices, institutional practices, unwritten and unstated assumptions of a populace, and, more generally, what Hans-Georg Gadamer (1900–2002) calls *prejudicia*.[78] These sources constitute an ethos. Hegel deconstructs different forms of an ethos in Western legal culture: the family, civil society, the organic constitution, and various forms of an international legal consciousness. I elaborate Hegel's exposition of the ethicality of such *ethê* in Chapters 7 to 10. Each of these forms of ethical life, though, presupposes different social relations between individuals *inter se*. In the Conclusion, I raise a series of questions that draw from Hegel's philosophy of the legitimacy of a modern legal order.

For Hegel, legal philosophy is "the thought of the world" and, as such, "it appears only at the time when actuality has gone through its formative process and attained its completed state" (PR Pref. 23). The legal philosopher "always comes too late" to recommend changes or to offer an ideal legal order. The legal philosopher can, at best, retrospectively make conscious what has hitherto been collectively unconscious in an ethos. As Hegel ends his Preface to *Philosophy of Right*, "[w]hen philosophy paints its grey in grey, a shape of life has grown old, and it cannot be rejuvenated, but only recognized, by the grey in grey of philosophy; the owl of Minerva begins its flight only with the onset of dusk" (PR Pref. 23). Perhaps Hegel's own life provides the best evidence of such wisdom. For Hegel reflected about the crises of his own life and of his own times. He did more than this, though, for he lived the crises of his times.

CHAPTER ONE

Hegel's Vocabulary

Hegel's vocabulary is not peculiar to himself. He is writing in the historical context of two deep intellectual traditions, each with its own vocabulary that Hegel takes for granted. Hegel's vocabulary is difficult to access in part because he does not set out his arguments in a nice analytically clear and succinct manner. His vocabulary also takes for granted an extraordinary breadth of Western literature, Greek and Roman history, Roman law, and incisive and thought-provoking metaphors. Indeed, Hegel's vocabulary only becomes apparent when situated in its cumulative context—that is, after one has digested the whole of his legal philosophy. This is especially so with such terms as *Recht, Sitte, Verstand, Vernunft, Sittlichkeit, Gesetz, Polizei,* and *Korporatione.* Perhaps the most important, yet unfamiliar, term in professional legal education today is *Bildung.*

1. *Bildung*

Hegel came to take *Bildung* for granted as a student at the *Stift* (the theological college). By *Bildung* Hegel intends "cultivation" or "education" (PR 187). But "education" is not just a matter of formal education. *Bildung* involves cultivation of the heart (the unconscious) and of the intellect. The individual develops her- or himself in both respects in context-specific life experiences. Mindful of Aristotle's explanation of *phronesis* (or practical reason) in Book VI of Aristotle's *Nicomachean Ethics,*[1] *Bildung* has a practical or action character. Drawing from Montesquieu, Hegel identifies three sources of *Bildung*: one's parents (love, trust, and obedience), one's teachers and instructors (formal education), and the education one receives generally from experiences in the world (1817/18, 86.109). When one becomes self-conscious, one becomes aware of oneself as separate from objectivity. Although the distinction arrives on the scene a century later with Karl Jung (1875–1961) and, more recently, with Northrop Frye (1912–1991), Hegel asks the philosopher to become conscious of the "collective unconscious" shared with strangers in a particular epoch of a particular ethos.[2] Hegel would be dissatisfied if we studied the self as if its elements were discoverable by empirical psychology. Instead, the philosopher must step outside her or his own immediacy with objectivity in order to observe the presuppositions of her or his philosophical consciousness as well as the presuppositions of the ethos in which the philosopher is immersed (PR 19R).

Hegel begins his exposition of *Bildung* with a theory of child development. Love characterizes a mother's relation with her children (PR 173A). Children develop from their initial immediacy with their parents to maturity when they are conscious of their world and of themselves in the world (PR 174). The child matures from her or his own efforts rather than from natural abilities, the gods, or the *polis* (PR 174A). Formal education and parental guidance render children increasingly independent and strong. Discipline helps the parent to break the arbitrary self-will of the child so that the child can gain a consciousness of the external world (PR 174A). *Bildung* is acquired rather than inherited from nature. Once acquired, the individual is lifted from the immediacy of parental love to the self-consciousness of one's separation from one's parents. One consequence of *Bildung* is that, unlike in early Roman law where children were enslaved, the child is not a thing to be possessed by the parent or the state (PR 175). The more that *Bildung* is inculcated into the individual's consciousness, the more autonomous is the individual from nature, family, and tradition. *Bildung* helps the individual to look inward into her or his feelings and beliefs on the one hand and outward to the objective institutions and posited laws on the other. As Hegel puts it, one "must work through the process of self-production both by going out of himself and by educating himself inwardly, in order that he may also become rational *for* himself" (PR 11A).

When individuals absorb *Bildung* as they mature, they become conscious of their separation from the objectivity of nature (PR 13R). In a tightly knit family, for example, the family members bond so deeply that they take family rituals and customs for granted. When a family member leaves the family for the city so to speak, she or he may not initially become conscious that she or he is autonomous from the prelegal practices of the family. The observing philosopher will be the first to recognize this autonomy. This autonomy marks the departure from the prelegal social order of the family. When the individual thinks, she or he begins to become separate from immediacy with objectivity.

Bildung encourages a transformation of meaning from immediacy to the mediation of concepts through the experience of time. When I think, I represent my immediacy in an objective world separate from myself. The more that I think about my representations, the more do I transpose my arbitrary impulses and desires "from the *form* of their immediate natural determinacy and from the subjectivity and contingency of their *content*" to the rational control by my will (PR 19). Through the acculturation inculcated by *Bildung,* one's act of thinking, not one's bodily impulses, controls and chooses one's objects. Posited laws and institutions are controllable by human beings in this way (PR 14). The process of becoming conscious of oneself may be painful. But the act of thinking draws us closer to social actuality: "only by making resolutions can the human being enter actuality, however painful the process may be" (PR 13A).

2. FREEDOM

Hegel is best known, along with John Stuart Mill (1806–1973), as the philosopher of freedom. Hegel's theory of freedom strongly differs, though, from Mill's. Mill separates the individual's freedom from the ethos in which the individual is situated. Hegel insists that one is not free unless one socially relates with strangers in the objective world to the point that the strangers no longer obstruct one's actions. Although both Mill and Hegel privilege the inner consciousness of the individual, Hegel fears that a presupposed separation of the individual from objectivity will have the consequence of reenacting the Terror. For, the individual will posit her or his arbitrary will within the boundary that separates her- or himself from objectivity. The critical condition of the inner will, for Hegel, is social freedom, and social freedom involves the dissolution of external constraints: "[w]ill without freedom is an empty word" (PR 4A). When the will is self-determining, the individual is free.

a) Subjectivity

One can gain a glimpse of Hegel's sense of freedom by retrieving his view of the great divide between antiquity and modernity. With modernity, according to Hegel, there arose a subjectivity wherein the individual thought on her or his own. As Hegel put it, "I am able to free myself from everything, to renounce all ends, and to abstract from everything" (PR 5A). Hegel lectures one year after the publication of *Philosophy of Right* that "[f]reedom is just thinking itself. Whoever rejects thinking and speaks of freedom, does not know what he is talking about."[3] All human beings, unlike an animal, are capable of thinking: "anyone can discover in himself an ability to abstract from anything whatsoever, and likewise to determine himself, to posit any content in himself by his own agency; and he will likewise have examples of the further determinations [of the will] within his self-consciousness" (PR 4R). Because such thinking emanates from within the individual, freedom is alive (PR 142).

In order to be free, I must be able to think about my choices in action. But is there any limit to my ability to think? Can I control all factors external to my consciousness? Do I live solipsistically through my own indeterminate abstractions or do I recognize myself in strangers and strangers in myself? Do not other human beings constrain the options available in my choices of action?

b) Two Senses of Unfreedom

Hegel offers two versions of the constraints that encumber one's freedom. In the one, I am unfree if my choices and actions are constrained by my own sensory impulses and appetites. In the other, the legitimacy of legality is drawn from the inaccessible *noumenal* realm which transcends the arbitrary impulses and desires. Let us address each in turn.

i) Freedom of Choice

With the first sense of unfreedom, I have the freedom to choose whatever are my impulses and appetites. Since each and all have this freedom of choice, each is constrained by the other's arbitrary impulses and appetites. The ultimate consequence is the domination of one by the other. There is no self-conscious reflection about the impulses and appetites. "Well, that is how I feel," students and professors are often heard to say. Constitutional adjudication often is said to concern the balancing of (arbitrary) values. Even Anglo-American general jurisprudence has been known to accept that legal reasoning can only go so far when the judge or lawyer must posit a value.[4] At that point, the posited value becomes the criterion of legality.[5] Legal philosophers often claim that posited social conventions legitimize legality. The arbitrary posit of values and facts is the "commonest" view of freedom, according to Hegel (PR 15R).

Hegel suggests that a freedom based upon the arbitrary values, drives, and needs is empty and lacking in intellectual coherence because the external world of institutions still confronts and controls human action. This is so at the same time that the individual fails to consider that such externalities are the objects of her or his consciousness.[6] The observed individual to whom I refer is the legal official.[7] Further, the subjectively posited values are arbitrary because, bound with the immediacy of the individual's identity with objectivity, they are not the object of thinking. The Enlightenment sense of an autonomous or self-determining individual is thereby ignored. Terror becomes a possibility. Moral and social relativism have their day in court. The freedom of arbitrary choices is oblivious to the possibility of the reflection about the content of choices or about how external social conditions might constrain such arbitrary will (PR 11). If the individual is allowed to choose as her or his impulses and appetites dictate, the individual flees from social relationships.

ii) Transcendental Unfreedom

Hegel raises a second sense of unfreedom. This sense of unfreedom claims a universality because it is purged of all historically contingent circumstances. Hegel's problem with this second sense of unfreedom is that what is taken as freedom is external from experience. The rights are empty of social-cultural content. As such, they lack determinate particulars (PR 5). The unfreedom is formal. Formal freedom excludes the content of freedom from consideration. "A will which resolves on nothing is not an actual will; the characterless man can never resolve on anything" (PR 13A). Indeed, if the observed official—whether a judge or lawyer or legal scholar/student or philosopher—deeply believes in the formal concepts, such as the concept of free speech, due process, or access to justice for example, the concepts perpetuate a "freedom of the void" (PR 5R). Instead, officials must nest the formal freedom in the appearance of phenomena. The abstractions of the former *noumenal* realm unify with the context-specific consciousness to create freedom.[8] Freedom accesses actuality only when it is concrete rather than theoretical. Hegel exemplifies this sense of unfreedom in his extensive analyses of Roman Stoicism, the French Revolution, and Hindu fanaticism.[9] The empty freedom, acting in denial of the existence of other finite strangers with their own immediacies, might "actualize" such freedom with a "fury of destruction," "fury of the void," and an "intolerance of everything particular" (PR 5A). Hegel exemplifies this prospect in his discussion of the "monstrous excesses" of Roman emperors (PS 480, 481) as well as of the "Hindu fanaticism of pure contemplation" which, when it turns to practicality, becomes "the fanaticism of destruction, demolishing the whole existing social order, eliminating all individuals regarded as suspect by a given order, and annihilating any organization which attempts to ruse up anew" (PR 5R). The twentieth century has experienced too many examples of freedom of the void to accept the freedom without questioning its viability. By destroying all institutions and particularity, the abstractions alone are believed to exist.

c) Positive Freedom

The above two forms of unfreedom could be avoided, according to Hegel, if the philosopher addressed the Enlightenment idea of a thinking subject. If I can think, I can create objects from inside my consciousness. The objects are thereby nested in a *phenomenal,* rather than an empty *noumenal,* realm of knowledge. As a human being, I am a creator, the source, the author of my concepts. Thinking is *my* activity: "[i]n this thinking-over the genuine nature [of an object of consciousness] . . . this thinking is *my* activity, this true nature is also the *product of my* spirit, [of me] as thinking subject. It is mine . . . or it is the product of my *freedom*" (EL 23). If free, I become "at home" with myself: "Spirit is here purely at home with itself, and thereby free, for that is just what freedom is: being at home with oneself in one's other, depending upon oneself, and being one's own determinant" (EL 24A2).

I am completely free when there is no objectivity that constrains my consciousness: "where there is no other for me that is not myself" (EL 24A2). I am free if external constraints are absent from my action. In the past, nature, a priori moral maxims, conscience, and customs were believed to constitute the unchangeable and unchanged objectivity. Such sources of constraints upon one's freedom were *external* to the individual's consciousness. Hegel introduces the idea that the individual makes the world part of her- or himself and then translates her or his self-conception into what has heretofore been taken as the uncontrollable objectivity. The individual creates an objectivity of consciousness that mediates between the individual and the objectivity of nature. I thereby become at home in nature.

Thus, there are levels of freedom. The more we think, the more is there a possibility to become free. If I do not reflect about objectivity, I do not access "the *truth* of this freedom because it does not yet have itself as its content and end" (PR 15R). My inner immediate self remains autonomous from the external objects posited externally by institutions and by strangers. The freest society is one where individuals think about their role in thinking and their reciprocal relationships with strangers. The reciprocal recognition of social beings, each becoming conscious of the process by which she or he has determined the stranger, is the condition of freedom.

This requires that I become conscious of my appetites and of my social relationships presupposed in formal freedom. I then become reconciled with objectivity when I refer "to nothing but [myself] so that every relationship of *dependence* on something *other* than [my]self is thereby eliminated" (PR 23). Freedom is thereby "rational."

This is a very different sense of freedom than John Stuart Mill's negative freedom. One is only truly free if there is no external objectivity that constrains one's actions. And this only occurs if I determine what would otherwise be such external constraints. Hegel describes this point in this way:

> that is just what freedom is: being at home with oneself in one's other, depending upon oneself, and being one's own determinant. In all drives I begin with an other, with what is for me something external. Hence, we speak of dependence in this case. Freedom is only present where there is no other for me that is not myself. The natural man, who is determined only by his drives, is not at home with himself; however self-willed he may be, the *content* of his willing and opining is not his own, and his freedom is a formal one. (EL 24A2)

Freedom exists when I, not nature, determine objectivity. Hegel's sense of freedom addresses the extent to which self-conscious action recognizes strangers and, more generally, that recognizes the universals that individuals share in an ethos (PR 15A, PM 476). Freedom thereby becomes a social, not an individual, matter: "in social ethics these two parts [inward purpose and the actualization of that purpose] have reached their truth, their absolute unity" (PM 486). The role of the legal philosopher is to identify the boundary of the collective unconscious and the relationship of the individual with others inside that boundary.

Hegel links his theory of positive freedom with the institutional context of objectivity. First, as John Rawls points out, the official or inhabitant is not passively resigned to the status quo of the institutional, procedural, and substantive legal structures.[10] Legal reasoning is the consequence of *my* work, not someone else's. Hegel explains in his 1824/25 lectures that even the intellectual trace of a rule to an external foundation is "devoid of any speculative thought" by the self-determining individual (PR 29R). Thinking is "actual" because it emanates from *my* consciousness (PR 29).[11] Rules are binding because they rest in just such an actuality of freedom: "[r]*ight* is any existence [*Dasein*] in general which is the *existence* of the *free will*. Right is therefore in general freedom, as Idea" (PR 29). Alas, Hegel is already explaining his sense of freedom with terms, such as *actuality, Idea,* and *will,* which we still need to understand. But before we proceed, other terms need clarification.

3. SELF-CONSCIOUSNESS

One such term is *self-consciousness*. When I am conscious of my act of think-ing and of the freedom to do so, I am conscious of *my* self as the object of *my* thinking. Who is this "I" that is the object of my consciousness? Clearly, I do not have fixed values or beliefs for I am constantly grow-ing as I think. In addition, I have infinite possibilities of choosing this or that action. If I am free, I choose a particular content to my action from a multiplicity of concrete social differences. I am self-conscious when I see myself playing a role in such a choice. I am free if I think for myself and, second, if I become conscious that I am constructing objectivity. At this point, I recognize myself as a constraint upon my actions. When I am free, I refer "to nothing but [my]self, so that every relationship of *dependence* on something *other* than itself is thereby eliminated" (PR 23). What Hegel intends by this assertion is that I cannot inform myself of my identity by informing myself of what I am not.[12] My representation of myself must not be separate from my thought.

Thus, for Hegel, the only constraint to my freedom is not an objective representation, such as a legislated rule, but my own thought about the content of the legislated rule. The subject must "work through the process of self-production both by going out of himself and by educating himself inwardly, in order that he may also become rational *for himself*" (PR 10A). I thereby comprehend that I construct the world that I have heretofore as-sumed to be an external uncontrollable objectivity (PR 153).

We shall see in Chapters 2 and 4 that before I become conscious of my own construction of objectivity, I am not aware of my self as separate from objectivity. I develop as I become aware of this separation. When I become aware of this separation, I have a will. This will distinguishes human beings from animals, as we shall see in the next chapter. I am not satisfied with being aware of particular capacities, character, propensities, and foibles of myself as a single being. Rather, I become aware of myself as the creator of objectivity. As such, objectivity is ever changing and progressively developing (PM 377). I come to know my role in constructing objectivity. I recognize myself in objectivity.

4. THE TWO STANDPOINTS OF SELF-CONSCIOUSNESS

Against the above background, we need to distinguish between two vantage points from which to study experience.[13] Hegel shifts from one to the other, from sentence to sentence. One has to appreciate from which standpoint he is writing in any particular passage.

The first standpoint is the observed consciousness. This is generated from a subject who is initially immersed in an ethos without being conscious that she or he is separate from its objectivity. In a tribe, for example, the tribal member accepts customs as if they were "a second nature." When the individual subject literally or metaphorically leaves the tribe for the civil society of the city or state, she or he still feels as if the universals of the city are beyond human control. The observed individual is not conscious of her or his autonomy from objectivity. As such, she or he does not yet have a will.

The second standpoint is that of the observing or philosophical consciousness that observes the development of the observed individual's will. Philosophical consciousness observes how civilization manifests the closing of the gulf between the will and objectivity of consciousness.[14] *Bildung* aids both endeavors. The philosophical consciousness, for example, slowly becomes aware that an abstract person, property, contract, crime, and legal legitimacy are the constructions by the will. The observed will passes through several presupposed structures that represent different relationships between the will and objectivity. Like the owl of Minerva, the philosopher looks backward in experienced time to retrieve the various presupposed structures of the relationship of the individual with the shared universals of objectivity. Hegel identifies several such epochs of objectivity: Greek tribes, the early polis, Socrates, the Roman law, Christianity, feudalism, the French Revolution, along with Abstract Right, the family, civil society, the organic state, and the world history of international legal objectivity.

The consciousness of the observed individual subtly and slowly merges with the philosophical consciousness until objectivity is reconciled with the will in an organic constitution. This apparent reconciliation, however, does not bring closure to the development of self-consciousness because the organic constitution, as a state, becomes conscious of its separation from the international objectivity of consciousness. The will thereupon continues its journey in the quest for freedom.

5. SPIRIT

What drives the observed individual (and, for that matter, the philosopher) to desire to be free from external constraints? Oedipus's, as much as Socrates', quest for truth begs the issue. Would we not be happier if we remained ignorant and if we just did not have to ask questions about our presupposed structures of consciousness? Would we not have peace of mind if we earned a minimal standard of income, only had to read e-mail, sat in front of a computer for a few hours each day, and went home to watch TV? Why should a law student or a legal scholar desire to think about the separation of the will from posited rules that she or he heretofore may have accepted as constitutive of "the Law"? Why does one desire to think at all? I shall return to these questions in the Conclusion chapter.

Suffice at this point, Hegel is skeptical about the possibility of an everyday passive "couch potato." There is something in a human being that generates a desire to become self-conscious. What is this generating factor internal to consciousness? Why would a family member desire to leave the family security for the alienating and psychological insecurity of private property? Why would a state desire to leave the security of its freedom from noninterference for the violent and political insecurity of territorial conquest? Hegel responds to these questions by holding out that a spirit, inaccessible through human language, precedes the subject and the object (PR 242). Love is entangled with this spirit.

Hegel continuously incorporates spirit as the ultimate motivating drive for *Bildung,* freedom, self-consciousness, and love itself. When Hegel writes of spirit, he is referring to something that is divine and to that end his translators capitalize the word *Spirit.* One might initially speculate that Hegel is writing about the Judeo-Christian Spirit, an invisible author or creator "out there" beyond human concepts and language. But such a religious project sets up "a *world beyond* which exists God only knows" (PR Pref. 20). The spirit that Hegel has in mind is immanent inside the human consciousness. To support his argument, Hegel admiringly brings in the historical Socrates into his arguments again and again. And one may recall that in *Apology,* Socrates cannot explain why he questions leading Athenian citizens. He is self-conscious that the generation of his questioning has dominated his being since childhood. Socrates asserts that:

> [a] divine and daimonic thing comes to me—the very thing Metetus made mocking allusion to in the indictment he wrote ["of not acknowledging the gods the city acknowledges, but new daimonic activities instead" (24b5)]. It's something that began happening to me in childhood: a sort of voice comes, which, whenever it does come, always holds me back from what I'm about to do but never urges me forward. *It* is what opposes my engaging in politics. (31c5–d5)[15]

This utterance might have been Hegel's. An inward *daimonic* force drives the individual to become conscious of her or his relationship with objectivity (PM 377A). This *daimonic* force is, I believe, the "God" that Hegel characterizes as "the march of God in the world" (PR 258A). Such a march of the divine emanates from *within* the individual's consciousness.

This inward project explains why Hegel understands Socrates as a tragic figure. On the one hand, Socrates lived through an ethos whose laws required that he be punished. On the other hand, Socrates, an observed individual, strove to become self-conscious of his relationship with the laws. In this striving for self-consciousness, "the breath of the spiritual world will . . . find its way into this solitude [of the abstract monadic individual]" (PR 153A). That is, Socrates turned inward into his own self-reflection. Looking backwards, like the owl of Minerva, the philosopher recognizes Socrates' contribution to the development of civilization at the same time that his community considered him a criminal.[16] Self-knowledge brings salvation as well as the Fall. Hegel challenges the philosopher to become aware of the philosopher's own ethos and how the observed individual relates to strangers through the shared objectivity of the ethos.

6. UNIVERSALS, INDIVIDUALS, AND PARTICULARS

We need to take a rest here and enter into Hegel's vocabulary once more. Hegel takes for granted three terms that need to be clarified: *universals, individuals,* and *particulars.* Hegel uses the terms in different contexts in his writings. In *Phenomenology of Spirit,* he begins with the individual's perception of the external world and then takes consciousness through several moments, including different forms of law, until the individual feels at one with a universality shared with others. In *Science of Logic,* Hegel takes one through the moments of the individual's consciousness internal to subjectivity. There is arguably only one such individual or what Hegel calls subjectivity in Hegel's logic. In *Philosophy of Right,* however, Hegel takes one through the emerging moments of a shared consciousness with strangers. By describing a legal order as "emerging" I do not mean "emergence" in the anthropological sense (although such an interpretation could be gathered from Hegel's *Introduction to the Philosophy of History*), but in the sense of a philosopher's recognition of a presupposed structure of consciousness that logically emerges from a previous structure. Hegel uses the three terms to describe this emergence.

a) Universals

Hegel begins his legal philosophy with an examination of stateless societies. He begins with different shapes of a tribal culture. The tribal member is immediate with tribal customs. The tribal member does not reflect about the tribal customs. The customs are uncontrolled and uncontrollable by the tribal member. The member lacks a will because she or he is not separate from objectivity. Accordingly, it just seems natural for the tribal member to associate the unwritten norms with Fate (*Moira*) or nature.

Now, the philosopher, who observes the emergence of the individual's will, observes how the tribal member (initially, a male) subtly and slowly becomes separate from the shared values and aspirations of the tribe as manifested through its customs. Hegel describes these shared customs as universals.[17] But he also describes other phenomena as universals, and so we need to continue this overview of the emergence of a modern legal consciousness to understand the term. Although the philosopher observes that the tribal member eventually becomes separate from the tribal customs as the member begins to think, the observed tribal member is unaware of this separation. With separation, the philosopher observes that the tribal member unknowingly gains a will. The will constructs concepts that mediate the separation between the observed individual on the one hand and the objectivity of nature on the other. The observed individual's lack of awareness leaves the individual, from her or his standpoint, as immediate with objectivity.

When the individual begins to recognize the concepts as the product of her or his own thinking, she or he becomes aware of her or his own will. Property and contract are examples of products of her or his will. Hegel describes these concepts as universals. Although the individual does not yet recognize strangers—this comes later in the development of self-consciousness—the individual believes that, because she or he is immediate with them, all other individuals share the same concepts. The difference is that in the tribal society the universals are unwritten, whereas in the emerging ethos they are self-consciously authored universals. When an individual contravenes such willed universals, the legitimacy of the objectivity of consciousness is also challenged. This requires that the philosopher begin to observe how strangers intentionally act towards strangers. And this, in turn, encourages the philosopher, in part three of *Philosophy of Right,* to observe how the willing individual recognizes strangers through shared universals in an ethos. When the individual recognizes other wills, a difficult process that I describe in Chapter 6, the objectivity of consciousness possesses legitimacy in *Recht* and *for* the subject.

One can already appreciate that Hegel's sense of a universal differs radically from Kant's. Kant distinguished between the *noumenal* and *phenomenal* worlds. In the former, the "individual" is abstracted from all biography and social-cultural context. The person is "rational" and, Kant believes, the shared maxims and categorical imperative are also "rational." The "sharing" takes place amongst rational persons in the *noumena*. The "sharing" in Kant's works thereby transcends human experience. Differences amongst individual rational persons are intellectual distinctions amongst rational persons. When this world of transcendental rational persons is taken as legitimacy, the philosopher distinguishes one concept from another without ever inquiring into the social-cultural context of *phenomena*.[18] Hegel argues that this super-sensible realm, separate from context-specific human consciousness, is lifeless.

As I shall explain in Chapters 3 and 4, Hegel's sense of a universal begins with Kant's *phenomena* and forgets about the *noumena*. Universals, for Hegel, are shared in context-specific circumstances. The universals are experienced. So, the universals vary from one structure of consciousness to another, from one ethos to another. As Gadamer puts it, the universals are "not appearance as opposed to reality but rather appearance as the real itself."[19] The universals do not represent a picture of concepts, such as the picture of a heaven or a perfectly good will. For Hegel, concepts are experienced in the phenomenal realm.

b) Individuals

Now, the second term that Hegel takes for granted, particularly in *Philosophy of Right,* is the individual. Hegel uses two different terms for what is translated into English as "individual." The first is *das Individuum. Das Individuum* is driven by appetites, desires, needs, and values. This individual is the same creative, spontaneous individual whom John Stuart Mill describes in his *On Liberty*.[20] But because the individual begins to think upon leaving the tribal culture and because she or he remains unconscious of her or his separation from the products of such thoughts, the arbitrary desires are concealed in the immediacy with indeterminate concepts. The individual her- or himself becomes an indeterminate abstraction or "person."

Hegel uses the term *der Einzelne* for such an abstract person. When the individual needs another and thereby agrees to a contract, the individual (*das Individuum*) is driven by appetites and needs to come to an agreement. And yet, once the individual has come to an agreement with the stranger, both are *die Einzelnen*. Both possess legal standing and are abstracted from their intentionality. This is the person that is guaranteed rights in a constitutional bill of rights, for example. "Everyone" is guaranteed "equality before the law," we see over and over again in today's statutes and treaties. In this vein, Article 16 of the *International Covenant on Civil and Political Rights,* 1966 provides that "Everyone shall have the right to recognition everywhere as a person before the law."[21]

The empirical individual (*das Individuum*) cannot be considered equal before the law because each individual differs from the next according to context-specific circumstances. Only *die Einzelnen* or abstract persons, cleansed of all values, a biography, an ethos, a history, and context-specific experiences, can be considered equal with such other persons. When we shift to the international legal order, Hegel refers to a state as *der Einzelne* because it is recognized as an abstract person.[22]

c) Particulars

If there are only universals in a discourse, then all individuals are the same. The universals are indeterminate. The philosopher can only recognize individuals as different if there is something other than the universals to differentiate them. An individual needs to will something that is other than the universals in order to compare the individual with the other individual. Put differently, if each of two strangers, each with a will, recognizes the other, there must be a third factor that differentiates the one from the other. Hegel calls this third factor, the particular. If the two individuals share the particular, then the universal unites with the particular. The shared universal becomes concrete in context-specific circumstances of particularity. The former indeterminate universal is embodied with content (PM 431). Each intentional individual subject (*das Individuum*) recognizes the stranger as different despite their shared universals.

From this, we can appreciate that there are two contexts of Hegel's use of a particular. In the one, that of nature as the universal, the particular is posited as a unit of the objectivity of nature. The empirical sciences accept this context of a particular. So too legal reasoning accepts the "facts of the case" as particulars posited "out there" in the naturelike objectivity. In the second context, that of self-consciousness, the identity of the particular depends upon the ethos as self-consciousness moves through experiential time. In order to understand Hegel's use of the word *particular,* then, one needs to appreciate the presupposed structure of consciousness that Hegel is describing.

If we take the legal culture of a tribe, for example, the tribal member feels immediate with the customs and rituals of the tribe. The custom may be that of the adolescent being required to live in the "wilds" on the outskirts of the territorial familiarity of the tribe. Or the custom may be that of the eldest family member burying the deceased body of a member killed in battle. The member experiences the particular custom as a "this" or "that." One is certain that one experiences the custom and that one experiences it now (PS 91). In this immediate experiencing of the custom, the tribal member lives through particularity. The member excludes from reality what is not here and not now. The particularity might be articulated as the psychological security of the ritual. Or it might be expressed as the economic security of the custom. Immersed in the immediacy of the tribe or family member, one cannot think about one's particular experiences as a tribal member without introducing concepts (PS 92).

If one begins to think about an experience of immediacy, the act of thinking supersedes and raises the particular into a concept that is universal (PR 21R). The particular is categorized as a "this" (PS 98). In order to know a specific "this" in all its particularity, then, one must be able to associate the "this" as a particular with the concept. The concept, though, is fixed independent of time and space. A concept is the standard or criterion against which one can say that one can claim to know a particular. Accordingly, before one can know a particular, one must have a prior understanding of the boundary of the concept which categorizes the "this" (PS 98).

Along these lines, the law student does not speak "the facts of the case." Nor does the lawyer perceive the "facts." The law student claims to know the doctrine or rule or other concept that categorizes the facts before the lawyer can claim to know the facts (PS 100). The concept, in a sense, is content independent before the claim of knowledge about "the facts." The law student supersedes the experience of particularity with the concept whose boundaries enclose the particular.[23] Rules, doctrines, and other concepts intervene or mediate between the law student and the experienced particularity. Hegel explains in the *Science of Logic* that although one ordinarily thinks about a particular, concepts are grasped as if there were no particular external to the act of thinking (EL 24A2). For this reason, Hegel uses the term *particularity* in the context of the objectivity of nature and the context of the objectivity of consciousness. What the law student knows is a mediating concept, not the particularity per se. The "facts of the case" are conceptually informed. But because there are no particulars external to thinking, the rules, doctrines and other concepts, as universals, cause particulars, such as "the facts of the case," to come into existence. As Hegel cautions, "[w]e learn by experience that we meant something other than we meant to mean" (PS 63). What the law student takes as the "facts of a case" is dissolved into something else that does not access the "facts" in the objectivity of nature (PS 110).

Thus, the lawyer knows something very different from what the witness originally intended with "the facts are such and such." The witness has experienced the event, and the experience is the particular of the lawyer's universals. The lawyer locates the witness's event within the boundary of a concept, such as property. As a lawyer, I come to know the facts through "the play of these *abstractions*" (PS 131). The abstractions may re-present or picture the experience. But the abstractions cannot really be known because they are reified from the witness's and even the official's experiences. Because of the gap between the intellectualization about the particulars and the experience of particulars, legal knowledge, to the extent that it is preoccupied with concepts (for example, rules, doctrines, and principles) addresses indeterminacies in the name of "practical law." Such an indeterminacy is the source of illegitimacy (PR 66R).

Hegel describes this inability to access particulars as "understanding" or *Verstand*. This is not Gadamer's sense of understanding.[24] We believe we know differences, as lawyers, when we distinguish one concept (such as, say, *mens rea*) vis-à-vis another concept (say, *actus reus*).[25] We distinguish one concept from another by linking it to a presupposed particular ("the facts") which we believe is external to the interplay of concepts. But this understanding intellectualizes the world to the point that legal reasoning becomes estranged from particularity. We become stuck in an optical illusion. We claim to know "the law"—we may even be examined on our claim—but we are really imprisoned in a supersensible world which excludes particulars. I shall explain this predicament more fully in Chapter 3. When the law student assumes that the law is composed of rules, principles, and other concepts, she or he leaps into a supersensible world which, like K in Franz Kafka's (1883–1924) *The Trial* (1925), seems unreal. H.L.A. Hart (1907–1992) accepts this viewpoint when he argues that the official must "step" from the prelegal into legality if the prelegal connotes the phenomenal and if the legal connotes the knowledge of concepts.[26] In contrast, Hegel claims that only the experiences are accessible as knowledge. One simply cannot access the intellectual differentiation of concepts (for example, rules) that, by themselves, lack particularity. Without particulars, concepts are indeterminate. They are "the most abstract and poorest truth" (PS 91). And this would require that law students, legal scholars, and legal philosophers address the particularity presupposed in the content of the rules, principles, and other concepts.

7. *Die Gesetze and das Recht*

We are finally ready to understand what Hegel signifies by the title of his book, *Philosophie des Rechts* (1821), commonly translated as the *Elements of the Philosophy of Right*. The "elements" to which Hegel's title refers are the various presupposed structures of consciousness that the philosopher recognizes in the social relations of observed individuals. What does Hegel signify by *Recht*?

a) *Particular Posited Laws and the Law*

There are two senses of law in Hegel's day: *Gesetze* (particular laws) and *Recht* (the Law). And there are two senses of *Gesetze*.

The first sense of *Gesetze* is familiar to the student of the common laws. In English, we refer to "the laws." French refers to "loi," and Latin to "lex." The noun, *Gesetz,* comes from the verb *setzen. Setzen* signifies "to posit or to lay down." This idea is associated with the belief in an author of expression.[27] A legislature or court is such an author. We can believe that expression is posited only if we also accept that there is an author, external to the expression, who posits that expression. We speak of the "founding fathers" of a constitution or the "intent of Parliament" or a Supreme Court's "holding" as if such authors originate the inscription *ab initio*. The writing signifies concepts such as doctrines and rules in leases, wills, contracts, property, and other instruments. Hegel has a special method of legal reasoning for this sense of laws: *Verstand*. Rules (that is, concepts) are decomposed into microconcepts, a shared criterion of the microconcepts is identified, the shared criterion or standard transcends the aggregate of microcategories, rules are raised higher in the supersensible realm of knowledge, the logical consequences for other rules are then distinguished, and technical forms and procedures are applied to "the facts of a case."

Hegel introduces a second and different sense of *Gesetz,* however. For Hegel, the author who posits this sense of *Gesetz* is not external to the subject. Rather, the rule is posited in the subject's consciousness. *Gesetzt,* as a participle, signifies "a law." *Gesetz,* as a verb, signifies "posited." If a rule is posited in one's consciousness, the legal rule is no longer "out there" separate from the individual's particulars. Instead, the laws are *Gesetze* in one's consciousness. The project of the philosopher is to retrieve such *Gesetze* presupposed in the consciousness of the individual. Each individual presupposes a structure with boundaries. One shares such a structure with others in an ethos. But their structure develops through time so that the philosopher can, indeed, recognize different structures. Each structure is a "moment" or "element" in the whole movement of consciousness, a movement whose totality constitutes *Recht.*

Now, Hegel's contemporaries also used a very different term to connote a very different sense of law. Here, they referred to "the law." This is the entry point for Hegel's use of the term *Recht.* I shall often refer to "the legal order" as synonymous with this sense of meta-law. French signifies "the law" as *le droit* instead of *la loi* and Latin signifies "the law" as *ius* instead of *lex.* Although Lon Fuller (1902–1978) understood law in this wide sense,[28] few contemporary Anglo-American teaching materials in any area of law assume or articulate this macrosense of "the Law." *Recht* incorporates the meta-law from the whole social, religious, moral, political and *les lois* (in the sense of particular rules) elements of the ethos. Hegel, who calls his classic the *Philosophy of Right,* understands *Recht* in this second wide and deep sense. Hegel takes *Recht* as "not merely civil right, which is what is usually understood by this term, but also morality, ethics [in the sense of ethical life as defined above] and world history [or international law]" (PR 33A). The German language builds upon the word *Recht* in order to frame *Naturrecht* (natural law), *Staatsrecht* (constitutional law), and *Völkerrecht* (international law). Already, we can see that Hegel's laws will hardly be recognizable in the contemporary Anglo-American treatises of various subject matters, such as administrative or debtor-creditor law. The law, for Hegel, is hardly the aggregate of particular rules, let alone legal rules posited by centralized institutions.

b) Sittlichkeit

To complicate matters, Hegel shifts his terminology two-thirds of the way through his treatise. He uses *Sittlichkeit,* instead of *Recht,* to signify "the Law." The root of this term is *Sitte* or custom. We might use the word

ethos to connote *Sitte.* But the root of *Sittlichkeit* is *sittlich* and *sittlich* signifies ethical. So, by focusing upon *Sittlichkeit,* Hegel will examine the ethicality of an ethos, not just the ethos. I shall elaborate what Hegel means
by "ethicality" in Chapter 6. I shall usually use the German, *Sittlichkeit* or
"ethical ethos" rather than the English word, *ethos,* in order to emphasize
the ethical element that Hegel intends in this part of his study.

Hegel makes great use of *Sittlichkeit* in contrast with the Anglo-
American preoccupation with *Gesetze* or the aggregate of particular rules.
So, for example, Hegel contrasts the undeveloped ethical life of the Greeks
with the developed ethical life of a state-centric modern legal order. The
undeveloped *Sittlichkeit* of the Greek tribes, for example, accepts that each
tribal member is bonded with the next so that customs seem like a "second
nature." The modern developed *Sittlichkeit* presupposes that the individual
is a thinking and self-determining being who recognizes other beings. In
the ethical life of modernity, each member of an ethos recognizes that she
or he is an individual separate from others and yet, when individuals share
universals, they bond into a reflective ethos of developed *Sittlichkeit.* Because the social relationships lie deep in the consciousness whose boundaries are shared, the universals seem like a "second nature." By privileging
Sittlichkeit as the object of study, the role of the philosophic observer is to
become conscious of the collective assumptions and expectations of individuals, to question the content of the assumptions and expectations, to
identify how individuals relate with each other through shared universals,
and to ascertain whether such universals are consistent with the drive of
the individual to become self-conscious.

c) Recht as Gesetze

And here is the twist. When that moment arises—when I recognize
a stranger through posited laws and institutions—then the universals of
the ethos are posited *inside* my consciousness. The universals are *Gesetze*
in Hegel's special sense of *Gesetze.* Because strangers share such universals with me, we bond with each other through the universals. Instead
of the universals being externalized to a supersensible world of concepts,
as with Kant, they become determinate because they are now particularized in one's act of thinking and thereby embody their consciousness with
particularity: "[t]o posit something as *universal*—i.e. to bring it to the consciousness as universal—is, as everyone knows, *to think*; when the content
is reduced in this way to its simplest form, it is given its final *determinacy*"
(PR 211R).

A particular rule—a *loi, Gesetz,* or *lex*—is thereby posited into the consciousness of observed individuals. Even the particular aggregate of discrete laws is no longer "out there" in objectivity, separate from the individual's consciousness. For Hegel, an object is posited in one's consciousness only when the object is particularized in the act of thinking represented in a social-cultural ethos in which the individual is situated. That is, consciousness is given body from the reconciliation of universals with particularity. This particularization mirrors the collectively shared universals in the ethos. *Recht* now exists in one's consciousness. *Recht* is actual—but more of this term, *actuality,* in a moment.

Accordingly, a particular rule is not binding because some institutional source posited it. Nor is it binding because judges and lawyers are bound by the *ratio* of previous decisions. Rules are binding when they are particularized in one's consciousness as if they were one's own (PR 219). One reflects, deliberates, and assesses the content of the shared universals in one's ethos: "all the contingencies of feeling [*Empfindung*] and opinion and the forms of revenge, compassion and selfishness fall away" (PR 211A). Only *Recht* is left (PR 211A). The rules, externally posited by a legislature or court, are no longer alien from one's consciousness. One is conscious of oneself and of the stranger through the shared universals represented by *lois. Recht* is now *Sittlichkeit.* The rules and institutions are now practical matters. They are binding because their legitimacy originates in one's consciousness through shared universals.

d) The Separability Thesis

Having introduced Hegel's vocabulary, one might already appreciate one of his messages. Hegel indirectly addresses a question which plagues contemporary legal theory: namely, does legality incorporate social relationships without resort to moral argument? Joseph Raz calls this the separability thesis.[29] We have noted that when Hegel writes about *Recht* he is not concerned with a section of a statute or of a paragraph in a higher court judgment. Rather, *Recht* incorporates the structure of consciousness that the individual shares with others about objectivity and about the role of the individual in constructing that objectivity. Binding laws are nested in the whole complex of unconscious beliefs and consciously posited ideals, religious practices, moral duties, social customs, codified laws, unwritten assumptions, judicial precedents, and all other manifestations of the collective unconscious. Such a wide spectrum of social sources constitutes the resource material for one to elevate presupposed structures of consciousness to objects of study and the relation of such structures to the individual immersed in any one ethos. Lord Devlin's (1905–1992) "anthropological morality," to which Hart and Ronald Dworkin (1931–) reacted with abhorrence, comes closer to Hegel's sense of an ethos.[30] Although Devlin, like Savigny, was content with uncritically accepting and identifying the *custos morum,* Hegel presses on to expect the philosopher to examine retrospectively how the observed individual becomes conscious of the customs in the ethos and then to study how the content of the customs presuppose social relationships in the ethos. This social relationship is represented by the shared universals in the ethos.

Thus, Hegel's sense of binding laws encompasses sociology, moral philosophy, political theory, art, the sciences, and anthropology, as well as the posited rules, forms, and procedures that one is taught in many professional law schools in North America today (PR 124R, 258R). Put more formally, laws include *Moralität* (moral duties), *Sittlichkeit* (ethical life), and public international law, the unstated assumptions and expectations that Lon Fuller privileged, and the posited rules of centralized institutions to the extent that they are incorporated into the consciousness of the individual. When Hegel entitles his book *The Philosophy of Right,* then, he is not necessarily speaking the same language as Ronald Dworkin's "rights as trumps."[31]

The modern legal order of a rights-oriented state is only one form of an ethos. Hegel also addresses the ethos of a nomadic tribe, the Greek polis, the Roman legal order, the European feudal system, the Chinese empire, German principalities, and the different ethical *ethê* of modernity (the family, civil society, the organic constitution, the abstract state in international law, the family of states, the state-centered international legal order, and world history that conceives the state as constrained by peremptory norms). Why are the universals of an ethos binding? The breadth of the sorts of issues that Hegel entertains for *Recht* is as stunning as his contempt for the lawyer of *die Gesetze* (in the sense of a discrete rule or *loi*). One cannot become an expert about rules and procedures without linking them to the legitimacy of the ethos in which one is immersed: "[i]n positive right, what is *legal* [*gesetzmäßig*] is therefore the source of cognition of what is *right* [*Recht*], or more precisely, of what is lawful [*Rechtens*]; the positive science of right is to that extent a historical science whose principle is that of legitimacy" (PR 212R). Because the individual's separation from universals marks modernity, the individual has a will. If that will recognizes other wills through shared universals, the separation from universals dissolves into a bonding between wills. Posited laws become legitimate and therefore binding upon inhabitants.

e) The Content of Gesetze (Posited Laws)

If the philosopher examines the relationship of the individual to strangers through shared universals, the philosopher's role is to become conscious of such relationships in the content of any particular rule (PR 211R). The philosopher must continually look backwards, more generally, into the collective memories of society in order to retrieve such relationships. The philosopher articulates the social assumptions and expectations shared by officials and citizens. If the law professor rests content with "learning the rules," decomposing rules into microrules, and then recognizing a value as the criterion of legal reasoning, the professor, according to Hegel, mimics the barbarian (albeit a higher level of civilized barbarian than the lowest in a hierarchy of barbaric societies): "[b]arbarians are governed by drives, customs [*Sitten*], and feelings, but they have no consciousness of these" (PR 211A). If the professional legal education expects the student to study the social relationships presupposed in the content of rules, *Recht als Gesetze* (the law as discrete posited laws) is no longer. In the *Recht* of self-conscious individuals, such discrete posited rules and doctrines become determinate in one's consciousness. How the philosopher is to do this is elaborated in Chapter 3.

8. ROMAN LAW

Hegel draws from Roman law throughout his works. Some background in Roman law is necessary especially to grasp his critique of legal formalism.

First, Roman law distinguished between the right of persons (*in personam*) and the right of external things (*in rem*). If one were not recognized as a person, then one had to be a thing. This was the case with the slave. As a slave, the human being, unrecognized as a legal person, could be sold and maltreated as a thing.[32] The slave lacked legal rights (such as marriage). A slave was regarded as property rather than as a legal person who could own property. As property, the slave could not own property although a master might confer property to a slave for the use and enjoyment of the slave.[33] A child also lacked personhood as exemplified by the fact that, from the early (510/509 B.C.E.–c. 264 B.C.E.) to middle

Roman Republic (c. 264 B.C.E.–133 B.C.E.), children, with the exception of a daughter who had become a Vestal virgin, could be abandoned, sold into slavery,[34] and even killed for misconduct. Adultery in the master's or husband's house exemplified misconduct.

Second, a human being did not exist, legally speaking, unless she or he was categorized as one of the three legal persons: *libertas, civitas,* and *familia* (PR 40A).[35] *Libertas* concerned the capacity to be a person with rights and duties. *Civitas* conferred a cluster of rights for citizens. *Familia* involved the capacity to have rights as a Roman family.[36] The family, being a single legal person, had to be represented by a head of the family: this was the *paterfamilias* (father/husband). If one lost his legal status in one of libertas, civitas, or familia, he lost his legal status in the other two (*capitis deminutio*). Without the legal status of libertas and, therefore, civitas, the human being could be conveyed as a thing. If I lost my capacity to have rights and duties by becoming a slave, for example, I also lost my Roman citizenship and my rights as the head of the family. In C.E. 212, the *Constitutio Antoniniana* conferred citizenship to all free persons (excluding slaves that is) in the empire. The citizen, who was *sui iuris,* was legally autonomous (self-legislating). If one were *alieni iuris,* one fell under the *auctoritas* of the paterfamilias. An alieni iuris could marry or divorce only with the consent of the paterfamilias.

Third, a special legal method reinforced the Roman differentiation of legal persons with their differing duties. One's rights and duties depended upon the initial categorization of an individual by the state's centralized institutions. If one were transmitted from one category to another (say, from a citizen to a slave or vice versa), legal opinions were needed. If the slave did not offend the legitimacy of the paterfamilias, the legal distinction might not affect the slave's material or social life.[37] That said, the legal category was assumed to constitute human existence. As an example, lawyers, particularly in the classical period of Roman law (31 B.C.E.–235 C.E.), strove to categorize human beings according to the forms of action in the *Twelve Tables* (451–450 B.C.E.) which had codified customary norms. Hegel asserts that in order to retain some legitimacy, Roman jurists of the latter period dissociated themselves from "unjust and abominable institutions" by "invent[ing] verbal distinctions on the sly . . . and even silly excuses" (PR 3R). As an example, a daughter could be categorized as a son in the early Republic (PR 3R). Clarity, analogical and deductive reasoning and, more generally, an intellectual refinement of categories characterized the jurists' role, especially during the latter half of the classical period of Roman law (100 B.C.E.–235 C.E.). Such a legal method can best be gleaned from the highly structured *Institutes* of Gaius (about 160 C.E.) as well as Justinian's *Codex vetus* ("old code," 529 C.E.).[38] Any one legal category was distinguished from another. Symmetry and all-inclusiveness characterized the whole structure of legal concepts.

Now, Hegel draws a series of conclusions from Roman law. First, Roman law recognized the separation of the person from external things: one was either a legal person or an external thing of nature. This person, though, was hardly the subject of Socrates' vein. When confronted with an alien objectivity, Socrates withdrew into his inward consciousness. He also insisted that he was an intentional subject. Instead, the Roman subject was only recognized as an abstract legal person emptied of intentionality.

Second, if a human being, like Socrates, withdrew into inward consciousness upon realizing his separation from external things of nature and from the polis, he would become estranged from the legal personhood which Roman law conferred onto the subject. Accordingly, as Hegel suggests in *Introductory Lectures on the Philosophy of History,* the Roman state itself took on an abstract existence, detached from the interests and lives of individual citizens, let alone of inhabitants (PH 203–04). Leading Roman law texts affirm that Roman jurists were isolated from the historical, social, religious, and political contexts in which they applied legal categories.[39] Legal categorization defined the subject to the point that the social relationships, with which Hegel is concerned, were a forgotten remainder.

More generally, the universals of Roman law were reified from social relations. The Roman law transformed intentional human subjects into abstract persons or things without particularity. If one were not defined as a legal person, the state institutions could execute the subject without the crime of murder being committed. Thus, an irreconcilable rupture severed the feelings, desires, and needs of the human subject on the one hand from universals of the legal order on the other (PR 357). Legal persons, abstracted from the biographies of an intentional subject, were defined by abstract or empty categories. All legal persons sank "to the level of private persons with an *equal* status and with formal rights, who are accordingly held together only by an abstract and arbitrary will of increasingly monstrous proportions" (PR 357).

This radical omission of intentionality from Roman law functioned as the source of Hegel's critique of legal formalism in his own day. Because of the absence of particularity in the person, the legal categories were "lifeless" (PS 477) and a "flight from the actual world" (PS 479). The legal person was a "sheer *empty unit*" (PS 480). Hegel is not going to leave the human subject stuck in such an abstract personhood. To call a human being a "person" is "an expression of contempt" (PS 480). Any "community" of empty units is a single formality whose rulers, such as Tiberius (14–37 C.E.) or Nero (54–68 C.E.), would identify social reality with the empty forms and thereby reinforce a "titanic self-consciousness that thinks of itself as being an actual living god" (PS 481).

9. THE PERSON VS. THE SUBJECT

This takes us to a further critical distinction that Hegel takes for granted: the person vs. the subject. In an undeveloped *Sittlichkeit,* such as tribal life or the polis, the member of the ethos identifies immediately with the shared institutions and customs without the mediation of concepts. Because the tribal member or citizen of the polis did not feel separate from customs and institutions, she or he was not a subject. Nor did she or he consider her or his immediacy separate from objects of nature. The subject enters into philosophy when the tribal members begin to feel autonomous from the shared customs and institutions of the ethos. Such separation suggests that there is a will. Roman law introduces such a sense of separation of the individual from universals of the ethos. However, the separation occurs in terms of the abstract indeterminate universals of the state. The person is defined by legal status. Social-cultural contingency is alien to the Roman sense of a person (PS 482). Before Roman law considers a human being free, the being must be recognized as a legal person. As Paul exclaimed when he was about to be crucified: *Romanus sum civis* ("I am a Roman citizen"). As a Roman citizen, Paul possessed a legal status that differentiated his abstract personhood from other intentional subjects—slaves, foreigners, migrant workers—solely on the basis of legal status.[40] The legal person, like Paul, is equal with all other persons precisely because of the absence of contingent, context-specific content in a "formal universality" (PR 35): the person is "a completely abstract 'I' in which all concrete limitation and validity are negated and invalidated" (PR 35R).

Roman law is a formal justice, for an intentional subject is masked by the abstract person.[41] The person characterizes an "empty understanding which mistakes this abstraction and *obligation* of its own for the real and the rational" (PR 200R). Hegel characterizes Stoicism with such an empty formalism. Stoicism dominated the philosophy in the classical period of Roman law (PS 477). When Hegel refers to one's "personality," he does not intend the human subject with a biography who experiences joy and suffering. He intends the indeterminate persons which, being abstract and empty of social relationships, are reified from the intentional subject. We can respect other persons and, at the same time, remain indifferent to the other's feelings, biography, or particularities (PR 49).

This empty person "is essentially different from the subject, for the subject is only the possibility of personality, since any living thing whatever is a subject" (PR 35A). When the subject interprets an external object, she or he has had context-specific experiences which she or he brings *into* the object. She or he embodies the object with her or his prejudgments and expectations. The latter have been experienced. Such prejudgments and expectations draw from the subject who is of a certain age, height, family, and personal biography, sitting in *this* room with diverse particular biological and personality traits. Such factors are abstracted from the contingent human being when the latter becomes a person. The subject is embodied with particulars. Her or his particulars need satisfaction (PR 124R). Each subject has a conscience with feelings of duty. Each subject differs in terms of intelligence, capabilities, *Bildung,* and other criteria of evaluation. The subject has the potential of becoming a person. The institutions recognize the intentional subject as a person. A person is equal with another person precisely because of the absence of the embodiment of content in the concept of the abstract person in contingent circumstances (PR 35). To the extent that the philosopher or judge associates legal existence with such persons to the exclusion of subjects, one addresses "pure phantasm[s]" (PM 6R).

10. ACTUALITY

The reification of personhood from subjectivity raises a further term in Hegel's vocabulary: *actuality (Wirklichkeit)*. When one uses the term *actual* in ordinary discourse today, it is juxtaposed with "oughts." And so, the legal official claims to base a legal decision or to interpret a decision as if it were grounded in the facts of a case. So too, the legal pedagogue is no doubt familiar with the student's exclamation that she or he needs to take "practical" courses in order to be prepared for the real world. Even "law and society" scholarship not infrequently considers the empirical social relationships as if they were observable facts. Hegel would reject each of these approaches in their infinite variety as constitutive of actuality. As Hegel explains, the mere arbitrary will, presupposed in empiricism and transcendental legal legitimacy, "remains infected with the conceit that, had it so pleased, it could also have decided in favor of something else" (EL 143A). All immediacies have the germ of something else. And this "something else" is immanent in the act of thinking. The legitimacy of the universals within and between individuals in the act of thinking rests within experience as self-consciousness (EL 41).

Actuality, for Hegel, concerns the extent to which shared universals are institutionalized in terms of the recognition of the thinking act that determines the self. The role of the legal philosopher is to observe whether individuals share such an actuality and, if so, how they do so in any structure of consciousness in any ethos of any epoch. The key to actuality is the extent to which one individual recognizes the stranger as a self-determining subject in a self-consciousness. This takes the philosopher to observe the character of the ethos in which the individual is situated (the family, civil society, the organic state, or the various *ethê* of the international legal order). What role does the individual play in such an ethos? How do individuals socially recognize each other? Do they recognize each other as members of the same ethos? Do they recognize each other in their actions? How is subjectivity manifested? What social associations inculcate the social identity of the individual with the social ethos? Do objective external things mirror the self-determined choices of the subject? Is it possible for the subject to be reconciled or bonded with the outer world?

These questions address how the observed consciousness relates to objectivity. Once the philosopher observes how an individual recognizes another in an ethos, the philosopher begins the task of examining the ethicality of the ethos (*Sittlichkeit*). This latter inquiry focuses upon the social content of rules and institutional practices. What "social content" signifies, in turn, is not some external, independent particular but the reciprocal recognition between strangers through the medium of shared universals such as legislatures, courts, and their posited rules (concepts) in the ethos (EL 74) Because Hegel locates knowledge in appearance (phenomena), existence is appearance (EL 131). Thus, the immediacy which generates the act of thinking is only a semblance of appearance; it is not a self-supporting and independent external grounding of the act of thinking (EL 131A). Appearance has immediacy in the subject's own consciousness. Accordingly, appearance contains possibilities within appearance (EL 143A). That is, immediacy is not equivalent to actuality because immediacy only has possibility, not the fulfillment of such possibilities.

Actuality lies immanent within the act of thinking in consciousness. If the philosopher can recognize the universals of her or his ethos and then identify how the individual recognizes others in the ethos through shared universals, she or he is a philosopher of actuality. Possibilities become actualized in an institutional world and in social relationships between strangers. And the role of the philosopher is to study possibilities as manifested in the content of posited rules, statutes, regulations, doctrines, and institutions.

II. THE CONCEPT

This leads to another distinction that one needs to grasp before joining into the movements of philosophical consciousness. Hegel makes a distinction between a particular idea (or concept) and the *Concept* as such, sometimes translated as the *Idea* (*Idee*). A particular idea or concept relates to the method of reasoning, associated with much constitutional analysis today, that Hegel calls *Verstand*. When universals unify with particularity and when the philosopher has returned full circle to the individual's act of thinking, we become aware of the Concept. The Concept is not "something far away and beyond" (EL 213A) nor a "law beyond law" of a universal legal order implicit in a narrative structure, to use Ronald Dworkin's pivotal notion in the final chapter in *Law's Empire*.[42] Rather, the Concept signifies how a self-determined thinking embodies concepts through movements of implied experienced structures of legal consciousness. The Concept incorporates all prior structures of legal consciousness through time.

The big question that *Philosophy of Right, Encyclopaedia Logic,* and *Science of Logic* address for lawyers and students of law today is "how is it possible no longer to consider rules, principles and institutions as units in an intellectualized world and further, to link such rules and institutions to concrete experiences of phenomena?" This will be considered in Chapter 3 when I elaborate Hegel's approach to legal reasoning. For now, it suffices to say that the subject is free if the social relationship nested in the content of rules is not external to the subject but immanent in the very movement of the subject's act of thinking. The legal philosopher thinks about thinking. The Concept, as the whole process of the movements of consciousness, is an *in itself* and, at the same time, *for* the subject. Freedom rests in the Concept. *In freie Wille, der den freien Willen will* ["The abstract concept of the Idea of the will is in general *the free will which wills the free* will," PR 27]. Since the reconciliation of universals with particularity produces a free will (PR 31), the Concept constitutes freedom.

12. THE LIVING GOOD

In the rights-conscious Anglo-American philosophy and culture today, it is difficult to entertain that there could be a sense of legality that does not privilege individual rights or some external intrinsic value such as social welfare. Deontology and utilitarianism are the traditions which general jurisprudence generally presupposes today. There is an alternative view of the identity of law, though. This hangs upon Hegel's special sense of the living Good. The Good is considered intrinsic (as opposed to instrumental) in that it is valued in and for itself. As Aristotle explains, "[i]f, then, there is some end of things we do, which we desire for its own sake (everything else being desired for the sake of this), and if we do not choose everything for the sake of something else (for at that rate the process would go on to infinity, so that our desire would be empty and vain), clearly this must be the good and the chief good" (*Ethics* 1094a19–20). If we could access such an intrinsic Good and if the Good were constituted from movements in self-consciousness, Hegel argues, we would be free. We would be free, that is, if the intrinsic Good were a structure of consciousness in an ethos through experienced time (PR 34A). The Good would be internal to the act of thinking. The Good would thereby be alive because thinking would be immanent in human experience: "[e]thical life is the *Idea of freedom* as the living good which has its knowledge and volition in self-consciousness" (PR 142). I fulfill or particularize the Good as I become self-conscious (PR 133A). The movement of consciousness lifts the individual as a member of a family or tribe from immediacy in the family/tribe to thinking in social actuality.[43] The Good is thereby nested in social relationships. Virtuous actions must not be isolated from an ethos (PR 150R). Alienation is overcome if objectivity and the self-consciousness are reconciled as a unity (PR 147).

It is apparent that one's reading of Hegel is misdirected if one locates Hegel's legal philosophy with reference to the leading legal philosophers of today. Alasdair McIntyre once urged us, for example, to return to a virtue sense of ethics.[44] Michael Sandel's *Liberalism and the Limits of Justice* focused upon the clash between a rights-based and a good-directed legal philosophy.[45] Ronald Dworkin too has privileged collective virtue, although he excludes the ethos as well as the consideration of the social relations presupposed in the ethos from a study of legitimacy. Joseph Raz has drawn from an Aristotelian idea of the Good to elaborate a theory of legal reasoning.[46] Raz systematically critiques Dworkin's theory of rights from such a teleological standpoint.[47] The problem with these approaches to legal philosophy is that the contemporary focus upon virtue or rights or the Good are external presuppositions that precede any thinking about the act of thinking. Such presuppositions are external to human experience by which Hegel means "self-consciousness." Such an external foundation of legality is arbitrary by virtue of its externality to consciousness.

Most importantly, the external foundation of legitimacy as exemplified above lops off the experience of time-consciousness from legal philosophy. Objectivity must be understood and justified in the context of time-consciousness. This experience of time is hardly a historicist project. As Hegel points out early in *Philosophy of Right,* historicism need only "consider the emergence and determination of right *as they appear in time*" (PR 3R). This is "a *purely historical* task." Instead, what is necessary is that the philosopher examine the content of the experience of time-consciousness. Such an inquiry would connect philosophy to the actuality of the relationships amongst strangers.[48] The philosopher plays a role in the retrieval of time-consciousness in such an ethos (PR 150R).

CHAPTER TWO

Hegel's Problematic

Hegel has a problematic that he is determined to overcome. The problematic infuses his lectures and each movement in his overall legal philosophy. The kernel to his problematic rests in his characterization of antiquity and of modernity. With modernity, the individual member of an ethos begins to think. Once the individual thinks, she or he becomes aware of her or his autonomy from the objectivity of nature. She or he also becomes aware of her or his own role in the construction of objectivity, only in this case the objectivity mediates between the individual and nature. The question that this subtle emergence of a self-conscious being in an ethos poses in legal philosophy is "why would such a thinking being be bound to the laws nested in objectivity if the individual were separate from the objectivity?"

The observed individual of antiquity was bound to *Moira* (Fate), nature, or customs as if they were uncontrolled and uncontrollable by human action. There was no subject and no object as a result of the immediacy. Such an immediate identity with objectivity, according to Hegel, characterized the early Greek tribes, the polis, and the pre-European tribes of North America. In a tribe, the tribal member felt immediate with the shared universals as if there were no mediating concept between the member and universals. Hart describes the undeveloped *Sittlichkeit* as "a small community closely knit by ties of kinship, common sentiment, and belief, and placed in a stable environment" where members live in a regime of "unofficial rules."[1] Although he does not offer a single example of an anthropological study establishing this characterization, Hart advises that "there are many studies of primitive communities which . . . depict in detail the life of [such] a society."[2]

In contrast, the observed individual of modernity possesses a self-conscious drive to think as autonomous from objectivity. When a tribal member begins to think about concepts that represent what the member of a tribe or polis has taken for granted as objective, she or he becomes autonomous from objectivity. That separation from objectivity privileges the individual's will to know the objective world. What had been considered an uncontrolled and uncontrollable objectivity in a tribal legal culture is now willed internal to the individual's consciousness. As long as institutions, posited laws, and other examples of objectivity remained external to the individual's consciousness, the individual remained unfree. The fundamental philosophic problem did not arise from "what is a unit of the state-centric legal order—a custom or rule or principle or policy?" Rather, the fundamental problem was that of legitimacy: "why would a thinking individual, no longer deferential to tradition, be bound to the laws of a state-centric legal order?"

Hegel's response to this question is, at one level, that a state-centric legal order could manifest the institutionalization of self-consciousness if the individual felt at home with the institutions and its posited laws. In order to feel at home with such laws, the institutions and laws would have to be the product of the individual's own act of thinking. The challenge for Hegel, then, is to elaborate a philosophy that reconciles objectivity with such an act of thinking so that objectivity will no longer constrain the individual's freedom. For the individual will recognize her- or himself in the objectivity that she or he has willed internal to her or his consciousness. The observed individual will thereby have "progressed" a great distance from the customs of the tribe and polis with which the member of the ethos had felt immediately at one. Although immediacy characterized the relation of a citizen with the polis, the relation of tribal members to tribal customs better exemplifies such immediate identity for reasons that will become apparent in a moment.

Tension permeates the subtle emergence of a thinking being from a stateless society such as a tribe. The tribal member, who has felt immediate with customs, is juxtaposed with the thinking being whose concepts mediate between the knower (of concepts) and the objectivity that has heretofore been considered uncontrollable. Such objectivity had, for millennia, been attributed to nature. Without journeying through an act of thinking, human beings, resembling animals in this respect, acted from appetites. Concepts, then, offer the opportunity for the thinking individual to escape from the constraints of nature. Thinking dissolves the tension between the individual's felt immediacy with objectivity on the one hand and the external objectivity as an *in itself*. But the question remains: "why would a thinking being still feel obligated to obey objectivity if the individual no longer identifies with it?"

This chapter will address Hegel's problematic. First, I shall explicate Hegel's notion of a prehistorical or prelegal stateless ethos. Hegel privileges two factors: the similarity of the natural being with an animal and the characteristics of the barbarian. Second, I shall isolate Hegel's hierarchy of societies. In this context, Hegel identifies various levels of barbarism, he elaborates the nature of legal consciousness in a barbaric society, and he emphasizes how progress materializes in civilization. Third, I shall connect Hegel's notion of civilization to the legitimacy of a modern legal order. Fourth, I shall historically contextualize the problematic in the troubled stateless condition of Germany in his own times. Finally, I shall elaborate why Hegel recognizes the modern state-centric legal order as the highest form of civilization.

I. THE LEGAL ORDER OF TRIBAL SOCIETY

Hegel begins his analysis of legitimacy by postulating a stateless society. The member of a stateless society feels immediate with objectivity as manifested by tribal customs. Concepts do not intercede at this point. The member feels so immediate with objectivity that objectivity seems uncontrollable and uncontrolled. Fate (*Moira*) and nature are usually considered constitutive of objectivity. Slowly, as the tribal member becomes self-conscious that she or he is separate from the tribe's customs, she or he begins to think on her or his own. The individual's concepts intercede between the individual and the objectivity. Personhood, property, contract, and crime exemplify such concepts. Although the philosopher is conscious of the mediation by concepts, the observed individual is not yet conscious that the concepts are the products of her or his own thinking. They are concepts with which one feels immediately bonded as one did with *Moira* or nature or customs. Such concepts are believed to constitute legal reality. As Gadamer puts it, those universals are "not appearance as opposed to reality but rather appearance as the real itself."[3] There is no representation or picture thought that mediates the individual's will vis-à-vis external things of nature. When the observed individual begins to represent objects, she or he leaves the felt oneness with the tribal customs and instead represents the customs as concepts.

a) The Animal and the Human

Hegel has two distinctions in his mind when he contrasts a stateless society from a state-centric legal order.[4] First, throughout his works, Hegel
distinguishes the physical from the spiritual. Animals are driven by physical needs and human beings by spiritual needs (PR 11A, 190A; PH 39, 49).
Hegel explains the difference early in *Philosophy of Right*:

> [t]he animal, too, has drives, desires, and inclinations, but it has no will and
> must obey its drive if nothing external prevents it. But the human being, as
> wholly determinate, stands above his drives and can determine and posit them
> as his own. The drive is part of nature, but to posit it in this "I" depends upon
> my will, which therefore cannot appeal to the fact that the drive is grounded
> in nature. (PR 11A)

The appetites of the animal are unmediated by thinking. Its appetites are
unlimited. The only constraint upon the animal's behavior is nature. The
human being is driven to know objectivity as mediated by concepts: "[i]t
is a trivial commonplace that man is distinguished from the animals by his
ability to think, yet this is something which is often forgotten" (PH 39).
The absence of mediating concepts guarantees that an animal has limited
means to satisfy its needs and appetites. And yet, its physical needs are
unlimited because no concepts constrain its behavior. As a consequence,
"savagery and unfreedom" characterize the animal (PR 194R).

As with the Epicureans and Roman Stoics,[5] Hegel likens human beings to animals when they lack a thinking capacity:

> [t]he natural man, who is determined only by his drives, is not at home with
> himself; however self-willed he may be, the *content* of his willing and opining is
> not his own, and his freedom is only a *formal* one. When I think, I give up my
> subjective particularity, sink myself in the matter, let thought follow its own
> course; and I think badly whenever I add something of my own. (EL 24A2)

So, for example, an "imbecile" is considered an animal if she or he commits a crime during a fit of rage. She or he must be treated as if an animal
(1817/18 W105). If the imbecile were a rational being, she or he would think
with concepts. One such concept might be a crime. The imbecile does
not know that she or he shares such a concept by virtue of the imbecility.
When a German attempted to assassinate Napoleon in 1809, for example,
the assailant could not acknowledge the relation of his act to a shared universal such as "thou shalt not kill." Accordingly, the assailant was stuck in
a prethinking condition (1824/25 W117). The "lowest" form of human being feels immediate with the objectivity as if no other human beings exist
independent of the objectivity (PH 49, 50).

When the tribal member begins to think about objectivity, her or his appetites are left behind (PR 190). Instead of positing her or his appetites (which are, after all, arbitrary), the individual reflects about concepts that represent objects of nature. The reflection liberates the individual from natural needs to spiritual needs (PR 194). When the concept's content is particularized with reference to a context-specific social relationship with a stranger, the mediation between knower and objectivity transforms consciousness into a social relationship with strangers (PR 192). Hegel describes the transformation in this way: "[a]fter the creation of the natural universe, man appears on the scene as the antithesis of nature; he is the being who raises himself up into a second world" (PH 44). The second world is a spiritual realm where consciousness seeks knowledge of objectivity as if its own determination (PR 194R).

Hegel adds that the ultimate end of thinking (and, therefore, of the *telos* of the human being) is to render the human being self-sufficient. This will be so to the extent that one thinks about objects as if the objects were one's own: "[b]ut man has knowledge of himself, and this distinguishes him from animals. He is a *thinking* being [his emphasis]" (PH 49). By thinking about concepts, the human being controls externalities as elements of her or his consciousness. One knows oneself through the consciousness of the objects. If one is self-sufficient, one no longer depends on external things of nature. Conversely, if dependent upon external constraints, one is unfree. If one is unaware that one has the capacity to be free through thinking, one is a natural being (PH 48).

Spirit enters this self-consciousness because spirit drives the human being to overcome immediacy. This spirit thereby distinguishes the human being as opposed to an animal. When the human being thinks, she or he turns inward into her or his consciousness, unlike an animal. Since the animal immediately identifies with the external world, the animal lacks spirit. The whole of history, according to Hegel, represents this drive of humans to leave the natural condition of animals.

b) Who Is a Barbarian?

We are now in a position to understand why Hegel considers so many peoples on the globe as barbaric (in his day as well as, if he were with us today, he would consider such in our own times).[6] The Greek word for barbarian connoted someone who "babbles." If one were not a Greek, one was a barbarian. The Greeks were highly cultivated, according to Hegel, and so they believed in an "absolute gulf" between themselves and the barbarians (EL 163A1). Except for Socrates, the members of the Greek polis lacked the drive to recognize themselves as the authors of objectivity (PH 79). Barbarians, conceived contemporaneous with Hegel, carry on this absence of self-consciousness. They therefore lack any personal responsibility of the harm they may cause to others' feelings or body (1822/23 W151). They do not act morally, that is. Barbarians are driven by biological motives (PR 211A). The barbarian lacks a sense of blameworthiness and even any sense of right or wrong: "among uncultured peoples a crudeness still rules over the concept of right and wrong. There is no consciousness of the extent to which my use of my property may be detrimental to others . . . Among us, the health of others is a more important right than is the running of a business" (1824/25 W 177). The barbarian lacks a sense of morality because the barbarian, immediately bonded with the tribe's universals, does not recognize other human beings as separate from any shared ethos. Knowledge involves concepts, the very substance that barbarians lack. Their decisions and actions, therefore, are arbitrary, violent, blind and irrational, formless, deferential to heroes, and punishable by revenge.

Revenge, not the punishment associated with the state, characterizes the consequence of harm caused by a barbarian. Revenge is motivated from the deep immediacy felt by the individual harmed towards the act of harm. Revenge is "undying, as with the Arabs, where it can be suppressed only by superior force or by the impossibility of putting it into effect" (PR 102). Punishment defers to concepts (1817/18 48. 57–58). As such, punishment requires reflection. Even individuals in a modern society, Hegel complains, mimic the days past of barbarism because they sometimes act from "delight in rationalization and fault-finding because it is easy to find fault, though [it is] hard to recognize the good and its inner necessity [from within the individual's consciousness of itself]" (1822/23 W198). Since history, law, and justice take form when human beings begin to think, Hegel excludes barbarism from world history, legality, and justice (PH 81), just as Hart excludes the tribal society of Rex I from legal philosophy as prelegal and just as Giorgio Agamben (1942–) excludes what is not state centric as "chaos."[7] Indeed, both Hart and Agamben are oblivious to the possibility that a tribal culture can be ordered[8] and, indeed, that the "prelegal" bodily and ritualistic character to a prelegal tribal culture is continued and concealed in the formalism of legal reasoning.[9]

Hegel adds a further insight about the difference between barbarians and thinkers. Thinking is active. When thinking is particularized, the thinking involves action. When I think, I am actively doing something. My will thereby actively brings the external passive things into my consciousness as thoughts (PR 113). By virtue of my will, I realize that I am separate from such things. The natural being, stuck in immediacy, is inactive. The objective world of nature and of the gods and goddesses is beyond the control of the natural body. The natural being is *acted on*, to use Spinoza's term.[10] The barbarian is mild, passive, humble, and possesses an "obsequious submissiveness" even in the face of "degradation" (PH 164). This active character to my willing is entirely absent in a barbarian, according to Hegel.

Such a passive life is characterized, Hegel claims, by the aboriginal peoples of the Americas, especially South America. Hegel describes the peoples as "physically and spiritually impotent . . . Even the animals show the same inferiority as the human being" (PH 163). Hegel describes them as "culturally inferior nations" (PH 163) and "obviously unintelligent individuals with little capacity for education" (PH 164). The aboriginal peoples exhibit "mildness and passivity, [and] humility and obsequious submissiveness towards a Creole, and even more towards a European" (PH 164). Hegel clearly considers the aboriginal peoples as lacking any self-consciousness and, thus, "it will be a long time before the Europeans can succeed in instilling any feelings of independence in them" (PH 14). "Their inferiority in all respects, even in statute, can be seen in every particular," Hegel continues, "for they still live in a natural state of lawlessness and savagery." In addition to being like animals, they are "like unenlightened children, living from one day to the next, and untouched by higher thoughts and aspirations" (PH 165). The indigenous populace of Spanish and Portuguese colonies experience the ultimate degradation of passivity by succumbing to slavery. Further, they lack a "communal existence without which no state can exist" (PH 165). Without a centralized institutional structure to bring order, the indigenous peoples are "savage hordes."[11]

In contrast, the European settlers carry "the advantages of civilization" when they journey to the Americas, Africa, or Asia. The most important advantage of civilization is said to be the desire of the settlers to determine themselves as self-conscious beings. A *terra nullius* is believed to characterize North and South America (despite the fact that over eleven million aboriginal peoples inhabited North America alone when the Europeans began to settle the continent). "America has a long way to go," Hegel claims, because of the absence of a centralized form of government, courts, written laws, institutions, police and other examples of a state (PH 168). Once a state structure takes hold in North America even slavery will be a mere "stage in the progress away from the purely fragmented sensuous existence, a phase in man's education, and an aspect of the process whereby he gradually attains a higher ethical existence and a corresponding degree of culture" (PH 184).

Hegel's attitude towards the Americas reflects his consistent hierarchy of societies. The hierarchy is based upon the extent to which individual members, in Hegel's opinion, self-consciously think through their shared institutions. At the low end of the hierarchy of prehistorical societies, there are "barbarian hordes." Law and justice cannot exist there, according to Hegel. Law and justice are only possible with "civilised nations" (PH 124).

2. THE HIERARCHY OF SOCIETIES

Once Hegel hinges his theory of law upon the difference between a passive animal and an inward-looking thinking subject, we are left with a series of questions. Throughout Hegel's *Philosophy of Right* and his *Introduction to the Philosophy of World History*, Hegel contrasts civilization with the "savage," "barbaric," "primitive" "hordes."[12] There are two related traits of such hordes. First, the savage hordes lack a state. Second, they lack self-reflection. Barbarians are passive, lack intellectual curiosity, are unfamiliar with formal education, and are driven by their biological appetites. The barbarian is said to be dull, open to "solitary brooding," clumsy, not in control of his actions, and driven by habit (PR 197A). In his 1819/20 lectures Hegel even describes "savages" as lazy. Even "primitive Germans" are said to spend their time "lying on bearskins" (1819/20 W156).

But why would a thinking being desire to escape from animalistic barbarism? How does the animal-human dichotomy work into Hegel's idea of a civilized society and, in turn, into his legal philosophy? And how is his view of civilization related to his legal philosophy? Indeed, why does Hegel begin his legal philosophy about the state-centric legal order with a stateless condition?

a) Levels of Barbarism

By studying a society in terms of the level of development of self-consciousness, Hegel believes that he can hierarchize barbaric societies (PH 122–23). At the lowest end of the hierarchy, there are Africans who live "in a completely barbarous condition" of a "primeval and completely natural state" where "man exists in his natural savagery" not unlike a dog (PH 177).[13] Living "outside the sphere of culture," African history "precedes culture and development." Aboriginal peoples of the Americas also occupy the lowest rank in Hegel's social hierarchy (PH 164–71). Hegel also locates the Mongols and Arabs at the bottom of the social hierarchy because they live a nomadic life (PH 156) and destroy institutions with no desire to replace them.[14] Hegel characterizes the Mongolians as driven by animal-like appetites. In contrast, the Teutonic barbarians, who invaded Rome, lived on a "higher" form of barbarism because they did not wish to destroy the Roman institutional structure. Along with the Arabs and Mongols, Hegel locates the Greeks, Romans, and Chinese at the lower rung of social hierarchy (PH 120–21, 134–35). Because the Orientals, for example, are "patriarchal," they lacked self-consciousness. The Chinese lacked institutional avenues for consent to posited laws. They also lacked any sense of freedom. As noted earlier, the ancient Greeks (except for Socrates) epitomized the identity of immediacy with objectivity.

The common phenomenon of a barbarian was the failure of a barbarian to recognize the barbarian's own role in the construction of what she or he eventually conceived as objectivity (PH 137–39, 79, 81). This failure likened the barbarians to animals. More generally, "[e]ven at the present time, we know of peoples which scarcely form a society, let alone a state, but which have long been known to exist" (PH 135). Unlike the Greek view, though, Hegel's sense of a barbarian had the potential to become self-conscious. This potentiality was exhibited through various forms of economic and social relationships such as hunting, pastoral life, agriculture, and city dwelling. Each such social form institutionalized higher and more complex methods of gathering food (PR 351).

b) The Legal Order of a Barbaric Society

The legal consciousness of a society varied with the corresponding level of social development, according to Hegel. He isolated two forms of barbarism, for example. One is grounded in private revenge, and the other defers to shared concepts that are greater than the aggregate of private interests. The former lies at the bottom of the vertical hierarchy of barbaric societies. The second approaches civilization. In order to appreciate this social hierarchy, so prominent even today in the constitutional adjudication about aboriginal customs in Canada, Australia, and New Zealand, and in the foreign policies of the industrial great powers, one needs to understand how radically different is the legal order of a barbaric society from that of a civilized one in Hegel's view.

For one thing, customs characterized the barbaric legal order. Customs were ingrained in the child's upbringing through festive celebrations, dances, and play.[15] Social rituals exalted nature because of the control of natural events (droughts, desert storms, plagues, epidemics, and disease) over the survival of the tribe. Such a legal order of the tribe radically differed from that of the polis.[16] The *nomos-physis* binary arrived on the scene after the polis was formed.[17]

Second, the tribal members followed customary norms without thinking about them. Hegel lectures in 1817/18 that "all simply did their duty, without moral consternation and without the vanity of claiming to know better. There was simple consciousness that the laws *were*" (1817/18 W126). There was a complete absence of self-consciousness about the separation of the tribal member from the customs (PR 211A).

Third, prior to the historical rise of the polis, even the gods were controlled by the customs, better known as Fate or *Moira*.[18] *Moros*, which meant "allotted part," functioned as the dominant source of law in the Minoan (2000 B.C.E.) and Mycenian (1500 B.C.E.) cultures. *Moira* wreaked chaos if any god or human being exceeded its jurisdiction. *Moira* was all controlling of human and divine action.[19] The tribal member did not feel separate from the shared customs. The tribal member recognized other individuals and social entities but not from moral duty: "the Greeks . . . acted on the basis of ethos; they were thus ethical without being moral," Hegel asserts in later lectures (1824/25 W126). Such an amoral ethos clashed with the possibility that members of an ethos acted from duty.

Finally, because the barbaric legal culture lacked the thinking individual, there was also a lack of system and order to the customs. Antigone just went out, for example, and buried her brother's body without wondering whether it was the right thing to do. The objectivity of nature in the prepolis culture existed "in a completely *external* and *fragmented* manner and conceal it [rationality] under the guise [*Gestalt*] of contingency" (PR 146R).

c) Progress

Civilization, justice, law, and philosophy arrive on the scene when the individual begins to think. Further, unlike the state of nature philosophers such as Thomas Hobbes (1588–1679), John Locke (1632–1704), and Rousseau where the human subject leaps from the state of nature to civil society in an all-or-nothing way,[20] the stateless society progresses from barbarism to higher levels of civilization before the individual leaps into civil society. More generally, one errs if one associates Hegel's sense of statelessness with that of the "state of nature" legal philosophers: Grotius, Thomas Hobbes, Samuel Pufendorf (1632–94), John Locke, Rousseau, and Hegel's English contemporary, Jeremy Bentham (1748–1832).[21] First, the traditional "state of nature" theories of law did not entertain the possibility that the human being could develop self-consciousness in the state of nature (PR Pref. p. 13A). For Hegel, continuity characterizes the movement from barbaric into modern societies. Hegel projects the Enlightenment possibility that even barbarians and slaves have the possibility of subtly and slowly separating from their ethos by gaining a consciousness of an "inner self [that] always tells him how things ought to be, and he finds within himself the confirmation or repudiation of what is accepted as valid" (PR Pref. p. 13A).

As a further difference between Hegel's stateless society and that of the state of nature philosophies, Hegel concludes at an early stage of his thinking that the social contract of the "state of nature" philosophies presupposed the desired outcome (NL 65). Instead, for Hegel, the outcome is socially and historically contingent. Non–state-centric social relations have not only been possible but have been the norm until the modern epoch.

Hegel's sense of statelessness differs from the state of nature philosophers for three further reasons. First, in contrast with Hobbes,[22] Hegel equips the individual in a stateless society with a language and reason. Second, Rousseau, like Lucretius (5/1 B.C.E.–65 C.E.),[23] had considered the individual free in the very "natural" condition that Hegel associates with barbarism and unfreedom. As Rousseau wrote, "[m]an was born free [in a state of nature], and everywhere [in civil society] he is in chains."[24] The state represents a continuous *movement* from the tribal member's immediacy with the Fate, nature, and tribal customs to higher and higher forms of individual self-consciousness. Self-consciousness reaches a high point (though not the final point) with an organic constitution, a phenomenon examined in Chapter 9. Hegel contextualizes legal legitimacy in a socially and historically contingent ethos rather than in the abstraction of individuals from such an ethos. Such an individual would not be satisfied by a ruler with an arbitrary will. Third, in contrast with state of nature philosophers, Hegel identifies two shapes or forms of a state: the external and the immanent state (PR 182). I shall examine these two shapes in Chapters 8 and 9.

At this point, Hegel builds a sense of social progress into his legal philosophy: "[i]t is important that we should recognise that the development of the spirit is a form of progress" (PH 125). Hegel continually writes about "development," "gradual progression," "progress," "a higher plane," and "culturally inferior nations" in *Philosophy of Right* and *Introduction to the Philosophy of History*. Progress is "immanent": it is not posited "out there" by some law reform commission study (PH 131). Progress begins with the savage hordes driven by animalistic instincts and ends. Progress is organic-like growth. For there to be progress, one can only understand the early stages of something in the light of something more developed. A hierarchy of societies is thereby built into Hegel's notion of progress. Further, any society at the lower end of the hierarchy will be able to develop into a stage at the higher end.

Why, then, does Hegel describe a state as a higher level of civilization than a clan or tribe or family? First, a clan or tribe or family, even if considered a "people," is "an indeterminate abstraction" (PR 279). Second, the formless mass constitutes lawlessness (PR 278R, 279A) or destruction (PR 302A). A tyranny or despotism, for example, is a "formless mass" that opposes all organized structure (PR 302A, 278A). Courts, government, a legislature, public authorities, and a bureaucracy mark such an organization (PR 279R). Without a centralized structure or organization, the mass cannot attain its interests in an orderly manner. The consequence is that "the masses will always express themselves in a barbarous manner" (PR 302R). For "*the many* as single individuals—and this is a favourite interpretation of [the term] 'the people'—do not live *together*, but only as a *crowd*, i.e. a formless mass whose movement and activity can consequently be elemental, irrational, barbarous, and terrifying" (PR 303R). The condition of "the many," Hegel says, hangs in the air over "the abstract individuality of arbitrary will and opinion, and is thus grounded only in contingency rather than on a foundation which is *stable* and *legitimate* [*berechtigt*] in and for itself" (PR 303).

One can now appreciate that when Hegel cautions that "the owl of Minerva begins its flight only with the onset of dusk" (PR Pref. 23), legal philosophy is no exception. The observing philosopher must retrospectively read how the social relationships inside a society have evolved to the present day. Only the civilized society is conscious of the difference between the lower and higher level of development. If a nation is recognized as a sovereign state, the nation has progressed toward a higher-ordered level of civilization (PR 351). Nations are treated as barbaric if they are "less advanced" than the higher order societies. Since customs share the immediacy that characterizes the natural being, customs manifest a lower stage of progress while mediating representations characterize a higher legal order (PR 349, 359). The role of legal philosophy is to recognize the stage of civilization that the legal consciousness of a particular society presupposes.

This historical progress towards higher and higher levels of self-consciousness, not the sovereign state per se, marks the "conquering

march of the world spirit" (PH 63). Such a spirit expresses "the divine process which is a graduated progression" (PH 64). Hegel also describes the
progress as the "march of God" (PR 258A). Why does progress share this
divinelike character? Because the immanent invisible drive to become self-
conscious generates progress, the social hierarchy has an inevitability about
it (PH 90). At the same time, manifestations of the divine are continually
changing (PR 152). Hegel has in mind here Socrates' own attention to the
daemonic drive as the generative origin of his interminable effort to become self-conscious.

As I argue in Chapters 8 through 10, the nation-state reflects just such a
progress (PR 144A, PS 437, PH 94). Hegel describes the progress through
levels of self-consciousness into a state in this manner:

> the nation's highest impulse is to comprehend itself and to realise in every area
> of its existence the concept it has formed of itself. The most important element
> is neither that of physical need, whatever its nature may be, nor that of formal
> justice, but of thought and intelligence as such. Free, disinterested, dispassion-
> ate consciousness is the highest achievement of the nation, and the same of
> true art. (PH 112)

The state is just one higher form of development from the natural forms
of a "savage horde" (Mongols), restorative invaders (Teutonic barbarians
of Rome), a tribe (Antigone's), family (the nuclear family in civil society),
despotism (Cicero's Rome), and civil society (possessive individualism)
(PH 137). The feudal constitutions themselves lacked the form of a state.
The feudal lord claimed title to land. The feudal lord exercised discretion
uncontrolled by any transcending rule of law. The inhabitants followed
manorial customs, however arbitrary their content. Self-consciousness carries "uncivilized" peoples to a higher level of civilization. And laws mark
such a higher level.

Finally, a state may "exist" in name only as in the case of a tyranny or
despotism where there is neither the rule of law nor a bureaucratic organization of state officials (PR 302A, 278R). With despotism, the arbitrary
self-interest of the ruler, whether a monarch or the *Volk*, lies behind posited laws. The ruled are "a destructive mass opposed to all organization."
Only a sovereign state possesses the possibility of the rule of law because of
the absence of determinate concepts to allocate jurisdiction in a despotism
(278R). Without a systemic order, Hegel continues in the latter passage,
the individuals "will always express themselves in a barbarous manner."

The lower forms of social organization fail to give form to the ruled. A
tribe, feudal principality, or tyrannical war lord who claims to represent a

"state," each exemplifies a "formless mass" without the internal organization of governments, courts, public authorities, legislatures, and the like to
be a state (PR 279R).[25] Such stateless social entities rank at the lower end
of the social hierarchy precisely because they lack a state. As Hegel writes,
"[b]arbarians are governed by drives, customs [*Sitten*], and feelings, but
they have no consciousness of these" (PR 211A). For there to be a state,
there must be a constitution with a generally accepted legitimacy, a common military, an organization of officials, and shared concepts whose content recognizes reciprocal relationships. In addition, the state's laws must
be systematic (PR211A). There has to be a *center*—a term Hegel frequently
uses to describe a state—determined by written laws vertically and horizontally linked to all offices and personnel of an organization.[26] Hegel
considers France as having such a center where, for example, the mayors
of the smallest village are appointed by the central ministry.[27] Harm to
the center of the legal order, this being the freedom of self-consciousness,
harms the legitimacy of the social whole. Hegel lectures in 1824/25 that the
civilized being becomes conscious that her or his acts may be detrimental
to others (1824/25 W177). Without a center, stateless societies lack systemic
and written laws (PR 211A). Further, they lack a "center" to social life (GC
77). The state offers such a center. In this respect Hegel shares the constitutional perspective of the common-law lawyers of the early nineteenth century. Only sovereign states were recognized as states in the international
legal order. States alone could claim absolute title of property to their territorial possessions (PR 260).[28] Such states could also enter into treaties
to which they consented to be bound. A tribal legal order was too inferior
to civilization, as represented by the state, to enter into binding treaties.[29]
Given the association of the state with civilization, the individual could
harm the state as "the center," independent of private harm caused to another individual.

3. THE TELATION OF LEGALITY TO LEGITIMACY
IN A CIVILIZED SOCIETY

Hegel's hierarchy of societies and his preoccupation with the relation of
the individual vis-à-vis strangers in any society leads to several elements of
his legal philosophy that we need to clarify at this point.

First, the legitimacy of a legal order takes a turn when heroes replace
private revenge. With private revenge, honor is defended in battle. There

is no sense of harm to the community as a whole. In the Trojan War, for example, Menelaus's vanity in Homer's *Illiad* is harmed when a foreign ruler abducts Helen, and Achilles's vanity is harmed when his boyfriend is killed by Hector. Similarly, Polyneices seeks revenge against his brother, Eteocles, in Sophocles' *Antigone* because Eteocles refused to give up the throne despite their agreement that the throne would be shared two years at a time. Because of the immediacy of the tribal member with the customs of the clan or tribe, an attack against the prestige of the tribal ruler is an attack against the very existence of the tribe. Legitimacy rests with the person of the ruler as represented by a symbol such as the spear in Wagner's *Götterdämmerung* (1876).[30] When Hagen causes treachery against Brünnhilde and Siegfried, Brünnhilde takes the spear in an act of personal revenge at the end of *Götterdämmerung*. A society breaks from such a level of social development, however, when the leader, such as Alexander, Romulus, Caesar, Augustus, and Napoleon, is recognized as a hero (PR 102R). Despite his own drive for power and prestige, the hero is conscious of the development of his society into a higher ranking on the hierarchy of civilized societies. Civilization is thereby advanced. Such occurs, for example, when the hero, such as Romulus or Augustus, founds a state. In the case of Napoleon, the hero lifts the feudal society into a state-centric civilization (PR 93A, 1822/23 W77–8).[31]

Second, although violence constitutes the origin of the state (PR 50)—a point that Walter Benjamin (1892–1940), Carl Schmitt, and Jacques Derrida (1930–2004) develop[32]—the violence is displaced once the rule of law and the self-conscious posit of shared concepts characterize the legal order.[33] The more that objectivity is the consequence of mediation through concepts, the more does a unit of legality displace the originary violence in the constitution of law: "[f]or although the State may originate in violence, it does not rest on it; violence, in producing the State, has brought into existence only what is justified in and for itself, namely, laws and a constitution" (PM 432).[34] Contrary to Derrida, the interpretative act, for Hegel, is sanitized of violence.

When the tribal member begins to reflect about the objectivity with which she or he has heretofore identified (as with nature, for example), however, the member withdraws into her- or himself and begins to dissociate from the objects with which she or he had felt immediate (PH 62). The member ceases to be a natural being who, animal-like, was driven by arbitrary appetites disguised as the objectivity of consciousness (PH 49). Such a natural being, according to Hegel, had lived a solipsistic life as if

she or he lacked any need for another individual to fulfill her or his appetites. When the individual begins to think, she or he thinks about concepts
which mediate between the individual and what the individual had heretofore taken as the uncontrollable objectivity of nature. The two moments
of immediacy and mediation radically differ. This gap between immediacy
and mediation permeates his theory of legal reasoning as I elaborate in
Chapter 3, and his philosophy of substantive law as retrieved in Chapters 4
to 10. In *Encyclopaedia Logic*, Hegel describes the gap as generated from "a
thinking journey" that elevates thinking above the sensible with "the *leap*
that is made into the supersensible when the sequences of the sensible are
broken off, all this is thinking itself; this transition is *only thinking*" (EL
50R). Such a leap characterizes the emergence of civilization from the tribal
society. This is so much so that Hegel emphasizes that those societies that
are characterized by immediacy (where objectivity is deemed to be Fate,
nature, or unconscious customs) must be excluded from any philosophical, historical, or legal inquiry (PH 12). Legal philosophy begins when a
society has left the immediacy of tribal customs for the self-consciousness
of humanly authored laws. Hegel considers the state as such an author.

Each individual member of an ethos possesses the potential to grow in
self-consciousness to the point that self-consciousness recognizes the knower's objects as her or his own. So too, progress emanates from the immediacy
of the tribal legal culture to civilization where self-consciously posited laws
and institutions manifest how individuals recognize each other inter se.

Hegel's explanation why immediacy characterizes the lowest form of
social life is best understood, perhaps, in his explication of Antigone's immediate identity with her unwritten tribal customs (PS 450; PR 166R; PH
17, 94, 202–03). Although I shall also discuss immediacy as manifested
in the "archaic family" in Chapter 7, Antigone's example is important in
this context because she acts as if there is no mediating knowledge between herself and the objectivity of nature. Indeed, she feels so immediate
with *Moira* that she does not consider herself bound to King Creon's edict.
When King Creon admonishes Antigone, "Did you know that this had
been forbidden?" Antigone replies "I knew. I couldn't help knowing. It
was everywhere." Creon exclaims, "And yet you dared to violate the laws?"
Antigone then gives her great defense, reread by Aristotle as the basis of
natural law (*Rhetoric* 1.13, 1.15):

> What laws? I never heard it was Zeus
> Who made that announcement.
> And it wasn't justice either. The gods below
> Didn't lay down this law for human use.

Antigone then continues that the human ruler, such as a king, never had the

> Power to trample the gods' unfailing,
> And I never thought your announcements
> Could give you—a mere human being—
> Power to trample the gods' unfailing,
> Unwritten laws. These laws weren't made now
> Or yesterday. They live for all time,
> And no one knows when they came into the light.
> Sophocles' *Antigone*, l.450–58.[35]

Antigone's sense of "what binds a law?" radically differs from King Creon's.

Unlike many a contemporary law student or professional law teacher, Antigone does not search her memory as to whether there is a rule that she ought to bury her brother's body. She was not taught how to find a custom in a book or a classroom. She does not debate with her sister or anyone else as to whether the content of the custom is wise or just. Antigone buries the body of Polyneices without thinking whether she ought to do so morally. If she had acted from a moral recognition of others, a duty would have interceded between herself and her knowledge of the custom. This knowledge would have lifted her thinking above her immediacy. She feels as if she has no choice but to obey the unwritten laws beyond her control and as if she feels immediate with such objectivity. Antigone *experiences* the laws just as she experiences the edict (that she ought not to bury the body), the prosecution, and the sentencing by the polis (PR 166R). Her father/half-brother, Oedipus, had committed incest for which the gods were wreaking havoc inside her conscience; her half-brother had committed incest with her mother and had begot herself; her little sister had initially refused to support her action against their uncle, the king, or to empathize with her suffering; her uncle is the king who issued the very edict which she disobeys; her brothers had killed each other on the battlefield; her uncle had ordered her to be stoned and then starved to death; and her first cousin and fiancé (Haemon) and her mother (the wife of her half-brother/father Oedipus) had committed suicide. Her world is inverted. Even the legitimacy of the polis is personally experienced in that the one brother, Polyneices, claims the authority of Thebes.[36]

Hegel explains that when individuals begin to think about concepts that mediate between self and the object with which one feels immediate, one begins to feel separate or autonomous from the custom (PH 58). The individual's thinking about thinking begins the progress of human development through increasingly sophisticated layers of civilization (PH 54, 55, 112, 125). Hegel suggests in *Introduction to the Philosophy of History* that the state represents the most advanced stage of civilization (PH 101, 137). There is no closure to the development to higher and higher levels of civilization, however. Indeed, the potential for the reconciliation of the knower's concepts with the knower her- or himself even proceeds through different shapes of international law. That said, the individual's consciousness of her or his own objects only begins, according to Hegel, when a state-centric legal order takes form (PH 142–43). For the state's officials deliberate and reflect about concepts before they posit written laws. The separation between oneself and the polis or state closes when the state is shared amongst self-conscious individuals (and here Hegel has the organic legal order in mind, as examined in Chapter 9). The state is an author.[37] This contrasts with the authorless laws of the stateless legal order.

4. THE PROGRESS FROM THE PRELEGAL PHENOMENA TO THE LEGAL PHENOMENA

The juxtaposition between immediacy, as represented by tribal customs, and mediation, as represented by the state, is important for history, law, and philosophy. Philosophy, history, justice, and law only begin, for Hegel, when the philosopher observes that a society has left the immediacy of a tribe for the self-reflection of civilization. Mediating concepts represent other concepts: they "are not truly the first [immediacy]; [for] mediation consists in having already left a first behind, to go on to a second, and in a going forth from moments that are distinct [because they are concepts of thought]" (EL86).[38] Like the leap from immediacy to mediation by concepts, the thinking individual mourns the loss of immediacy (EL 86A2). As Hegel expresses at one point, "this prehistorical period lies outside the scope of our present investigation" (PH 134).[39] In like vein, Hegel describes a radical rupture between the immediacy characteristic of a tribal society and polis with the mediations by concepts in civilization: "[t]he Greek heroes step forth in a prelegal age, or they are themselves the founders of states, so that right and social order, law and custom [*Sitte*] proceed from them, and actualise themselves as their individual world, *remaining connected to them*."[40] The legal philosopher is left with Hegel's caution that one must exclude the prehistorical and the prelegal from philosophy.

The prelegal phenomena are also excluded from what contemporary Anglo American general jurisprudence considers "legality." There are three aspects of the prelegal world that general jurisprudence excludes today. One concerns the "prelegal" tribal legal orders which allegedly lack secondary rules to ascertain the succession of rulers. The second aspect concerns the exclusion from general jurisprudence of the prelegal experience of immediacy. Third, general jurisprudence excludes the very phenomenological experience of thinking that precedes the presupposed external foundation of binding laws.

To take an example and only as an example, Hart uses similar terms as does Hegel regarding the leap from the prelegal tribal legal orders to the modern in his *Concept of Law*.[41] Hart extends the exclusion of the phenomenological differences to legal officials who are "haunted" by the loss of experiential meaning in a prelegal world once legal officials leap into the modern legal order.[42] Further, when Hart addresses his differences with other scholars, he admits that he is personally "haunted" by the clashing values in which they find themselves.[43] Hart makes a rigid rupture between the multiplicity of immediacies in the prelegal experiences and the rule of recognition of such experiences: the rule of recognition is a discrete "approximation," frozen in experienced time, of the multiplicity.[44] This exclusion of the prelegal world of experience and collective memories remains with us today, for example, in Canadian court decisions about aboriginal claims to property, indigenous customs, and self-government.[45]

The progress from the immediacy of the prelegal world to the mediation in the modern world offers the opportunity for an individual to philosophize, according to Hegel (PH 143). The philosopher's role is to observe how the individual becomes increasingly self-conscious from the development of one presupposed structure of legal consciousness to the next. This very drive to become increasingly self-conscious creates the need for a state, according to Hegel: "[b]ut we must not for a moment imagine that the physical world of nature is of a higher order than the world of the spirit; for the state is as far above physical life as spirit is above nature" (PR 272A). The state, I shall argue in subsequent chapters, is only one more step on the ladder from the prelegal to civilization. For example, Hegel himself calls the state-centric legal order "objective mind" (PM 535–52) as opposed to "absolute mind" in *Philosophy of Mind*. With absolute mind, institutions are no longer external to the individual's self-consciousness. This is only possible, if it is possible, in an international legal consciousness, I shall argue in Chapter 10.

The progress from the prelegal to the legal civilized world impacts upon what is the legal unit of the legality. For, what is a legal unit (for example, a rule or policy) in legal reasoning depends upon the legitimacy of the legal order. A crime does not exist unless the criminal act challenges the very legitimacy of the legal order, as we see in Chapter 4. The lawyer's

intellectual trace after the latest case in the common law system is misdirected if the latest case is posited in a legal order that lacks legitimacy.
And a modern legal order lacks legitimacy if the self-conscious individual
is not bonded with her or his rules and institutions. The units of legality,
then, shift into issues about legitimacy. Legitimacy, in turn, addresses religious practices, art and philosophy, social practices, traditions and rituals,
institutional relationships, and the usual posited rules and policies with
which the lawyer and even the Anglo-American philosopher are familiar
(PM 553–77). Thus, instead of a bonding with a reified objectivity, such
as occurs in the Roman legal order, the subject intentionally bonds with
experienced objectivity (PR 94). The subject and her or his ethos thereby
reach a higher stage of development from the unreflective immediacy of a
tribe. The philosopher observes this development of self-consciousness. So
too, justice and goodness only become possible when the individual has
become self-conscious of her or his recognition of strangers. This recognition, again, is manifested by universals (such as legislatures and courts as
well as rules) which they share together (PR 93A). A hierarchy of societies,
progress, and social relations between individuals are thereby built into
Hegel's legal philosophy.

5. HEGEL'S GERMANY AS A STATELESS SOCIETY

Hegel had reason to be preoccupied with the difference between a prelegal and a modern legal order. For the Germany of his day, in Hegel's
view, shared many of the characteristics of a premodern legal order. In
particular, he believed that Germany was a stateless society at a time when
sovereign states were consolidating themselves in Europe and extending
their dominions throughout Africa, Asia, and North America. The stateless condition of German principalities began to be an issue in the 1760s.
Influenced by Adam Ferguson's *Essay on the History of Civil Society* (1767),
Hegel concerned himself with the issue of statelessness in the marginal
notes (1800) to his essay, "The German Constitution" (1798–1802).[46] Hegel
begins the essay with the famous line, "Germany is no longer a state . . .
and they [the older teachers of constitutional law] believe that it is only in
name that they can describe the German state as an empire or body poli-
tic" (GC 6, 74). Germany was composed of many small feudal principalities which lacked the organization of a state (GC 66). The members of the
principalities also lacked any sense of an ethos that was greater than the
sum of its parts either internally or externally vis-à-vis other German prin-

cipalities. Hegel facetiously explains in the essay that the constitutional law professor could no longer describe Germany as a state because one would have to concede consequences which flowed from the concept of a sovereign. Instead of constitutional lawyers addressing such a difficult question, they called Germany an "empire" (GC 14).

This is not to say that Germany, being stateless, lacked laws or even courts. Rather, German-speaking peoples lacked a unifying state which was internally organized with a centralized form of government and a monopoly of violence, on the one hand, and which was externally recognized as a state by other states on the other: "[i]n Europe's protracted oscillation between barbarism and civilization [*Kultur*], the German state has not fully accomplished its transition to the latter, but has succumbed to the convulsions which accompany it; its members have broken away to complete independence, and the state has dissolved" (CG 97). With respect to internal sovereignty, laws were drawn from feudal notions of possession, private actions, and power without the sense of public authority [*öffentliches Recht*] as exercised by the states of France, Spain, England, Denmark, Sweden, Holland, and Hungary. Each had grown into a single state by pacifying and uniting those social elements that threatened to undermine the state's legitimacy (GC 62, 77).

What did Hegel mean when he described Germany as stateless? The German provincial assemblies lacked both social bonding and the interlinking of centralized governmental offices. With respect to external sovereignty, each principality regarded the other as foreign. The expansion of feudal estates worked against Germany's existence as a state (GC 56–57). Instead of being internally organized in a pyramidal structure, Germany was disorganized, stuck in feudal forms of government, and "disintegrated into a mass of states whose mode of subsistence is fixed by solemn mutual treaties and guaranteed by major powers" (GC 66–67). Each principality had its own legal jurisdiction, its own monetary system, and a monopoly of coercion inside the territorial boundary of the principality. Hegel urged that Germany construct a centralized public authority in the shape of a pyramid (GC 40) because, without such a center, a state could not exist. The monarch functioned as the ultimate center of the state. And laws, instead of being customary norms, had to be "known by thought, it must be a system in itself, and only as such can it have any validity among civilized [*gebildeten*] nations" (PR 211A). A common educational system built upon the humanities would educate the elite in a manner necessary to perceive and work for the interests of the state. Customs, education, religion, culture, [*Bildung*] and language helped to unify the state (GC 19, 21).

Hegel raises a second concern about the stateless condition of Germany. In place of the feudal order, a new international legal order had taken formation in Renaissance Italy and had then expanded to incorporate Spain, Portugal, England, and France by the sixteenth century. The parties to the Treaty of Westphalia, 1648 had not recognized Germany as a sovereign state (GC 74). The will of foreign states had determined Germany's future. Without their protection, the authority of the principalities would collapse (GC 74–75). Napoleon's military victories marked the vulnerability of German principalities to external state military action. War had exposed the need for German principalities to protect themselves from external aggression. In order for Germany to be recognized as a sovereign state, there would have to be a radical shift in the legitimacy of the German legal orders from feudalism to a state-centric organization with shared prejudgments and expectations. But this would require a sense of legitimacy that was greater than the aggregate of the parts. The old form of multiple feudal principalities had disguised the emergence of actual social and political forms (GC 62).

Hegel explains in "The German Constitution" that Germany could become a state like the others:

> the illiberal demand that laws, the administration of justice, the imposition and collection of taxes, etc, language, customs, culture [*Bildung*], and religion should be regulated and governed from a single centre is not fulfilled in Germany; on the contrary, the most disparate variety prevails in these matters. But this would not prevent Germany from constituting a state if it were organised in other respects as a political authority. (GC 25–26)

But to be a state, Germany had to be much more than a mere shell to regulate and protect private economic or social interests. Rather, there had to be a centralized organization. Unless the principalities united into a secular state, inhabitants lacked the opportunity to bond with strangers who shared universals with them. If inhabitants participated in and self-consciously authored the laws and institutions of a German state, they would feel at home with the objectivity of their institutional legal structure. Once recognized as a state in its external relations, no other state could legally interfere into the domestic affairs of the members of the legal order. Here, Hegel is just repeating the accepted principle of Emmerich de Vattel (1714–67), if not Hugo Grotius (1583–1645).[47] Hegel continually urges in his essay that the German political elite recognize the new international legal order presented by the Treaty of Westphalia, 1648.

Given the domestic and international context in which Germany was situated, then, Hegel needed to justify why the laws of a state would be binding upon an individual who emerged from a stateless condition to a state-centric international legal order. The rule of law had to depoliticize the arbitrary acts of feudal rulers. And an apolitical public service was needed to displace the feudal lords and kings. Most importantly, Hegel had to explain why individuals would feel bonded with such apolitical laws and public service. Unlike ancient Greece and Rome and unlike tribal societies, the individual would now be autonomous and yet feel at home with objectivity.

In addressing Germany's stateless condition, Hegel had before himself several options. One was Fichte's idea of an Ephorate which supervised the actions of rulers.[48] However, such state representatives would supervise themselves for they were ultimately responsible for creating or abolishing the Ephorate. Another option was to associate legitimacy with the general will much as did Rousseau. But how could the general will be institutionalized in civil society constituted by a contract between arbitrary wills? In either case, the terror of the French Revolution remained a possibility. Although I shall expand upon this in later chapters, Hegel believed that a legal order could only avoid terror if the philosopher focused upon a self-reflective social bonding as constitutive of the reconciliation of subjectivity with centralized institutions. Such a self-reflective social bonding privileged the recognition of each individual inter se. In place of the undeveloped bonding of a family member with the universal customs of the family, Hegel privileges reflective subjects who are acculturated into a reflective *Sittlichkeit*. The reflective individual feels "at home" in such a *Sittlichkeit* because one participates in the deliberation and reflection about the content of posited laws and because one recognizes oneself through the objective institutions. Hegel believed early in his career that such a social bonding is greater than the aggregate of individual rights.[49] The state might well represent such social bonding. I shall explain in Chapter 6 that in his mature legal philosophy twenty years later Hegel emphasizes that the self-reflective social bonding manifests the ethicality of the reciprocal recognition amongst strangers.

The condition of German statelessness goes hand in hand with the paramount concern of Hegel's day: freedom. One is considered free to the extent that other human subjects, other human constructions (such as the state), and other external objects—nature and territory—do not constrain one's freedom to act. Hegel asks whether there is an immanent structure in an individual's consciousness where the above external objects do not constrain the individual's actions. The starting point for such an inquiry is the immediacy or presence with which the individual identifies objectivity. The individual can no longer blame the Fate, nature, the gods, polis, God or a feudal ruler as the determinative source of one's actions. This intentional act appears for the first time with Socrates, although Hegel does suggest that Antigone went inward into her consciousness when she opposed the newfound state of King Creon (PR 166R).[50]

6. THE STATE-CENTRIC INSTITUTIONAL LEGAL ORDER

We have seen that Hegel claims that Western legal culture reflects a slow and distinct actualization of the potentiality of self-conscious subjectivity.[51] Hegel argues that the historical Socrates exemplifies the first thinking being who breaks from the immediacy of objectivity. When Meletus charges Socrates with corrupting the youth of Athens, Socrates defends himself in terms of his lack of intent to do so (*Apology* 25d–26a). Socrates admonishes that "it's the greatest good for a man to discuss virtue every day, and the other things you've heard me discussing and examining myself and others about, on the grounds that the unexamined life isn't worth living for a human being" (*Apology* 38a). Socrates withdraws into himself to the point that he subjectively impersonates objectivity, as the Speech of the Law, in *Crito*. Hegel insists that Socrates' student, Plato, just could not recognize the new phenomenon of subjectivity that Socrates had exhibited. Indeed, Plato constructed arguments justifying a state, arguments that would prevent the formation of a family or the protection of property independent of the state (PR 185R). Subjectivity emerges, however, in the Roman legal culture where subjectivity is recognized as a reified legal person (PR 185A). Christianity turns subjectivity inward to love, romanticism, and the eternal salvation of the individual's soul.

When Hegel addresses subjectivity in a "civilized society," the individual's thinking about objectivity is contingent and initially arbitrary. There is no yardstick to balance any conflict between individuals. The individual's arbitrary desires oppose tribal customs. This opposition feels "wrong" (PR 81). Why? Because the individual has unknowingly just emerged from a tribe where one had felt immediate with the shared assumptions and expectations of other tribal members. If the individual opposed the shared tribal customs, one would be separate from them. One would thereby possess a will. The will, though, would be arbitrary, because the individual would not think about choices which confronted the individual. The observed individual's arbitrary will would challenge the legitimacy of the tribal ethos and, for that matter, the legitimacy of any legal order, such as the feudal, where the individual accepts objectivity as an externally posited "given." Conflict and violence would characterize the conflicts of arbitrary wills in the emerging individualist ethos. The philosopher, observing the relationship between individuals, becomes aware that the individual is separate from the customs and, in place of the customs, there are objects created by the individual's consciousness. An objectivity of consciousness emerges.

When the observed individual begins to separate from the universals of the tribe, a thinking process links with the will. The separation of the individual from external things generates a subject and objects. The objects are external things of nature and of consciousness. There are two types of objectivity now: the objects constructed in objects posited by nature and those in consciousness. The possibility of freedom arises when the individual recognizes that objects, heretofore located in an external objectivity, are the construction of consciousness and when the objects are shared with others through laws and institutions. When the objectivity is in fact determined by the individual's consciousness, the objects are binding upon the individual (PR 124R). This process of recognition is slow and painful. It requires the individual to become distant from what she or he has hitherto taken as universally uncontrolled and uncontrollable— Fate, nature, or unwritten customs. The individual becomes aware of her or his own conscience, duties to others, intentionality, and social relations with strangers in a socially contingent world. Because one has constructed this world in one's own consciousness, one recognizes strangers as also self-determining through the shared act of thinking. This shared act of thinking exists, despite differences in temperament, intelligence, desires, and need. *Bildung* works to make the observed individual self-conscious capable of reconciling objectivity with the individual's subjectivity. *Bildung* also works to encourage the philosopher to become conscious of how strangers reciprocally recognize each other.

What Hegel is describing here are two radically different senses of legitimacy. In the one, the tribal legal order and the legal order of the polis are legitimate if the member of the tribe or polis is immediately bonded with the community without the mediation of concepts. Hegel's project is to describe how such a "beautiful life" dissolves as the tribal or city member, such as Socrates, begins to think on her or his own. In the second, concepts intercede between individual and the shared objectivities of nature and of consciousness (PR 217R). Each legal concept—the person, property, contract, crime, blameworthiness, and intentional wrongdoing—marks one logical phase in the development of legal consciousness from the immediacy of the tribe and polis. The individual becomes a subject. Each shape of consciousness signifies how individuals socially relate to each other inter se (PR 217). Despite the apparent break from the prior external constraints (such as customs) in which the observed individual finds her- or himself, there invariably remain further external constraints upon self-determination (PR 81A).

As long as the individual is a subject, there must be an object. Subjective freedom emerges when the individual bonds with shared objects, such as institutions of the state and the rules posited by such institutions, but when she or he does so from reflection about the content of the shared objects. This self-conscious reflection contrasts with tradition external to consciousness and with the arbitrary will disguised by objectivity (PR 104). The universals manifest how one individual socially relates to another, both as self-determining subjects. With such interpersonal recognition, as I shall explain more fully in Chapter 6, the ethos will be ethical (PM 486). If the individual can recognize her or his self in all objectivity, there is no longer an external constraint on the subject's freedom to think (PR 23). The laws are no longer externally posited as objectivity. The laws are recognized as the mediation between the subject, as knower of objectivity, and the known objects in consciousness. It is not just posited rules that manifest such mediation. Rather, moral duties, religious practices, ethnic assumptions, and world history are incorporated into legality (PR 33A). Legality dissipates into a quest for legitimacy in a modern legal order.

Legal Reasoning

It is one thing to recount the logic of freedom within the subject's consciousness. It is another to understand how Hegel relates the logic of freedom to legal reasoning. When we turn to theories about legal reasoning today, we might ask whether there is a special method that lawyers and judges adopt to fulfill objectives in a statute or to fulfill legal rules posited in precedents. So, for example, contemporary constitutional analysis in the United States or Canada often takes a "fundamental interest" or "constitutional value" as an objective or "given" standard and then examines the means that a legislature chooses to fulfill the "given." The courts elaborate detailed tests and doctrines concerning the means. The "givens" are usually posited in a text called "the Constitution" or in the intent of the Founding Fathers or in unwritten conventions such as the "rule of law" or the "independence of the courts." In like vein, Joseph Raz accepts that reasoning can take one only so far until one must post a "given" value.[1] Hegel's theory of legal reasoning is, in contrast, an antimethod in that he attempts to explicate the activity of thinking immanent in the movements of legal consciousness *before* the official ever posits the fundamental interest or objectivity of a statute. Legal reasoning is and can be presuppositionless, Hegel claims. Before one assumes that there are values or rules or a state in an objective world, one must investigate the activity of thinking. As Hegel says in *Lesser Logic,* it is absurd to know the world intellectually as if posited by objectives, rules, or values "out there" beyond human consciousness, before the philosopher or even the observed official has any capacity to think (EL 10R). We need to explain and justify the act of thinking in concrete circumstances. Accordingly, legal reasoning must bracket any objective or "given" or presupposition. Instead of working within intellectual differences amongst rules and other concepts in objectivity, Hegel directs his attention to human experience as constituting legality. In order to set up Hegel's theory of legal reasoning, I address his metaphor of an inverted world, how meaning is transformed in the inverted world, the consequences of the identity of law in the inverted world, and the role of the philosopher in the inverted world. These are the themes of sections one to four.

Against the background of this metaphor, I turn in section five to Hegel's insights about the intellectual differentiation of rules in a seemingly uncontrollable objective world. Hegel calls this *Verstand*, which associates legal units with externally posited rules. Concepts are "self-standing" or discrete units, isolated from the phenomenal world of appearances which, in contrast, are conditioned by experiential space and time.[2] A concept (and a rule or principle is a concept) is self-standing when it only relies upon itself for knowledge. *Verstand* begins when one subject intellectually produces an indeterminate abstraction that is fixed in time and space. But this fixity in space and time contradicts the sense of experienced time that is exhibited as the thinking being moves through implied structures of consciousness. *Verstand* reifies legal units vis-à-vis social phenomena.

From Hegel's critique of *Verstand*, I turn in sections six and seven to Hegel's theory of legal reasoning that aspires to institutionalize *Vernunft*. *Vernunft* links concepts with particular context-specific social experiences of the subject who is immersed in an ethos of which she or he feels an intimate part. The family, civil society, the organic legal order, and various shapes of the international legal orders exemplify such ethê. In this way, Hegel links the posited rules and values with the legitimacy of the legal order as a whole (or of *Recht*) because legitimacy hangs upon the self-determining subject and such a subject is self-determining if, as an act of thinking, she or he feels at one with the objectivity of the ethos. *Vernunft* incorporates such a broad spectrum of research materials that one needs to ask whether legal reasoning is really anthropology. I explain in section eight why this is not so and proceed to explain, in section nine, that the identity of legality rests with truth about the content of rules.

I. THE INVERTED WORLD

As an introduction to Hegel's theory of legal reasoning, one needs to grasp the radicality of his method. Hegel offers a metaphor to aid us in this regard. Although he had scientific laws in mind when he wrote *Science of*

Logic and *Lesser Logic,* his metaphor also extends to written and unwritten human laws. The metaphor, introduced in his early essay, "On the Nature of Philosophical Criticism" (1802),[3] elaborated in important passages of *Phenomenology of Spirit* (PS 143–65) and explained in detail in *Science of Logic* (SC 499–511), imagines the world as inverted. Hegel is not the first to use this metaphor.[4] With the aid of the inverted world analysis, Hegel is able to reread the two dominant traditions of legal thought of his time and of ours.

a) The First Legal Supersensible World

The first supersensible world, which Kant describes as the "thing-in-itself," is juxtaposed to appearances. Like the dog owner who feels insulted when one steps aside to avoid the dog on a pathway, the subject feels immediate with her or his object, in this case a dog. The immediacy is indeterminate because there is no constraint upon the subject's beliefs or intuitions. The immediacy identifies with itself. Truth lies in the essence of this immediacy (SC 499). Appearance lacks the essence that Kant (and Hart) located in the noumenal realm of knowledge. Thus, appearance is an illusory show whose essence is an abstract reflection (SC 500–01).

So, there are two sides of the supersensible world. The essence or criterion of a rule is posited as an indifferent, indeterminate abstraction. Appearance is contingent, unessential, and ever changing (SC 501). The one side is the negative of the other. Hegel locates laws in appearance, however. Laws are "immediately present" in appearance (SC 503). Laws mirror appearance. When one claims an essence for an appearance, the unity is a law of appearances (SC 502). That said, laws are indifferent to appearance because laws are abstract reflections. Because there is an untranslatable gap between the thing-in-itself as essence and the appearance, a focus upon the former erases the latter (SC 501). Each depends upon the absence of the other.

For example, to take the Hegel/Hart distinction between legal versus prelegal, legality depends upon the absence of prelegal phenomena. Legality is fixed in time and space. The prelegal phenomena, excluded from legality by general jurisprudence, manifest change. The distinction, like the North Pole versus the South Pole, could have been the other way around (EL 119A1). Each concept is conditioned by the other, and each concept thereby exists in relation to the other. There is still a remainder to the essence of legality, though. The remainder is the content of a law (SC 505). Put differently, a law is empty of being (immediacy) in the first supersensible world. Legality is what the legal is not (the prelegal in appearances).

In explicating the first supersensible world, Hegel begins with the separation of objective facts from subjective values, or the thing-in-itself from appearance. This dichotomy works through much professional legal education and adjudication today. First, legal reasoning, whether of the classroom or the courtroom, is presupposed to be objectivity as the locus of legality. Second, ever more pressing in former colonies of the European states, there is the distinction between a legal and a prelegal world. This distinction, introduced by Hegel[5] and accepted as a "given" by Hart's *Concept of Law*,[6] works to exclude the prelegal tribal legal orders from the concept of legality. Third, the distinction also excludes bodily experiences—associated with subjectivity—from legality. What the observing philosopher and observed legal official accept as legal "actuality" is a supersensible world that is above and separate from human experience. This world is what Hegel considers the "first supersensible world." It includes the rules and principles, the statutes and judicial decisions, and state institutions, all of which are considered objective, measurable in space and time, and the object of legal analysis. The "given-ness" of the externality reinforces the assumption that objectivity constitutes the "practice of law."

Such a supersensible world presupposes that legality and legitimacy are external to human experience, experience being understood as consciousness. Stuck in the first supersensible world, the philosopher intellectually differentiates concepts by clarifying their boundaries, identifying their features or criteria, and analogizing from one concept to a revised concept. Such concepts, being external to experience, are lifeless, frozen in space and time, and inauthentic (in the sense of being reified) explanations as to how one concrete individual differs from a stranger, and vice versa. Being external to experience, the units of legality are estranged from social relations. As such, their social content matters little. They are, to use a common phrase from general jurisprudence, "content-independent."[7] At best, the first supersensible world merely copies or re-presents actuality. Such has often been the effort of the law and society and access to justice movements.[8]

The problem is that when rules and the particular institutions are posited external to consciousness, they are hung so high, Hegel explains, that only experts who specialize in the knowledge of them can claim knowledge of them (PR 215R). Even then, knowledge of the supersensible world is inaccessible because our knowledge is conditioned by appearances. We can only evaluate the institutions and rules in terms of appearances. This requires that we turn to the only thing that philosophers can know: consciousness. Thus, what philosophers need, according to Hegel, is a second supersensible world that encapsulates both the noumena and ever-fluctuating particular experiences. This second supersensible world is constituted from a reflective *Sittlichkeit,* as elaborated in Chapters 9 and 10.

b) The Second Legal Supersensible World

If the abstract rules and institutions were incorporated into the consciousness of individuals, the populace would be able to access them. This possibility always exists in the earlier first supersensible world. But it only becomes an actuality in a second supersensible world which joins the abstractions to subjective consciousness. The individual now becomes conscious of her- or himself through mediating rules and institutions which the individual shares with strangers as each recognizes the other through the rules and institutions. The individual's self-consciousness becomes the center of the inverted world. Hegel describes the second supersensible world as "the world of appearance and the world-in-itself" (SL 505). The content of the second supersensible world is distinct from the content of appearance (or what Kant describes as "phenomena") in the first supersensible world.

In particular, the second supersensible world does not necessarily represent, as consciousness, the intellectual differentiations of the first world. And yet, the second supersensible world is above the world of appearance in the first (SL 507). The second world contains not only simple, changeless laws but also flux and multiplicity (SL 507). "That which was previously law [that is, primary and secondary rules per Hart] is accordingly no longer only one side of the whole whose other side was Appearance [the prelegal] as such, but is itself the whole" (SL 506). The second supersensible world is both sensuous (because it includes appearance) and supersensuous (because it explains more than one single instance). It contains the immediacy of experience but also reflected indeterminate essence of existence. It is the multiplicity of social experiences (or implied structures of consciousness) which embodies determinacy but also the determinacy in respect to this content (SL 508). Appearance now has a ground that is in appearance rather than in the first supersensible world.

The second world does not take the social relationships between individuals per se as legal actuality. The first supersensible world required that one would retrospectively "leap" from the legality back into the phenomenologically prelegal world in order to access the fluctuating social relationships. If the latter scenario were followed, the "legality versus prelegal" would be hierarchically reversed. There would remain an externality to the act of thinking. Only, in this case, the externality would be prelegal experiences rather than the "legal" world of intellectual abstractions. This would continue the old problem of founding knowledge in an externality to structures of legal consciousness. Accordingly, the second supersensible world does not suppose that the two worlds oppose each other: "[b]ut such antitheses of inner and outer, of appearance and the supersensible, as of two different kinds of actuality, we no longer find here" (PS 159).

Hegel's point is that the second supersensible world contains the phenomenal *and* the *noumenal* worlds. There is no externality in itself, whether the externality be the "practical law" of abstract rules and institutions or the "law and" world of legal sociology, psychology, political science, or anthropology. The particularity of appetitive drives, needs, and values are now unified with the shared universals which manifest how one individual recognizes another. The individual will now feel "at home" (*Dasein*) with such a unity.

The metaphor of the inverted world makes the point that actuality only lies in appearances (the phenomenal world), not in the objectivity presupposed in the first supersensible world. Any educational structure or judicial institution that only aims to clarify, decompose, and intellectually differentiate concepts lifts the philosopher and the official into the make-believe world of the first supersensible world. The traditional analytic role of philosophy and law is removed, though, in the second supersensible world. In its place, the official observes how individuals recognize each other in contingent, context-specific differences through mediating concepts and institutions. Nothing is external to the second supersensible world—no presupposition, no rule of recognition, no state. Accordingly, freedom in the second supersensible world is positive because it is internal to the process of appearance itself.

The idea of the inverted world is that before the philosopher or official presupposes that centralized institutions, with their externally posited rules, are sources of binding laws, the philosopher must work her or his way through disorder (PS 144).[9] Relating this point to the observed official or observing philosopher of the contemporary legal order, we usually assume that legislatively and judicially posited rules are fixed in time and space. Certainty marks the possibility of access to justice if posited rules are considered equivalent with justice. But before such an institutional order exists (analytically speaking), continual flux characterizes social relations. What is a binding unit of law—whether a written rule, a constitutional value, a policy, or a social interest, for example—appears ambiguous and opaque. But the inverted world renders such certainty illusionary. The posited statutory and judicially posited rules do not even copy the dynamic movement of social relationships. The metaphor of the inverted world thereby brings into question whether posited rules are fixed or even binding despite their apparent objectivity. The sources thesis of Joseph Raz,[10] the rule of recognition of Hart,[11] Kelsen's foundation of legality in a *Grundnorm*,[12] and Dworkin's "law beyond law"[13] are put to the side or bracketed. Legal philosophy always comes on the scene too late to be able to instruct the law professor or judge as to how we ought to design a just society.

Instead, first, the inverted world locates the subject as the center or source of objectivity. Second, like the individual who stands before a life-sized mirror, what the first supersensible world presupposed as objectivity is now determined by the subject's consciousness. Objectivity—the legal institutions, the statutes, the precedents, treatises, conventions—is now nested in the individual's consciousness. The individual acts. In the first supersensible world, the individual is acted upon. In the second, one becomes conscious that one actually determines what had heretofore been projected as objectivity. In like vein, the individual's consciousness is mirrored through the universals of rules and institutions.

Hegel uses the metaphor of an inverted world to explain the possibility that the legitimacy of an institutional structure rests in the immanent thinking of a self-determining being. Laws are no longer binding because some external institution has posited the rule of recognition nor because a posited rule accords with some one *Grundnorm* or set of moral principles such as "equal respect and concern." Of course, the subject in the inverted world is not the empirical subject with an arbitrary will, a concept that I shall address in the next chapter. The subject must struggle with her- or himself and with strangers who, like the subject, are immediacies. But each individual recognizes strangers in the inverted chaotic world. Peace will reign in the inverted world only when each individual reciprocally recognizes the other. What is taken as a binding law in an inverted world is determined by the individual as she or he recognizes strangers as well as her- or himself.

How is it possible for a philosopher or observed legal official/inhabitant to comprehend such an inverted world? The key is that the observed subject becomes the center of the world. Four characteristics color how the observed subject is at the world's center. First, instead of gazing outward, I, as a subject, turn inwardly into my self-consciousness. This consciousness structures how I read texts and interpret the acts of officials. Second, my process of thinking is continually moving because it emanates from my consciousness. Third, I presuppose my structure of consciousness before I even begin to become conscious about it. Fourth, although my initial immediacy to any stranger denies and excludes the stranger from my legal reasoning, I become conscious that I determine the stranger as I read myself in the stranger and as the stranger in my consciousness. I become conscious of my role in such self-determination. And my structure of legal consciousness continually leads to a new structure of consciousness with no closure in sight.[14] I become conscious of an emerging structure by recognizing that the old one constrained my ability to comprehend my awareness of my self-determining role in my determination of objectivity. The consequence of these four elements of the inverted world is that I determine myself as I recognize strangers in the inverted world. More, I determine particular laws as well as the legal structure as a whole. My self-determination legitimates the legal order and its units.

2. THE TRANSFORMATION OF LEGAL MEANING IN THE INVERTED WORLD

Legality, then, is the reverse of what one might often take for granted as objectivity. As just noted, this does not suggest that the inverted world turns the prelegal world on top of the intellectual differentiations of a *noumenal* realm as law and society scholars often presuppose. The positing of the prelegal above the legal would imagine the inverted world in a physical sense of sensation: a preestablished, independently existing world of phenomena or the prelegal would oppose the elements of legal reasoning. That would retain a hierarchy with a different content. If that were so, we would relapse into the former world of abstract constant unities in the first supersensible world. We would try to access the essence of the prelegal world by intellectually differentiating a new set of concepts from context-specific phenomena.

   Instead, all presuppositions, values, and habits are now incorporated into one's consciousness. No external presupposition founds legitimacy. In the first supersensible world, the prelegal was the nonlaw. The prelegal was *ab*-original. Now, the inverted world is both the prelegality and legality, both *in-itself* and *for-itself*. The legal and the prelegal depend on the other and this, inside the appearances of experience (that is, of consciousness). Both the prelegal and the legal of the first supersensible world have thereby dissolved (SC 509–11). Appearance is redefined in the second supersensible world. The inverted world makes the point that actuality is itself contradictory. As a consequence, "the law of one world . . . is confronted by an *inverted* supersensible world where what is despised in the former is honoured, and what in the former is honoured, meets with contempt" (PS 159). Or, as Hegel puts it in *Lesser Logic,* according, then, to the law of the inverted world, what is *like* in the first world [of statutes and precedents] is *unlike* to itself [that is, the prelegal multiplicity of particular experiences in subjectivity], and what is *unlike* in the first world [that is, the prelegal] is equally *unlike to itself* [that is, posited as abstract rules and institutions], or it becomes *like itself* [that is, a multiplicity of social differences in the prelegal world] . . . this means that what in the law of the first world [posited rules] is sweet, in this inverted in-itself is sour, what in the former is black is, in the other, white. (PS 158)

There can be no closure that will give the philosopher or the observed official peace of mind as she or he may have experienced in the first supersensible world. The law student must continually struggle. And the resource material of the competent law student/scholar/lawyer, we shall see, is very different from the aggregation of rules and arguments. Legality becomes actual and therefore legitimate.

Actuality is finally understood as both the truth projected in the abstract constant rules about the inaccessible *in-itself* and the perversion of such a world. But the perversion is a good perversion (PS 160). This is so for two reasons. First, the legal consciousness of the observed official inverts itself when it begins to reflect about its thinking process. That which is inverted (the first supersensible world of constant abstract laws) is a false actuality or "practical law," to use the familiar excuse of law students for choosing courses that summarize the forms of empty rules. The true actuality is the instance of the legal form. The second or inverted world encapsulates the instance and its dissimilarity. The new world constantly changes. This change repeatedly overthrows the abstract rules and institutions that the official had taken for granted in the first supersensible world (PS 156).

The inverted world is a good perversion, second, because it embodies both the legal and the prelegal. What the observing philosopher had formerly recognized as chaos or prelegal now constitutes binding laws. Legal and prelegal, North Pole and South Pole, render the other determinate in a self-defining relationship. All social differentiations are internal to the second supersensible world: "[t]hus the supersensible world, which is the inverted world, has at the same time overarched the other world and has it within it . . . Only this is the difference as *inner* difference, or difference in *its own self,* or difference as an infinity" (PS 160). As a consequence, the rules and institutions that were the objects of analysis are brought within experience. The legal/prelegal dichotomy collapses into consciousness itself. Actuality is appearance qua appearance. And this is in constant flux.

Again, the inverted world raises issues that might seem counterintuitive to Anglo-American general jurisprudence. We legal officials often take the world of courts and legislatures and precedents and regulations as constitutive of the phenomenal world. But the inverted world suggests otherwise. For the inverted world offers the possibility that the individual's acts are located in experience. The inverted world is not a supersensible or transcendental structure of objectivity superimposed upon legality. The inverted world turns everything inside out and upside down so that the courts, institutional structure, precedents, and statutes are, as elements in a binding legal structure, mere appearances. They are determined by the subject. This subject breaks from Beingness (or immediacy) between her- or himself and objects. The dog is no longer an element of the identity of the solipsistic dog owner. Although the observed subject might desire to dominate others in this inverted world, she or he comes to recognize the stranger through action. Hegel's inverted world thereby describes appearance which ontologically precedes what the legal philosopher might take as legal objectivity. Such an appearance even precedes statehood, lawyers, judges, law schools, and philosophers. Indeed, the inverted world represents a world before legal language has assigned a sign to a posited rule and before legal consciousness has become structured with a boundary between subjectivity and objectivity. Legality is thereby turned back into itself before the legality/prelegality is presupposed. Legal philosophy is transformed into a circle that turns back into itself rather than being imprisoned in abstract rules posited by the external "the Constitution" or the "intent of the Founding Fathers" (EL 147), PR 267R).

Once the legal philosopher gets this far, one becomes aware that one has read the exterior world of posited rules and institutional sources through presuppositions that one has hitherto taken for granted. The most important such presupposition has been that laws are binding because of their institutional source in the state bureaucracy. We become aware of one more thing: namely, that we have presupposed a structure of consciousness that located the observed subject as being autonomous of the objectivity of consciousness as represented by state institutions such as courts. Once we become conscious of these two propositions, philosophy takes on a new role. For legal philosophy must now retrieve different implied structures of legal consciousness. The identity of a legal unit is nested in the social relation of one individual with another. Institutions, such as a legislature or court, will manifest, as a possibility, such a relation. When all inhabitants share such social recognition to and from the other, the institutions are universals as are their posited rules. My process of self-determination lies at the center of both the prelegal and the legal because both are inside the second supersensible world. Each continues itself in its stranger for each now recognizes its stranger in the inverted world. The appearance of the first supersensible world dissolves in favor of a second world where the legal and the prelegal recognize their dependence upon each other by virtue of the self-determining process of thinking.

3. THE CONSEQUENCE OF THE INVERTED WORLD

Because the legal versus prelegal distinction is dissolved into experience, life is assimilated into the radically different idea of legality. In the first supersensible world, a human experience was an instance of laws posited by institutions. A law as an abstract rule, then, was reified from living experiences in appearance or phenomena. This indifference to the instance was all the more solidified the more that consciousness changed. This was so because the posited laws were fixed in time and space. What is more, as intellectually constructed modes of the explanation of experience, laws enabled science (that is, legal officials) to manipulate life (PS 153). But when the second supersensible world overarches the first into a unity of laws and appearances, the constant flux of appearance is introduced into self-consciousness (PS 160). Indeed, the humanly constructed laws become alive.

As a consequence of Hegel's inverted world analysis, what was formerly posited external to the subject's consciousness—the statutes, precedents, courts, and bureaucracy—is brought into the subject's consciousness. Life, for Hegel, is not Kant's pure transcendental ego. No. Nor does life involve the scientific or even the "internal" point of view towards the content of a legal standard.[15] Nor are laws externally posited separate from subjectivity. Laws are binding upon inhabitants when the inhabitants bring cognitive experiences *into* the objectivity of rules and institutions (PS 162). The observing official and philosopher observe that inhabitants incur a process of thinking which encloses abstract laws. Laws thereby become alive in contrast with the dead abstractions of the first supersensible world within which legal officials often remain content to work. As Gadamer notes in *Truth and Method,* the organic being draws into itself everything which is outside it.[16] Life is nourished by what is alien to it.[17] Instead of the constant, abstract, externally posited rules and procedures of courts; governmental bureaucracy; and the police constraining the freedom of the observed subject, the subject's own consciousness constrains itself. I am "at home" in such an inverted world because I am its center. I help build a legal order as mine and then I recognize myself and strangers in such a legal order. I am free.

In this manner, life displaces the social alienation in the first super-sensible world. As fixed abstract forms, laws in the first supersensible world were the most important part of social alienation. But consciousness in the inverted world comprehends life by becoming inwardly aware of how the abstract forms had concealed experience. Because contradiction is internal to the inverted world, the process of legal self-consciousness lacks closure. The inverted world closes the unbridgeable gulf that had plagued the in-accessibility of the knowledge of objects in the first supersensible world. The legal official is finally brought into direct contact with the objectivity of consciousness through practical action.

The structures of legal consciousness grow immanently from within the consciousness of the subjects. The philosopher recognizes such struc-tures as if she or he were gazing at a mirror. Institutions and posited laws are now located in appearance qua appearance. What opens up in this appearance is the constant play of differentiating experiences that, when uniform, constitute the law of particularity. Plato's world of pure forms lacks any such movement or change. In addition, despite the role of inten-tionality in Socrates' defense, Plato's world of transcendental forms also lacks any room for such a subject-centered actuality. Changes in concrete experiences (that is in structures of consciousness) require that officials retheorize the nature and identity of law.

4. THE INVERTED WORLD
AND THE LEGAL PHILOSOPHER

The inverted world metaphor exists in the ethos in which one lives. This takes one to the social bonding of the clan and of the city in antiquity.[18] The challenge for Hegel is to describe how an ethos emerges when in-dividuals begin to represent their former identity of immediacy that had characterized the clan or family.[19] With the dissolution of the immediate bonding with objects in the family, an inward-looking subject can only re-present the immediacy. Romanticism, the quest for salvation, conscience, and inward self-consciousness become separate from objectivity. This separation introduces the first supersensible world. It raises the possibil-ity that an individual has a will. In the ethos of Greece, for example, there was no such subject because the individual identified with the objective laws of Fate, Nature, and the polis. The philosophical consciousness rec-ognizes the collapse of such a beautiful ethical life with the rise of the self-conscious individual. Such a subjectivism, best represented by Socrates, is imagined as corrupt from the standpoint of the immediacy of the tribe and then of the polis (PR 185R).

How is it possible for a questioning individual, such as Socrates, to be bonded with the rules, institutions, legislature, and adjudicative procedure where there is no *Volk* or common religious experience today as there was in the clans and city-states of ancient Greece? If there is war, insurrection, or natural disaster, why will the citizen have a duty to sacrifice her or his life for the state? To kill another human being for the state? To ask, as a journalist or cabinet minister, how many of the enemy have been killed today? Hegel feared that the emerging "community" of his day might become "hollow, spiritless and unsettled" as had been the legitimacy of the kings and princes of the German principalities (PR 138A). Further, there was a risk that, as with Socrates, the Stoics of Rome, and the romanticists of his contemporary Germany, the individual would "flee from actuality and retreat into his inner life" (PR 138A).

5. WHY IS *VERSTAND* UNCONNECTED WITH ACTUALITY?

We are now in a position to address the nature of legal reasoning. Hegel has a term to describe the legal reasoning in the first supersensible world: *Verstand*. *Verstand* is the method of logic that reinforces the external presuppositions that Hegel disfavored. When philosophers and legal officials use *Verstand* as their method, the abstract laws become estranged from appearance. The possibility of actuality is inaccessible. Hegel explains that this is so because of the self-standing character of a concept. He elaborates what he means by this in *Inner Logic* and *Philosophy of Mind*.

a) A Self-standing Concept

As I explained in Chapter 2, the act of thinking begins with the moment of immediacy in an individual's consciousness. The mind intellectually constructs a concept. In the first supersensible world, such a concept stands by itself as a discrete unit. Such a concept is isolated from space and time and, therefore, estranged from the experience of immediacy which the concept represents. *Verstand* reinforces the first supersensible world by decomposing such a discrete and self-standing concept. The parts of the concept are taken as the "reality" or "practice" in that the more one decomposes a concept into its discrete parts the closer does one access legal reality—or, so it is believed in the first supersensible world.[20] The parts stand for or are the metonyms for the concept as a whole. The parts and the concept itself are abstracted from the time and space experienced in the immediacy. The unit of analysis is fixed in time and space (PM 389R). But such a discrete fixed abstraction contradicts the beginning of the act of thinking: that is, the moment of immediacy in consciousness. *Verstand* is stuck in such a contradiction: the lawyer, law student, or legal scholar—or, indeed, the legal philosopher of general jurisprudence—cannot break from the division of the world between the subjectivity of immediacy and the objectivity of fixed abstract concepts.

In this light, the philosopher of *Verstand* is caught in an intellectual world where differences are intellectually constructed in terms of concepts. The philosopher thinks *about* or "think[s] over" or re-presents the immediacy of subjectivity (EL 2R). We think *about* intuitions; we reflect *about* them. Both subjectivity and objectivity remain "out there," separate from the thinking being. The representing concept is distinguished from immediacy. The act of thinking mediates between the initial moment of immediacy on the one hand and the object which represents the immediacy on the other hand. Representation (*Vorstellung*) mediates by categorizing the immediacy. The representation confers form onto the particular immediacy of the subject. The categorizing representation displaces the immediacy as the object of study (EL 3R). Such a category is self-standing because "there is nothing to be thought with a concept save the concept itself" (EL 3R).

Thus, if the philosopher remains stuck in an intellectual world of concepts, the representation is alienated from the immediacy. The fixed representations, such as posited rules by the state, are erroneously taken as "genuine" or practical constituents of legality. The reasoning involves intellectual distinctions about the rules. Since social phenomena draw from such moments of immediacy, legal reasoning, as *Verstand,* excises social phenomena from what the legal philosopher and lawyer take as legality (EL 6R). What is taken as "the law" is the "empty" first supersensible world with no return to the prior immediacy of subjectivity (EL 192A).

Hegel calls this "picture thinking." At one end of the concept-social spectrum, there is the self-standing concept. At the other end there are the social phenomena. The legal reformer who works through *Verstand* cannot access the social phenomena despite the need of the reformer to address the relation of legality with social phenomena. The self-standing concept never perfectly fits with the social phenomenon it represents. Hart himself echoes *Verstand* (and the first supersensible world) when he admits that a rule merely "approximates" or "very nearly reproduces" social phenomena.[21] The representation through the act of intellectualization leaves the inner immediacy (or what Hegel calls "being") of the subject in favor of a representing concept (PR 454). The former immediacy is represented. Any claim that analytic reasoning is "practical" law is thereby fantasy. Such a claim remains imprisoned in the decomposition of concepts (rules) into their parts, without returning to the moment of immediacy which began the process of thinking. To access actuality, the philosopher returns to the observed subject's immediacy that the intellectualization represents.

b) Interaction of Concepts

Hegel is dissatisfied with *Verstand* because the philosopher remains "imprisoned" in an external world that posits representations without retrieving the immediacy with which the act of thinking began. *Verstand* becomes important in this loss of the immediacy. Immediacy is excluded from legality as prelegal. For the units of observation are concepts rather than the immediacy experienced by individuals in social phenomena. One concept is exclusively represented in terms of another concept: freedom in terms of necessity, culture in terms of nature, actus reus in terms of mens rea, a legislature in terms of a court, civilization in terms of barbarism. The aim of the philosopher in the first supersensible world is to clarify self-standing concepts, to categorize the concepts, and to identify the boundaries of the concepts inter se. From the philosopher's "hundreds of assurances about reason, knowing, thinking, etc.," the concepts gain self-acceptance in the philosopher's discourse "through endless repetitions of one and the same [statement]" (EL178R). With the introduction of concepts, then, there is a leap from the prelegal into the legal world, as both Hegel and Hart express, and the philosopher forgets that she or he has forgotten about the prelegal immediacy that was experienced.

c) Verstand's Representation of a Multiplicity of Particular Experiences

When legal analysis remains imprisoned in the first supersensible world, what is erroneously believed to be legal knowledge is estranged from subjectivity. The legal official, preoccupied with particular rules of objectivity, aims "to state what is right and legal [*Rechtens*], i.e. what the particular legal determinations are" (PR 2R). With *Verstand,* the particular determinations are other concepts/rules. Rules are verbalized as "concepts of right or of such 'concepts of right' as are defined in this or that legal code" (PR 3R). But the codes, whether of debtor-creditor law or tax law, real estate law or constitutional law, lack any explicit reference to presupposed structures of legal consciousness or social communication (PR 3R). A statute posits "general determinations of right, propositions of the understanding, principles, laws, and the like" (PR 3R). The judge or lawyer can identify a definition by virtue of the etymology of a word and this abstracts a concept from a context-specific experience. The more contradictory the rules in the abstract acts of intellectualization, the more difficult does one find it to posit a general definition. For, a definition claims to be universal whereas contradictions render such universality impossible. But, as Hegel (and Hart) point out, such a definitional approach to legality possesses shortcomings (PR 2R).[22]

d) Difference as a Difference Between Concepts

The self-standing concept becomes the object of decomposition into its parts. With *Verstand,* what is taken as difference is an intellectual difference amongst concepts. Social differences are immaterial and, indeed, forgotten. The more minute the parts and the clearer the identity of the shared features of concepts, the closer does one access the concepts of law. The distinctions between concepts approximate truth (PR 31R). Hegel explains such formalism of *Verstand* in this manner: "in the empirical sciences, it is customary to decompose what is found in representational thought [*Vorstellung*], and when the individual instance has been reduced to the common quality, this common quality is then called the concept" (PR 32A).

Hegel's description of the decomposition process of a self-standing concept may be familiar to the legal scholar whose methodology is *Verstand.*[23] Hart and Raz perhaps have best described and used this method in general jurisprudence today.[24] The official clarifies the boundaries of a concept (that is, a rule or principle). The official then decomposes the concept into its microfeatures. The official then identifies a common criterion of the microfeatures. The criterion constitutes the essence of a revised concept. The concept constitutes the knowledge of the perceived "facts of a case." The official, though, never accesses such facts because she or he is caught in a network of concepts. One concept is justified in terms of another concept. The philosopher's role is to describe and clarify "the pathology" of the system of concepts so decomposed in the objectivity of consciousness.[25] The system is even said to have "a life."[26] The boundary of the concept encircles a territorial-like metaphysical space. By discerning analytic truths about the boundary of a concept in an a priori manner, one "hopes that by doing so, we will learn something interesting, important, or essential about the nature of the thing the concept denotes."[27]

Hegel describes *Verstand,* much as does Hart, as the decomposition of a concept into distinct elements that are also self-standing independent of the particularity of social relationships. The microparts of a concept are inseparably bound together into a supersensible world that is erroneously taken as social existence. This is the first supersensible world. Thinking is the negation of something that is immediately experienced. Put differently, "it is a mistake to assume that, first of all, there are objects that form the content of our representations, and then our subjective activity comes in afterwards to form concepts of them, through the operation of abstracting that we spoke of earlier" (EL163A2). Actuality is this forgotten immediacy when the philosopher enters into the act of mediation about the immediacy, a mediation where individuals recognize each other such as happened in the second supersensible world (EL12R).

6. HEGEL'S CRITIQUE OF *VERSTAND*

Verstand has several elements that stand out as conducive to social alienation according to Hegel.

For one thing, with *Verstand,* social relations are excised from an analysis of intellectual differentiation (PR 26R). Hegel describes the analysis of a concept in this manner: the method "takes an object [*Gegenstand*], proposition, etc. given to feeling or to the immediate consciousness in general, and dissolves it, confuses it, develops it this way and that, and is solely concerned with deducing its opposite—a negative mode which frequently appears in Plato" (PR 31R). The cumulative aggregate of such analyzed concepts stands for a system of concepts emptied of all social particularities despite the rhetoric of making distinctions about differences.

Second, this focus upon the intellectual differentiation between concepts deters officials from scrutinizing the substantive content of a concept. Because particularities are not addressed in the clarification of the boundaries and the differentiation of concepts, legal knowledge is entirely formal. If the "philosopher" retrieved the content of the concepts, philosophy would link an indeterminate concept with the social ethos in which the philosopher and the observed subject are immersed. The "content-independence" of legal arguments is a good thing according to some contemporary legal philosophers.[28] Such content-independent reasons may be considered the units of legal objectivity.[29] The key to the formalism of *Verstand* is just this content independence. Hegel's complaint with *Verstand,* not surprisingly, is that the clarification and intellectual differentiation of concepts is "entirely superfluous," as his handwriting indicates (W13, fn 23).

Instead of focusing upon *Verstand,* Hegel relates truth to the content of concepts/rules. Legal truth addresses the relation of the particularity of the social content of rules with their form. This relation addresses the presupposed structure of consciousness. But if such a structure were excised from the analysis of concepts, as in *Verstand,* and if legal analysis ignored the recognition of individuals inter se, rules (that is, concepts) would lack legitimacy. Even the mere application of the rule to posited facts fails to address the ethos in which the official and litigants play a role. For the social events may be represented as concepts and, even if this is not so, the social event is enclosed inside the boundary of the rule/concept. Even legal historians, if they string concepts into a systemic explanation of social events, may become imprisoned in a theoretical world of concepts. Although we believe that we are "learning the law,"[30] we "learn" empty concepts and posited facts without considering the social differences that constitute the meanings. Hegel lectured in 1824/25 that, "To think that the concept will determine everything is a prejudice. It is not true, because there is an immense sphere into which the concept does not descend . . . The concept proceeds through a specific development, up to a specific point of detail in its determinations, but these determinations remain universal (1824/25 W13). As a consequence, *Verstand* "unconsciously achieves the opposite of what it intends" (PR 3R).

Third, the irony about *Verstand,* according to Hegel, is that although the philosopher and observed subject may believe that they are dealing with social practice, they are trapped in an intellectual world that only recognizes concepts as the units of legality. The particular experiences are enclosed by the concepts. The concepts are applied to posited facts but the latter also become concepts. The social context-specific content is immaterial to the analysis of concepts. Accordingly, this theoretical education "stops short at the universal and so does not reach actuality" (PR 207R).

Against this background, it would seem that Hegel would view a great deal of his (and our) professional legal education as theoretical. First, legal analysis composes general rules from an endless multiplicity of detailed micro-rules (PR 189). The decomposition of such rules draws from "the material of finitude and individuality [*Einzelheit*] whose extent is infinite" (PR 216R). Second, we may believe that we are satisfying social needs or accessing social phenomena by decomposing rules when in fact we are only decomposing rules *about* food, shelter, and clothing into more microconcepts. Any one concept is related to another concept. Instrumental rationality, a form of knowledge I examine in Chapter 8, becomes highly specialized to such a point that individuals have "an inability to feel and enjoy the wider freedoms, and particularly the spiritual advantages, of civil society" (PR 243).

Indeterminacy plagues *Verstand.* How so? Because the boundary of a rule/concept is another concept, the relations between concepts miss the context-specific drives, needs, and values of particularity. Most importantly, the intellectual differences between concepts miss the particularity of the social relationships presupposed in the content of the concepts. Even context-specific events are categorized as concepts, although we are deceived into believing that they are "facts." The social event, represented as a concept, is subsumed inside the boundary of a concept when the rule is applied to the posited facts (PR 3). The facts are taken as objective. Both the rule and the facts are posited external to and onto the subject. As a consequence, for Hegel, such an analytic approach to the philosophy of law is "pseudo-philosophy." The authority of a rule becomes a mere "half-measure" (PR 31R) and "one-sided" because it fails to incorporate the social ethos into the content of the rules. Sarcasm permeates Hegel's treatment of *Verstand.* The closest that the formalist method of knowledge accesses social contingency is to subsume the facts, themselves swallowed in objective representations, under a category (PR 3R). As a consequence, the pursuit of logical consistency amongst concepts "has nothing to do with the satisfaction of the demands of reason and with philosophical science" (PR 3R).

Fourth, legal institutions lose any connection with experiential prejudgments or *prejudicial.* Social meaning, according to Hegel, draws from the intentionality of the subject, not from the criterion of some concept. The criterion intellectually transcends the control of the subject. The criterion is external and above the subjectivity. The institutional risks being estranged from actuality, "the [external] institution has thereby lost its meaning and its right [to exist]" (PR 3R). Or, as Hegel also emphasizes, "[t]his method leaves out of account what is alone essential to science—with regard to content, the *necessity of the thing* [*Sache*] in and for itself (in this case, or right [that is, of legally binding concepts]), and with regard to form, the nature of the concept" (PR 2R). The association of legitimacy with institutional sources when the institutions themselves are empty of any relation with actuality merely continues a rhetorical and reified shadow of actuality. In order to confer content into the relation of self-standing concepts with actuality, we need to recollect what went on before we represented concepts with concepts. With *Vernunft,* we bring to consciousness what we had forgotten during our preoccupation with the clarification, decomposition, and differentiation of concepts.

7. *Vernunft*

Hegel offers a form of reasoning that coheres with the inverted world analysis. *Vernunft* holds that an authentic philosophic method must focus upon the emergent presupposed structures of consciousness. Savigny's historicism had left no such role for the subject. So too, Kant's transcendental referent had held out that intuitions without concepts were blind. By applying concepts to sensible experience, we worked the latter into unities—that is, into a "sense." A judgment thereby incorporated inclinations of the body into the individual's will.[31] Once we bring inclinations into a judgment in this manner, though, we lose the possibility of universal moral rules. The latter are located in a *noumenon* rather than knowledge of phenomena.[32] I shall now examine Hegel's differentiation of legitimacy from truth, how *Verstand* fails to access such truth, how *Vernunft* differs from *Verstand,* the retrospective role of the philosopher of *Vernunft,* and how legal reasoning can institutionalize *Vernunft.* Only a speculative philosophy rooted in *Vernunft,* according to Hegel, deserves the name *philosophy.*

a) Truth of the Content of Rules

For Hegel, the legitimacy of a binding law depends upon truth. Truth addresses the relation of the form of a concept with its particularized content. The particularity is the very act of thinking through which subjects are "becoming." Through this content, individuals reciprocally recognize each other. Without a particularization in its content, a concept is indeterminate in scope. I do not relate to "this" or "that" external representation. I do not have an idea of this or that rule. If rules are reconciled with my subjectivity, the rules are "mine." The subject embodies (confers the experiential body into) the content of rules and institutions. The particularity of an object of consciousness, such as a rule, becomes my own thinking. For Hegel, the social particularization of an indeterminate concept incorporates the subject's implied structure of consciousness or, in Hegel's terms, "the whole preceding exposition and development of thinking" that observed subjects have considered their own (EL 213A). The philosopher's role is to unconceal such implied structures "however painful the process may be" (PR 13A). Such implicit structures of consciousness manifest how the act of thinking links with objectivity. The implicit structure itself, not the institutions or discrete posited rules, "gives itself the form of external thereness" (EL 213). Hegel argues that both the empiricism of Locke and the rationalism of Kant and Fichte miss this nexus of objectivity with the subjective consciousness.[33]

b) Reason

Philosophy, for Hegel, involves reason (*die Vernunft*) rather than the intellect (*der Verstand*). *Der Verstand* involves the analysis of the interrelation of concepts in an intellectual world. The English term most frequently used to translate *Verstand* is *understanding*. As noted in Chapter 1, *understanding* erroneously suggests Gadamer's very different use of the term (*understanding* as experiential knowledge). We had better translate *Verstand* as *intellect* or, better, as *intellectual knowledge*.[34] Hegel believes that Kant had been preoccupied with *Verstand* when he had considered concepts as things-in-themselves. Again, much as Hart describes of "meaning," *Verstand* presupposes that a concept has an essence.[35]

The fixity of a concept in time and space, described as such by *Verstand*, is accepted in contemporary Anglo-American jurisprudence.[36] The importance of *Verstand* is exemplified in law courses that introduce the student to the vocabulary and method of analytic distinctions between concepts. Perhaps Hart best describes *Verstand* in his Introduction to *Concept of Law*.[37] As noted earlier, both Hart and Joseph Raz exemplify *Verstand* in their essays about concepts.[38] Also noted earlier, Raz suggests that because intellectual distinctions can only take one so far, the official must ultimately posit a value to end the struggle to reconcile intellectual contradictions or, as Hegel puts it "establish [*festsetzen*] for the sake of establishing" (PR 214R).[39] *Verstand* thereby privileges a professionally trained elite of expert knowers of indeterminate concepts, knowers who ultimately posit their arbitrary wills behind the legal analysis of concepts or the posit of constitutional values (PR 215–16).

Vernunft, in contrast, involves synthetic reasoning in that particulars are added to the analysis of concepts. This particularity is a singular context-specific experience that the individual brings *into* her or his self-determined concepts as she or he recognizes strangers. In this way the experience of reciprocal recognition between strangers links the self-determined act of thinking with appearance. After all, the philosopher began the enterprise of philosophy with immediacy. And immediate knowledge involves mere appearances, not pure concepts in a *noumenal* realm (EL 45A). The appearances become determinate.[40] Because jurists tend to associate subjectivity with such appearances and law with objectivity, the speculative reasoning that Hegel advocates is often excluded from both philosophic and lawyers' reasoning in general jurisprudence.

What becomes important with such an exclusion of concrete experience in *Verstand,* as noted above, is the presupposed legitimacy of the posit of an arbitrary will by a state official or institution. *Vernunft,* in contrast, is concrete in that it relates indeterminate concepts with contingent, context-specific experiences. *Vernunft* crosses the boundary between the *noumenal* and phenomenal worlds. Concepts are actualized in the individual's social experiences. Hegel thereby collapses the distinction between the rule/value, is/ought, law/politics dichotomy by locating concepts inside the structures of consciousness of the observed subject. Values are implied from the universals shared with strangers in one's implied structure of consciousness. The observed subject is ultimately free when she or he becomes conscious that the subject shares the concepts with strangers through laws and institutions that they have constructed. Hegel calls such a consciousness, Reason or *Vernunft.*

The philosopher cannot discover or learn *Vernunft.* Nor can the philosopher analyze, theorize, or institutionalize *Vernunft* by occupying an office in a faculty of education or of law or, for that matter by being called professor of philosophy, in a university that prides itself in the production of skills. I shall explain why this is so in Chapter 8. *Vernunft* synthesizes concepts with contingent, context-specific experiences. This synthesis is marked by an interesting contrast between an act of representation and the experience of immediacy or presence with an object. Instead of distinguishing concepts as we do with *Verstand,* we access *Vernunft* through the immediate identity of self with object. The individual most successfully accesses *Vernunft* if she or he has reached the highest standards of *Bildung.*

Hegel's philosophical method, then, is an immanent process of the retrieval of the act of thinking. The philosopher observes how concepts mediate between immediacy and the objects of nature. The philosopher also observes how the content of the mediation differs from one ethos to the next. Because the retrieval is immanent in the act of thinking, consciousness is "an immanent progression and production of its own determinations" (PR 31). If the philosopher limited the study of law to the intellectual distinctions amongst a priori concepts, the concepts, being representations external to the philosopher, would have to be posited *onto* the observed individual's particular context-specific experiences. Such an act of thinking would be violent. Even if the concepts were applied to what are held out as "the facts" of a case, the concepts would have to be posited from the vertically higher concepts *onto* the concepts about "the facts." The "facts" would become an instance of the intellectually differentiated concept. But with *Vernunft,* the subject is initially immediate with objectivity and then the philosopher recognizes the objectivity in the subject's implied structure of consciousness.

Such a structure, though, is not peculiar to each individual. Rather, it is shared in a social-cultural ethos in which the philosopher and observed individual live. An ethos manifests the possibility of reciprocal recognition. It is just such an ethos that inculcates immediacy into the collective consciousness of the populace. How does the philosopher recognize when one structure of legal consciousness is evolving into another? The philosopher identifies when a populace begins to challenge what it had heretofore taken for granted without deliberation. Athenian democracy, for example, had evolved into a hollow, spiritless, and unstable social order which had no space for the rise of an intentional subject according to Hegel. Aristophanes mocked the polis (PR 138A). Faced with such a hollow structure of consciousness, Socrates retreated into his own inner consciousness (PR 140R). The role of the legal philosopher is to make conscious what has hitherto been unconscious in terms of how someone like Socrates relates to others through shared unconscious values.

The philosopher of *Vernunft* looks backward into the structures of legal consciousness implied in any particular society at any particular epoch of time. In this way, *Vernunft* is recollective of the collective unconscious. In the passage with which I began this book,

> [a]s far as the individual is concerned, each individual is in any case a *child of his* time; thus philosophy too, is *its own time comprehended in thoughts.* It is just as foolish to imagine that any philosophy can transcend its contemporary world as that an individual can overleap his own time or leap over Rhodes. If his theory does indeed transcend his own time, if it builds itself a world *as it ought to be,* then it certainly has an existence, but only within his opinions—a pliant medium in which the imagination can construct anything it pleases. (PR 21–22)

Put differently, the philosophic method that Hegel advocates and manifests describes phenomena rather than constructs justificatory arguments about a priori concepts. Reason, for Hegel, involves the movement of structures of concepts immanent to the act of thinking.

There are two points that one needs to bear in mind in this respect. First, the logic of the immanent movement of legal consciousness lacks any externally posited presupposition. Most disciplines of study carry a presupposition with them. Political science, for example, presupposes that the state is the object of study. The study of law usually presupposes that the rules of legislatures and courts bind inhabitants by virtue of their source in the state's bureaucracy. To be sure, Hegel admits that a philosopher presupposes that philosophy must begin with something that is either immediate or mediated (SL 67). But legal reasoning, according to Hegel, claims that the legal philosopher must not come to her or his subject of study with any presupposition about an externally posited source of legitimacy.

The absence of any such presupposition in Hegel's method—at least as Hegel sees his method—helps to explain why most of Hegel's analysis in *Philosophy of Right* concerns a stateless condition. Each structure of legal consciousness is socially and historically conditioned. Structures of consciousness relate to nature, objectivity, subjectivity, and the collective unconscious of the subject. The philosopher must retrospectively identify the boundaries of objectivity and subjectivity in the implicit structures of consciousness of the observed actors. Such structures will vary from society to society and from epoch to epoch.

Second, as Gadamer would caution,[41] Hegel's approach to philosophy is not really a method. For one thing, a method suggests a technique to reach a goal. Such reasoning is instrumental. *Verstand* is characterized by such instrumental reason, a point that Max Horkheimer (1895–1973) and Theodor Adorno (1903–1969) picked up over a century later in their powerful *Dialectics of Enlightenment*.[42] Because *Verstand* accepts the externally posited source of reasoning as a "given," the immanent process of thinking "is precisely what the understanding always describes as incomprehensible" (PR 7R). Even a philosopher needs to become conscious of the boundary of her or his own presupposed structure of consciousness in an ethos. Further, a "method" suggests that there are rules about thinking in a certain way. Hegel's aim, though, is retrospectively to identify the rules that any particular ethos might have. The philosopher observes how nonphilosophers also feel immediate with "the law." There is no external factor or criterion that mediates between subject and law. In sum, Hegel's "method" is hardly what one might consider a "scientific" method.

c) Legal Reasoning as Vernunft

Let us contrast how a philosopher might reason as *Verstand* and as *Vernunft*.[43] Let us take the monarch as the object of study. With *Verstand*, the monarch is a mere concept. Reasoning as *Verstand* differentiates the concept of the monarch from other concepts, such as of the legislature or the electorate. This is *Verstand*. The concept represents the monarch. The concept of the monarch—or a court or legislature or a right—is located in a network of self-referring concepts. In such a view, though, one could, at best, have faith in the unity of the parts of the analyzed concept (PR 280R). As Hegel notes, "[t]he concept of the monarch is therefore extremely difficult for ratiocination—i.e. the reflective approach of the understanding— to grasp, because such ratiocination stops short at isolated determinations, and consequently knows only [individual] reasons [*Gründe*], finite viewpoints, and *deduction* from such reasons" (PR 279R). If the monarch were the object of *Vernunft,* however, the concept of the monarch would relate to the context-specific social phenomena that particularize the concept. Such a synthesis of concept and particularization would be "*entirely self-originating*" much like Hegel describes of the logic of freedom.

Hegel cautions that there is little point to analyze concepts in a manner that parses sentences from "predicates, principles and the like" (PR 269A). The latter parsing involves "formalistic thinking [*Formalismus*] that endeavours to rationalize away [*wegzuräsonnieren*] the substantial and concrete nature of the thing [*Sache*] in favour of *individual* aspects which belong to its external appearance and of abstractions which it derives from these" (PR 319R). Such rhetoric turns on "the art of allusions, turns of phrase, half-utterances and semi-concealment" (PR 319R). The legal reasoning in the sense of *Vernunft* inquires into the beliefs and ideals embodied in customs, religious practices, intermediate social institutions, posited codes, the social relations between men and women, languages, political and legal institutions, and the social-cultural practices of such institutions. This inquiry renders conscious the implied structure of the collective unconscious. Legal studies need to unconceal the spirit of social actuality from the reified old forms.

Hegel is not the first constitutional lawyer to associate the units of legality with such a wide spectrum of resources: Aristotle was another.[44] Hegel builds legal units from *social* relations rather than from the intellectual differentiation of rules. Unless rules are contextualized in social relations, choices are made as if human beings were abstracted from the social world. Instead, rights and duties are articulated in the context of an ethos. Particularity (the desires and inclinations) is identified from a medium (a universal). The universal joins with particularity to manifest the presupposed social relationships between strangers. Hegel thereby connects his method to actuality, a term I introduced in Chapter 1 (PR 320). Actuality may be unwritten and unconscious behind the ratiocination of statutes and precedents.[45] Further, the jurist must have a "disposition" to seek out such social actuality (PR 270R). Only philosophical consciousness—not the instrumental and analytic method of legal reasoning—can comprehend a particular judicial decision as *Vernunft*. The jurist must identify how immediacy between subject and objectivity is manifested in reciprocally recognized relationships in an ethos. Legal reasoning, then, is directed to the immanent relationships between individuals in an ethos. But the judge or philosopher may well share a presupposed structure of consciousness with the observed subject's immediate identity with objectivity. The role of the philosopher or judge is formidable (PR 320).

8. ANTHROPOLOGIST OR PHILOSOPHER?

It is tempting to describe Hegel's theory of legal reasoning as an anthropological exercise. The Roman Stoics, such as Seneca, and the Roman Epicureans, such as Lucretius, as well as modern legal philosophers, such as Locke and Rousseau, had claimed a temporal origin to the state. Even leading Anglo-American legal philosophers, such as Hart, have asserted or implied that a modern legal order anthropologically develops from a "rudimentary and primitive" or "prelegal" one.[46] *Philosophy of Right* also draws heavily from historical and anthropological sources (PR 32, 19R). This is especially so when Hegel distinguishes civilization from barbarism as outlined in Chapter 2 (PR 32R, 349, 351). Hegel's lectures just before his writing of *Philosophy of Right* also suggest an anthropological method. There, he claims that the modern state has its historical roots in the family or clan (1817/18 122R). We evolve historically from the nomadic life of savages (1817/18 103), to an agricultural community (103), to a trading class (1817/18 104), and to a universal class of public servants (1817/18 105). Even the corporation is a historical phase that has replaced the nuclear family of the town: "[i]t is very often the case with us that states developed out of corporations, e.g. through feudalism . . . As third estate [Stand] the people in turn formed corporations, by means of which they took advantage of the weakness of the state to secure privileges for themselves" (1817/18 125R). More generally, "[t]he ensuing stage of history is always higher, and this is the perfectability of spirit . . . In sublating its phenomenal form, the spirit of the age [*Zeitgeist*] attains in the transition a higher stage" (1817/18 126R). The intimate association of a social practice with an ethos reinforces the anthropological character of the object of study.[47]

That said, Hegel has in mind in his mature legal philosophy a philosophical, not an anthropological, method. The different forms of *Sittlichkeit*, I shall explain in Chapter 6, presuppose universals that strangers share. Hegel's mature legal philosophy describes the recognition of the stranger as the central issue in ethicality. It is not any social-cultural ethos with which Hegel is concerned. Rather, legal reasoning focuses upon the logical progression of presupposed structures of consciousness that increasingly recognize a self-conscious subject's role in subjective and objective legal consciousness. There are no interrupted moments in linear progress: no "two steps forward and one step backward." Further, a historical event is not the same as the structure of consciousness. Each structure of consciousness is the logical foundation of the next. As Frederick Copleston suggests, the movement from one structure of consciousness into a higher level of consciousness (and, therefore, of civilization) is a thinking movement for Hegel, not a historical one.[48] This movement of thinking is what Hegel describes as Reason or *Vernunft*.

If Hegel were following an anthropological method, he would not initially concern himself with private property and begin with the family as a social institution. Indeed, Hegel admits that we might be able to have a family, such as takes place in some nomadic tribes, without private property (PR 32A). Hegel first examines property, however, when the individual begins to think because it is a shape of consciousness that preconditions the possibility of a family *where a self-conscious subject is possible*. The anthropological genesis of a subject's social institutions come on the scene before the philosopher becomes conscious of what is transpiring in the observed subject's self-conscious relation with objectivity (EL 83A). The observed subject brings such institutional practices and their products into her or his consciousness. The observed subject thereby holds her- or himself responsible for the content of any one rule or institutional act. Legal knowledge becomes practical rather than theoretical. The philosophic perspective recognizes how this role of the subject with objectivity is transformed from the feeling of immediacy with customs to a reflective ethos.

Accordingly, an anthropological origin to a legal system is of no concern to Hegel except by way of example to his argument. Rather, he aims to explain why the posited rules and institutions of a state are binding when the inhabitants are internally driven to become self-conscious through acts of thinking. The act of thinking is immanent in an already existing social ethos (PR 31R, 189R). Even morality, according to Hegel, is located in social relationships. The observed subject (and philosopher) cannot separate her- or himself from social relationships. The inhabitant may not even opt from the public character of the state's laws: "if no state is there then reason [the reason associated with the progress of self-conscious will] demands that one be founded" (1822/23 W67). Historically, a state comes first and then the civil society with property, contracts, and institutions arrives on the scene (1819/20 W188). Indeed, even in Hegel's own terms, the origins of history—a stateless society of barbarians—is a mythological "prehistory." He rigidly distinguishes between barbarism and civilization in order to render experienced time possible. Although commentators of Hegel's works have often understood the organic legal order as the final moment of history,[49] this entirely misses the time-consciousness of *Vernunft*. There is no historical closure to the development of presupposed structures of legal consciousness. *Recht* involves a cumulative process of the subject becoming ever more conscious of her or his role in determining and mirroring laws and centralized institutions.

9. TRUTH AND THE IDENTITY OF LAW

The philosopher's role in all this, though, is not, as appears to be the case today, that Hegel's philosopher become the specialist of applied ethics, a market economy, public policy, human rights, or gender politics. Nor does Hegel's philosopher aim to clarify concepts such as "free speech," the nature of a right, or the concept of law itself. Further, too often the contemporary legal philosopher assumes that legality is constituted from what lawyers and judges claim they do. The rules and values posited by state institutions are often considered authoritative or binding. We have all been reminded: the law student must learn to think like a lawyer. The philosopher's role (and that of the lawyer or judge) are too important for that. For the legal philosopher's objective is the search for truth, according to Hegel.

This is the entry point for the contemporary lawyer or legal scholar to appreciate Hegel's laws. When the lawyer or judge examines the binding character of a legal rule, the object of study is a proposition. The clarification of the boundary of the proposition and the consistency between propositions identify a legal unit. The judge plays the role of a disinterested third party who appeals to concepts that transcend the particular context-specific experiences of the parties. The judge appeals to a rule (this being a concept) as the unit of legality. Of course, human values are important, though our lawyers, legal scholars, and judges often find difficulty in running too far or fast with them. When we humans are weighed down with subjectivity, we defer to representations (*Darstellungen*) of a concept in hopes that we access objectivity. When we recognize the contingency of knowledge, though, we fall back upon subjectivity as the ultimate referent of legal reasoning. Both judges and philosophers acknowledge that posited human values or beliefs end the otherwise infinite ratiocination of rules.[50] The values function to evaluate the content of the rules.[51] We try to relate such values to their source in the institutional bureaucracy of the state-centered legal order to legitimize our beliefs as binding on others.

The philosopher's role, as well as the lawyer's, does not end here, though. This trace of a legal unit to some external founding authorizing origin may be true or untrue. Contemporary legal philosophers are comfortable, more often than not, when they associate legitimacy with such an external legitimizing origin such as habits of obedience and when this origin is recognized as a rule of recognition. Hegel's point in this enterprise is that the content of such a legitimizing externality, as well as the content of the rule of recognition, are immaterial if the legal philosopher or the legal official are only concerned with "what is the identity of the unit of legality?" Hegel's facetious comments about the rule-chasing lawyer are as vivid as are Cicero's.[52] Hegel might also describe the policy expert of today as a mere "pseudo-philosopher." Why? The concept-chasing lawyer or policy expert fails in the quest to access truth of a legal unit. Hegel proceeds to examine how the posit of a value relates to a presupposed structure of consciousness that the subject—the official widely defined—presupposes.

Truth lies, then, in the social relationships presupposed in the content of a concept or rule. Such a rule manifests an implied structure of consciousness where individuals may or may not reciprocally recognize each other. But because the subject's structure of consciousness evolves over time, truth wanders through time. A philosophy of law is a narrative about experiences in time-consciousness. An analytic syllogism does not address such. One reads the rules and institutional acts through an opaque window. The challenge is for the philosopher to identify the spirit of one's epoch, better understood as *Weltanschauung.* For Hegel, legal existence rests in the act of thinking about an event during the experience of time. The content of statutes and precedents incorporates the social-cultural assumptions and expectations that one takes for granted when one intellectually distinguishes one rule from another. The observation about the presupposed self-conscious recognition of strangers through shared mediations, such as institutions, religious practices, and all the other indicia of *Vernunft,* would be the objective of legal education. I shall expand upon Hegel's theory of legal education in Chapter 9. The importance of the act of thinking prior to any presupposed external foundation attributed to an authorizing origin is otherwise missed by legal philosophers. Sources external to consciousness, such as a hypothetical state of nature (Hobbes), habits of obedience (Bentham and Austin), the regularity of social behavior (Hart and Coleman), an invisible author (Rousseau), an

a priori thought (Kelsen), bonding (Hart and Raz), or an idealized rationally cohesive narrative (Dworkin), are removed from the act of thinking.

Truth, though, is not accessed by such a trace of authority to some
exteriority to self-consciousness. One cannot pass through the process of
thinking from such a superficial act of learning. The identity of the social
phenomena in the content of a rule, the examination of how the content
of such rule represents how each individual recognizes the other, and then
the nexus of such social recognition with the presupposed structures of
consciousness in an ethos: such inquiries involve speculation, Hegel admits. The philosopher must not rest content with the mere accumulation
of speculative ideas. Hegel explains his point more clearly in this way:

> The *truth* concerning *right, ethics, and the state* is at any rate *as old* as its *exposi-
> tion and promulgation* in *public laws and in public morality and religion.* What
> more does truth require, inasmuch as the thinking mind [*Geist*] is not content
> to possess it in this proximate manner? What it needs is to be *comprehended*
> as well, so that the content which is already rational in itself may also gain a
> rational form and thereby appear justified to free thinking. For such thinking
> does not stop at what is *given,* whether the latter is supported by the external
> positive legitimacy of the state or the mutual agreement among human be-
> ings, or by the legitimacy of inner feeling and the heart and by the testimony
> of the spirit which immediately concurs with this, but starts out from itself
> and thereby demands to know itself as united in its innermost being with the
> truth. (PR Pref. 11)

There simply is no closure to the pursuit of self-consciousness by observed
individual or deserving philosopher. The human subject can evolve to
higher and higher levels of self-consciousness where the individual recognizes her- or himself in the stranger and the stranger in her- or himself.
To this end, Hegel begins with the stateless society that characterized the
Germany of his day.

This absence of closure, manifested by the thinking being, marks Hegel's
problematic of a modern state-centric legal order. For if an individual gains
a consciousness of her or his separation from the universals of one's tribe
or polis, why would one feel obligated to follow the laws of the newfound
state-centric legal order? In order to set the stage for this fundamental
question, we need to turn to Hegel's explanation of the moment of immediacy with objectivity when the former member of the tribe or polis unknowingly emerges from an implied structure of consciousness centered
about a thinking being.

CHAPTER FOUR

Persons, Property, Contract, and Crime

Hegel begins his *Philosophy of Right* with what he calls Abstract Right. It is sometimes said that Abstract Right represents the state of nature where monadic individuals are abstracted from biography and socially contingent relationships with others. Others suggest that Abstract Right begins with the Kantian autonomous person who, by virtue of being purged of inclinations, can reason about universal maxims. There is a problem with both accounts: namely, that at the same time that Hegel describes *Recht* as abstract he also describes it as being immediately determinate (PR 34–39). Hegel begins *Philosophy of Right,* for example, with "[t]he will which is free . . . as it is in its *abstract* concept, is in the determinate condition of immediacy" (PR 34). What does Hegel mean by this assertion? How can a person's will be abstract and indeterminate and yet, at the same time, be immediate and determinate? Hegel restates the apparent contradiction as follows:

> At first, will appears in the form of immediacy; it has not yet *posited* itself as intelligence freely and objectively determining itself, but only *finds* itself as such objective determining. As such, it is (1) *practical feeling,* has a *single* content and is itself an *immediately individual, subjective* will which, we have just said, feels itself as objectively determining, but still lacks a content that is liberated from the form of subjectivity. (PM 469R)

How can the will be objective and yet be immediately subjective?

Hegel's explanation, which Hegel does attempt in a dense paragraph (PR 34A), lies in the stateless condition from which the thinking (and therefore civilized) being emerges. We need to bear in mind the two levels of consciousness: the observing philosopher and the observed subject. The observing philosopher, though not entirely aware of what is going on, is ahead of the observed individual. I shall begin in section 1 by explaining how the retention of an immediacy with objectivity prevents the observed individual from becoming aware that she or he is autonomous of the objectivity which concepts construct. The immediacy also deters the individual from being conscious of her or his own role in the construction of the concepts. In section 2, I shall then identify a series of concepts that the individual wills as she or he emerges from the tribe: personhood, property, contract, and crime. Because of the immediacy with such concepts, the individual does not accept that objectivity could be otherwise. The individual remains a natural being because of this close association of immediacy with objectivity. The individual cannot imagine that there are other beings. Violence and the unlimited desire to assimilate and conquer territory characterize this solipsistic being. That said, in section 3, I shall reconstruct two arguments, with examples, as to why there are limits to the inviolable right to private property in Abstract Right. Then, in section 4, I shall retrieve how ethicality emerges in the individual's recognition of a stranger by virtue of being a contractee. In section 5, I shall recount how the philosopher comes to realize at this point that a new objectivity has interceded between the observed individual and the objectivity of nature. When an observed individual contravenes or undermines the newfound objectivity, she or he challenges the very legitimacy of the objectivity of consciousness. The latter must punish the criminal in order to return the objectivity to its proper legitimacy. The criminal's act is contrary to the criminal's interest as a rational person who has the potential to be self-conscious. This has implications for sentencing by deterrence and by rehabilitation.

I. THE IDENTITY OF IMMEDIACY WITH OBJECTIVITY

Returning to Chapter 1, I distinguished between two forms of self-consciousness. The one is the observed subject who, immersed in an ethos, is unconscious of her- or himself and of her or his separation from objectivity. The second, the philosophical consciousness, observes the subtle and slow development from such immediacy to the mediation of concepts that represent objectivity. With the latter concepts, the observed individual continually tries to determine objectivity so that she or he can become free of external constraints to her or his action. The observed individual believes that she or he is free of external constraints only to find that such a freedom is an illusion that needs to be overcome. What the observed subject takes as objectivity, including formal institutions and laws of the external state, is only a shell that conceals social relationships that the philosopher (and the observed subject) need to lift from immediacy into the thinking about concepts. The philosopher struggles to become self-conscious in her or his observations about such relations of the observed individual to objectivity, just as does the observed individual.

So, Hegel begins with an observed individual who is emerging from her or his consciousness in a tribal legal order. Although the individual still remains immediate with the tribal customs, she or he is separating from them as she or he leaves the tribe for the individualist culture. The individual unself-consciously thinks about concepts that represent the newly emerging objectivity of consciousness. The individual feels unaware of any humanly constructed mediating concept between the self and the objectivity of nature even though the individual has become separate from such objectivity upon leaving the tribe. The absence of awareness about the mediating concepts renders indeterminacy to the concepts. The indeterminacy is characterized by a lack of particularity in the content of the concepts.

The separation of the emergent individual from objectivity goes hand in hand with the development of a will. The will, though, is not quite existent because the will represents an awareness that is still absent in the emerging objectivity. The autonomy of individual from the objectivity of nature, in contrast, is observable by the philosopher.

The philosopher observes that the content of the concepts with which the emergent individual feels immediate are indeterminate. They lack no limit because they are shells that lack particular content by virtue of the immediacy of the observed individual with them. The concepts—for example the concept of property—would become determinate when the individual self-consciously thinks about the content and when the observed individual brings content into the concepts. That moment will only arise when strangers recognize the concepts as their own. The contract is the first such moment of recognition of the stranger. Until that moment of consciousness, there seems to be no limit to the scope of the individual's objectivity of consciousness (though I shall argue in section four that there is such a limit even in this early moment of self-consciousness). I shall now proceed through various moments of the emerging objectivity of consciousness: personhood, property, contract, and crime. I shall do so with a view to understanding how legitimacy emanates from the increasing self-consciousness of the subject.

2. THE DEVELOPMENT OF THE WILL FROM IMMEDIACY

The philosopher observes that the observed individual is separate from objectivity in contrast with the observed individual who still feels immediate with objectivity.[1] So, objectivity is determinate (from the viewpoint of the observed individual) and indeterminate (from the viewpoint of the philosophical consciousness). The observed individual is not aware that she or he is a subject. The individual does not yet know that she or he thinks on her or his own—that is, that she or he has any intentionality, desires, conscience, morality, or other internal factors that philosophers generally associate with a subject. Nor is the observed individual aware that the objectivity that she or he considers all controlling is really historically and socially contingent. The individual still retains the tribal presupposition that there is an objectivity that is uncontrolled and uncontrollable. Consistent with such an assumption, the observed individual is a mere accident to ethicality: "[w]hether the individual exists or not is a matter of indifference to objective ethical life, which alone has permanence and is the power by which the lives of individuals are governed" (PR 145A). The individual is lost in "merely a play of the waves" (PR 145A). If the individual identifies with institutional sources, the individual forgets that she or he is autonomous from the objectivity of posited enactments and institutions (PR 140f). The complete immediate identity of the individual with objectivity empties the individual of any particular content such as a biography or intentionality. Further, there does not appear to this individual any other objectivity than the one with which she or he identifies. The individual is alone in the world. She or he recognizes no other individual. She or he assumes that everyone else accepts the objectivity that she or he is constructing in her or his consciousness.

a) The Philosopher's Observation of the Separation of the Subject from Objectivity

To the philosopher, this immediacy has dissolved into the mediation of concepts. The concepts mediate between the former immediate observed individual and the objectivity with which she or he had felt at one. The philosopher becomes aware that the concepts emanate from the subject's consciousness. There are two sets of objects now. There is the objectivity of nature, the gods, Fate, and customs. I refer to this as the objectivity of nature. And there is an objectivity which is constituted from the subject's concepts. I call this the objectivity of consciousness. The objectivity of consciousness intercedes between the subject and the objectivity of nature. Concepts are objects of consciousness.[2]

Only the philosopher becomes aware of the separation of subject from the objectivity of nature, and only the philosopher is aware that the person itself is a concept emptied of conscience, intentionality, and other internal factors. The philosopher is not yet aware of any institutions, such as courts or legislatures. Nor is the philosopher aware of any state. The philosopher is only aware that the subject has begun to think after having departed from the tribal culture (PR 41A). Hegel characterizes the unaware subject as a "natural being." The individual is not natural in a biological sense. Rather, she or he is natural in the sense of having bonded with the objectivity so deeply that the objectivity seems like a "second nature."

b) The Abstract Person

Recalling the difference between a subject and a person, explained in Chapter 1, the philosopher only recognizes abstract persons at this early moment in the emergence of consciousness. The individual feels bonded with the abstract person because of the determinate immediacy as she or he leaves the tribe. But precisely because of that immediacy, the abstract person, as a concept constructed from the consciousness of the observed individual subject (the subject being the "same" as the "individual" emerging from the tribe), is a key element of the seemingly uncontrolled and uncontrollable objectivity. Hegel explains the abstract person in this way:

> Personality begins only at that point where the subject has not merely a consciousness of itself in general as concrete and in some way determined, but a consciousness of itself as a completely abstract "I" in which all concrete limitation and validity are negated and invalidated. In the personality, therefore, there is knowledge of the *self* as an *object* [*Geganstand*], but as an object raised by thought to simple infinity and hence purely identical with itself. In so far as they [as observed individuals] have not yet arrived at this pure thought and knowledge of themselves, individuals and peoples do not yet have a personality. PR 36R)

The abstract person lacks intentionality, conscience, human values, or any other element of subjectivity. Although the person has determinate content as *this* subject who has an arbitrary will as she or he emerges from the stateless condition of a tribe, the person in objectivity with which the subject feels immediate is "pure self-reference" and "infinite, universal, and free" (PR 35). Being empty of any particularity as a person, the person's identity has an infinite scope.

Thus, a contradiction, unknown to the tribal culture, permeates the emerging structure of consciousness (PR 35A). On the one hand, a finite determinate subject feels immediate, as she or he did in a tribe, with the objectivity that the subject is constructing. On the other hand, the subject is unknowingly separate from the objectivity. The subject even feels the objectivity as determinate (by virtue of immediacy). But the concepts of the objectivity are indeterminate, abstracted as they are from space and time by virtue of the separation of the subject from the objectivity (PR 42R, 42A, 56). This objectivity is of consciousness rather than of nature.

Because the term *person* is so common in international human rights treaties and in constitutional bills of rights, let us focus upon the character of this abstract person. The person exists without a biography, parental nurturing, assumptions, expectations, a family, schools, a market economy, a state, race, religion, or gender. The person is even purged of human feeling and intentionality. There are no mediating institutions between individual persons and objectivity. The person does not experience time and space (PR 42R, 42A). The abstract person exists behind a "veil of ignorance," to use the concept of John Rawls.[3] The appetites, desires, and values of immediacy are particulars that are absent from the abstract person. As Hegel puts it, "[i]n formal right, therefore, it is not a question of particular interest, of my advantage or welfare, and just as little of the particular ground by which my will is determined, i.e. of my insight and intention" (PR 37). Since immediacy characterizes the structure of consciousness of the emerging thinking subject, the subject, like the former tribal member, lacks any awareness of being autonomous of objectivity. The subject believes that objectivity is determinate because there is no other objectivity or stranger existence. But because of the immediacy, the objectivity is pure.

The philosophical consciousness, however, is aware of the observed individual's unawareness of separation. The philosopher therefore observes that the observed individual's mediating concepts in the objectivity of consciousness are indeterminate precisely because the observed individual fails to comprehend them as mediating concepts (PR 34). But by virtue of its indeterminacy, such a person is a monad isolated and indifferent to other persons as persons. The person does not depend upon any other person or institution for its existence. Interestingly, even the nuclear family can be such an abstract person (PR 169). Strangers are mere external things like trees, tools, and automobiles. Things exist "out there" beyond the consciousness of the person. They need to be seized in order for the person to lack external constraints upon her or his will. But even other abstract persons are things to the person whom the philosopher observes. Each person is capable of being appropriated by the other as a thing.

All this reinforces a formalism in the consciousness of the observed individual. The formalism is produced from the immediacy with objectivity. The abstract person is a unit in the objectivity. Hegel explains the formalism of the objectivity when he addresses impulses and choice in *Philosophy of Mind*:

> The nominal [formal] rationality of impulse and propensity lies merely in their general impulse not to be subjective merely, but to get realized, overcoming the subjectivity by the subject's own agency. Their genuine rationality cannot reveal its secret to a method of outer reflection which presupposes a number of *independent* innate tendencies and immediate instincts, and therefore is wanting in a single principle and final purpose for them. But immanent "reflection" itself carries it beyond their particularity and their natural immediacy, and gives their contents a rationality and objectivity, in which they exist as necessary ties of social relation, as rights and duties. It is this objectification which evinces their real value, their mutual connections, and their truth. (PM 474)

The abstract person is just such an objectification of subjectivity. And the objectified indeterminate person wills only what the person self-determines. There is no other person at this point in the subject's consciousness. The person refers to itself for its identity (if this self-referral is possible without a comparative other person or particular). Anything that stands opposed to the person, whether an external thing or even an external subject with wants and desires, is null and void (PR 39). As in Roman law, all that exists is either the abstract person or external things.

With the help of *Bildung,* the drive to become self-conscious takes possession of one's body, the body being "immediate existence" (PR 48). This "possession" takes place by virtue of the superimposition of concepts upon the body (immediacy). By thinking about and through concepts, the individual develops her or his body by becoming self-conscious. When the individual does so, she or he takes possession of her or his body through the concept of personhood. This person, though, is distinct from the personhood of strangers (PR 57). This is the first stage of self-consciousness. The individual, who fails to develop her or his self-consciousness, also fails to take possession of her or his body. The body becomes a thing, and the individual becomes a slave whose body is conveyed to a master (PR 57R).

c) Property

The second concept of objectivity is property. Like the person, property is an abstract and indeterminate concept. Both concepts emanate from the subject's consciousness and the capacity of the subject to bring her- or himself *into* concepts so that she or he only recognizes her- or himself as an abstract person who owns property. There are external things of nature "out there" beyond the concepts of the abstract person and of property. The concepts mediate between the knower of the concepts and the external things [*Sachen*] of nature.

i) The External World of Nature

The external things are products of nature. Both territory and even animals are such products of nature. Territory is *terra nullius* (vacant land) to this unaware will since no other person exists to possess or own the territory (1817–18, 20R.22). All external things are passive, relative, and impersonal. They lack form.

Only the human being can confer form onto a thing because only the human being is self-conscious (PR 42). A thing is relative in the sense of being used or usable like a tool (PR 43). Even an animal is usable as having a relative value (PS 109, PR 44A). Hegel, like Kant, draws heavily from Roman law in this respect.[4] A thing lacks form until the human will confers a concept onto the thing. Since the human subject now has a will and since external things of nature are passive, impersonal, and of relative value, the human subject has "an absolute right to imbue something external with one's will" (1817/18, 17R.20). Property is a concept that is superimposed (in thought) upon an external thing. The legitimacy of the person to do so is absolute because there is only an indeterminate abstract person who confronts separate passive things that are *nullius*. The property interest is thereby inalienable and imprescriptible (PR 63A). The thinking individual, driven by a will, has begun to emerge from an immediate identity with the tribe's customs in favor of thinking subjects who confer concepts which mediate between the subjects and external things of nature.

ii) The Violent Seizure of a Thing

The first stage of the will, then, is the physical seizure of a thing (PR 54). The subject may use any instrument to seize the thing: the subject may even use weapons (PR 55R). We need to note several points about the seizure, though. The seizure is temporary. Further, since the individual still feels immediate with the objectivity of nature, the physical seizure of things in nature, to the observed individual, seems natural (PR 55). Again, there are no other self-determining subjects who differ from me: all other things, including strangers, are "out there" for seizure. I am not yet aware that I have a consciousness that intercedes between myself and the objects of nature. There will always be something else needed to fulfill my arbitrary will: "external objects [*Dinge*] extend further than I can grasp. Thus, when I have a specific thing in my possession, something else will be connected within it" (PR 55A). The desire to possess the absent things will drive the subject to desire to seize more and more things.[5] The abstract person conceals a living subject who, driven by appetites and impulses, is a possessive individualist as long as she or he is unaware of others and as long as external things are absent from the person's will.

This violent seizure of external things arises in two contexts in Hegel's arguments about legal philosophy. In one, the individual seizes a particular thing, such as a pencil or plant or animal. In the other, a state takes possession of a territory. The state does so by conquering another state— after all, the state, as an abstract monadic person in this early moment of self-consciousness, does not recognize another state as existing because of the immediacy that characterizes the state's identity with nature and with objects of consciousness. I develop this moment of international legal consciousness in Section 3 of Chapter 10. All territory for this state is *terra nullius* (PR 50, 55, 58). The Roman principle of *res nullius occupanti cedit* ("a thing belonging to no one is ceded to the occupant")[6] remains with constitutional lawyers today.[7] The seizure of territory generates the claim of absolute and radical title to the territory by a state so that aboriginal peoples have, at best, a *usufructory* right (to use the land but not own it). In either case, violence constitutes the initial moment of the objectivity of consciousness. As noted in Chapter 2, this very violence gives cause to Walter Benjamin, Carl Schmitt, and Jacques Derrida, following Hegel, to claim that the very constitution of a state rests in violence.[8] Again, Derrida and Stanley Fish (1938–) insist that the violence continues into the very interpretation of the texts of the constituted state.[9] Hegel, though, claims that "the original, i.e. immediate, modes of acquisition and titles are in fact abandoned" (PR 217R).

iii) The Conferral of a Form on the Seized Thing

The early act of the will confers a form or concept *onto* the seized single thing (PR 103). The person embodies the thing with its will (PR 59R, 59A). The form (*Vorstellung*) represents the single thing "in its totality" (PR 54A, 56). The thing is thereby assimilated into one's personhood (PR 56R). Again, the person, being empty of biography and other particulars of the body, is not the empirical person of immediacy. The person is a rational autonomous person that one might liken to Kant's rational person except that Hegel's person is immersed in phenomena. My violently seized thing is intellectually transformed into the concept of property once I confer a form onto the thing. That said, because the person exists by reference to its own immediacy, the violence of the seizure of an external thing is recognized as legally binding only when the subject confers form onto the seized thing and only when other persons recognize the form as property. This arises in a contract—a concept that I shall address in a moment.

At this point there are three elements that characterize the will. First, the abstract person makes an external thing into property by imputing her or his will into the physical possession of the thing. Hegel puts this point this way: "[i]n property, my will is personal, but the person is a specific entity [or unit, *ein Dieses*]; thus, property becomes the personal aspect of this specific will. Since I give my will existence [*Dasein*] through property, property must also have the determination of being this specific entity, of being mine. This is the important doctrine of the necessity of *private property*" (PR 46A). Second, the will of the observed individual feels immediate with her or his construction of the concept of property although the concept unknowingly intercedes between the individual's immediacy and the external things. Third, the observed individual takes possession of her or his own body and confers a form onto it (PR 57). The conferral of form onto external things of nature is critical to the identity of the abstract person as well as of property: "[t]he free spirit consists precisely in not having its being as mere concept [that is, as the person] or *in itself*, but in overcoming [*aufheben*] this formal phase of its being [that is, immediacy] and hence also its immediate natural existence, and in giving itself an existence which is purely its own and free" (PR 57R). The observed individual translates into her or his personhood what she or he is as a possibility in immediacy: namely, the possibility of being an owner of property, as a concept, over things of nature.

The consequence of the conferral of form onto the possessed external thing is that nature is displaced into "an *independently existing* externality" (PR 56). This externality is the objectivity of consciousness. The objectivity of consciousness intercedes between the observed individual and the objectivity of nature. In this way, "[t]his reality, in general, where free will has *existence*, is the *Law* (Right)—the term being taken in a comprehensive sense not merely as the limited juristic law, but as the actual body of all conditions of freedom" (PM 486). This is the genesis of the formation of *Gesetz* (PM 485). It is also the genesis of the legal formalism about which I shall expand in the next chapter. This objectivity of consciousness ceases to be contingent in the time and space that the individual has experienced immediacy (PR 56, 42A).

iv) Signs Representing Property

In addition to the conferral of a form onto an external thing, the will signifies the form. The sign "indicate[s] that I have placed my will in it" (PR 58). Boundary stones or the planting of trees or a flag, for example, signify ownership of territory. So too, the registry for mortgages signifies ownership. Such signs provide indicia, first, of the claim to have placed my will into the thing and, second, the exclusion of the property interest from other persons (PR 58A). Thus, the thing is not the external object that it is (a chair, a book, an automobile) but a sign that signifies one's will to strangers (PR 58A). The sign links one's person with the emerging construction of objectivity (PR 60). The thing has now been transformed from a physical object into a sign about the person's will (PR 58A). At this point, once the signification representing a person's will is shared with other persons, there arises the possibility that the sign can be exchanged.

Hegel points out that the relation of the will to property undermines the contemporary understanding of a *usufructory* right. Even today, courts assign a usufructory right to aboriginal peoples to fish and hunt on lands that they cannot own, for example.[10] If they do not use the land for such a purpose, the right of usufruct may be annulled and reverted to the proprietor. This usufructory right, Hegel now claims, rests upon an "empty distinction" between possession and property (PR 62R). Similarly, the feudal distinction between the full and unconditional use of land on the one hand and the rent or tithe on the other[11] lacked rational coherency with the will's creation of a property interest. Property willed by a subject, however, suggests the complete and free ownership of external things (PR 62). Such ownership transforms the physical possession into the "security, stability, and objectivity" of a form (PR 217A).

The rule of law now enters the story (PR 103). Legality does not follow the arbitrary empirical desires of immediacy. Legality is constituted from concepts that mediate between the immediacy and the external things of nature. The mere possession of a thing does not signify a property interest in the thing. We cannot speak of equality of needs as contingent at this point in time. The desire to fulfill economic needs returns the philosopher to the moment of immediacy. The philosopher can only speak of equality in the context of the equality of the abstract right. Property is the legitimate claim to possess a physical thing (PR 45). Property is private in the sense of excluding others from the thing (PR 46). The things of nature are now humanized in the sense that a concept of individual self-consciousness (property) has overladen the things. The objectivity of consciousness unknowingly intercedes between the emergent individual and the objectivity of nature.

3. PERSONHOOD AND PROPERTY AS PARTICULARS IN OBJECTIVITY

Property, then, exemplifies how an empty concept (the abstract person) can link with the external natural world of things, all while the observed subject is not conscious of such nexus. The person remains in the phenomenal realm. Contrary to Kant, the noumena is now an element of the phenomena (PR 44R). There are no moral duties at this moment of consciousness. This would be so only if the philosopher turned to the subjectivity rather than the objectivity of consciousness. This objectivity constructed from her or his consciousness also contrasts with the objectivity of nature. Personhood and property are the first two concepts constructed from the objectivity of consciousness. Hegel's philosophy of law thereby remains inside the human experience. And yet, this very experience objectifies concepts as legal units that are alienated from the felt immediacy of the subject who emerges from a tribe.

Bearing in mind Hegel's sense of actuality, a concept explained in Chapter 1, the abstract person begins the fulfillment of the potentiality of actuality as it claims ownership of the thing. After all, because the person is initially empty of all intentionality and all social relations by virtue of its immediacy with objectivity, the appropriation of a thing as property gives content or embodiment to the person. But the embodiment is abstract because, by virtue of immediacy, the individual is unaware that her or his arbitrary will has posited the embodiment of the person.

Is the appropriation of a thing a particularity that embodies content to the person? By owning property, the individual becomes a person. But is such a property-owning person socially and historically contingent? Even in a contract where two persons recognize each other as persons, do the persons recognize each other as social beings rather than as abstract persons? That is, does the person suddenly possess the content of a biography? Does the person have the sort of personality that is the object of psychology studies? Is this abstract personality the object of *Bildung*?

Without private property, the will cannot develop in the appropriation of things from within as arbitrary immediacy nor without consciousness. Because private property is recognized in an abstract objectivity with which the person is immediate, there is not, as yet, any consciousness of the experience of time and space. Space and time are abstracted from conscious-ness—that is, from experience. The right to private property is recognized as part and parcel of abstract personality in an objectivity of consciousness. The subject feels immediate with such objectivity. From the philosopher's observation, however, the subject is an empty abstract person who owns empty concepts which intercede between the subject and nature: "my right to a thing is not merely possession, but as possession by a *person* it is *property,* or legal possession, and it is a *duty* to possess things as *property,* i.e. to be as a person. Translated into the phenomenal relationship, viz. relation to an-other person—this grows into the duty of some one *else* to respect *my* right" (PM 486). This objectivity of consciousness generates Abstract Right.[12]

Although perhaps counterintuitive, the formalism of this objectivity of consciousness portrays a sense of the fulfillment of actuality. The observed subject feels at one with objectivity even though, from the philosopher's observation, the subject is autonomous of the objectivity. By physically seizing an external thing, the observed individual's will is actualized. In addition, though, the subject, heretofore unrecognized as acting from an arbitrary will because she or he is unaware of separation from objectivity, wills property as *that subject*'s. All this takes place without the observed individual aware of what is happening. The observed consciousness is only aware of an objectivity of nature. Personhood and property seem to be nested in such an objectivity of nature even though an emerging objectiv-ity—the objectivity of consciousness—has interceded between the individ-ual and nature. Private property, not social or economic needs, is the first requisite for freedom, according to Hegel (PR 45R).

4. THE PEREMPTORY NORM OF FREEDOM

We have observed how violence characterizes the property of the seized thing that becomes the object of entitlement. Violence also generates the initial state's seizure of a territory that is overlaid with the form of prop-erty. The question that arises, in this context, is whether there is a limit to the initial violence towards the external objects of nature and of conscious-ness. Hegel suggests that the originary violence is displaced by the confer-ral of form over the things and territory. Legality takes form as it were. As Hegel puts it succinctly:

> For although the State may originate in violence, it does not rest on it; vio-lence, in producing the State, has brought into existence only what is justi-fied in and for itself, namely, laws and a constitution. What dominates in the

> State is the spirit of the people, custom, and law. There man is recognized and treated as a *rational* being, as free, as a person; and the individual, on his side, makes himself worthy of this recognition by overcoming the natural state of his self-consciousness and obeying a universal, the will that is in essence and actuality will, the *law*; he behaves, therefore, towards others in a manner that is universally valid, recognizing them—as he wishes others to recognize him—as free, as persons. (PM 432A)

Precisely because the forms lie inward in the subject's consciousness, can the individual claim title and then alienate property in all "things"? Are there some "things" that remain internal to the will?[13]

a) Why the Right to Property Is Limited

Hegel makes two arguments as to why the acquisition of the right to property is not unlimited.

The first argument draws from Hegel's claim that property carries an inviolability in the objectivity of consciousness (PR 43, 47, 48). Hegel states that the person, being an indeterminate concept, has an "absolute *right of appropriation* which human beings have over all things [*Sachen*]" (PR 44). The point is, though, that such a right of appropriation exists because of the self-consciousness. Gans reports that Hegel expands upon this point in his lectures: the free person "has the right to make his will a thing [*Sache*] or to make the thing his will, or, in other words, to supersede the thing and transform it into his own; for the thing, as externality, has no end in itself, and is not infinite self-reference but something external to itself" (PR 44A). If someone else alienated my property claim to a thing against my will or against the will of a state, my drive to become self-conscious would be cancelled (PR 57). If a person infringes such an internal spirit to become self-conscious, the intervention is void. For if I cannot reflect about myself as I possess and then claim title to things and territory, I cannot even begin to confer a will into a seized thing. For a will is an expression of *self*-consciousness. If I lack a will, I do not think. Indeed, as noted in my chapter two, I resemble an animal if I do not think. A contract or statute to authorize a master to deny my right to property is therefore null and void (PR 66A). Nor may a contract or statute withdraw or deny one's personhood or freedom of expression for the same reason of the nexus of personhood and free expression with the drive to become self-conscious.

The second argument against the unlimited appropriation of things is that philosophical consciousness (though not observed consciousness) recognizes, as explained above, a separation of the immediacy from the objectivity of consciousness. Persons and property manifest such an objectivity.

As a consequence of this separation, the subject arbitrarily wills a form into things external to consciousness. The artist or writer or scientist, for example, creates an external product. One may *"alienate individual* products of *my particular physical and mental [geistig] skills* and active capabilities to someone else and allow him *to use them for a limited period"* (PR 67). As Hegel explains, "[t]he distinctive quality of intellectual [*geistigen*] production may, by virtue of the way in which it is expressed, be immediately transformed into the external quality of a thing [*Sache*], which may then in turn be produced by others" (PR 68). The product may be patented or copyright protected (PR 69R). The new owner "appropriate[s]" the words that I have communicated. The new owner also appropriates the invention that I created.

She or he does so at a price, though, because the product has gained an exchange value to which all consumers are associated. Ordinary skills may not be patented because I have not extended my will to produce the product. What is appropriated is "a series of discrete and abstract *signs*" (PR 68R). But the act of creation itself cannot be alienated. It is not an external thing, an externality which the structure of consciousness presupposed. That is, the subjective genesis of the arbitrary will expresses an inalienable inner will (PR 68). I cannot sell the possibility of my personhood (as expressed by my creative acts) without undermining my very autonomy from the objectivity of consciousness (PR 69R).

b) Master-Slave as Example

Hegel uses slavery to exemplify the above two arguments for the limitation on the acquisition of things. Slavery assumes that the slave is a passive external thing of nature such as a tree or flower. As such, the slave may be the object of possession, title, and an exchange value. The slave is believed to lack the capacity to be self-conscious: that is, to have a will (PR 57R).[14] As a thing, the slave is external to the owner who violently seizes the thing and then imputes her or his will into the thing. The slave, as an external thing, thereby becomes the property of the master (EL 163A1).

Hegel claims, however, that both the master and slave, as human beings rather than animals, have the potentiality to have a will. Because the master and slave believe that the slave lacks a will, the slave lacks any consciousness that she or he is autonomous from the objectivity of nature, and the slave is believed by the master and the slave to be parts of such an objectivity of nature. The slave, as an observed individual, is considered a "natural" being by the master because of the slave's absence of self-consciousness. The master feels immediate with the slave as property just as if the master might feel immediate with his villa or vineyard or conquered territory. In Hegel's words, the master and slave, by virtue of their immediacy with the objectivity of nature, lead a "conceptless existence." Both master and slave accept that the slave lacks the potential for self-consciousness. As such, the slave, for the master, is a mere external thing that may be bought and sold and, for the slave, the master alone is a subject with a will.

This implied structure of master-slave fundamentally contradicts the possibility of self-consciousness in all humans. All human beings, however unconscious, have *the potential* to displace the violence of natural existence with the conferral of thought into the seizure of things. As humans rather than as animals, we can think. Yes, we have animal-like appetites, inclinations, values, beliefs, and all the other particulars that embody an arbitrary will. But such particularity manifests only an early unconscious moment in the development of a thinking being and of civilization. Each subject, by imputing an arbitrary will into a thing, gives oneself "an existence which is purely its own and free" (PR 56R). This transformative project, integrally dependent upon an unconscious subject who has the potential of self-consciousness and who is autonomous from objectivity, recognizes the slave and the master as "on the way to truth." Despite the fact that the slaves might have experienced a far harsher fate in Africa than in the Indies and despite the fact that slave owners may have contracted a property interest in the slave, "the enslavement of Negroes is an institution that is wholly wrongful, one that contradicts the right that is truly human and divine, and that the institution must be abolished" (1824/25, W14).

Slave laws are void. Why? Because one's distinct personality and self-consciousness are "inalienable" and "imprescriptible." The inalienable and imprescriptible elements include "my personality in general, my universal freedom of will, ethical life, and religion" (PR 66). As a consequence of this relation of objectivity to the inalienability of self-consciousness, one just cannot alienate one's own will. We may now add this to the above two arguments as to why the right to private property is limited. Legal legitimacy rests upon such an inalienable will. Legitimacy of the objectivity of consciousness presupposes that a will is autonomous of the objectivity of nature and of the objectivity of consciousness. Legitimacy of the latter presupposes, therefore, a subject and an object. Any objectivity of consciousness that confers the status of slavery to a human being is thereby "false" [*unwahren*] precisely because it denies and undermines the human being's inalienable drive to become self-conscious (PR 57R). Such a law authorizing slavery is "absolutely contrary to right" in that it contradicts "the *concept* of the human being as spirit" or self-consciousness (PR 57R).[15] Because an objectivity that legalizes slavery fails to address the social recognition owed by the master to the slave and vice versa in the content of the objectivity of consciousness, ethicality is absent from the content of such objectivity. The objectivity is illegitimate (that is, not binding upon all individuals capable of becoming self-conscious). The slavery held out as an element of the objectivity of consciousness contradicts the very genesis of the self-consciousness. All human beings have the potential to be a subject because all have the capacity to think (PR 21R). If the slave realized that she or he had a will, the slave would think rather than merely feel. Once the slave is aware of this, she or he becomes aware that she or he helps to construct the master as master through the objectivity of consciousness. If the slave were a free will, the slave would recognize her- or himself in the master. Once one becomes conscious of one's subjectivity, one becomes conscious that one, as a subject, produces the contingent structure of slavery.

Accordingly, the abolition of slavery is not a moral or "ought" duty drawn from the noumenal realm of the categorical imperative. Rather, slavery does not exist if all human beings have a will. Thus, for Hegel, the slave is responsible for her or his own predicament: "[b]ut if someone is a slave, his own will is responsible, just as the responsibility lies with the will of a people if that people is subjugated. Thus the wrong of slavery is the fault not only of those who enslave or subjugate people, but of the slaves and the subjugated themselves" (PR 57A). The slave, as an observed consciousness, is not yet aware that she or he has a will, that she or he is autonomous from the objectivity of nature as well as of consciousness, that she or he constructs the objectivity of consciousness, that the latter is therefore contingent rather than uncontrolled by nature, and that therefore the slave can will her or his social recognition of and by strangers. The philosopher is left to conclude, then, that there is, indeed, a limit to the extent to which a human being may violently possess and then confer title onto things because some "things" in an objectivity of consciousness are human beings. This limit rests in the very inward subjectivity that drives observed individuals to become self-conscious.

c) Peremptory Norms of Subjectivity

Hegel identifies several peremptory elements of this subjectivity. These peremptory norms exist before any state exists and, indeed, before any observed individual who emerges from a "natural" tribal consciousness recognizes a stranger represented in the objectivity of consciousness. There are at least two sets of peremptory norms in the very genesis of legality.

First, immediacy includes bodily inclinations. Taking a distinction from Edmund Husserl,[16] the body is both biological and experiential. If the individual sells her or his body into slavery, she or he cannot even begin the project of becoming self-conscious as an autonomous thinking being. The slave has sold her or his immediacy to the objectivity of nature. As such, the selling of one's body is null and void (PR 57, 57R). One has an inviolable right over one's body (PR 43, 47, 48). Accordingly, life itself is inviolable (PR 70). Suicide, as an offence against life, is null and void: *"life* is not something external to personality, which is itself *this* personality and *immediate*. The *disposal* [*Entäußerung*] or sacrifice of life is, on the contrary, the opposite of existence [*Dasein*] of *this* personality" (PR 70). That said, the individual may have to sacrifice her or his life for the ethos when the ethical life of the international legal consciousness is imprisoned in a certain shape as described in Chapter 10 (PR 70A). Aside from life, conscience is also an element of immediacy. As such, an external or self-inflicted constraint upon conscience offends the very presupposed immediacy of philosophy (PR 66, 66A). So too, religious freedom is an important inalienable and imprescriptible element of immediacy (PR 66).

Second, when we turn to the context of mediation, the elements of subjectivity that condition the striving to think about the mediating concepts are also inviolable (PR 66). One important element of mediation is thinking. Accordingly, constraints upon the act of thinking also contradict the very possibility of mediation by concepts between the knower and objectivity. More generally, the ethicality of the ethos itself is indispensable to the very legitimacy of the modern objectivity of consciousness, as we shall see in Chapter 6. One cannot even begin to think about thinking as if it were denied (PR 66). In sum, peremptory norms enter into Hegel's argument in the very first moment of consciousness when the individual's consciousness separates from the immediacy with the tribal customs.

Copyright protection, for example, draws from the initial mediation between the individual and the objectivity of nature: "[b]ut the author of the book or the inventor of the technical device remains the owner of the *universal* ways and means of reproducing such products and things [*Sachen*], for he has not immediately alienated these universal ways and means as such but may reserve them for himself as his distinctive mode of expression" (PR 69). Hegel distinguishes between the ownership of a thing—which is the consequence of the exercise of one's internal will—and the legitimacy which ownership confers onto another person to manufacture the original object of creation (PR 69R). Further, Hegel explains that one may alienate the external products of that subjectivity but not

the legitimacy to create the products (PR 69). The legitimacy and therefore the legality to sell or use an object is external to the inalienability of
the right of property. Since the object is the product of the creator's will,
the creator alone may decide upon its external use or value. What is alienated is the form, not the content, with which the author confers property
into an external thing of nature. Since it cannot be precisely determined to
what extent the creator has given form to an external thing, the intellectual
property cannot be constrained by posited laws. The only constraint to the
freedom of intellectual property is the honor of the author (PR 69R). Any
form may endlessly be altered in many different ways so that ownership is
a mere "superficial imprint" upon an object. Ownership is part and parcel
with the inward will that drives the individual to continually overcome
external constraints upon her or his freedom. The power to sell or use an
object is external to such an inward freedom.

5. CONTRACT: THE DEPENDENCE UPON A STRANGER

The philosopher recognizes personhood and property by observing the
unaware individual who subtly becomes separate from the objectivity of
nature as she or he leaves the immediacy of tribal customs. The observed
individual still feels immediately bonded with this objectivity of nature
without being aware of her or his autonomy from it as a thinking being.

a) Interpersonal Recognition

When thought lifts the individual from immediacy into personhood,
the first moment of consciousness emerges (PR 42). There is one duty of
the person at this moment: the duty to respect strangers as abstract persons.
This duty involves an indifference to the stranger's feelings, biography, or
other particularities because only abstract persons exist at this point (PR
49). The person and property—the two concepts which the autonomous
subject constructs in the first moment of self-consciousness—are emptied
of particularity.

The above duty to respect strangers as persons arises when the observed
individual enters into a contract. When the person enters into a contract,
each contractee recognizes the entitlement of the other contractee to property since the person, in the first moment of Abstract Right, is nothing except property. Each person recognizes the other person in order to assure it
of existence in an otherwise life-threatening struggle between a master and

a slave, both of whose consciousnesses have not yet developed from immediacy. Social inequality arises after the immediate consciousness of the subject has appropriated things and transformed them into property. In this moment of the possession of things, the person desires to fuse with things of nature: "[t]his means that in the consciousness of their self-identity they [the persons] know themselves to be identical with others through the mediation of external existence, and they accept one another as mutually free and independent" (1817/18, 31.34). The recognition of the other's property claim, though, is incorporated into the objectivity of consciousness.[17] The observed individual exists in a formal and reified structure of empty concepts. This explains why Hegel lectures that "human beings are equal, but only as persons, that is, only with respect to the source of their possession" (1822/23 W49).

There are always external things, though, that the person desires to appropriate in the moment of recognition of the stranger by entering into a contract. The individual will only begin to gain peace of mind when she or he recognizes human beings as persons like her- or himself rather than as external things. But personhood and property, by themselves, cannot assure reciprocal recognition between the contractees because each may withdraw its arbitrary will from the contract. The observed subject is only dependent upon the other contractee. If reciprocal recognition differs from dependency, is the latter an intentional phenomenon? Or is it a will that is recognized by institutions such as a legislature or a court? If so, is the legal recognition abstracted from all socially and historically contingent meaning? Is a person conferred legal status by institutions in the objectivity of consciousness? In order to respond to these questions, we need to return to several elements of philosophical consciousness.

First, the philosopher realizes that property is the consequence of thinking about a concept. The conferral of a form onto the thing involves such thinking. Thinking incorporates concepts which, in turn, intercede between the knower and the things of nature. The philosopher is not yet aware of the particular capacity, intelligence, work effort, and intent of the observed individual in willing the form into the thing (PR 43R). The philosopher is constrained at this point by the empty concepts of personhood and property. The abstract person, emptied of intentionality, is the object of consciousness.

Second, the claimant to property does not recognize another intentional subject. Even when the claimant recognizes a person by entering into a contract, the persons are not recognized as intentional subjects. The intellectual conferral of a form onto a thing ignores the space and time experienced by the observed individual in immediacy (PR 56, 42A). After all, the willing individual, at this second stage of the observed individual's self-consciousness, still identifies immediately with its objectivity of consciousness without realizing that she or he is autonomous from the objectivity of nature and even of consciousness. The property-holding claimant only recognizes a contractee as immediate with objectivity, like itself. Accordingly, it would be premature to describe the relationship between property owners in a contract as "inter-subjective" or a "social bond."[18] For Hegel, the existence of property at this point in the will's development could hardly introduce a dialogic community.[19]

The contract is an inter*personal,* not an intersubjective, transaction. The eventual contract itself institutionalizes a shared objectivity of consciousness between two abstract *persons.* The intentional subject feels immediately identified with the abstractions of personhood and property as if there were no objectivity of consciousness. When the contract is performed, it is a form, not subjectivity, which is performed. How could two persons possess a social bond when they are not aware of their own subjectivity nor that of strangers? How could there be an ethical relationship when both are believed to be cleansed of all intentionality? Hegel urges the philosopher to recognize the possibility of an ethical relationship. But at this moment, the best that the philosopher can recognize is an ethical relationship between abstract disembodied persons: "Be a person and respect others as persons" (PR 36) or "Respect yourself and others in their ownership as persons" (1817–18, 31R.35). But the imperative directs that we respect persons as persons, not subjects as intentional subjects.

Third, property, to be property, is private to the abstract person. Communally owned property is just not possible (PR 46). The property is exclusive to the will of the person. Plato's *Republic* did not allow for private property because Plato was describing an ethos where the philosophical consciousness had not yet recognized a separation of individual from the shared objectivity of consciousness in the polis (PR 46).[20] This concept of property is not yet actual because there are no other persons whom the individual, as an abstract solipsistic monad, considers as things. That only occurs when such a person realizes that it needs others in order to fulfill its arbitrary will that has heretofore been considered by the solipsistic individual as universally shared with others (PR 43R).[21]

Finally, there are two things happening in Hegel's argument. There is an empty autonomous person "out there" in an objectivity of consciousness. Only the abstract person is recognized by others in contract. Second, there is a subject, driven by spirit, who feels immediate or bonded with the objectivity of personhood, property, and contract. The latter objectivity is constructed from consciousness in contrast with the objectivity of nature with which the tribal member had felt immediate. But the newly constructed objectivity of consciousness is purged from the particularity of desires, impulses, needs, and the like. Precisely because of the absence of particularity from the abstract person, the person is indeterminate. When faced with a stranger with a biography and desires and appetites and values, the stranger is considered a thing. A struggle for life ensues. In order to retain autonomy from the objectivity of nature, the person must recognize the stranger. The abstract person cannot monologically recognize itself. It cannot refer to itself. The ownership of private property cannot do that. The person can only recognize itself if the stranger also recognizes the person.

Influenced by Fichte,[22] Hegel argues that the person recognizes the stranger and the stranger recognizes the person's arbitrary will by agreeing to a contract. The contract stipulates how two monadic abstract persons can coexist despite their autonomy from each other and despite their otherwise unlimited desire to acquire the stranger as a thing.[23] The contract renders determinate particularity to the indeterminate concept of personhood.

Or does a contract render determinate particularity? The contract represents concepts shared between two arbitrary wills that are concealed by their personhood and the claim to property. Further, the contract is not actual until it is enforced in particular contingent circumstances. Further, through the universal (the terms of the contract), each contractee recognizes the other's right to property.[24] But the one recognizes the other as an abstract person, not as a subject with appetites, desires, needs, and an intentionality. The particularity of personhood and of a contract is property in an objectivity, not subjectivity. The one recognizes, not the intentional will of the other, but the property interest of the other person. But the property interest is a *form* conferred onto a seized object. As a consequence of these factors, the contract is inter*personal,* not intersubjective: "[c]ontract presupposes that the contracting parties *recognise* each other *as persons* [my emphasis] and owners of property" (PR 71R). Further, the recognition is directed to the objectivity of consciousness with which the observed individual feels bonded: "it is a relationship of *objective* [my emphasis] spirit, the moment of recognition is already contained and presupposed within it" (PR 71R). The intentional subject is a remainder.

b) Form over Content

In a contract, space and time remain abstracted from experience as consciousness. Once signed, sealed, and delivered, the experienced time and place of the contract become irrelevant. The contract becomes the unit of the objectivity of consciousness. A contract is often erroneously taken as actual because the parties still feel immediate with it. The value of the property is exchanged as a universal sign, however different the particular intentionality of the owners (PR 77). Such form, estranged from concrete particularity (but not from the particularity as property) characterized Roman contract law, for example (PR 77R, 79R).[25] Roman legal classifications were "superficial groupings" based on formalities external to the contingent arbitrary wills of contractees (PR 77R). The problem is that such formalism becomes alienated from the experienced time and place of immediacy and from unaware subjects with intentional wills.

The contract offers a "rational middle" between two abstract persons.[26] The arbitrary will of the contractee is fulfilled at the same moment that the form displaces the seizure of the arbitrary will: "I no longer own property merely by means of a thing and my subjective will, but also by means of another will, and hence within the context of a common will . . . [This] constitutes the sphere of *contract*" (PR 71). The terms and conditions of the contract remain separate from the impulses, desires, and needs of the arbitrary will. The community that is constructed is an empty abstraction. The contract is a mere "form and shape of community," not an actual community of subjects with intentional wills (PR 75).

Precisely because of the formalism, a contract can create neither a marriage nor a state (PR 75R). In Chapter 7, I shall examine how, if a marriage continues as the amalgam of two arbitrary wills, it simply will not last. What is needed is a recognition and respect of one member of the marriage to the other. Similarly, in Chapter 8, I shall explain that, according to Hegel, a contract cannot generate an organic constitution because a state must have a legitimacy greater than the mere aggregate of private arbitrary wills. The state must be a universality whose legitimacy is valid *in itself* and *for* subjective self-consciousness. If arbitrary wills remain independent of any shared universals, the legitimacy of the universals will be forever challenged (PR 81R).

c) Actuality as Performance

If the contract remains a mere concept or set of concepts, when is its content actualized? When it is performed, the performance of a contract gives body to this form (PR 71A, 78, 79). I recognize the thing I seized as the property of another and I perform such a recognition: "I have hereby alienated the thing [*Sache*] I own, that it has *now* ceased to be my property, and that I already recognize it as the property of the other party" (PR 79R). The will is now particularized. The arbitrary wills of possessive individualists are displaced by the common interest through their contract.

First, Hegel explains in his 1824/25 lectures that, after the person has conferred a concept onto a passive external thing and then assigned a sign to represent the concept, the individual thereupon sells what she or he cannot use (1824/25 W65). The exchange of the surplus value links concrete context-specific experiences with the objectivity of consciousness. Second, the human being is now driven by something higher than her or his arbitrary will in the performance of the contract. This "something higher" is thinking. The whole process of thinking about the seized things leads to the performance of the contract: the arbitrary will of the possessive individualist is long displaced by the thinking process—the seizure of an external thing, the conferral of form onto the thing, the shared exchange value of the form, the contract, and the performance of the contract (1824/25 W66).

Prior to a contract, we have seen, the owner exclusively owns a property interest in a thing of nature (although this exclusivity is subject to the peremptory norms of subjectivity just noted). The contract, though, displaces such exclusivity: "in identifying my will with that of another, I *cease* to be an owner of property" (PR 72). The initial arbitrary will is transformed into a rational will and this, in turn, is exchanged with another rational will into a unity of different rational wills (PR 73). The common interest of the two contractees produces joint ownership in place of the exclusivity of private property. And yet, each contractee is an abstract person that lives forever. This contrasts with the finiteness of the observed subject. Thus, the arbitrary wills of concrete subjects are not entirely institutionalized in the common interest of the contract (PR 73). That is, the contract is generated from arbitrary wills, each with its own particularity. The problem is that when a concrete subject dies, the property, if jointly owned, devolves to the surviving party to the contract. However, if two arbitrary wills enter into an agreement as common, rather than as joint, owners, the assets devolve to the estate of the abstract person. Hegel tries to resolve the contradiction by stating that the relationship is mediated threefold: the contractee "*ceases* to be an owner [because of the exchange value] of property, *remains* one [because she or he retains a remainder not conveyed to the contract], and *becomes* one [because the contract becomes a new form of property]" (PR 74). The form (the abstract person) links with the content (the death of the subjectivity of the party) to sustain the formalism of the objectivity of consciousness.

The point is that when the contract is performed, the performance expresses the arbitrary will behind the form. This contrasts with alleged uncivilized societies. Here, the form of the contract and its performance may coincide (PR 78A). However, even in performance, the observed subject is unaware of the universal shared with a stranger-contractee. The consequential bond in the performance of the contract is a reified bond—reified, that is, from subjectivity. The bond lies between two equals, yes. But the equality is between two abstract persons, not intentional subjects. The bond of a contract is abstracted from the earthly world. What is performed is property, not the intentional will of an embodied subject. The bond exists in thought alone. The contract, once again, is interpersonal, not intersubjective.

As a consequence, blameworthiness is not relevant when a contract is breached. For the person remains empty of intentionality in the emergence of the objectivity of consciousness as Abstract Right.[27] The breach is an either-or situation because the contract joins two abstract persons. A breach of contract, unless it involves deceit of other circumstances below regarding crime, concerns a civil wrong, not a criminal wrong, because the breach does not contradict the legitimacy of the whole objectivity of consciousness by denying the full existence of the other person. Further, the contract is constituted from the formalities of equal empty persons, not from the expectations and assumptions of intentional subjects. Lon Fuller's claim that a contract presupposes unwritten assumptions and expectations that phenomenologically precede such formalities would take the lawyer in the wrong direction according to Hegel.[28] The contract exists between two empty persons who own property, itself an abstraction from the embodied subjects and even from external things of nature. Persons, property, and the contract are intellectualizations that have displaced the particularized intentional subject, while the subject remains unaware of her or his autonomy from willed objects. Subjectivity, at least at this point in Hegel's argument, is left as a remainder to the objectivity of consciousness.

6. CRIME

Until this point in the philosopher's observation of the will, the observed individual remains unaware of her or his autonomy from the objectivity of nature. The question is, "how does the observed individual shift her or his consciousness from the Abstract Right of the objectivity of consciousness with which she or he feels immediate to a subjectivity of intentionality from which the objectivity is reified?" Intentional subjectivity comes into its own at the end of Hegel's section on crime. But how does intentionality flow from criminal law?

Hegel examines criminal law in two places in *Philosophy of Right*. One arises from an ethos where an observed individual increasingly becomes autonomous from the objectivity of consciousness and yet, where the individual still believes that she or he is immediate with objectivity, the latter being an objectivity of consciousness lacking any intervening concepts (PR 82–103). This presupposes that the increasingly individualist society remains stateless. The second set of passages concerning crimes concerns the administration of an institutionalized civil society (PR 209–29). I intend to examine the first set of passages in this chapter because here Hegel elaborates the nature of crime and the nature of law generally. I shall begin by briefly outlining the context in which Hegel elaborates his theory of crime and his theory of the binding character of laws. I shall then turn to his rejection of deterrence and rehabilitation as adequate forms of punishment.

a) The Context

To understand Hegel's theory of crime, one needs to situate Hegel's statements in the context of his argument. I have recounted how Hegel is preoccupied with explaining why a thinking individual, who thinks on her or his own, would be bound to the objectivity of consciousness as Abstract Right. The criminal law, when the individual confers form onto a seized thing and then contracts with others in order to fulfill her or his arbitrary will, is not administered by a state. Rather, Hegel is concerned here with the relation of a crime to the legitimacy of the objectivity of consciousness as a whole before he even introduces a state. Indeed, we have hardly mentioned the state until this point in my retrieval of Hegel's argument about the nature and identity of law. There are no courts nor parliaments nor even a state. The observed individual does not knowingly incorporate her or his values, passions, desires, and other inclinations into the objectivity of abstract persons, property, and contract. The observed individual begins to become conscious, though, that she or he is autonomous from the objectivity of nature. That said, the individual is not yet fully conscious of this autonomy.

Although generated in violence, the emerging objectivity of consciousness shifts into the products of thinking. This thinking links with the legitimacy of the objectivity of consciousness as a whole. Yes, harm is caused to an individual contractee who was mistaken or deceived, or whose contractee signed the contract without an intent of fulfilling it. Indeed, in Roman law (from which Hegel draws the distinction between private and public wrong), theft (*furtabine*) and robbery (*rapina*) are categorized as *criminal privata*.[29] A victim could sue a thief civilly. But there is another harm that Hegel wants us to consider. This is the public harm. Here, the very legitimacy of the emerging objectivity of consciousness is challenged by an observing individual. The philosopher recognizes this objectivity of consciousness but the observed individual remains unaware of it at this point.

b) Legitimacy

Hegel takes up the same issue here that Socrates recounts in the "Speech of the Laws" in Plato's *Crito*: "why is the objectivity of consciousness binding upon a thinking being such as Socrates?" At this stage in Hegel's argument, the philosopher is not concerned with the justice or injustice of a particular rule in the objectivity of consciousness nor with the procedure institutionalized in the objectivity. Rather, the philosopher addresses "why is a legal rule binding?" The pressing issue for Hegel is to explain and justify why human beings are bound to the universals of a social ethos that emerges from the immediacy of a tribe or the polis? This emerging ethos will have intentional subjects who do not yet recognize their own separation from the objectivity.

If an objectivity of consciousness is going to correct a wrong to itself, there must be some justification why it has a higher claim to legitimacy than does a mere contract between the arbitrary wills of inhabitants (PR 81A). With a public wrong, Hegel shifts from the abstract person whose property claim is privately harmed to the legitimacy of the objectivity of consciousness of which abstract persons, property, and contract are mere units in the objectivity. *Recht* exists as *Recht* or an *in itself* independent of the subjective consciousness: "an injury to *one* member of society is an injury to *all* the others" (PR 218R). Again, if the objectivity of consciousness fails to cancel the crime, the crime "*would otherwise be regarded as valid, and the restoration of right*" (PR 99). That is, the criminal's arbitrary will would become the universal.

Thus, it is impossible for the objectivity of consciousness to leave a crime unpunished without compromising the legitimacy of the shared universals that have heretofore been willed. A criminal act denies the legitimacy of the objectivity of consciousness. The purpose of the conviction and sentence is not to cause suffering to the criminal but to right the wrong to the universals of the emerging ethos. The objectivity of consciousness needs to retrieve its legitimacy from the criminal's arbitrary will. The formality of the contract hides such an arbitrary will (PR 82). "*Crime [Verbreche]* is any form of coercion whereby *the principle of the will is attacked* and *right is infringed as right* [my emphasis]" (1817/18, 45.50). The criminal causes harm to the very legitimacy of the universals of the emergent objectivity of consciousness that privileges property, personhood, and contract.

Hegel's concern for the legitimacy of an objectivity of consciousness contrasts with Kant's. Kant had cautioned that one must not inquire into the historical or even the philosophical origin of the legitimacy of an objectivity of consciousness because the state represented the Idea of an objectivity of consciousness—that is, a rational will of the *summum imperium* (supreme political authority).[30] Further, if the philosopher inquired as to why a concept is binding upon a thinking being, the philosopher would, according to Kant, raise "pointless questions that threaten the state with danger if they are asked with too much sophistication by a people who are already subject to civil law."[31] Kant's Idea of an ideal legal order even prevented the citizen from examining the revolutionary basis of a legal order.[32] Kant urged the proscription of sedition, revolt, and the execution of the head of the state even if the head "has misused his authority."[33] Indeed, Kant continued, "the slightest attempt" to unconceal the legitimacy of binding laws in civil society is "high treason" and deserving of "no lesser punishment than death." As Kant ended the *Grounding of the Metaphysics of Morals,* the philosopher just could not question a presupposition in a moral order.[34] Nor could the philosopher question the condition for a legal order.[35] Hegel was unhappy with this closure of the movement of time-consciousness.

Why is the legitimacy of the objectivity of consciousness challenged by a criminal, according to Hegel? Because the legitimacy of the objectivity of consciousness rests with the free will of an observed individual. Personhood, property, and contract are the initial consequence of the actualization of such a free will. They are universals once one person recognizes the stranger through a contract. When an individual injures the free will by supplanting such universals by her or his own arbitrary will that she or he wills another to follow, harm is caused to the universals of property, personhood, and contract. Unless the criminal's act is cancelled, a new objectivity of consciousness would emerge, one that is based on something other than the self-determination of the individual's self-consciousness. The legitimacy of the emergent objectivity of consciousness is cancelled, according to Hegel, by private or public acts that institute slavery or child labor, for example. So too, if a public authority institutes capital punishment or if an individual commits suicide, this undermines the legitimacy of the objectivity of consciousness.[36] Each challenge to the objectivity of consciousness undermines the free will that generates the objectivity of consciousness.

Hegel most clearly explains his theory of punishment in his 1817/18 lectures, the year before he wrote *Philosophy of Right*. With a crime, the legitimacy of the emerging social ethos is annulled (1817/18, 46.52-3). The annulment takes the form of retribution—"the bringing to naught of the nullity brought about by the crime" (1817/18, 47.56). Hegel's explanation again sounds remarkably similar to the Speech of the Laws in *Crito*. What is injured by a crime is *"Recht* as *Recht."* What is mine is negated in such way that, "if I were to allow it to happen, I should lose not only what belongs to me but in general the capacity for ownership, the universal [element] of my being, which in such a case is not recognized. Here right as right is infringed, the universal [element] of the free will" (1817–18, 45.50-1). Without universals that presuppose the immanent individual self-consciousness, the individual has no legal rights as trumps against any external institutions of the state.[37]

If I take up arms or even act against the shared universals of the objectivity of consciousness in a particular ethos, I implicitly claim that my actions are binding upon others. Socrates would have argued along similar lines if he had accepted exile rather than the sentence of death. He also argued the same in the *Gorgias* (493c494a, 507e–508a). That is, I claim to represent still different concepts that strangers ought to accept in comparison with the universals that reciprocal recognition shares. I implicitly cancel the objectivity of consciousness. I destroy the legitimacy of the objectivity of consciousness that is built upon the possibility of my own free will (PR 92).

c) Mistake and Deceit

The tribe or clan of the stateless society has dissolved when the tribal members begin to realize that they are autonomous from the objectivity of nature. They seek security in the mediating concepts of property and contract. They need to accept the *legitimacy* of the structure of consciousness (PR 86). If one individual harms a property interest or contract of the subject [*Dasein*], civil compensation cancels such harm (PR 98). The harm is private between two subjects. But when one injures the objectivity of consciousness *in itself* (that is, as *Recht* as *Recht*), harm is caused to the shared universals of objectivity as well as to the private property (PR 99).

Hegel identifies three forms of public harm to the objectivity of consciousness: first, the harm caused by mistake; second, the harm caused by deceit; and third, the harm caused when a property holder or contractee pretends to respect the other as a person but really intends to undermine the very legal structure that protects such persons. In deception, the parties implicitly accept the contract. The institutional mechanism of universal *Recht* enforces the contract. However, in deception, one party merely pretends to accept the contract and the decision of the adjudicative institution. The other party is deceived: "[t]he arbitrary will of the other party may delude me with a false semblance as regards what I acquire, so that the contract may be perfectly in order as a free mutual agreement to exchange *this specific* thing in its *immediate* individuality [*Einzelheit*], although the aspect of what is universal *in itself* is lacking" (PR 88).[38] The deception effectively undermines the binding character of the contract and the changing, yet abstract, universals such as property, personhood, and contract (PR 87). The universality must override the subjective will of the deceiving individual in order to sustain the legitimacy of the objectivity of the ethos as a whole (PR 89). In contrast with the unintentional or mistaken wrongdoer, the deceiver is punished because the deceiver indirectly infringes or challenges the legitimacy of the objectivity of consciousness as a whole by deceiving the other party to the contract (PR 89A).

d) The Criminal's Harm to Her- or Himself

We can now appreciate that the criminal's act even causes harm to her- or himself as a self-conscious being (PR 100). The criminal has rights, such as due process, because she or he has the capacity to become a self-conscious individual: "[b]ut the ugliest man, the criminal, the invalid, or the cripple is still a living human being; the affirmative aspect—life—survives [*besteht*] in spite of such deficiencies" (PR 258A). If an institution causes harm to the ugliest man, the criminal, the invalid, or even the slave without addressing the universals willed by all, the institution "hangs in the air" on an "insecure footing" (PR 265A). For the criminal causes public harm against the very legitimacy of the objectivity of consciousness. The criminal needs this legal structure in order to have and enforce his own individual right to property (PR 100R). No individual and no organized group may claim legitimacy to exercise violence or to bind legal persons contrary to the legitimacy of the universals of the emerging, though incomplete, consciousness of objectivity. If one person is allowed to undermine the legitimacy of this particular shape of the objectivity of consciousness, then the personhood of all others is also negated.

Until the criminal commits harm to the universals of the objectivity of consciousness, the criminal implicitly accepts that she or he too is a rational person who confers form onto seized things and who enters into contracts. The intent of the criminal is not an issue here. When the rational person harms a stranger in a manner that harms the shared universals of the objectivity of consciousness as a thing-in-itself, the philosopher cannot be concerned with the extent of harm or suffering caused to strangers (PR 99R). Nor is the philosopher preoccupied with the fact that the criminal may not have expressly or even implicitly consented to the offence to the universals implied in the objectivity of consciousness and under which she or he is charged (PR 100R). Rather, the philosopher is concerned with the very need for an objectivity of consciousness where individuals can become self-conscious and therefore free.

e) Deterrence and Rehabilitation

In the same way that the criminal act treats the victim as a nonperson, so too the universals of the emerging individualist ethos treat the criminal as a nonperson if the criminal is used as a means to fulfill objectives independent of the universals. This occurs with the punishments meted for deterrence and rehabilitation. The latter forms of punishment fail to address the very relation of punishment to the legitimacy of the objectivity of consciousness as a whole. Instead of addressing the latter's legitimacy, deterrence and rehabilitation examine the psychological propensity of an individual to cause a crime (PR 99R). Hegel explains that "[i]n so far as the punishment which this entails is seen as embodying *the criminal's own right*, the criminal is *honoured* as a rational being" (PR 100R). We would respect the criminal's freedom only if we treated her or him as a person who was recognized as an abstract person before the legitimacy of the objectivity of consciousness. If a person is punished in terms of rehabilitation or deterrence, the shared universal concepts are revised by accepting the criminal's act as a new element of the consciousness of objectivity. This creates a new evil without addressing the old one by the punishment. Rehabilitation and deterrence treat the criminal as a "harmful" nonthinking being who must be rendered "harmless" (PR 100R). Such forms of punishment examine the psychological character of the criminal (PR 99R). The appropriate— and the only—response to a criminal's act is to restore the legitimacy of the emerging objectivity of consciousness by force if necessary. If appropriate in the circumstances, the head (such as the monarch or president) of the objectivity of consciousness may pardon or give mercy to the criminal after such punishment has been whetted: this differs from trying to reform or deter future criminal acts (PR 282A). By doing so, the Abstract Right, as the first moment of the objectivity of consciousness, is restored. This includes the restoration of the criminal as a person. The legitimacy of punishment, then, is not the state as an external source or force, nor the need to reform the intentionality of the criminal, nor the need to deter acts by other subjects but the very inalienable self-consciousness that renders the binding character to the objectivity of consciousness.

Rehabilitation and deterrence differ from Hegel's retributive theory of punishment. The retributive theory understands punishment as an evil which needs to balance against the evil act of the criminal (PR 99R). If authorities attempt to deter or rehabilitate the criminal, they merely displace one evil for another, the collective evil for a particular evil. Instead, punishment must address the very legitimacy of the objectivity of consciousness as a whole. For, justice is only possible if the objectivity of consciousness is legitimate. After all, justice, history, and law only begin (according to Hegel) when the individual thinks about concepts that intervene between the individual and the objectivity of nature. This is the point when the members of an ethos emerge from the prelegal into the legal world. Once violently established, the objectivity of consciousness will need institutions and posited laws to enforce the concepts of the objectivity of consciousness. The arbitrary will of the ruler certainly will not do that because her or his will fails to access the universals of the objectivity of consciousness. Similarly, the arbitrary will of the *Volk* will not access the objectivity of consciousness but rather will remain immersed in the unconscious subjectivity. Once the objectivity of consciousness is legitimate (that is, generated from the will to be self-conscious), the units of the objectivity are binding. In addition, the philosopher can then examine the possibilities of justice. Punishment, by retrieving the legitimacy of the emerging objectivity of consciousness itself, restores the latter as an *in itself* constructed by the self-conscious will (PR 99).

Deterrence and rehabilitation thereby express contempt for the will of the criminal as a rational being who has the potential to become self-conscious. Why? Because issues involving deterrence and rehabilitation fail to address how the criminal's act recognizes the self-consciously posited universals shared in the presupposed objectivity of consciousness, the observed individual (a judge or lawyer or legal scholar or student) plays in a make-believe world of laws that lack legitimacy. I showed in Chapter 3 how the individual could break from such a world with *Vernunft.* By annulling such shared universals of the objectivity of consciousness, the criminal demonstrates disrespect for her- or himself as a being who has possibilities to *become* self-conscious. Punishment annuls the criminal's annulment of universals: "[t]he cancellation [*Aufheben*] of crime is *retribution* in so far as the latter, by its concept, is an infringement of an infringement" (PR 101). If the objectivity of consciousness failed to cancel the crime, the criminal's act would support the will of new concepts based upon the criminal's act (PR 99). The purpose of the conviction and sentence is not to cause suffering to the criminal but to "right the wrong to the universals of the emerging ethos." It is impossible for the objectivity of consciousness to leave a crime unpunished without compromising its own legitimacy. A crime annuls the universality. Punishment annuls such an annulment. Justice thereby enters the picture as punishment rather than as revenge as in a tribal culture. Interestingly, by upholding the shared universals of the objectivity of consciousness, punishment protects the rule of law rather than the rule of arbitrary will (PR 103).

f) Is Hegel's Philosophy of Punishment Counterintuitive?

Let us turn now to certain well-known passages that counter the contemporary liberal support for rehabilitation and deterrence. For one thing, Hegel claims that "[i]n so far as the punishment which this entails is seen as embodying *the criminal's own right,* the criminal is *honoured* as a rational being" (PR 100R). Hegel goes further. Although rehabilitation and deterrence are commonly offered in sentencing hearings today, Hegel states that the effort to reform how the criminal behaves or the effort to deter future acts of crime as the grounds of punishment "is like raising one's stick at a dog; it means treating a human being like a dog instead of respecting his honour and freedom" (PR 99A). Further, the punishment, in an effort to rehabilitate or to deter criminal acts, institutionalizes a new evil without addressing the old one by punishment. Hegel leaves room for institutional authorities to pardon or grant mercy to the criminal after the punishment has been whetted. But this differs from the reform or deterrence of future criminal acts (PR 282A). Because it comes after the criminal is punished, how is it possible to honor a criminal as a person by punishing her or him? What does Hegel mean by a "rational being"? Why are deterrence and rehabilitation contemptuous of the criminal? How do deterrence and rehabilitation treat a rational person like a dog?

One needs to appreciate, again, that Hegel still has not introduced the state into the objectivity of consciousness. Rather, Hegel is concerned here with the relation of a criminal harm to the empty shared concepts (personhood and the like) binding upon the autonomous self-conscious individual. When harm is caused to the universals of the objectivity, the emergent structure has to reassert or restore itself as legitimate.

Now, Hegel takes on two forms of punishment. When philosophic consciousness is aware of the formation of an objectivity from concepts that intercede between the observed individual and the objectivity of nature, that very objectivity may be harmed. The personal harm is no longer an issue. Public wrong, not private wrong, deserves punishment. However undeveloped because of the observed individual's lack of awareness of the nexus of the objectivity to her or his subjectivity, the objectivity is legitimate because it is constructed by a thinking being. The criminal challenges the incomplete *Recht* as *Recht,* not as a private wrong.

So, the criminal, by stealing or killing, wills a different claim to universality (such as "respect that man who carries a gun") than that which the observed individual and the philosopher have come to recognize as binding because of the immanence of personhood, property, and contract from the autonomy of the observed individual. A criminal act harms *Recht* as *Recht.* The core universal of this emerging idea of a objectivity of consciousness, founded as it is on the drive of the individual to become autonomous from objectivity, is that every human being, as opposed to an animal, has the potential to be a person, to own property, and to enter into contracts. Without such a potentiality, freedom would not exist as a possibility (PR 95). Again, as Socrates explained in the "Speech of the Laws" in *Crito,* the capacity to exercise free will involves a universal element that is harmed when someone causes a particular harm. Hegel insists that if one commits a crime, the victim loses the potential to own property and to be a self-conscious subject. Slavery is thereby a crime against humanity because the potential to become self-conscious distinguishes humans from animals.

The philosophic consciousness is not concerned here with the criminal's intent. Nor is the philosopher concerned with the harm or suffering caused to a victim of the crime (PR 99R). Nor is the philosopher concerned with the fact that the criminal may not have expressly or even implicitly consented to the legislation under which he is charged (PR 100R). Rather, the objective *Recht* punishes a criminal so as to cancel the criminal's act and thereby to restore the legitimacy of the emerging ethos of self-consciousness (PR 100).

And yet, punishment restores the criminal's will as well as the wills of all by reaffirming the legitimacy of the objectivity of consciousness. The honor of the criminal is denied if the sentencing institutions treat her or him as if she or he is a "harmless" animal or a thing which is existent external to the objectivity of consciousness (PR 100R). The cancellation of the cancellation of legitimacy restores the shared universals amongst willing subjects. The crimes against slavery (PR 57, 57R, 57A), capital punishment for minor offences (PR 101A), and discrimination against ethnic groups (PR 209R)—all of which cause public harm against the objectivity of consciousness—would be expelled from the objectivity (PR 101R). Though generated in violence, the rule of law now prevails—or so Hegel believes.

7. THE TURN TO INTENTIONALITY

In a criminal wrong, the individual will challenges the legitimacy of the posttribal objectivity of consciousness. Revenge had characterized the tribal society. Punishment now displaces revenge (PR 103). Philosophic consciousness is now aware that there are universals valued *in* and *of themselves* despite their genesis from experience rather than from nature, Kant's noumenal world of things-in-themselves, conscience, or tradition. By punishing the criminal for nullifying the legitimacy of the objectivity of consciousness, the criminal can become conscious of her or his role in the actual construction of universals in the objectivity by her or his actions. Punishment will induce the criminal to accept the objectivity of consciousness as her or his own (PR 104A). If universals are legitimate, Hegel claims, the philosopher can begin to address issues of the identity of the units of the objectivity of consciousness as well as the elements of justice and the Good. When the observed individual becomes conscious of her or his participation in the construction of universals in the objectivity, she or he will have emerged into the civilized world of thinking, especially thinking about the nature and identity of law (PR 100R).

This suggests that with the advent of crimes, the observed individual, as well as the philosophical consciousness, is becoming aware of her or his own *intentionality*. This intentionality goes hand in hand with an awareness of the objectivity of consciousness as separate from the subject. When such an awareness takes hold, though, the philosopher must retreat to a study of the inward self-examination of the observed individual. The philosopher must observe whether and the extent to which the individual recognizes the universals as her or his own. Since such universals manifest the shared presuppositions of the individual and strangers in the objectivity of consciousness, objectivity is now joined with the intentionality of the subject. It may be, for example, that the criminal is bonded with a nuclear "family" which, in turn, is alienated from other intermediate institutions such as religious, educational, and political institutions.

The philosopher is beginning to see that the objectivity of consciousness, when linked with the contingent particularities of subjectivity, constitutes an ethos. The concepts of the objectivity as an "in itself" must join with the intentionality of the subjectivity "for itself." The philosopher must retrieve the relationships of strangers in an ethos in order to address whether intentional subjects share the universals of the objectivity of consciousness or whether the latter is in fact evolving into a different identity. Social relationships constitute the universals of the objectivity as well as the particularity of intentional subjectivity. Legitimacy (and the identity of laws) thereby takes on a wider scope than the habits of obedience, the rule of recognition, social facts, conventions, or the original intent of the founding fathers offers. Social actuality enters into the picture.

CHAPTER FIVE

Legal Formalism

Hegel's fear of the arbitrary will directs him to the legal formalism of the two dominant traditions of legal philosophy with which I introduced this book. In the one case, Fries, Savigny, and other romanticists claimed that legality was grounded in the emotions and values of the *Volk*. In the second dominant legal tradition, elaborated by Kant and Fichte,[1] legitimacy was separated from the legality of phenomena. The arbitrary will was silently incorporated into both senses of the objectivity of consciousness. Something more than the identity of a legal unit (such as conscience, a value, custom, rule, or policy) was needed in order that the thinking individual consider the objectivity of consciousness binding. In an effort to understand that "something else," Hegel exposes the formalism of the two dominant legal traditions of his day.[2]

This chapter offers an outline of Hegel's critique of legal formalism. His critique generates his later excursus into ethicality and the shapes of ethical ethê. I shall begin by returning to Hegel's phenomenological description of how an individual thinks. I shall then turn to his description of the moral content of such thinking. Hegel privileges in this regard intentions and the personal knowledge of circumstances in one's acts. Hegel finds both elements of intentionality problematic because the arbitrariness of the will displaces ethicality in both traditions.

I. THE RELATION OF ARBITRARY VALUES TO THE FORMALISM OF THE OBJECTIVITY OF CONSCIOUSNESS

The first possibility of intentionality, represented by romanticism and historicism, is the conscience or "the heart" of the individual (PR 136). Hegel defines conscience as "that deepest inner solitude within oneself in which all externals and all limitation have disappeared—it is a total withdrawal into the self" (PR 136A). When I become disillusioned with the "hollow, spiritless, and unsettled existence" of indeterminate concepts in the abstract shape of the objectivity of consciousness, I look inward into my own consciousness to try to find an actuality which I can take as real (PR 138A). Socrates' withdrawal from Greek life exemplifies such a turn to conscience (PR 138R). Socrates describes his withdrawal as a "sort of voice" that encourages him to question the universals of the objectivity with which Athenian citizens had felt immediate (*Apology* 31d). Hegel complains that, according to the utilitarian school of thought, officials aggregate the values, desires, and interests of individuals as if this would determine the social welfare (PR 123, 123R). As already noted, contemporary theories of legal reasoning suggest that a judge must ultimately posit a value or fundamental interest when the judge runs out of the ratiocination of concepts.[3] The rhetoric of rights not infrequently colors this posit of a value (PR 126R). Even the foundation of constitutionality is believed to rest on the ultimate subjective values or posited social facts.

Hegel's problem with this effort to link conscience to the objectivity of consciousness is that the observed individual becomes stuck in self-absorbed inwardness without actively recognizing strangers (PR 138A). That is, the subject or the state's officials posits arbitrary values without becoming aware whether and how the content of the values presupposes social recognition amongst strangers. To focus on the latter, the philosopher would have to examine the content of the concepts in the conscience's objectivity of consciousness. This would, however, undermine the traditional philosopher's role which was to accept posited values as "givens" in the objectivity of consciousness. All the philosopher did was to posit inward values from tradition and to coerce strangers to follow her or his values (PR 139, 139R).

We might return to act utilitarianism as one example of the imprisonment of the inner consciousness of posited values. In this philosophy, there remains a rupture between my conscience and the transcendent yardstick of the greatest happiness of the greatest number. First, the official jumps from the aggregate of all consciences to a specific rule without an assurance that the resulting content of the rule manifests the reciprocal recognition in the ethos: that is, the ethicality of the ethos. Second, we do not know whether the aggregate works towards the good rather than evil. The computation of a multiplicity of consciences is all that matters (PR 126). Third, there is no necessity that the individual interest coincides with the universals of the community (PR 125). As a consequence, an "empty vanity . . . transcends the sphere of cognition" (PR 140R). All that matters is that the philosopher (or judge or scholar) has a good heart, good intention, and good conviction. One's good intention renders the outcome good. Conversely, the separation of the subject's conscience from the abstract objectivity of consciousness or Abstract Right renders the universals devoid of the actuality in subjectivity (PR 131A). The Good is dead. Only if the Good is "concrete" in socially contingent experiences is there a living Good (PR 144).

If a posited value or rule is considered binding because its content coheres with a ruler's or the *Volk*'s arbitrary will, formalism has a field day. There is no assurance of goodness or of intersubjective recognition in the substantive content of the posited value or rule. Legality is thereby reduced to "a purely *external letter*, indeed an empty word, for it is only my conviction which *makes it a law* and a binding duty for me" (PR 140R). Even an appeal to the will of the highest court, a founding text, or the intent of the Founding Fathers as the source of legitimate laws does not help. In fact, this merely camouflages intentionality, for each presupposed source is nested external to the subject's consciousness. Behind the formality of the arbitrary value or rule, text, or "intent of the Founding Fathers," there are "countless *individual convictions*" (PR 140R). There is no way to distinguish important from unimportant collective intentions, good from evil. Even the appeal to rights becomes mere "play" where "it is I who am excellent and master of both law and thing; I *merely play* with them as with my own caprice, and in this ironic consciousness in which I let the highest of things perish, I *merely enjoy myself*" (PR 140R). Worse, the rights conceal vulgar coercion. Accordingly, Hegel concludes that it is simply "monstrous" to portray any posited value or rule as legitimate and, by implication, as legal.

Hegel has the romantic subjectivism of Fries, Friedrich von Schlegel, and Savigny in mind when he describes his contempt for the empiricism that conceals the posit of an arbitrary value. Hegel would also have in mind the contemporary claim, noted in earlier chapters, that the positing or balancing of values must ultimately determine the outcome of a dispute when the ratiocination of rules runs out. With the dominating romanticism of his day, legality becomes the mere "image produced by my conviction" (1822/23 W122). Romanticism fails to recognize the reciprocal recognition of strangers in an ethos. Subjectivity reigns supreme behind the formalist rhetoric of individual rights without the needed focus upon how one subject recognizes another in the social relations presupposed in the content of the right. If the official desired to retrieve such subjectivity, the official would have to examine the content of the concepts that the rights otherwise leave to the arbitrary will of the subject. Instead, the strongest conscience determines the outcome of any social relationship. The outcome depends upon power relationships rather than upon rational choices. Officials pretend to know the objectivity of consciousness when, in fact, their rhetoric lets them posit their own arbitrary wills. The rhetoric of values and rights is *"empty* of all ethical *content* [*die Eitelkeit alles sittlichen Inhalts*]" in that the mere inscription of rights, rather than the social relations of subjects inter se, is what matters (PR 140R). The problem is that formalism privileges the subject as if a monad. The subject basks in the glory of self-knowledge and truth, both of which are "poised above an immense void, conjuring up shapes and destroying them" (PR 140A). It is unforgivable for the philosopher to admit having erred in such a situation (1819/20 W123).

Interestingly, negative freedom, a term examined in Chapter 1, encircles the random choices posited by such arbitrary impulses (PH 94). The objectivity of consciousness protects the freedom of choices posited by the arbitrary wills. There is no need for such a "free" individual to gain *Bildung* or to elevate her or his development beyond the first moment of what Hegel considers civilization. The boundary that protects the *inner sphere of life*, to use J. S. Mill's term, reinforces the freedom of the individual to arbitrarily posit values by instinct without the mediation of thought. Justice is not possible with such a view of freedom because justice addresses how the objectivity of consciousness reconciles with the individual's self-consciousness. Nor is *Bildung* possible. Indeed, the educated subject experiences more in a single day than the uneducated subject in her or his entire life (1819/20 W156). Even freedom of the press, if understood in terms of a protective boundary about arbitrary values, is the product of "completely uneducated, crude, and superficial thinking [*Vorstellung*]" (PR 319R). "Formalistic thinking [*Formalismus*] endeavours to rationalize away [*wegzuräsonnieren*] the substantial and contrete nature of a thing [*Sache*] in favour of *individual* elements which belong to its external appearance and of abstractions which it derives from these" (PR 319R). The taint of animalistic revenge, authorized by European legal codes of Hegel's day, remains concealed in legal formalism in the "residue" of private prosecutions.

Paragraphs 140, 140R, and 140A of *Philosophy of Right* reconstruct Hegel's critique of this version of legal formalism. First, however well intentioned, *pure hypocrisy* (this is Hegel's term on several occasions) colors the effort of an official (such as a judge) of the objectivity of consciousness to universalize her or his arbitrary intention (PR 140).

Second, evil may result from the formalism. One might believe that the subjectively posited arbitrary value is legitimate (and consistent with democracy) if an appropriate institution posits the value within its jurisdiction. But Hegel claims that this perspective may well lead to terror. The risk is that the posit of the arbitrary value as the foundation or source of legality may become reified from the social relationships in an ethos. Raz elaborates such a possibility in his theory of "exclusionary" "artificial reasoning" which transforms a subjective value into an objectivity where the social relations presupposed in the content of a particular decision or rule are excluded from legal reasoning once the decision is rendered.[4] Aside from the illusion of objectivity, Hegel argues that if the official stops reasoning here and claims to bind all inhabitants by the official's positing of an arbitrary value, illegitimacy may be restated (and perverted) as the good. The positing of the subjective value may be the consequence of an evil conscience. The illusion of objectivity is worsened if the official need only find "*any* good reason" for the decision—even a hypothetical reason. The intent of the official determines nothing (PR 140R).

Third, the basic problem with the formalism that follows the posit of arbitrary values is that no effort need be made to identify how one subject recognizes a stranger. Such recognition is presupposed in the content of the posited value. What exists are abstract goods which "being completely lacking in content, can be wholly reduced simply to meaning anything *positive* at all—anything, that is, which has any kind of validity and which, in its immediate determination, may even count as an essential end (such as doing good to the poor, or caring for myself, my life, my family, etc.)" (PR 140R). A claim that justice is constituted from posited arbitrary values is empty of content since "any content one pleases can be subsumed under the good" (PR 140R).

2. THE LEGAL FORMALISM OF MORAL RULES

This takes us to the second version of intentionality in Hegel's day (and ours): the legal formalism of moral rules.[5] As I noted in the Introduction and Chapters 1 and 3, Kant had distinguished between two forms of knowledge: the *noumena* (a priori) and the *phenomena* (appearance). Kant claimed that one cannot intellectually access one's rational or noumenal self. One only knows one's rational being through intuitions about one's phenomenal self. One's intent can be imputed from one's actions in the phenomenal world.[6] Thus, the good will, situated in the *noumena,* is external to one's day-to-day actions in the phenomenal realm. The most important action in the phenomenal realm is the recognition of a stranger in action. Since one's actions in the phenomenal realm are influenced by bodily inclinations, the moral maxims derived from the *noumenal* realm are mere "oughts" or duties. The most important "ought" is dignity, which Kant defines as something that lacks a price. Such a dignity is nested in the *noumenal* or "ethical" realm.[7] If I fail to accord dignity to others, I lack a moral well-being even though I am happy.[8]

a) The Separation of Legality from Morality

The legal units, according to Kant, are posited in the phenomenal realm external to the good will of the rational person in the *noumena.* As such, legality is separate from morality. In *The Metaphysical Elements of Justice*, Kant uses different terms to describe legality: *externally legislated, acquired, objective, positive, contingent*, and *arbitrary*.[9] The externality of laws to morality is manifested in the state's ultimate title to all territory, the state's monopoly of coercion, the abstract character of citizenship, and the possibility of legislated slavery.[10] In sum, an untranslatable rupture persists between the *noumenal* realm of moral action and the appearances of externally posited laws. Even Kant's Idea of a rational legal order, explained in a moment, is an "ought" external to experience.

This gulf between legality and morality offers an enormous challenge to Hegel. For why would a thinking being feel bound to moral laws that remain external to her or his experiences? The posited laws of the objectivity of consciousness, for example, may compel the individual to act against her or his moral conscience. In an effort to explain why a thinking being would feel bound to posited laws, Fichte elaborated how the external legal order could institutionalize freedom.[11] Fichte claimed that although rights are natural in that they exist without a state, we need the state in order to institutionalize the conditions for the rights to be effective. But a legal person, though legislatively guaranteed equality before the law, is external to the self-conscious subject. The subject is left a monad without social relations with strangers. The gist of Fichte's rights thesis is that the empty rights protect the individual human subject so that she or he could posit whatever she or he chose as good (PR 132). The rights are abstract indeterminate concepts. Lawyers and judges become expert knowers of such rights. But the rights are only known in a theoretical world, not in a phenomenal actuality.

The effort to address the moral intentionality of the will of a subject results in the very separation of moral actions from legality. Legal responsibility depends upon the rights posited external to the observed subject's reflective consciousness (PR 132). Precisely because of the gap between "is" and "ought," self-consciousness, being stuck in phenomena, is deprived of "all ethical worth and dignity" (PR 132R). Legitimacy remains separate from subjective values. Either the values are arbitrarily posited as truth, as in the case of the first form of legal formalism, or they are posited as rules separate from moral intentionality. All that is required is that there be a universal rule that all rational persons, purged of a socially contingent biography, would accept. That would only be possible if the universal rule were empty of content. It is as if Kant plumped the autonomous rational person in the midst of a society oblivious to the social and anthropological context in which the subject is situated, as if the human being were a monad with no biography, no values, no expectations, and no assumptions.

The only way Kant and Fichte can overcome the separation of legality from morality is to assess any particular legislated rule in terms of the Idea of a rational legal order. The Idea is an ideal paradigmatic structure. By Idea, Kant intends "a necessary concept of reason to which no corresponding object can be given in sense-experience."[12] The Idea is self-sufficient, something valued as an end-in-itself in the *noumena*. The Idea represents a perfection that we cannot find in socially contingent conditions. Thus, although legality is situated in the phenomenal world of experience, its legitimacy lies in the Idea of law in the *noumena*. Despite the intuition that Ronald Dworkin's *Law's Empire* manifests a Hegelian legal philosophy (which might explain the extraordinary hostility to his philosophy in Anglo-American general jurisprudence), Dworkin has Kant's Idea of law in mind when he describes the "law beyond law" nested in the legal narrative.[13] The categorical imperative is a similar element of the Idea. As perfection, the Idea of a rationally deduced legal order is something towards which we ought to strive. Just because the Idea of a legal order is not socially contingent, this does not mean that inhabitants and rulers cannot strive to institutionalize it.[14] The Idea of a perfect legal order is the spirit, not the letter, of the constitution.[15]

The above sense of an ideal legal order does not help Hegel. Kant offers an indeterminate concept (respect to the person as an end *in itself*) without the possibility of particularizing the good will. Once again, the idealization of a legal order is separate from the subjective freedom of the individual in experience.[16] Instead of linking posited laws with subjectivity, the Idea of law prolongs such a rupture. One is considered free if the posited rules replicate the abstract rights in the Ideal legal order. Subjective experience is never addressed. To the contrary.[17] The Idea of a legal order takes the individual into an even emptier world than the institutional rights and duties that Fichte and Kant initially offered as separate from morality.

b) Hegel's Critique of the Transcendental Referent

It is apparent by now how Hegel would respond to this second form of intentionality. Kant and Fichte fail to contextualize the categorical imperative in a socially contingent ethos. Kant and Fichte flesh out moral intentionality as if the individual had no biography, assumptions, expectations, education, ethnic or religious upbringing, or, more generally, social relations with strangers. Fichte's rights, in particular, are stuck in the *noumenal* realm of a priori concepts that are emptied of social-cultural content. The legal rights conceal how one subject recognizes another as a subject through the medium of the rights. Without a social-cultural content, then, the volition of the subject is also worthless, however well intentioned (PR 124). The "mutually independent" rights holders in the objectivity of consciousness are purged of all particular needs and desires. The rights, being contentless, are mere formal shells abstracted from particular needs and desires (PM 491, PR 37).

Accordingly, rights talk is the rhetoric for "uncultured people" (PR 37A). The rhetoric is "lopsided" because of its content independence. The formalism of rights consciousness camouflages extreme poverty in phenomena and officially sanctioned coercion that is imposed upon individuals in phenomena. So too, the empty rights discourse ignores the social identity of the subject with intermediate organizations that intercede between the subject and the objectivity of consciousness. One's intentionality is constituted from multiple determinate elements of a finite being (PR 105). The finite being wills her or his presence in everything she or he does (PR 107A). But as Peter Gabel exposed, the role of the judge in a rights culture conceals such phenomena and focuses instead upon the formal boundary between one individual's arbitrary will and that of another's without examining their context-specific relationship (PR 38).[18]

Hegel explains the problematic of legal formalism in his early essay, *Natural Law* (1802–03). A legal concept supersedes a multiplicity of context-specific objects of nature. Once such a supercession is universalized as a rule that all moral persons ought to follow, the multiplicity of particular experiences are forgotten. The act of intellectualizing about context-specific needs and desires thereby cancels the latter (NL 438/39, 79–80).

Posited legal rules may well try to replicate the ideal legal order. But the rules and the ideal are emptied of particulars: that is, of social phenomena. Legality is modeled after an ideal social relationship. Universals, such as personhood, property, and contract, become dead precisely because of their emptiness of social relationships. Conversely, the external objectivity of consciousness will appear hostile to the social relations between subjects inter se. Indeed, the external objectivity of consciousness will be incomprehensible to the observed subject. Kant's sense of legality is open to such a lack of spirit and life. Indeed, Kant perpetuates the hostile struggle of arbitrary values that had characterized the legal formalism of the romanticist tradition of legal philosophy. Only Kant does so by denying a role for the intentional subject. What is left is a reified legality external to human subjectivity.

The externality of the objectivity of consciousness from moral subjectivity leads to another consequence. "Respect for persons" is often offered as the ultimate criterion for constitutional analysis today, for example. But "respect for persons" is an indeterminate concept. It is an abstract duty done for duty's sake (PR 133). The duty is located in the objectivity of consciousness separate from any beliefs, biography, or socially contingent content. Hegel likens this reified objectivity to the intrinsic Good that Aristotle held external to human action: "if I know nothing apart from the fact that the good is my duty, I do not go beyond duty in the abstract" (PR 133A). If a duty is nested in the objectivity of consciousness and if the latter is estranged from the self-consciousness of the subject, it is empty. For the objectivity remains constituted from indeterminate concepts. The subjectivity is the arbitrary will which does not consider how an individual acts towards strangers. In order to reconcile the duty of abstract objectivity with the self-consciousness of subjectivity, the philosopher and the observed individual must rationally link the particular content of a right to the duty. The right thereby becomes determinate and nonarbitrary (PR 134). The right becomes a member of actuality. Once again, the challenge, for Hegel, is to unify indeterminate concepts with the particularization of the will. This would involve the incorporation of one's psychological inclinations and one's empirically conditioned biography into a judgment. These are the very socially contingent factors that Kant (as well as Hart and Dworkin) excludes from legality as "inclinations" of the phenomenal world. Unless the objectivity of consciousness is reconciled with subjectivity, "dignity" becomes a mere rhetorical device to help the observed subject feel at home with the empty objectivity. At the same time, the philosopher observes how alienated from actuality has the observed subject become.

Even the appeal to dignity (what Hegel calls a "pure and unconditional duty") possesses "the character of formalism" and "empty rhetoric" (PR 135R). First, even if one acts in a particular way, there is no criterion to decide whether a particular desire or need is a duty. One cannot jump from an idealized indeterminate concept (dignity) to a particular socially contingent desire or need. Second, despite the rhetoric of dignity, the objectivity of consciousness—because it is located in the phenomenal realm—may well exclude human beings from the protection of rights. Slavery, infanticide and capital punishment may well be possible. Indeed, it makes sense that Kant's text concerning geography, untranslated into English to this day, exemplifies how the radical rupture between the moral objectivity from subjectivity reinforces an outright Eurocentric racism towards the indigenous peoples of the world.[19] Third, the basic problem with the separation of the subjectivity from the objectivity of consciousness is that the universals of morality and of the objectivity of consciousness are emptied of human experience. Dignity misses the social-cultural context of the human subject in an experienced time and place unless the individual official ultimately relies upon conscience or the familiar "I know it when I see it." But that collapses the formal concept into the arbitrary values posited in the first version of formalism. Finally, by universalizing legitimacy in ideals such as Kant's Idea of law, one negates the particular social contingencies that envelop the theoretical world of rights consciousness. Dignity lacks any criterion for the differentiation amongst particular desires and needs other than the formal contentless principle of noncontradiction between universal abstract concepts. Such a principle of noncontradiction does not help. For where the principle is empty of content as it is, there can be no contradiction (PR 135A). There is nothing to prevent terror. Indeed, there is nothing to prevent the "complete absence of human life" (PR 135R).

The jurist of the formalist objectivity of consciousness produces an illusion that laws are rational when, in fact, they are irrational because form, not the substantive content of the human laws, matters for formalism (PR 211, 211A). Such formulaic laws misrecognize that the forms (that is, concepts or rules) represent actuality. The forms are constituted from a fixed linear time and in relation to other self-standing forms (PR 157, 257). This is precisely Hegel's complaint against the abstract objectivity of consciousness. Such objectivity is "empty," "formulaic," and "abstract" vis-à-vis the social relationships in presupposed structures of consciousness. Any abstract objectivity, as a consequence, is alien to the social experiences between strangers. The society will lack cohesion and will risk erupting into social and political chaos, if not revolution. The reform of such empty laws will be "ad hoc" and irrational since the attention of reformers will be directed towards the differentiation of "oughts" rather than to the social relationships presupposed in the substantive content of the concepts.

A judgment rendered in the arbitrary objectivity of consciousness applies a concept (better known as a rule today) to a context-specific experience. But because of the rupture between self-consciousness and the objectivity of consciousness, reasoning is preoccupied with the legitimacy of the form of the rules/concepts in the objectivity, not with the truth of the content of the rules/concepts in social actuality. Legal judgments are considered binding in terms of their form. Legal reasoning addresses whether one rule is consistent with another. And the examination of this consistency assumes that the concepts are a priori and legitimized in an authorizing origin in a noumenal world, a world which Kant himself believed was inaccessible because we only have representations of such rules/concepts. Concepts give order to the multiplicity of intuitions. If one incorporated substantive empirical content into the quest for the binding quality of a rule, one would thereby cross the boundary between concepts and immediacy. One would be returning to the empirical realm of the perception of sensations and thereby seek the truth of a rule in experience rather than the identity of a legal unit in the *noumenal* realm. Indeed, truth in knowledge would now constitute legitimacy.

Reasoning in the formalism of objectivity of consciousness has a limited role: namely, to distinguish one concept from another without examining the presupposed reciprocal recognition amongst strangers in the content of the concepts. *Verstand* plays to formalism. The legitimacy of a concept remains in the *noumena*. Instead, the project of Hegel's philosopher is to observe the legitimacy of any concept that mediates between observed individual and the objectivity of consciousness. The denial of such a role for a utopia entirely misses that the philosopher's project is immersed in phenomena. The philosopher never crosses the rupture from phenomena to the *noumena* as Kant claims. The philosopher, like the observed consciousness, remains immersed in phenomena. But with the *Verstand* of formalism, universals are binding upon all subjects because of the consistency of the form of one concept form (independent of its content) vis-à-vis the form of other concepts. *Verstand* (the differentiation of self-standing concepts) wins in the law exam. This strange legal knowledge excludes the particularities of human experience. Legal formalism conceals the continued unexamined arbitrary will in the name of the rule of law.

3. HEGEL'S EXIT

Hegel overcomes the formalism of the two traditions of legal philosophy by reconciling the objectivity of consciousness with self-consciousness. He does so by introducing the ethical ethos or *Sittlichkeit*. The individual is situated in the ethos of a family, civil society, organic legal order, and/ or international legal order as well as in intermediate organizations. Instead of applying the abstract rules of the rational person from the *noumena* onto the context-specific subject, rationality itself is immersed in a social-cultural context with collectively shared assumptions and expectations. The formalism of the objectivity of consciousness excises the social-cultural context from the optical illusion of an objectivity that is claimed to be "practical" or "real." In order to explain why individuals have duties towards each other, however, Hegel finds it necessary to explain the social interrelations of individuals represented through the medium of collectively shared institutions and concepts in an ethos. The objectivity is only one side of such an ethos. The ethos also includes religious practices, beliefs, collective memories, rituals and political practices, all of which presuppose social relationships among observed individuals. Hegel situates the reciprocal social relationships in the universals assumed in any one implicit ethos. More importantly, Hegel explains why an individual would desire to proceed to higher and higher levels of intense and rigorous social relationships with strangers once located in any ethos.

Here, influenced by his own self-education and the Enlightenment more generally, Hegel relies upon *Bildung* and *Vernunft* to reconcile the objectivity of consciousness with subjective freedom. Because objectivity is constituted from universals shared amongst strangers and because subjectivity is constituted from reciprocal recognition of strangers, objectivity is reconciled with subjectivity. Influenced by his friend Hölderlin, Hegel introduces the role of love to generate why the formerly monadic concealed subject would desire to recognize strangers. The philosopher now examines social relationships entertained in the substantive content of the indicia of an ethos.

The latter social relationships raise the issue of the ethicality of an ethos, something that I examine in the next chapter. Indeed, such social relations constitute the crux of ethicality for Hegel. The inquiry of "nobler minds" evaluates how the content of shared assumptions, collective memories, and expectations of an ethos presuppose and represent how individuals reciprocally recognize each other. The "nobler minds" examine actuality. The official becomes consciously aware of her or his implicit self-centered action towards others. This explicit awareness is a "higher ground" of freedom than the earthly ground if abstract persons were emptied of a biography, collective and private memory, or context-specific embodied meanings. The relationship of the subject with strangers becomes the center of the "higher ground" in a *Sittlichkeit*. In doing my duty in a *Sittlichkeit*, I am with myself [*bei mir selbst*] and free (PR 133A). Spirit (or this drive to become self-conscious) constitutes the ethicality of a state-centric objectivity of consciousness. More, Spirit explains the evolution of law from the earliest times of human development to the mature moments of civilization. Spirit is never content with any particular structure embedded in consciousness.

The legitimacy of a modern legal order (that is, of a state and an international state-centric legal order) develops from human consciousness. As Hegel expresses, "[t]he *ethical world*, on the other hand, the state, or reason as it actualizes itself in the element of self-consciousness, is not supposed to be happy in the knowledge that it is reason itself which has in fact gained power and authority [*Gewalt*] within this element, and which asserts itself there and remains inherent within it" (PR Pref 12–13). Legality is nested within the social relationships of a particular society. The philosopher's role is to recognize the implied structures of consciousness in such an ethos and then to identify the presuppositions that address the extent to which the observed individual recognizes strangers through shared universals. Such a role links the legal philosopher to the study of freedom in any particular ethos. The clarification, decomposition, and differentiation of concepts, by themselves, would never access the reciprocal recognition of strangers in an ethos.

CHAPTER SIX

The Ethicality of an Ethos

We have reached the point where Hegel introduces the most original element of his theory of law: *Sittlichkeit*. What Hegel intends by his notion of *Sittlichkeit* is not easy to grasp. S. W. Dyde translates *Sittlichkeit* as "the ethical system." Alan White translates it as "ethicality." Knox and Nisbet translate *Sittlichkeit* as "ethical life," thereby risking the imputation by the Anglo-American legal scholar that *Sittlichkeit* concerns individual moral action, as that is addressed in the philosophic study of contemporary ethics, rather than the manner in which a community shares values and assumptions that concern how strangers recognize each other. Most contemporary English commentators use the term "ethical life" for *Sittlichkeit*. What does *Sittlichkeit* signify?

Let us parse Hegel's term, *Sittlichkeit*. *Die Sitten* are customs. *Die Sitte* denotes a more abstract character to customs than does a description of the content of a particular custom. It is tempting, therefore, to associate *Sittlichkeit* with an ethos.[1] An ethos, however, is an anthropological notion that need have little to do with ethical relationships. *Sittlich* denotes honesty, good character, moral cleanliness, and pure character. *Sittlichkeit* represents the abstract noun of the adjective, *sittlich*. *Sittlich* is an adjective connoting an ethical ethos. Hegel is not interested in any ethos but in an ethical ethos.[2]

Another of Hegel's terms, *Moralität,* needs clarification. Hegel distinguishes *Moralität* from ethicality. Ethicality, for Hegel, draws from the *Sitte* or bonding of an individual with others into a community. Henry Jones, a turn-of-the-twentieth-century English ethicist and Hegelian, explained that "[t]he bond must be inward, not outward; it must be essential, not accidental; it must be such, in a word, that the parts fall asunder into meaningless abstractions when the bond is broken."[3] Because thinking characterizes the modern human being and distinguishes modernity from the ancient world, according to Hegel, a society is ethical if the subject self-consciously recognizes strangers in the ethos. The ancient Greek societies lacked any such sense of ethicality. Why? Because members of a tribe or polis lack any consciousness of their separation from the shared universals of the community and, therefore, they lacked any independent role in the construction of universals (PS 440, 441, 444; 1824/25 W33). In like vein, the citizens of the polis lacked morality because they did not intentionally act from duties towards others (1822/23 W126, 1824/25 W126). Although lacking morality, the Greek polis was an ethos (because its members were dependent upon and bonded with each other). In contrast, the Roman Stoics were preoccupied with an individual's duties to others. The source of Stoic morality was one's inward intentionality. However, the Stoic sense of morality, according to Hegel, was reified from day-to-day social relations in the Roman ethos. Indeed, the Sage was so idealized that few, if any, human beings lived the life of the Sage. For actuality to manifest morality, all individuals had to participate as moral actors in the ethos (1822/23 W126). Social bonding exists if individuals are no longer excluded from participation in the community (1817/18 159.247–48).

This need to connect moral duties with the ethos in which one lives raises two elements in a *Sittlichkeit* or ethical life (PR 142). First, Hegel writes, *Sittlichkeit* is "the *Idea* [Concept] *of freedom* as the living good." Returning to my Chapter 1, the Concept embodies all movements of consciousness. One acts towards others from self-conscious choices. One can only act self-consciously, however, if one is free from external constraints. Freedom is interconnected with various shapes of self-consciousness, as we saw in earlier chapters. Because of the indispensable relation of freedom to self-consciousness, freedom is an intrinsic good valued *in* and *for itself*. But because freedom exists through action, rather than through pure contemplation, freedom is lived. Hegel remarks that such a living freedom, being valued as an intrinsic end, contrasts with Book X of Aristotle's *Nicomachean Ethics* (1177a10–1178a7) where Aristotle argues that pure contemplation is the supreme element of *eudaimonia* or happiness (PR 156A).[4]

Second, ethicality is the "motivating end" and "foundation" of self-conscious action. An ethos, as we saw with a tribal ethos, does not necessarily ensure that its members are self-conscious. The ethos may also be tyrannical, elitist or the like, isolated from everyday life, or disguised as a liberal state in sheep's clothing. The alienation of an ethos from moral duties possesses the key problematic for Kant's theory of morality, according to Hegel. For moral duties are identified and grounded in the *noumena* which, by Kant's own theory, one cannot access as knowledge (PR 147, 150, 150R). Ethicality, for Hegel, draws from phenomena. The philosopher must address how one subject recognizes another through shared assumptions, expectations, conventions, practices of institutions, and posited laws whose legitimacy Kant had externalized in the *noumena* realm (PR 144, 145).

In order to do so, the philosopher must continually focus upon the relation of the thinking being to the objectivity of consciousness. One can hardly do more harm to Hegel's legal philosophy than to become stuck in Abstract Right, for example, without addressing such a relationship. In Abstract Right, as recounted in Chapter 4, the observed subject is still immediate with objectivity. Only in this case, the objectivity is of consciousness rather than of nature as with a tribe. The concepts are indeterminate because they lack particularities in their content—particularities such as a biography, religion, desires, needs, and intentions (PR 37). The subject, being immediate with universals, is unaware that she or he has created the indeterminate concepts. Because of the immediacy with objectivity, the subject believes that everyone else in the society shares the same universals: "the will of others is the existence [*Existenz*] which I give to *my end*, and which is *for me* at the same time an other [emphasis added]" (PR 112).[5] Hegel insists that "any intentions which the will of others may have with reference to my will, which gives itself existence [*Dasein*] in property, are irrelevant" (PR 112A). Although a contract embodies (that is, particularizes) the otherwise indeterminate concepts, the contract represents common interests between arbitrary wills. The freedom of a person will only be assured when the one will recognizes itself in the stranger. At that point, a bonding develops between subject and stranger. Because legitimacy concerns such bonding independent of a particular arbitrary will, philosophical consciousness turns inward into the inner consciousness of the individual towards strangers.

Two traditional views in Hegel's day concerned moral action toward strangers (PR 114). First, the subject who is immediate with objectivity seizes, colonizes, and fuses the stranger into the thinking being's consciousness. The stranger loses her or his own social difference from the thinking being. Second, the subject acts as if the stranger is an abstract person. This conceals the monad's posit of its own arbitrary will. Hegel offers a third sense of moral action: the subject might raise her or his inner intentionality to universals shared between the individual and the stranger. The individual now has moral duties that stem from experience. Experience is no longer isolated from the objectivity of consciousness. I shall now identify six elements of such intentional moral action in experience: blameworthiness; ethicality; why the subject would desire to recognize the stranger; immediacy, mediation, and the ethos. I shall then examine the time-consciousness of ethicality and the institutionalization of ethicality.

I. BLAMEWORTHINESS

So far, so good. But how does the philosopher recognize the observed subject's intent? Hegel identifies two factors: personal knowledge of the circumstances and actual *mens rea*.

a) Personal Knowledge of the Circumstances, Consequences, and Universals

In the first stage of intentionality, the observed subject only knows two things: first, the indeterminate concepts of personhood, property, and contract; second, the objectivity of nature (such as that a blackbird is black or that an acorn will fall to the earth by the force of gravity). Hegel associates the first stage of intentionality with the "natural being." This being is unaware of her or his autonomy from the objectivity of consciousness. As the individual becomes increasingly conscious of her or his separation from objectivity, a rupture exudes between the individual and the objectivity. The individual in the first stage of intentionality, however, does not yet think (PR 115). The objectivity with which she or he feels immediate seems "natural."

When the individual begins to think about the objectivity of nature and of consciousness, the individual becomes aware of her or his existence as autonomous from both objectivities. Morality enters into one's consciousness when one acts from recognition of a stranger. One's knowledge and intent now become important. I now realize that my action may alter the external objectivity. I am now aware that I am responsible for the consequences of my action even though I may not have intended them. My intent will be implied from the circumstances (PR 115A). I am blameworthy.[6] My property causes harm to another if I physically control the external thing that is the source of harm (PR 116). I am accountable for the purpose of the deed's objective as constructed from circumstances (PR 117). I must recognize the consequences of my action.

The classic example of the importance of intentionality, according to Hegel, is that of Oedipus. Oedipus did not know that the stranger whom he had killed along the road was his father. Nor did he know that the widow whom he gamed to win as his betrothed was his mother or that his children were also his sisters and brothers. Oedipus, if he had known all these circumstances, would never have desired to marry his mother or father his siblings. After Oedipus became aware of the circumstances, he lived in tormenting anxiety because the universals of the tribal ethos, with which he identified immediately, had no place for personal intentionality and, therefore, of blameworthiness. He remained a natural being and yet accepted guilt as an intentional being. Oedipus would have been blameworthy, according to Hegel, only if he had known of the circumstances in which he had wedded his mother (PR 117A). One is only blameworthy for foreseeable consequences (PR 118). Foreseeable consequences address one's mens rea (PR 118A). One is not blameworthy for acts if she or he acts under a mistake of fact (PR 118). Blameworthiness also addresses one's knowledge (or lack thereof) of the universals. I am responsible for what I know about the circumstances, the consequences, and the universals that I wrongly accept as "givens" (PR 118A).

b) Actual Mens Rea

In addition to my personal knowledge of the circumstances, foreseeable consequences, and universals, my moral action towards strangers depends upon my actual intent. The observed subject intends an action as her or his own (PR 121). One commits murder not for the sake of murder but for the pleasure or positive advantage intended in the murder (PR 121A). When I intend an action, my desires, needs, and impulses motivate my action. There remain external things of nature. But I bring my intended concepts *into* the objectivity of nature so that the latter is no longer a constraint upon my freedom (PR 119). Intention relates my *mens rea* with an external object. If I try to justify something in terms of my intent, I isolate the thing and relate my subjectivity to the thing. But if I fail to account for my intent, I return to the first moment of the objectivity of consciousness. I have an arbitrary will opposed to external things. The gap between the will and objectivity remains.

In sum, when the philosopher observes the relation of the observed subject with the objectivity of consciousness, the philosopher must address two issues: first, the actor's knowledge about the circumstances, consequences, and shared universals; second, the actor's actual intent to cause harm against a stranger. If one sets fire to a building, it matters naught whether the fire spreads, according to Hegel. The initial fire threatens the whole external building: "[t]he stone belongs to the devil when it leaves the hand that threw it" (PR 119A). An intentional subject thinks and is aware of her or his separation from shared universals. She or he has a will. As such, the individual's intent vis-à-vis other individuals becomes important (PR 120). Such a concern for others is excluded from the social relationships of children, imbeciles, lunatics, and others (PR 120R).

2. ETHICALITY

When the philosopher observes how the observed individual recognizes strangers in context-specific circumstances, the philosopher studies the ethicality of the ethos (PR 152).[7] The individual remains autonomous from strangers, but the individual is conscious of her or his recognition of strangers. One will be ethical if and when one's action recognizes universals because the universals represent *shared* concepts and institutions with strangers. The legitimacy of an individual's action rests in such ethicality. The question that one needs to face today is whether Hegel's legal philosophy ever entertains that the monadic subject recognizes the stranger as a stranger independent of the immediacy and concepts immanent in the subject's consciousness. This is the question that Emmanuel Levinas (1906–95) poses and answers in the negative.[8] I shall now summarize Levinas's critique of Hegel and then claim that Hegel does offer ethicality as the focal point of legal philosophy.

a) Levinas's Critique

For Levinas, the stateless world lacks language and consciousness. There are no subjects or objects in this stateless world. Once we begin to think about an object, Levinas says, we begin to desire to colonize, assimilate, expel, and develop strangers in the mirror of ourselves. Indeed, such a desire to know strangers rests at the foundation of totalitarian regimes. Let us examine Levinas's attack on Hegel.

Hegel understands the leap from the prelegal to the legal, from the immediacy of the tribal culture to the mediation of civilization, in terms of the thinking consciousness of the individual. Levinas finds the thinking consciousness problematic because, Levinas claims, the thinking individual aspires to enclose all external objects into the boundaries of concepts of the thinker. Put differently, when I think about the stranger, I represent the stranger as a concept and bring the stranger into the boundary of my consciousness. Since immediacy connotes being for Hegel, Levinas elaborates an ethicality that is otherwise than being.

Levinas claims that Hegel's observed individual brings concepts back to the immediacy with which Hegel began his project. The stranger becomes immediate with the identity of the observed subject.[9] The assimilation of the stranger takes place inside the intellectual consciousness of the individual. When I know the stranger, I comprehend the stranger's body as *my* concept.[10] Concepts form a system or structure of intelligibility. But this system is premised upon a subject-centered philosophy.[11] Hegel's philosopher attempts to recoup the separation of the subject from objectivity by returning the stranger as a nameless singularity into the subject's immediate identity (that is, being) with objectivity.[12] By doing so, according to Levinas, Hegel returns the individual to absolute knowledge: there is no longer a stranger who can constrain the individual's freedom because the stranger has been assimilated into the subject's consciousness.[13] And yet, the stranger, as an experiencing being, still remains unperceived and unconceived "out there" beyond my autonomy just as Hegel had found problematic to freedom through the movements of his legal philosophy. The stranger is a remainder to my consciousness. If I cannot recognize the stranger in terms of my concepts, I exclude the stranger as nonknowledge or as outside science. What cannot be assimilated into the subject's consciousness is either a posited romantic subjectivism or a remainder.

Totality wins the day. Colonialism, imperialism, the mass expulsion of ethnically different peoples, domestic repression, and war are the inevitable and only instrumental means to continue to "know" the stranger.[14] With Hegel's paradigm of knowledge, my knowledge begins with my immediacy with universals, such as we saw with the archaic tribal culture. But as I think, I become separate from the tribal universals. I gain a will. I will that external objects come inside my thoughts. I am continually driven to absorb all that is external to my consciousness and to bring it into my consciousness. The never-ending drive to do so, we saw in Chapter 2, has a *daimonic character*. If I become self-conscious of my role in the representation of the external things and human beings, I access "ultimate wisdom and absolute thought" in the Western view of culture, according to Levinas.[15] Though the stranger may differ from my concept of the stranger, I measure the stranger in terms of my concepts. My concepts represent sameness as a criterion of comparison inside my consciousness.[16]

b) Reciprocal Recognition as Ethicality

There is an important point that one needs to appreciate when reconstructing Levinas's critique of Hegel's philosophy of law. In one interview, Levinas admits that his reading of Hegel borrowed wholesale from Franz Rosenzweig's critique of Hegel.[17] Levinas expresses his own caution in his interpretation of Hegel's phenomenology: "[t]he Hegel who frightened him [Rosenzweig]—was it the real Hegel or Meinecke's Hegel?"[18] Friedrich Meinecke (1862–1954) had traced the development of national German feelings in the nineteenth century, elaborated a theory of "reasons of state" in modern history, and tried to balance morality with power.[19] However, Meinecke failed to situate the reasons of state in an international objectivity of consciousness based upon the reciprocal recognition of states and the peremptory norms that Hegel claimed for the objectivity, as I explained in Section 4 of Chapter 4 and as I shall explain regarding international legal consciousness in Chapter 10. Further, when Levinas refers to Hegel, he has *Phenomenology of Spirit* in mind, and he invariably cites *Phenomenology* as his source for reconstructing Hegel's phenomenology.

Hegel wrote *Phenomenology* at the start of his scholarly career and completed it in 1805, however. Further, although Hegel wrote *Natural Law* (1802–04) and "The Constitution of Germany" (1798–1802) at the turn of the century, his legal philosophy did not mature until fifteen years after this writing and over ten years after *Phenomenology*. In addition, his earlier works about law concentrated upon natural laws of the Newtonian character, not humanly posited laws. This was also so with his *Science of Logic*, published between 1812 and 1814. Although Hegel's speculative logic and his critique of various schools of legal philosophy, elaborated in my Introduction and in Chapters 3 and 5, share many common themes with his mature legal philosophy, Hegel does not begin rigorously to focus upon the nature and identity of human laws until his lectures on legal philosophy at Heidelberg in 1817, *Philosophy of Mind* (1817), and *Philosophy of Right* (1821). And yet, Levinas takes *Phenomenology of Spirit* as the representative text for Hegel's philosophy of law and justice. Levinas's Hegel is not the Hegel of the philosophy of law.

Levinas's interpretation of Hegel's legal philosophy is suspect. Be that as it may, although Hegel begins his description of the enclosure of external things by the will in *Philosophy of Right* much as Levinas describes generally of Hegel's phenomenology, philosophical consciousness and the observed individual soon realize that the observed individual cannot fulfill its arbitrary will without an authentic *recognition of,* rather than a mere dependence upon, the stranger. Further, although Levinas is right that the observed individual is only free when she or he returns to her or his will as the object of self-determination, Hegel insists that the return is through the mediation of concepts and institutions shared with the stranger and, further, that this freedom can only take place if the observed subject recognizes the stranger as also worthy of freedom.

The subject only begins to recognize the stranger when subject and stranger enter into a contract together, not when the subject wills property into the external things and when the stranger is considered such an exterior thing as Levinas assumed. With a contract, as Hegel explains, the subject does not assimilate the stranger into her or his consciousness except to the extent that their arbitrary wills share common interests. The continual effort of the subject to assimilate external things into her or his consciousness only prevails in the first moment of Abstract Right. Further, the subject does not permanently depend upon the stranger because the stranger may withdraw her or his arbitrary will from the contract if her or his arbitrary will is not fulfilled or if, as in the case of slavery, the subject begins to deny the stranger's control of her or his own body. Hegel realizes that there needs to be a stronger recognition of the stranger than what a contract offers. This awareness takes place in the punishment for a criminal act that contradicts the universals of the objectivity of consciousness as an *in itself.* When the subject recognizes the stranger as a person, rather than as a thing of nature in the objectivity of nature, the subject faces a constraint which restricts her or his freedom unless both subject and stranger reciprocally recognize each other as self-determining.

Contrary to Levinas' reading of Hegel, the process of recognition never closes—not even in the sovereign state. What is critical to appreciate in Hegel's philosophy of law is that legal legitimacy (that is, why is a posited rule binding?) depends, not upon the immediacy of the subject as Levinas suggests—an immediacy which Hegel claims can never be retrieved once we begin to think—but upon the social recognition of the stranger by the subject and vice versa. In Hegel's effort to reconcile the formalism of the objectivity with subjectivity, ethicality is never accessed in a final form. Hegel identifies shapes of reciprocal recognition in various forms of a family, the external state of civil society, the organic legal order, and various *Sittlichkeit* of the international legal order. To associate Hegel's legal philosophy with the monadic subject, let alone the monadic subject of the moment of property in abstract objectivity of consciousness, is reductionist and misdirected. In Hegel, as in Levinas, the recognition by the "I" of a stranger puts the "I" into question. With Hegel, this is the consequence of the continual movement of self-consciousness. We never reach the totality that Levinas attributes to Hegel's philosophy of law. Indeed, the continual movement of self-consciousness to ever more rigorous forms of social bonding even displaces the contemporary acceptance of a state-centric international legal order as I argue in Chapter 10.

We can live in an ethos, such as civil society where legal formalism and unrestrained competition for property reign, without the reciprocal recognition between self and stranger. However, when one lives in an ethos of reciprocal recognition, ethicality exudes. The shared interrecognition of subjects bonds them into a community, a community which is greater than the sum of the self-determining immediacies. This community embodies social differences (PR 154). An objectivity of consciousness is legitimate, according to Hegel, if the institutions and posited laws, social values, and collective memories represent shared universals between observed subject and stranger. The objective of the philosopher (and of the legal official) is to examine the extent to which any one ethos exhibits such legitimacy. Mere emotional or national bonding amongst individuals will not ensure such legitimacy. After all, the archaic clan members bonded together. So too, Kantian moral duties, even if fulfilled in action, do not ensure legitimacy because the individual moral action may be separated from the reciprocal social recognition (PR 146R). Actuality is constituted from the reciprocal social relationships between individuals. Actuality, as such, manifests ethicality. Ethicality involves neither duties nor impulses. Rather, ethicality involves the reciprocal recognition between observed individual and stranger (PR 150R). The subject is only free to the extent that she or he "belong[s] to ethical actuality" (PR 153). The universals of an ethos are no longer alien from the stranger or from the subject's social action as happened with legal formalism (PR 147).

This is a roundabout way to explain why I entitled this chapter "The Ethicality of an Ethos." Hegel aims, in part III of *Philosophy of Right,* to make us conscious of the collective unconscious senses of ethical ethê that we have experienced in Western culture. Each ethical ethos presupposes a different structure of consciousness and therefore a different set of social relationships. The philosopher, as does the observed individual, lives through such different levels of self-consciousness in each ethical ethos (PR 145). Each structure is one phase or moment in the cumulative movement of the Idea *in and for itself* (PR 143).

c) Ethicality and the Identity of Legal Units in Objectivity

Needless to say, Hegel's inquiry is hardly what law deans, lawyers, or even the public might consider "law" today. Political science, sociology, or anthropology, yes. But law? Hegel contributes to contemporary legal philosophy by directing our attention to the importance of the recognition of the stranger in structures of consciousness. Such an inquiry incorporates what Hart and Dworkin exclude from legality as "anthropological morality."[20] Although Hegel excludes the tribal legal order as "prelegal," there is a sense in which his consideration of social relationships presupposed in the content of posited laws is also "prelegal." The study of time-consciousness requires *Vernunft* rather than the familiar *Verstand*. This is not a matter of accepting the implied structure of consciousness of officials but of identifying the extent to which their structure of consciousness presupposes if and how observed subject and observed stranger recognize each other. Such consciousness raising overcomes the legal formalism and reification, examined in the previous chapter, of the social relations in any ethos.

Simply put, the thrust of Hegel's ethics is that one's rights and duties are embodied in a social context and in a particular social context at that. Instead of locating morality as separate from legality as did Kant, morality and legality are fused into an ethical ethos. Ethicality grows immanently through *Vernunft* from immediacy to the recognition of others' context-specific experiences. It is a moot point here, addressed in the Conclusion chapter, whether time and space are experienced rather than abstracted from experience as linear time and territorial space. To be sure, though, the legal formalism of balancing posited values or of the balancing of rights does not help in this development. Further, instead of dividing law into a public and private realm, the private and public arguably dissolve into a unity, it would seem. (I shall suggest in the Conclusion, however, that Hegel's institution of ethicality fails in this regard.) A binding "law" incorporates the assumptions, expectations, institutions, and posited rules that observed individuals share with each other. This anthropological morality constitutes the ethos. The inhabitant feels "at home" with the posited laws and institutions as if the latter were the product of the inhabitant's will. The ethicality of such an ethos manifests the relation of the observed individual with strangers through such assumptions and expectations. The rules of the ethos are posited in one's consciousness (*Gesetz als Sittlichkeit*).

d) Kantian and Hegelian Ethics

Hegel believes that his approach to ethics fundamentally differs from Kant's and Fichte's. If I can act in accordance with a will that could be universally shared with strangers, then I would morally act according to Kant. If I could purge my being of all bodily inclinations, my personhood would be universal. All such persons, purged of bodily inclinations, would presumably have a duty to follow such a universal rule. My personhood and moral duties would not be historically or socially contingent. In Hegel's vocabulary, such persons would lack particularity. The good will would be abstract in that it would be located in an "intelligible world." It would remain untouched by the particular social-cultural values, beliefs, desires, intuitions, and other motivating factors in a phenomenal world. The good will would also remain untouched by the social relations of one individual with another. All persons in the intelligible world would be equal since there would be no contingent difference between one moral person and another. Differences would exist between concepts rather than between beings. The philosopher would not make rational choices immersed in social relationships. The time-consciousness would be detached from intellectual differences amongst concepts. As a consequence, the moral rules would be "oughts." Since I inevitably incorporate my values into my choices, my moral life remains unfulfilled. I have duties towards others. If my moral life fulfilled my duties, I would have a pure will with divine pretensions. Since only the divine has such a pure will, the divine can be considered purified of all bodily inclinations.[21] Kant's moral maxims and categorical imperative are socially empty of contingent content by Kant's own admission. The consequence, according to Hegel, is that "there is no room in living reality for empty notions like that of pursuing goodness for its own sake. If someone intends to act, it is not enough for him simply to pursue the good; he must also know whether this or that specific thing is good" (PH 80). In the everyday contingencies of life, one is immersed in an ethos in which one finds oneself. The latter introduces ethicality. Ethicality, not morality, is the name of the game.

Hegel describes Kant's moral universals as empty because they lack a relation of legal form to the social relations between individuals. Put differently, Kantian duties are radically separate from the phenomenal knowledge which is experienced through time and space. If the philosopher

examines social relations presupposed in the content of a legislatively or judicially posited rule, she or he would be concerned with "oughts" or duties,
according to Kant.[22] However, as a consequence from Hegel's standpoint,
if morality were stuck in a *noumenal* realm, moral duties would "evaporate
. . . into a complete powerlessness which I can endow with any content
whatever, and subjectivity of spirit becomes no less impoverished in that
it lacks any objective significance" (PR 141A). The talk of rights and duties "easily verge on empty declamation, because it [the declaration] refers
only to something abstract and indeterminate" (PR 150R). An arbitrary
will posits the content of a moral form of a priori argument. In like vein,
constitutionally entrenched "fundamental freedoms," to the extent that
they are analyzed as a priori forms, really represent unfreedom for they
are external to the ethicality of the social relationships between individuals
(PR 149A). As I pointed out in Chapter 3, for example, Kant considers an
inquiry into the legitimacy of a legal order as treasonous (PR 139A). Even
in the famous tract "What is the Enlightenment," Kant strongly urges the
freedom to think about concepts and to question their legitimacy but, at
the same time, he acknowledges the paradox that intellectual freedom is
only possible with "insuperable barriers" to it.[23] Further, morality is separate from legality.[24] The social relations of individuals are thereby ignored
or lost (PR 132R). The Kantian version of morality, then, withdraws the
moral being from the biographies, inclinations, and historical contingency
of structures of legal consciousness. If the philosopher were to incorporate
the latter factors into moral considerations as Hegel counsels, knowledge
would no longer be theoretical.

In opposition to the Kantian separation of legality from morality,
Hegel urges the study of the social relationships presupposed in the content of what Kant takes as moral duties universally accepted in *noumena*.
Such social relationships are manifested through intermediate social organizations, such as the family, corporation, class, or the state, or the international legal order. One's duties are situated in one's role in such social
organizations rather than in a priori concepts. A concern with ethicality
requires that one become conscious of one's role in an ethos and of the
shared universals of the ethos. This consciousness raising renders ethicality reflective. Subject and stranger gain a reflective *Sittlichkeit*. Thus, legality and morality do not exist in separate spheres of human action, as the
"is" and the "ought." Both legality and morality "must have the ethical
as their support and foundation" (PR 141A). By locating duties in social
relationships, the separation of legality from morality dissolves into an
ethos. Instead of being "abstract" (that is, empty) duties, moral duties are

"concrete" (PR 141). The moral duties of the a priori realm are now situated in the context-specific social relations between individuals. Moral duties mirror the self-conscious action of the individual in any one ethos. A legal order embodies both subjectivity (and all its manifestations, such as arbitrary will, feelings, desires, and rational will, in different *ethê*) and objectivity.[25] Contrary to Kant, moral duties become an element of legality. Legality also incorporates the social relationships between individuals (PR 128). Thus, "what is a binding legal unit's identity?" (that is, its legitimacy) dissolves into issues about ethicality.

Hegel emphasizes that this concern for ethicality arises from the advent of modernity for, in contrast with antiquity, the modern individual is capable of becoming self-conscious (PR 124R). The arbitrary will may well characterize a particular structure of legal consciousness such as what he will describe as civil society. But, as I just explained in the previous chapter, Hegel is dissatisfied with the arbitrary will as the source of ethicality because each will struggles with the next to the point of death. With ethicality, the lawyer or judge, as an observed subject, must focus on the several relationships of the content of a rule. So too, the philosopher must become conscious of the different structures of consciousness of an ethos experienced through time. Different criteria will characterize different ethê: the arbitrary feelings of a monad (Fries), the subjective spirit of a *Volk* (Savigny), the accumulation of personal happiness (Hume), and the autonomous moral reasoning (Fichte and Kant). The unit of legality, to be legal, must be legitimate and legitimacy rests in the ethicality relations of an ethos. Objective freedom is finally reconcilable with the subjective freedom of the observed subject and stranger alike. Without such reconciliation, the posited laws and institutions, such as courts, legislatures, and public authorities, lose their social actuality and therefore their legitimacy as institutional sources of binding laws (PR 145).

e) Freedom

When one experiences Objective freedom, one knows oneself as the author of objectivity so that one feels at one with the family or the state. Such a freedom is "infinitely more firmly based than the being of nature" because the observed subject recognizes objectivity as having been constructed by her- or himself (PR 146). Subjectivity dwells in an ethical ethos because the subject becomes increasingly self-conscious of her or his social relationships with strangers. The subject knows her- or himself as the source of truth, laws, and moral duties towards strangers (PR 140f). The subject realizes that the objective institutions are human constructions: "[i]t is not the thing [*Sache*] which is excellent, it is I who am excellent and master of both law and thing; I *merely play* with them as with my own ca-price, and in this ironic consciousness in which I let the highest of things perish, I *merely enjoy myself*" (PR 140f). But with this self-knowledge, the subject becomes aware of her or his separation from objectivity and of an alienation from objective institutions "and knows *itself* as that which *wills* and *resolves in a particular way*" (PR 140f).

The problem is that this self-aware subject knows that she or he is alienated from objective institutions and, thereupon, may turn inward oblivious to other self-conscious subjects. To bring content into such an inward-thinking individual, the individual must become aware (that is, be a "spiritual witness") of the different presupposed universals through which the individual recognizes another human subject. Such a conscious-ness will immanently grow from the thinking being (PR 31, 261). The in-dividual is ever at home with the objectivity manifesting as it does the interrecognition of thinking beings through the shared concepts and insti-tutions: "[t]he *right of individuals* to their *subjective determination to freedom* is fulfilled in so far as they belong to ethical actuality" (PR 153). Objectiv-ity, in the form of rules and institutions, is no longer alien to the subject. The subject becomes a member of the social whole. Only ethicality will color the ethos since the bonding is the consequence of reflection about the relations of I and thou.

Subjectivity is now incorporated in an ethical community. Why ethical? Because the members of the community reciprocally recognize each other (PR 141A). Thus, the philosopher must uncover an implicit structure that the subjectivity of the individual wills as her or his own. In a reflective *Sit-tlichkeit,* the individual is self-conscious of her or his autonomy and of her or his recognition of strangers. This recognition of strangers inter-se is mani-fested through shared intermediate social associations, such as the family, the corporation or public authorities, or through participation in state in-stitutions such as the legislature or the judicial institutions (PM 198).

By actively thinking about her or his relationship with strangers in her or his ethos, the observed individual thereby becomes conscious of the im-plicit universals in the implicit structures of the objectivity of conscious-ness. The individual must critically think with the aid of *Vernunft*. Public education is critically important in such a development of self-consciousness (PR 153A). Consciousness of the relation of the individual to the systematic character of the legal order makes a posited enactment concrete (PR 156A).

3. WHY WOULD THE SUBJECT DESIRE
TO RECOGNIZE THE STRANGER?

So far, we have seen that Hegel's theories of *Bildung,* freedom, and self-consciousness begin with the observed self who emerges from tribal immediacy. The difficult question, one which has preoccupied others and which I consider in the Conclusion,[26] is "why would the self ever desire to begin the act of thinking which recognizes a stranger?"[27] In order to think about an object, there has to be a subject as well as an object. Hegel offers that, in the first moment of thinking, the objects are external things of nature that, once possessed, may be transformed into property by one's conferral of a form onto the possessed thing. But how does Hegel address the ethical relationships between individuals? Hegel needs to incorporate intersubjectivity into his theory of law.

Philosophical consciousness observes, as Hegel argues in the *Lesser Logic,* that the problem especially arises because two persons, as immediacies, need a third particularity in order to be different (EL 12, 116R). If the third were the arbitrary will of the immediacy, then the philosopher would have two immediacies that appeal to external arbitrary values and interests. The external values would transcend the relationship between the two immediacies. What the philosopher needs, to be consistent with her or his project, is some third or particular that is nested immanent to the relationship between the two immediacies. The act of thinking itself is just such an immanent particular shared between the two immediacies (EL 88A). The third is the act of self-determination itself. And the act of thinking constitutes self-determination or freedom. Freedom becomes a necessary concept of logic. One becomes at home with oneself [*bei sich*] so that one no longer depends upon or refers to any external object for one's existence (PR 23). One "becomes" through the act of thinking. In this act of thinking, one forgets the arbitrary wants, needs and values which figure so importantly in the romanticist philosophy of law. The philosopher observes a beginning where the individual, as a subject now, produces her or his own objects for her- or himself (EL 17).

But can logic explain why one immediacy desires to think? As Hegel says, logic concerns the relationship between concepts. Hegel explains that "[t]his development of immediate ethical life through the division of civil society and on to the state, which is shown to be their true ground, is the *scientific proof* of the concept of the state, a proof which only a development of this kind can furnish" (PR 256R). Independent of the logic of freedom, there has to be something internal to human consciousness that generates why the observed individual would want to think.

There are at least two indicia of a noncognitive drive immanent in the subject's desire to think. The first indicia suggests that an invisible drive presses observing and observed consciousness to venture from one moment of consciousness to the next. When the philosopher observes how the subject shifts from property to contract, for example, the philosopher observes that the will exists *"for the will* of another person. This relation [*Beziechung*] of the will to will is the true distinctive ground in which freedom has its *existence*" (PR 71). Hegel continues that "I no longer own property merely by means of a thing and my subjective will, but also by means of another will." Hegel realizes that the subject still uses the stranger for the former's own self-interest and this understates why contract is a shallow basis to claim the legitimacy of the legal order over and above the amalgam of arbitrary wills. Such legitimacy becomes an object of consciousness when the subject or a stranger commits a crime against the objectivity of consciousness as a whole. When this happens, the subject must act in an "essential relation [*Beziehung*] to the will of others" (PR 113). To continue Hegel's point, when Hegel readies the philosopher for a shift from morality to the ethicality of different ethê, both the objectivity of consciousness and the intentionality of *Moralität* are one-sided because each exists independent of the other. What is critical is the ethical relationship between subject and stranger: "[t]he sphere of right and that of morality cannot exist independently [*für sich*]; they must have the ethical as their support and foundation. For right lacks the moment of subjectivity, which in turn belongs solely to morality, so that neither of the two moments has any independent actuality" (PR 141A). Each of the Abstract Right and of Morality fails to be ethical in the sense of the reciprocal recognition of strangers in the structure of observed consciousness.

The second indicia of a noncognitive drive to think arises from the fact that, without addressing Hegel's preoccupation with ethicality, it is difficult to understand Hegel's whole project in part III of *Philosophy of Right* as the assimilation of the stranger into the thinking of the subject as Levinas claims for Hegel's phenomenology. When Hegel introduces civil society, he advises, for example, that although "each individual is his own end, and all else means nothing to him" in civil society, "he cannot accomplish the full extent of his ends without reference to others; these others are therefore means to the end of the particular [person]" (PR 182A). The organic legal order emerges from civil society precisely because individuals recognize the stranger as a stranger rather than as a means or as an object of the subject's subjective consciousness. This drive to recognize the stranger, as a stranger, lacks closure. To the extent that subject and stranger, as a stranger, share ends, universality exists in the ethos. Hegel likens the march of an immanent desire to recognize the stranger as unmoved and, indeed, divine (PR 258, 258A, 270R). What is the nature of this noncognitive generating force that drives the subject to recognize the stranger through institutions, values, and laws?

This question takes us back to Hegel's adolescent education at the *Stift* with his comrades, Schelling and Hölderlin. At the *Stift* and during Hegel's depressions as a tutor during the 1790s, Hölderlin encouraged Hegel to consider the potential of love in the relationships between individuals. Then, upon leaving the *Stift,* Hegel led a lonely and monadic life as a tutor. He also longed for the recognition that Schelling was receiving as a philosopher. Hegel privately thought about the nature of friendship, particularly his friendship with Hölderlin and Schelling at the *Stift*. There is something in friendship that is unexplainable. One stands by one's friend through "thick or thin." Friendship causes one to break from one's solipsistic outlook in deference to the feelings and interests of one's friends. We unconsciously do so. Hegel picked up the notion of love, manifested through friendship, as the reason why a subject would desire to recognize and socially relate with others through a community. Hegel's privileging of love is not unfamiliar to general jurisprudence.[28] Love takes Hegel to ethicality. "Ethicality" addresses the relation of a subject with strangers in a presupposed structure of legal consciousness.

Love bonds individuals together. This love does not link individuals together through emotional feelings nor through the romantic love of Harlequin romances.[29] The "rightfully ethical [*techtlkich sittliche*] love" excludes "the transient, capricious, and purely subjective aspects of love" (PR 161A). Nor does ethical love play to a role for sexuality. Nor is it what Hegel's friend and contemporary, Friedrich von Schlegel, described in *Lucinde* as rendering a marriage ceremony superfluous and, indeed, a formality that camouflaged the physical surrender of seducers (PR 164A). Ethical love, even in marriage, is "exalted above the contingency of the passions and of particular transient caprice" (PR 163). Indeed, the moment of feeling [*Empßindung*] in marriage is "unstable" (PR 163A). Nor is Hegel's sense of love what we refer to today as "Platonic love." Nor is love the immediacy that one knows when one sees it—what Peter Gabel and Duncan Kennedy once described as "inter-subjective zap."[30] Hegel's sense of love displaces the individualistic and arbitrary will of romantic, sexual, and free love. The kernel to Hegel's sense of love is that one loves another by recognizing the other as a stranger rather than as an inversion of oneself as Levinas suggests of Hegel. Hegel transposes the natural feeling to desire the other as a sexual partner into the higher form of love as social recognition.

The recognition generated by love is authentic. How so? First, one is conscious of the stranger as self-determining, acculturated in the ethos by *Bildung,* and continuously striving to know one's presupposed structures of consciousness. That is, the subject assumes that strangers share one's own self-consciousness as an Enlightenment figure. Second, one recognizes oneself in the stranger despite the difference between the subject and the stranger. Love is the intuition of oneself in the stranger. Love is alien to nature because nature obstructs one's loving of a stranger. I no longer see the stranger as constraining my freedom when I recognize the stranger as a friend. An early stage of this experience of love might be a contract where the parties recognize their dependency upon the other. However, this dependency does not cohere with a self-determining subject. Accordingly, the philosopher observes a third moment in the relationship of a subject with a stranger where the stranger is recognized as a stranger "by regarding the other as other" (PR 7A).

Now, love, according to Hegel, is a "disposition" whereby one is self-conscious of one's individuality "within this unity" with another subject (PR 158).

There are three experiential moments in the development of love, then. First, "I do not wish to be an independent person in my own right [*für mich*] and that, if I were, I would feel deficient and incomplete" (PR 158A). Second, "I find myself in another person . . . I gain recognition in this person [*daß ich in ihr gelte*], who in turn gains recognition in me" (PR 158A). I become self-aware and thereby recognize myself in the stranger and the stranger in myself. The two moments are a contradiction: the subject needs the stranger and the subject recognizes her- or himself in the stranger. Hegel is quick to emphasize that *Verstand* cannot resolve this contradiction: "the understanding cannot resolve it" (PR 158A) and "*adequate cognition* of this identity [between subject and stranger] belongs to conceptual thought [*dem denkenden Begtiffe*]" (PR 147R). Third, the resolution of the contradiction is the ethical relationship that contrasts with the immediacy that initiated the thinking individual. Something independent of the act of thinking (and Hegel's logic) drives the subject to recognize the stranger as a stranger rather than as the inversion of the subject. This drive is alive as well as ethical (and logical) (PR 147R).

The family is Hegel's best example of the first two moments of love. Hegel explains love in the family in this manner: "[t]he family, as the *imme-*

diate substantiality of spirit, has as its own determination the spirit's *feeling* [*Empfindung*] of its own unity, which is *love*" (PR 158). One is a *member* of a family and acts from the love towards others. In a family, unlike the civil society to which the male adolescent seeks security, love displaces the individual self-interest of each member of the family. In love, "I am not isolated on my own [*für mich*], but gain my self-consciousness only through my renunciation of my independent existence [*meines Fürsichseins*] and through knowing myself as the unity of myself with another and of the other with me" (PR 158A). Love is thereby the natural form of *Sittlichkeit*.

More generally, love intertwines my subjective feelings and self-interest with an institutional objectivity which I share with others (PR 158A).[31] In the developed (or civilized) society, I am aware that I am autonomous from strangers. At the same time, though, I am aware that I share universals with strangers. When I will concepts (such as property, a contract, a legal rule, or a jury verdict) and when I feel bonded with such concepts, I recognize strangers (at the same time that I am separate from them) through the shared universals. I identify with my particular experiences and, at the same time, I identify with shared norms. The sharing renders them universal. By my recognition of the objectivity of consciousness, I recognize strangers with whom I share the objectivity. I can now dialogue and reason with them.[32] The shared meanings, represented by universals, render mutual respect and understanding between individuals possible. Goodness is actualized through such love.

Love unifies members of the family in such a manner. The family member recognizes that she or he is separate from the shared traditions of the family and yet, by participating in those traditions, the individual implicitly recognizes other family members. Contrary to Kant, love (not sexual desire) generates the desire to marry and form a family. So too, love drives the individual to bond with social organizations, such as a guild or corporation, and, ultimately, with institutions of the state and of the international legal order. The form and extent of the relationships of individuals with the shared mediums of the objectivity of consciousness embody ethicality.

Hegel suggests that this sense of love as recognition becomes critically important in a modern society. In modernity, the subject thinks about concepts and these, in turn, mediate the relationships between individuals. Once we mediate our social relations with concepts, we need faith and trust in strangers (PR 147R). We have to have faith that we are correctly representing strangers "out there" beyond our intuitive self-consciousness (that is, immediacy).[33] On another level, the mediation of our relationships objectifies love in a manner that philosophers may access through *Vernunft*.[34] Love is presubjective and preobjective.

Love would be Hegel's response to the contemporary distinction, noted above, between legality and legitimacy. For when legality is analyzed without relating it to legitimacy, a concern for ethicality is lacking, and therefore love is absent. Hegel describes the emergence of evil from the Fall of humankind in *Genesis* as the situation when the subject's thought is separated from "picture-thinking" or representations (PS 772–75). When legal scholars and legal officials only consider the "law" as constituted from rules and the jurisdiction of state institutions posited by the judge's or the legislator's arbitrary will, we perpetuate evil. The separation of legality from legitimacy is one such example of evil.

4. IMMEDIACY, MEDIATION, AND THE ETHOS

Hegel distinguishes two opposing forms of an ethos.[35] The first attributes immediacy between individual members of an ethos and the universals of the ethos. The second manifests a separation of the individual from the universals of the ethos. The individual is separated from such universals and from other individuals by virtue of possessing a will. This ethos is reflective. Because only a reflective form of an ethos entertains the possibility of the separation of individual members, ethicality only addresses the reflective *Sittlichkeit*.

a) Undeveloped Ethicality in a Living Community

In the first form of an ethos, the individual is so bonded with the community that she or he feels immediate with the community's universals as if there were no mediating organizations or rules or officials between the individual and the customs of the social order. So, for example, one participates in a family or a tribe as if she or he did not control or create tribal or family customs (PR 152). The family member accepts the legitimacy of customs without question. The members may believe that their objective ethical life is grounded in an "unmoved mover" such as nature or the Judeo-Christian God (PR 152) or, on occasion, in an eternal justice "which alone has permanence and is the power by which the lives of individuals are governed" (PR 145A). Hegel offers the extended family, clan, or tribe as the best examples of the immediate or "natural" bonding of an individual with an ethos. Although contemporary legal philosophy has retrieved this notion of an undeveloped *Sittlichkeit* as a ground to critique liberalism,[36] legal philosophers have also excluded the immediacy of an undeveloped *Sittlichkeit* as prelegal to a modern state-centric legal order. Legal philosophy in the latter tradition posits a concept—the rule of recognition or of social fact—rather than with the bonding of the undeveloped *Sittlichkeit*.[37] Hart's influential student, Joseph Raz, has also excluded the units of legality from the bonding manifested in an undeveloped *Sittlichkeit* despite his emphasis of the importance of social bonding to the legitimacy of legality.[38]

b) Reflective Ethicality

Hegel identifies a second form of an ethos. This is a reflective *Sittlichkeit* where the observed individual recognizes that she or he is separate from the universals of the ethos, yet she or he feels bonded with them because they are the product of her or his reflection and deliberation as well as the recognition of strangers. One can best understand Hegel's idea here by returning to his phenomenology of the will. Because I participate in the creation of the legal institutions and rules, I am bonded with them. But because I reflect about their content, the ethos is a reflective one.

Hegel sets out two requisites for bonding in a reflective ethical life. First, one needs to bond with the objectivity of consciousness as a social whole. This bonding incorporates social assumptions, expectations, intermediate associations, and even religious practices. Second, the bonding must be the consequence of one's thinking, deliberation, and evaluation. This requires three elements: first, the individual's active reflection about the content of rules and institutional actions; second, reflection about how the individual relates to strangers as presupposed in the content of the rules and institutional actions; and third, reflection about one's recognition of strangers as ethicality. These elements of self-awareness constitute the social actuality from which Hegel draws in his critique of legal formalism: "the self awareness of individuals . . . constitutes the actuality of the state" (PR 265A). Since an invisible source (spirit) drives one to become self-aware, spirit provides the ultimate truth for a presupposed structure of legal consciousness (PR 263A).

Hegel explains that with a reflective *Sittlichkeit,* faith and trust surround the belief that reflection ought to resolve conflict (PR 147R). But when we have an undeveloped ethos, there is a "relationship which is immediate and closer to identity than even [a relationship] of *faith* or *trust*"

(PR 147). Hegel identifies three forms of a reflective *Sittlichkeit*: civil society, the organic constitution, and various forms of an international legal order which eventually manifests the recognition of a stranger.

Although custom characterizes an undeveloped *Sittlichkeit,* custom is also important in inducing the bonding of a reflective *Sittlichkeit* (PR 151). On the one hand, a custom may originate from faith or trust through *Verstand* (PR 147R). Over time, the faith is so deeply felt that the representations become a *"second nature"* (PR 151). An individual, though separate from others by virtue of her or his will, relates to a stranger through such immediate bonding. On the other hand, spirit begins to become permanent when the individual's bonding with the objectivity of consciousness is the consequence of the actions of each individual will rather than of the unconscious acceptance of external things as in the consciousness of nature. In a reflective *Sittlichkeit,* reflection and deliberation become the operative factors in constructing the objectivity of consciousness.

As long as an individual follows a norm from an unconscious habit, however, she or he lacks self-consciousness, let alone the drive to become self-conscious (PR 151A). In addition, the individual does not socially relate or communicate with strangers if the habit is unconscious. Self-conscious action and the relation of one with another, we observed above, are the two elements of ethicality.

Although Hegel gives a place for customs, as Savigny most certainly did, customs alone lack the ethicality that is a possibility with modernity. The ethical character of a custom comes into play in two circumstances. First, the observed individual becomes conscious that human agents actually create customs. As one becomes conscious of the content of a custom, one becomes self-conscious. I feel that I am "at home" with them since I am conscious of them as mirrors of my inner will. Second, in this self-conscious action as manifested in the consciousness of the universals of a custom, one relates to strangers (PS 350). The custom is a universal but also a particularization of the universal: "[t]he laws proclaim what each person is and does; the individual knows them not only as his universal objective thinghood, but equally knows himself in them, or knows them as *particularized* in his own individuality, and in each of his fellow citizens" (PS 351). The particularization manifested by a custom embodies meaning through which communication between two individuals is possible. So, in *Phenomenology of Spirit,* for example, customs function as universals and particulars in a nation, so a custom becomes a "universal language" (PS 351) or "a universal public meaning open to the light of day" (PS 466).

5. THE TIME-CONSCIOUSNESS OF ETHICALITY

The philosopher of a modern legal order, then, must be capable of identifying the relation of the individual with the shared universals of an ethos over experiential time. When Hegel examines such an ethos, he retrieves how the observed individual recognizes strangers as strangers. Hegel's subject at this point is very different from the monadic subject whom Levinas attributed to Hegel. The observed individual especially recognizes strangers in her or his family, the corporation, and class (PR 255). The retrieved social actuality—which highlights the recognition and therefore the ethicality of an individual with strangers through universal laws and institutions—no longer presupposes laws and institutions as external to the subject's social relationships with others. Although there are many criticisms of this prospect, not least of which is the claim of Levinas and others that the individual is swallowed into a monad's universality,[39] Hegel claims that the objectivity of consciousness will be reconciled with the social relations of individuals in an organic state-centric legal order only to find the latter itself as an inadequate reconciliation immersed in an international ethos. I shall feel bonded with the universals despite my separation from them. I shall feel bonded with strangers as a consequence of my *Bildung*. For I have gone into myself and extracted truth for myself about my recognition of strangers. My action is thereby self-conscious. Since I am conscious of my social recognition of strangers, the ethicality of the universals, which manifest my social relations with strangers, is alive. Hegel explains that the subject and the stranger each loses her or his abstractness as a self-sufficient monadic self. Each remains "'really' distinct but 'ideally' one" (PR 128). Ethicality is consolidated since, despite my separation from others and from the shared universals with others, there is no further object with which I do not socially relate (PR 144A).

Alas, ethicality is never conclusive. For the retrieved ethicality that lies immanent in the social actuality of any one objectivity of consciousness produces a different social network through the experience of time. Indeed, the movement from the social actuality immanent in legal forms is never ending through experiential time. Each structure of legal consciousness actualizes the recognition of one individual with another. Hegel describes the structure of legal consciousness, where ethicality fully characterizes the structure, as "realised freedom." Such a realized freedom is *the absolute and ultimate end of the world*" (PR 129). The realized ethicality is the living Good: "[the Good is] *realized freedom, the absolute and ultimate end of the world*" (PR 129).

6. THE INSTITUTIONALIZATION OF ETHICALITY

What, then, is the role of a judge who acknowledges ethicality in the adjudication of disputes? The judge needs to relate the objectivity of consciousness to the subjective freedom (PR 124R). The judge does so by focusing upon the substantive content of the objectivity. Such content manifests the relationship of the individual with strangers and how that relationship is coherent with the presupposed structure of consciousness of the ethos in which the judge is immersed. Such an inquiry will ensure that the decision of the judge, as well as the transcendent rules to which she or he refers, are binding (PR 128).

Even if the official recognizes the relationship of an observed subject with strangers, immersed in a particular ethos and manifested through the laws posited by an organic constitution, the official remains a stage or two behind what is actually transpiring between presupposed subject and stranger relationships (PR 132R). The official looks backward to the development of self-consciousness and becomes aware of social actuality although the observed subject is not so aware as yet. A particular judicial decision becomes an element of ethicality, for the content of the decision addresses how the observed individual socially relates to the universals of the ethos through which official and observed individuals play a role. If a litigant is incapable of recognizing her or his relation with such universals (by virtue, for example, of mental disability), her or his legal responsibility is diminished (PR 132R). If the individual is intellectually capable of self-consciousness but acts from passion against the universals, the individual must be punished. The critical point is that the official understands a legal problem in the contingent context of the ethicality. This requires that officials examine the social content of rules.

Thus, the usual distinction between a right and a duty collapses in Hegel's preoccupation with ethicality (PR 155A). When one uses the term, a *right,* in the ethicality between individuals, one no longer uses a "right" as a formal concept. The content of the right, as a legal form, presupposes different social relations between one individual and another. The content of the right is intermingled with its form and is meant differently depending upon the structure of consciousness presupposed in a particular ethos (PR 33A). A legal duty is derived from one's social ethos and, in particular, from one's role in the social ethos (PR 2R, 149A). Cognitive inclinations are joined with duties. Such inclinations are not "of the heart" but of rational or self-conscious choices (PR 2R). By fulfilling duties in social organizations, the individual is liberated and feels "at home" with the organizations (PR 149).

Hegel seems to radically change the whole world which legal formalism had taken as a "given." Instead of seeing the state as external to the individual and instead of viewing rights as opposed to the state, the individual experiences her- or himself as *belonging* to the objectivity of consciousness. Instead of moral duty being abstracted from socially contingent circumstances, morality is intermeshed with social life. Supported by a wealth of anthropological and historical examples that would humble the Anglo-American legal philosopher of today, Hegel explains that there is something ingrained in the individual's subconscious that drives her or him on and on to recognize other social beings. This "something" is love or, more generally, spirit. And it is spirit that drives Hegel himself to elaborate the institutionalization of the legal consciousness that I shall now examine more closely.

CHAPTER SEVEN

The Shapes of Family Laws

This is the point where Hegel brings in the family as the first form of an eth-ical ethos. Hegel has already introduced freedom as the product of logic and of *Vernunft* in legal reasoning. This method has taken him to privilege the religious, moral, social, and political assumptions of any particular ethos in any particular epoch. Once the philosophical observer has recognized that an ethos exists, the philosopher needs to identify the pillars of the structure of consciousness that individuals assume in such an ethos. This explains why Hegel considers the family as so important to any analysis of a modern legal order. The individual family member identifies immediately with the customs, rituals, and practices of the family. So much so that she or he does not feel autonomous from the family. And yet, the universals inculcated in family members build the objectivity of the "civilized" legal orders.

Against the background of the immediacy that characterizes a family, Hegel identifies a different role for the family in different presupposed structures of legal consciousness. This is important. For one thing, some commentators have used Hegel's reading of the nature of the family in one epoch of legal consciousness, such as the archaic family, as representative of another, such as a civil society. Further, when one takes Hegel's state-ments about the gendered division of labor as offensive to today's social values, such an interpretive approach is reductive. Why? Because such a gendered interpretation freezes the development of both male and female in one particular structure or "shape" of legal consciousness contrary to Hegel's logic of freedom and of the ethicality of an ethos. Male and female become isolated from the immanent movement of consciousness through time. Hegel insists that the structures of legal consciousness continually develop into higher and higher forms of consciousness as the individual becomes ever more conscious of her or his role in constructing the objectivity of consciousness. Thus, we cannot reduce Hegel's sense of a family to one particular set of relationships between men and women. Nor is there one idea of a family, such as the nuclear family, as representative of the ethical ethos. There are several shapes of the family as an ethical ethos.

In an endeavor to explain why this is so, one needs to have several points clarified. When Hegel discusses the role of a member in the ethos of a family, he describes someone who is unaware of her or his separation from the universals of the family. The individual lacks a will. Without a will, the individual is not conscious of her or his role in the family. The individual just acts as a family member. The observed member of the family, however, differs from the role of the philosopher who looks backward to the structure of consciousness presupposed by family members. I shall, in my first section, clarify this distinction. After returning to the application of the distinction, I shall clarify the following: first, what Hegel signifies by a family member being a "natural being"; second, the need for contextualization in the immanent movement of legal consciousness; and third, the progression of the self-awareness of the observed subject and the philosopher to higher and higher levels of self-consciousness. After clarifying the above three issues, I shall identify, in section 2, five very different forms of the family that correspond with different moments of legal consciousness. In Section 3, I shall examine the social function of the family in the civilized legal orders. I shall conclude by emphasizing how the role of the family, as an ethical ethos, moves through experiential time. Time may be experienced in distinction from the time on a clock.[1]

I. CLARIFICATIONS

a) The Two Forms of Consciousness

Hegel's discussion of the family is not easy to follow. One reason is that Hegel sometimes, such as with his description of a woman in the family of a civil society, concentrates on whether and the extent to which an observed family member is conscious of her or his separation from the family. On other occasions, such as his description of Antigone or of the male child who leaves the archaic family for civil society, he describes the relationship from a philosopher's point of view. Both forms of consciousness recognize that in a reflective *Sittlichkeit,* the observed subject—woman or man—struggles to break from her or his immediate identity with the family because the modern subject, as opposed to an animal, thinks. When one thinks, a subject represents an object. The representation cannot return to the presence of the self as a oneness with the family. This struggle differentiates a human being from an animal. When Hegel describes a woman as emotional and subjective, like a passive plant (PR 166A) and preoccupied with raising a family (PR 164A), he is describing the observed woman in one particular epoch of the family—that of the civil society of his own times. But the observed woman may play a different role in a different shape of legal consciousness such as in the organic legal order or in world history, two forms of *Sittlichkeit* that I shall soon develop in Chapters 9 and 10.

The philosophical consciousness enters into the discussion of the family in this context. The philosopher may observe that the parents play an important role in educating the children of the shared universals of the society. Philosophical consciousness recognizes higher and higher structures of the self-conscious autonomy of the observed individual vis-à-vis the shared universals of an ethos. This movement, and the philosopher's consciousness of it, counters any possible reduction of a family member's role to any particular ethos. The social organization of the family and the role of its individual members will never remain the same over time. There is going to be an immanent development of philosophic consciousness as the philosopher recognizes different structures of legal consciousness. All family members will also develop by becoming conscious of their respective roles in the family and in other social institutions.

The self-conscious role of an individual family member in the ethos of the family and of the grander society is thereby an object of anthropological proof. The philosopher examines social practices in which the family member is immersed. The practices manifest the extent to which the family member is conscious of her or his autonomy from the shared universals in the family. Hegel is not concerned with the philosopher's intuitions about such a self-consciousness. Rather, the philosopher needs to adduce empirical, historical, and anthropological evidence to reach such a conclusion. Hegel explains this in his transition from *Moralität* to *Sittlichkeit*:

> [t]he *ethical* is a subjective disposition, but of that right which has being in itself. That this Idea as the *truth* of the concept of freedom cannot be assumed or derived from feeling or from any other source, but, in philosophy, can only be *proved*. Its deduction consists solely in the fact that right and the moral self-consciousness can be seen in themselves to return to this Idea as their own *result*. (PR 141R)

Hegel does not bring closure to any one form of a family as an ethical life.

b) A Family Member as a Natural Being

This raises the need for another clarification. Hegel often describes the family as a "natural" ethical life.[2] The temptation is to associate a family member, in this case the woman, with a nuclear family and a social role that is determined by her biology. Hegel describes the observed woman in the family of civil society in terms that have been interpreted as biological. Hegel, for example, compares a woman's role to that of a passive plant: "[t]he difference between man and woman is the difference between animal and plant; the animal is closer in character to man, the plant to woman" (PR 166A). The woman fails to attain *Bildung*: "[w]omen may well be educated, but they are not made for the higher sciences, for philosophy and certain artistic productions which require a universal element. Women may have insights [*Einfälle*], taste, and delicacy, but they do not possess the ideal" (PR 166A). The woman is said to be "passive and subjective" (PR 166). The state is even said to be in danger if women controlled the government for they might rule by emotional contingency rather than by universal rules. The husband represents the family as its head [PR 171].[3] Hegel also uses the pronoun *him* to describe the monarch.[4]

Hegel maintains that the woman remains a natural being in civil society, acting from unmediated feeling and an arbitrary will. Women remain at home in the ethos of a civil society. Women are said to contrast with the male adolescent who leaves the family for the grander individualistic world of civil society. Such a male creates his own family in civil society. The male has the potentiality of legal personhood and, as such, the male pursues his individual self-interest in the economy. Natural immediacy with one's mother characterizes the relation of the male with his mother. Intellectual free will characterizes the father to whose authority the son deepens in deference. The male thinks about external things of nature and transforms them into instruments of his will.[5] Hegel states that when the self-contained ethical life of the family in civil society dissolves due to the natural death of the father or to the divorce of the parents, the brother "leaves this immediate, elemental, and therefore, strictly speaking, negative ethical life of the family, in order to acquire and produce the ethical life that is conscious of itself and actual" (PS 458). The woman remains in the family. As Hegel lectures, "[a] girl's vocation [*Bestimmung*] consists essentially only in the marital relationship" (PR 164A). The actuality of which Hegel speaks here is civil society, only one shape of *Sittlichkeit*.

When Hegel writes about natural being, then, does he have biological nature in mind or does he intend the culturally induced "second nature"?

The reduction of gender relationships of the family to a fixed role over time seriously misses the role of philosophical consciousness as it observes the woman as a subject in different relationships of presupposed structures of legal consciousness. It also misses the continual movement of the consciousness of both the observed woman and the philosopher as they develop to higher and higher forms of self-consciousness through experienced time, a point I shall clarify soon. It also misses that Hegel describes different forms of a family in different historical epochs. The shift from the archaic family, for example, to the nineteenth-century nuclear European family (or even as read through twentieth-century eyes by contemporary commentators) entirely avoids the continual flux of the observed individuals through experienced time. Finally, the biological reading of the family risks a reductive categorization of the woman. Such a reductive reasoning fails to appreciate Hegel's intent to break from the objectivity of nature as biologically determinative of *Recht*.[6]

Legal and political commentators have been quick to accept such a reductive reading of Hegel's legal philosophy. They often have believed that Hegel presupposed the woman as a natural being determined by the objectivity of nature. The biological differences have been said to represent women with feelings and men with reason.[7] Hegel has been said to support the domination of man's consciousness over woman's unconsciousness,[8] and Hegel has also been interpreted as locating the woman as the origin of human consciousness.[9] Hegel's interpretation of Sophocles' *Antigone* has been taken as his view generally of women.[10] Hegel has been held to accept that women are like Antigone who is slowly deprived of life and who is granted a passive role vis-à-vis the male who, in turn, deprives her of liberty, her nature, love, and her choices of her life.[11]

When Hegel describes a family member as a passive, emotional, or natural being, however, the logic of his phenomenology suggests that, from the standpoint of the philosophical consciousness, Hegel is describing the feeling of immediacy which the family member experiences vis-à-vis the family's rituals and customs. Anglo-American general jurisprudence is already aware of this sense of naturalness, albeit more generally, since Hart describes it on several occasions in his works as I noted in previous chapters.[12] Hart describes the regime of Rex I, for example, with the very sense of immediacy that Hegel describes of a tribe and of a "natural being."[13] The family member feels so much at one with the family that she considers the customs of the family as if they were an uncontrollable second nature. Hegel describes the family, for example, as the "immediate of *natural ethical spirit*" (PR 157). The "nature" that Hegel attributes to a woman is a concept in the objectivity of consciousness, not the objectivity of nature. The family is "natural" because family members feel immediate with the universals of the family. Here, Hegel follows a long and deep tradition of Plato and Aristotle,[14] despite the determinative sense of nature adopted by Hobbes, Grotius, and Pufendorf. As Hegel explains in the Preface and Introduction (PR 11), the shape of consciousness as a second nature has not yet taken the form of rationality (that is, of a self-conscious will who is knowingly autonomous of the objective institutions and statutes which reconcile with subjectivity).

Antigone manifests such a natural being when she exclaims, in her defence of having buried the body of her deceased brother, Polyneices, contrary to Creon's edict, "no one knows when they [that is, customs] were first put forth" (457). No one is conscious of the historical origins of the customs because customs lack a distinct and assignable author. The unwritten tribal customs are felt immediate in the lives of family members.[15] As I explained in Chapter 2, Antigone personally experiences the unwritten tribal laws just as she experiences the prosecution and enforcement of King Creon's edicts. How could a family member such as Antigone consider her experiences as mediated by the concepts of a thinking being? Hegel does not close his analysis by pointing to Antigone's immediacy with the customs of her clan, though. And it is a misreading of Hegel's legal philosophy to generalize about his opinion on the role of women in a contemporary late-twentieth-century family from his view of Antigone's example. Indeed, Hegel contrasts Antigone's identity with unwritten customs in terms of King Creon's identity with the polis of Thebes. The object of Hegel's analysis, as an "authentic" philosopher, is to express how the human spirit, represented by Antigone and Creon, is driven to become more and more conscious of the autonomy of the observed individual from the shared universals of the familiar ethos and how each such individual becomes conscious of this autonomy and her or his subsequent recognition of other human beings in the ethos.

c) The Immanent Movement of Legal Consciousness

Before I address the role of the family in different presupposed structures of legal consciousness, one further point needs to be clarified. We saw in Chapter 2 that the most important factor, for Hegel, in differentiating civilization from precivilization is the state. A society either has a state or it does not. A tribal society lacks a state. The tribal family, as the first shape of a family in the development of human consciousness, is stateless. When

Hegel examines the family as a form of ethicality, however, the philosophical consciousness has become conscious of the relation of the individual's separation from others in an ethos. And this, Hegel assumes, situates the family in a civilization where there is a state. Hegel identifies several such ethê: civil society, the organic legal order, and the several forms of the international legal order. In civil society, the state is external to the subject's consciousness. The state, in like vein, is external to the family in such a shape of legal consciousness. In the organic structure of consciousness, the individual feels bonded with the objective structure of consciousness. The family, in such an ethos, functions as an intermediary between the family member and the organic structure. The immediacy of a family even characterizes various ethê of the international objectivity of consciousness. In sum, once Hegel begins to examine the nature of the family—so often considered independent of the various forms of a state-centric ethos today—the philosopher needs to situate the family in the implied structure of consciousness of a particular ethos. Civil society is the first such state-centric structure. There, individuals recognize that they are separate from each other and that each individual (and the family as a legal person) has a will.

This movement of the consciousness of the observed individual undermines any reductionist claim about the role of men, women, and children in a family. Indeed, it softens any fixed idea of "what is a family." The immediacy, which Antigone had experienced in her tribal family, for example, slowly dissolves as family members become conscious of their increasing autonomy from the customs of the tribal family. If Hegel were to fix the familial role of a woman to that of Antigone's family, the *movement* of the woman as an observed consciousness and the movement of the philosopher as a philosophical consciousness would be foreclosed. Spirit, one must recall, is precisely the continued drive to become self-conscious through experiential time. The spirit strives to become free from external constraints, such as the customs of the archaic family. As the spirit continues its journey, the observed subject becomes conscious that she or he is the stranger to objectivity, whether the objectivity is constituted from unwritten customs of the family, the customs and social practices of the guild, class or public authority, or the written laws posited by the external state. Recognition of the stranger thereby becomes self-recognition and vice versa.

The point needs emphasis. The spirit develops through self-consciousness over experiential time. Biological reductionism loses this time-consciousness. Hegel's philosophy of law is not imprisoned with one fixed shape of legal consciousness. If it were so, Hegel would return to the very formalism of *Verstand* which he steadfastly rejected. We would differentiate the woman, as a concept, from the man, as a concept. Like the inverted world metaphor, however, we play different roles in different shapes or structures of legal consciousness through experiential time.

Now, the reason why we need to understand Hegel's comments about the family in the context of time-consciousness is as follows. When Hegel concerns himself with the role of women as exemplified by Antigone, he is concerned with the family in a stateless tribal society. When Hegel describes the role of the woman in the ethical ethos of the family in *Philosophy of Right,* however, he is addressing modernity. This involves a family member who has a will by virtue of being conscious of her or his autonomy from the objectivity of consciousness in the family and in civil society. We have observed that the philosopher need not be concerned with prehistory or prelegality, according to Hegel. A state, external to the subject, figures highly in a modern ethos. The woman acts as if she were a natural being in civil society because she does not yet feel separate from the family customs. She experiences immediacy with such customs. One needs to be cautious, therefore, when addressing the role of women in a reflective *Sittlichkeit,* such as civil society, for some observed family members may reflect about the family's universals and others may remain immediate with them.

Further, civil society is an, as yet, incomplete form of ethicality precisely because it presupposes that the individual, separate from others, seizes property in a market economy for the family security. The formal relations that protect the right to property and contract are reified from the social bonding needed to keep the family together. The individual is alone, a unit, a thing to be manipulated, a means to the ends of the arbitrary wills of others, in a civil society (PR 176). Finally, when Hegel ends his section on the family in *Philosophy of Right,* he reminds us that he is not finished with the role of the family for "[m]arriage is still only the immediate [form of the] ethical Idea" (PR 176). Although Hegel says that the family is the primary root of the state in civil society for reasons that I shall explain in the next chapter, ethicality, as the social recognition by one individual of another, develops through the experience of time. As such, the genderized roles in civil society—like any social relationship in any ethos—dissolve with the dissolution of civil society. The whole point of the dissolution of any one presupposed structure of legal consciousness is that the observed subject becomes conscious of his or her changing role in the production of the actuality of universals.

2. FIVE SHAPES OF THE FAMILY

The above three factors—the two forms of consciousness, the cultural sense of a natural being, and the continual movement of self-consciousness through experiential time—work together to give shape or form to different senses of a family. I shall now identify each such shape of a family. Hegel is clear about one shared feature of all forms of the family. The family is generated from something invisible, love, not from a contract as Kant had claimed. Love is a subjective phenomenon. One is a *Mitglieder* or comember of a family. The family member is not the abstract person purged of biography and intentionality. To the contrary. Each member embodies her or his social relations with the family members with experiences that induce assumptions, expectations, rituals, and practices that family members share amongst each other. Each member accepts each other's opinions without question—at least as long as the opinions conform with the universals of the family. One such universal, for example, is deference of children to the authority of the father. In Hegel's view, the family in civil society owns property communally.

a) The Tribal Family

Hegel discusses the archaic family in detail in his description of Antigone's appeal to the binding unwritten traditions of her tribe.[16] He most clearly describes this form of a family in the early paragraphs of chapter VI of *Phenomenology of Spirit* and in two passages in *Philosophy of Right* (PR 144A, 206R). Antigone believes that there is no distinct and assignable author of the laws to which she feels bound. The family members feel so deeply and extensively bonded with the tribal customs that no member would dare contravene them. The customs may not even be communicated through the spoken word. Rather, they are communicated through gestures of the body: dances and rituals communicate the laws. Greek tribal life cannot abstract a time or space from one's very experience.[17] When King Creon sentences her to death by starvation in a cave, such a sentence is unfamiliar and, indeed, beyond tribal memory according to the Haemon (l.692–96), Tireisius (the King's blind advisor) (l. 1000), and the inhabitants (l. 790–804). The tribal members lose their bonding even with the city's laws because of the unusual sentence.

The tribal family enforces its customs by causing angst in the unconscious of the family member. This angst may well be transferred from one generation to the next. Sophocles begins his play, for example, with Antigone expressing angst about her father/brother's incest and then about her leaving her brother's body unburied. The divine laws work through the anguish that would haunt her if she disobeyed the divine laws and allowed the body of her brother to rot in the sun (l.458–70). Antigone does not permit her pride to excuse herself from answering to the gods which oversee the family's customs (l. 458). If Antigone were to disobey the customs, this disobedience "would have grieved me" (l. 468). The justice of the divine laws rests in the netherworld (the underworld) (l. 451). The customs of the tribal family are binding upon its members because the members feel at one with them. Because of the immediacy, Antigone is not aware of being autonomous from the family's tribal customs. Thus, the family member lacks a will. Only when the member has a will can we speak of the individual as a subject separate from the universals of the ethos. Only then can there be a possibility of an ethical relationship amongst individuals.

Now, Hegel explains in chapter VI of *Phenomenology of Spirit* that familial customs seem so uncontrollable that they are like a second nature. Although there were good utilitarian reasons why the eldest of a family should bury the deceased body of a brother/son killed in battle rather than to allow the body to rot in the desert sun and then to cause disease, for example, the tribal family attributed the binding customs to *Moira* or Fate. In the totemic legal culture before a city ever emerged (and before there ever arose a conflict between divine laws and human laws), even the gods were subject to *Moira*.[18] There was no thinking individual in such an ethos. That lack of a thinking being explains why Hegel attributed barbarism to the most undeveloped tribal legal structures. The individual felt so immediate with nature that the customs seemed humanly uncontrolled and uncontrollable (PS 450): the human being could not influence or "repeal" the natural events of drought or disease or desert storms. Tribal customs, though described by Hegel as divine laws, evolved from a dependence upon nature. The customs seemed natural. As Antigone exclaimed when King Creon, her uncle, cross-examined her for violating the city's laws, one does not know when the customs first originated. A custom, after all, has no distinct origin in time or place (a legislative enactment does have such).

b) The Family in Civil Society

The tribal family and the family in civil society remain two separate transient forms in the development of self-consciousness. The tribal family may have been generated from an arranged marriage or a contract. Once a family exists, traditions of the family determine the partners' present and future. The genesis of the family in civil society is love. In the marriage, the family does not arise by virtue of the conferral of legal status onto the two people in love. Love motivates each separate individual to unify into a legal form, the family (PR 203R).

i) Marriage

Each partner in a marriage recognizes her or his dependence upon the other.[19] In civil society, family members manifest this dependence by enforcing contracts and criminal law. The security of the market economy displaces the security of the family. Property now secures the former peace of mind assured by the family. In civil society, each individual is separate from the next and, therefore, each has a will. The marriage manifests the separation of two individuals with separate arbitrary wills. The wedding vows recognize the separate wills of two independent subjects. Before falling in love and marrying, each subject has a will that competes with other wills in a market economy: both are "infinitely particularized individuals" (PR 163R). Hegel explains that "marriage arises out of the *free surrender* by both sexes of their personalities, which are infinitely unique [*eigen*] to themselves" and, as such, "it must not be concluded within the *naturally identical* circle of people" who lack a distinct personality of their own (PR 168).

Accordingly, Hegel frowns upon arranged marriages, so common no doubt in the tribal family, because such marriages lack the self-conscious choice expected in the development of spirit (PR 161). Hegel also objects to associating a marriage with a contract to marry (PR 163R). A contract presupposes two separate arbitrary wills which continue after a contract has been signed. The contract thereby lacks the ethical relationship between two separate individuals into a oneness (PR 163A). So too, romantic love is not the grounds of marriage (PR 161A) because it lacks the self-conscious rational choices expected of the free will. Upon marriage, one marriage partner renunciates her or his autonomy from the other. In place of autonomy, one fuses with the partner into a single person, the family (PR 158A, 162). Marriage thereby sustains the ethical relation of one individual's recognition of the next: marriage produces "rightfully ethical [*rechtlich sittliche*] love, so that the transient, capricious, and purely subjective aspects of love are excluded from it" (PR 161A). Each family member reciprocally recognizes the next.

Love generates the relationship that is institutionalized as a marriage in civil society. The genesis of the family in love as reciprocal recognition, then, is independent of any positive laws that recognize the status of marriage. The genesis is also independent of the intellectual assimilation of one partner over the other. However, the subjective genesis of a family creates an "unstable" relationship which always raises the prospect of dissolution because each partner may eventually act from an arbitrary will rather than from the fused will that initiated the partnership (PR 163A): "there [can] be no merely legal [*rechtliches*] or positive bond which could keep the partners together once their dispositions and actions have become antagonistic and hostile" (PR 176). The legal formality of a marriage, according to Hegel, brings stability to the otherwise subjective union of two individuals: the marriage transforms the merely subjective love into "a *spiritual union*" or "*self-conscious love*" (PR 161). Dyde translates the marriage as "legal ethical love." The ethical relation incorporates the respect and self-conscious dependence of the one individual upon the other so that "love, trust and the sharing of the whole of individual existence [*Existenz*]" characterize the relationship (PR 163). The marriage bond, in turn, becomes "a *lasting* and inherently [*in sich*] universal union" (PR 203R).

In sum, what begins as "the arbitrary moment of the particular need [that is, the arbitrary will] of the *single individual* [*das bloß Einzelnen*] . . . is here transformed, along with the selfishness of desire, into the care and acquisition for a *communal purpose,* i.e. into an *ethical* quality" (PR 170). Each subject becomes conscious of the other through the legal form of the marriage. Each recognizes the other. As a consequence of the reciprocal recognition by the legal form, "the transient, capricious, and purely subjective aspects of love are excluded from it [marriage]" (PR 161A). I become a *member,* not a unit, of a family. I am happy if other units of civil society recognize me as a member of the family. The legal recognition of two partners in love displaces the biological or romantic origins of love (162R). Love is transformed into a "rightfully [that is, legitimate in the wide sense of *Recht*] ethical [*rechtlich sittliche*] love" (PR 161A, 163).

ii) The Family Property

Both formerly separate individuals, each with her or his own will, now recognizes that she or he fuses with the other into a single collective person (PR 167). Now that the family is an ethical ethos (PR 164), the family gains a singular will. Such a singular will representative of the family performs two social functions: first, it possesses and confers a form onto external things of nature; second, it educates the offspring. With respect to the first, the family, as a singular legal person, possesses rights to property and assets: "[t]he family, as a person, has its external reality in *property*; and only in the latter, in the shape of *resources,* does its substantial personality have its existence [*Dasein*]" (PR 169). Here, Hegel is heavily influenced by the Roman law of the family (PR 162, 163) and well he should since, as I showed in Chapter 1, he associates Roman Stoicism with the very legal formalism which characterizes his description of civil society (PS 477). As with Roman law of the classical (or imperial) period (30 B.C.E.–250 C.E.),[20] the individual family member does not attain legal status in civil society until she or he leaves the family, the father dies, or the family dissolves into divorce (PR 159). The children (that is, the male children) are legal persons [*rechtliche*] when they come of age (PR 177). Former family members become "self-sufficient and rightful persons" (PR 180) who provide for the food, shelter, financial resources, costs of education, and other social needs that the family formerly provided (PR 159).[21] They too may create their own families. Individuals may now hold private property. They may also act according to their self-interest. The child develops into adolescence, is transformed from an infant to a member of the family, falls in love, and then journeys into civil society. The male family member begins to identify with the economic framework of such a civil society (PR 201A, 255, 265). Civil society continues and the family—or, at least, this shape of a family—reinforces the structure of consciousness of civil society as the amalgam of separate arbitrary wills. An official of the state in civil society may adjudicate disputes between husband and wife if one or both allow their arbitrary feelings to overwhelm the ethical unity of the family (PR 176).

iii) The Father as Head

Hegel draws another element from the singular legal status of a family in civil society. The family, as a single legal person whose content is composed of several members (not units), needs a single head to represent the family vis-à-vis other legally recognized persons in civil society. To this end, Hegel assigns to the husband the headship of the family for legal purposes much like the monarch represents the person of the state in international law: "[t]he family as a legal [*rechtliche*] person in relation to others must be represented by the husband as its head" (PR 171). Until the male child grows into adolescence and leaves the family, there just has to be one member or some surrogate or trustee to represent the family vis-à-vis other persons in the legal order. As with Roman law, Hegel assigns such a representative role to the male father or husband.

iv) Education

The primary social function of the parents of a family in civil society is to educate their offspring, particularly the boys. This function continues into an organic structure of consciousness as I shall elaborate in Chapter 9.

Since the family originates from love, this phenomenon continues as the parents educate the children to become ethically related with each other and with others in civil society. Trust, respect for the other, the human values of the community, and other ethical relationships are transferred through the family from one generation to the next. In addition, the parents need to awaken the desire of the child to become self-conscious. Interestingly, this requires that the parent coercively lift the child from the self-interested desires "still entrammelled in nature" to the universals of an ethical community which lies potentially immanent in any family (PR 174, 174A).

Hegel is unclear at this point. There are passages where he suggests that the objective of the family is to inculcate *Bildung* in a presupposed structure of legal consciousness which he categorizes as civil society (PR 175). On other occasions, it may be that the family in civil society should teach skills to the child or student without questioning the presupposed universals of the market economy and of possessive individualism that structure civil society (PR 182A, 187R). Clearly, the external state of civil society has the legitimacy and duty to supervise and influence the child's education (PR 239, 239A). "Communal arrangements" need to be provided for such education. But since the structure of legal consciousness in civil society is the market economy which institutionalizes the right of private property, freedom of contract, and crimes, public education, it would seem, needs to be a skills-based training for the marketplace.

c) The Family of the Organic Constitution

Hegel identifies a role of the family in the structure of an organic legal order. I shall describe such an organic structure of legal consciousness in Chapter 9. Suffice at this point for me to suggest that Hegel associates the organic character of the objectivity of consciousness with the domestic reconciliation of the subjectivity with the objectivity of consciousness. One important reason why the individual inhabitant feels reflectively bonded with such an organism, I shall elaborate in the next chapter, is that she or he belongs to intermediate social organizations which, in turn, mediate her or his values with the state and vice versa. The family is the most important such intermediate social organization of the organic legal order.[22] Accordingly, the family functions as a filter to acculturate and educate the child into the shared universals of the organic community.

Thus, although there remains a family in civil society, the shape takes on a new social role in an organic legal order. So, for example, the male child's departure from the family for the greater material goods in the individualist economy is a negative in that the individual is no longer immediate with family members. When the individual becomes a citizen of an organic structure of consciousness that reconciles objectivity with subjectivity, however, the individual leaves the "long, disconnected experiences" of civil society and raises her or his consciousness from the accidents of his status and wealth in civil society to "the calm of simple universality" (PS 451). At that point, the family is merely "an unreal impotent shadow." As a mediating social institution in the organic legal order, the family becomes an intermediate social organization that mediates between the individual and the universals of the objectivity of consciousness. The family no longer functions to acquire property in civil society. That it does. But the family accomplishes more. The family becomes a social organization that mediates the arbitrary will of the individual with the universals of the overall ethos. I shall examine this closer in Chapter 9.

d) The Family as the Ethnic Nation

We are not quite finished identifying the different forms of a family as described by Hegel. Commentators, quite rightly, have been preoccupied with the role of the family in a state-centric objectivity of civil society. But Hegel continues his phenomenological description of the family in the final paragraphs of *Philosophy of Right* and in his *Introduction to the Philosophy of History*. He does so by identifying two forms of the family in an international legal consciousness. One is what today we call the ethnic nation. The second is a family of nations.

An ethnic nation shares a common language, historical symbols, common religious values, a shared collective memory, and other commonalities that constitute the group as an ethnic nation.[23] Hegel defines the ethnic nation as having a community with a "common natural origin or a coming together of scattered family communities under the influence of a dominant power or a voluntary union prompted by interdependent needs and their reciprocal satisfaction" (PR 181R). As with the domestic forms of a family, spirit drives the ethnic nation to seek recognition as a state. The ethnic nation, like the family of the domestic legal order, embodies social actuality even though the international legal order only recognizes states as legal persons. Such an actuality may erupt from the formal constraints of the state. The territorial boundary of the state is one such formal constraint. In each shape of state-centric self-consciousness, the state, like the individual subject in the domestic shapes of legal consciousness, is a mere accident. With the collapse of the family into civil society and from there into an organic legal order and from there into an ethnic nation, one is cautioned against reducing the nature of the family to some one set of social relationships such as those that characterized Antigone's life world.

Although Hegel suggests at one point that the nation is a natural phenomenon because its members, like a tribal family, are united by a common blood origin (PR 181R), he more often emphasizes his now familiar theme that, like a tribal family, the nation is like a "second nature" because religion, language, ethnicity, and customs unify the nation so intimately that individuals feel bonded with the members of the nation. The reflective bonding grows as individuals increasingly become psychologically and economically dependent upon each other.

Laurence Dickey and H. B. Nisbet suggest that Hegel considers such a nation as synonymous with the Greek polis.[24] The nation's supreme achievement is "spiritual self-consciousness" (PH 145–47). H. S. Harris suggests that the shape of self-consciousness in the form of a nation may have different forms of development.[25] The Mongolian invaders lacked any self-consciousness and, therefore, were a "formless" unconscious mass. Without form, the Mongolian invaders lacked a nation and could only wreak a destructive havoc. When the Teutonic tribes invaded Italy, however, they had a consciousness of themselves as a *Volk* and, accordingly, desired to replace the Roman legal and political structure with members of their own tribes. Without such self-consciousness as a *Volk,* the individuals are a *vulgus* (a very low class) rather than a *populus* (PM 544).[26] A mere aggregate of individuals, without the form of a nation, is a "shapeless, wild, blind force" that is self-destructive and lacking in law (PM 544). If a nation lacks the form of a state, the nation is "a futile and useless mass" (PM 549). Hegel believed that England of his day exemplified such a futile and useless mass of individuals.

e) The Family of Nations

The second shape of the family in the international *Recht,* Hegel says, is the family of nations (PR 339A). Such a family historically existed in his day, he believed. The family members shared collective values and memories, assumptions and expectations, and rituals and practices in their relations with each other. As I shall argue in Chapter 10, the international *Recht,* like the family, travels through several presupposed structures of consciousness. When states evolve from abstract monadic persons to reciprocal recognition of each other as states, they begin to take the form of a family. Hegel describes the family of nations in the context of "world history." A "spirit of the world" emerges from within the interstate relations which dominated (European) international law in Hegel's day. This spirit of the world initially takes the form of the "family" of European nations (PR 339A). Hegel explains that "[t]he European nations [*Nationem*] form a family with respect to the universal principle of their legislation, customs, and culture [*Bildung*], so that their conduct in terms of international law is modified accordingly in a situation which is otherwise dominated by the mutual infliction of evils [*Übeln*]" (PR 339A). The assumptions and expectations among the family of nations are unconscious; they are *prejudicia* or prejudgments and expectations. A state may invade another state's territory, for example, because family members inhabit it. Like the archaic family, the family of nations exists as an ethical ethos because the family members recognize each other, albeit without thinking, through their shared cultural, legislated, and customary norms (PR 339A).

3. THE SOCIAL FUNCTION OF THE FAMILY

The family represents a form of *Sittlichkeit* for three reasons. First, in a stateless society, the unwritten laws of the family or clan are associated with divine laws (PS 456, 457). Although it may be difficult for the contemporary lawyer to appreciate that "prelegal" and "prehistorical" tribal cultures possess legally binding norms,[27] Hegel claims that families may be nested in the objectivity of consciousness even though there is no state in the objectivity. The family that Hegel addresses here is not the nuclear family of today but the clan or extended family whose unwritten customs constitute the beginning of thinking: immediacy.

Second, the chief characteristic of the family is the immediacy between the family member and the universals of the ethos of the family. Hegel considers the family member as a "natural" being. The family itself is "the natural phase of ethical life" (PH 113). This natural phase is not a determinative sense of physiochemical nature. Rather, it is a figurative sense which Plato (in *Laws*), Aristotle, and Hegel call a "second nature." Hegel asserts that this second nature "binds the members of the family together" (PH 101). One acts because, as a member of the family, one ought to do so. On occasion, the family member, against her or his better judgment involving reflection about the consequences, commits a crime against the state out of loyalty to the family.

Finally, the family performs different social functions in different presupposed shapes of legal consciousness. For example, because of the immediacy between the consciousness of family members and the universals of the family, the family, as a clan or tribe, represents a "natural" or undeveloped *Sittlichkeit*. However, this is only one form of presupposed structure of legal consciousness. Another is a reflective *Sittlichkeit*. And there are several different forms of reflective *Sittlichkeit* which Hegel identifies in modernity.

As a consequence of the variety of roles that a family plays in the different shapes of ethical life, the family is ignored or, at least, plays a different function in the philosophies of Thomas Hobbes, John Locke, and Jean-Jacques Rousseau. Each of these earlier legal philosophers excludes the family from the modern legal order. For Thomas Hobbes, like Lucretius (99–55 B.C.E.),[28] the state of nature lacks the social relationships characteristic of a family. Indeed, natural beings, for Lucretius and Hobbes, even lack a language. Once one acquires a language, one can make contracts and, when that happens, the beings of civil society can never return to the state of nature.[29] The family is also hardly relevant in the state of nature of John Locke and Jean-Jacques Rousseau.[30] Similarly, because of the immediacy characteristic of the undeveloped *Sittlichkeit* of the family, contemporary Anglo-American legal philosophers, taking their cue from Hart, exclude any legal order characterized by immediacy or presence from the object of study of legality and legal legitimacy. For Hart, immediacy takes two forms. One is the immediacy characteristic of the legal order of a tribe. The other is the immediacy as conscience and emotion: "feelings of compulsion or pressure."[31] The prelegal moment of immediacy in the family, according to Hart, "*haunts* much legal thought" as if it were "a *chain* binding those who have obligations that they are *not free to do what they want* [my emphasis]."[32] And yet, Hart steps from the prelegal into the mediation of concepts and their justifications on faith.

4. CONCLUSION

The self-conscious will proceeds through shape after shape of ethê. In each ethos, the individual feels fulfilled. That fulfilment is short-lived, for the observed subject soon recognizes a still further constraint on her or his freedom. Freedom is important because the individual is driven to become self-conscious as autonomous from objectivity. Such external constraints continue the need for the observed individual to develop her or his consciousness since the constraints are constructed in an objectivity of consciousness (PR 156A). This movement of self-consciousness is "intensely actual" in the context-specific experiences of the subject. The family is one shape of such a personally intense actuality.

The law student today might well be expected to learn about "family law" as if it were "out there" in the posited rules of an objectivity resembling a "second nature." Because the implied structure of legal consciousness fails to reconcile such an objectivity with the subjectivity of family members, the family law succumbs to legal formalism. The reciprocal recognition of family members vis-à-vis each other and vis-à-vis individuals exterior to the family becomes a remainder to the analysis of concepts posited by legislatures and courts. Such a remainder would only become the object of study if the student examined the social relations presupposed in the content of the rules allotted to the subject-matter of family law and if the student examined the social relations in the context of the time-consciousness of the ethos. The externality of the objectivity of consciousness does not entertain an evaluation of social relations between individuals (PR 156A). Nor can the legal scholar, in such an approach, study the role of the family in any particular ethos in which the observed individual finds her- or himself. The legal formalism of family law, unfortunately, idealizes and separates the family law from the actuality of a self-conscious subject and the ethos. Such a subject continually grows in self-consciousness as she or he becomes ever more conscious of her or his role in the implied structure of legal consciousness which is presupposed in this formalism.

Hegel's primary concern is to raise into philosophic consciousness the structures of consciousness that observed family members presuppose. The philosopher must also become aware as to how the boundaries of such structures have obstructed the autonomy of such members as they begin to think. This requires that the scholar raise to consciousness how shared universals inside and outside the family constrain the observed individual's actions. There is not just one form of obstruction to the observed subject's freedom. There are several: the tribal family, the family as a self-generating unit in civil society, the family as an intermediary in an organic society, the family as an ethnic nation, and the family of nations leading to "world history." Hegel is describing the family, whether in his comments concerning *Antigone* in *Phenomenology of Spirit,* the nuclear family in *Philosophy of Right,* and the family of nations in *Introduction to the Philosophy of History* as examples of these very different forms of a *Sittlichkeit.* There is not just one family. There are several very different families in Hegel's philosophy of law.

The family does continue its form as a community in a cumulative way from shape to shape of self-consciousness. In addition, each shape of the family grows independent of the objectivity of consciousness, whether the objectivity is external to subjectivity (as in civil society) or is embodied with subjectivity (as in an organic legal order). However, in each case, the philosopher recognizes a very different relationship between the family member and the shared customs of the family. The ethical relations of family members lie immanent in the continuous immanent transformation of the family into higher and higher forms of self-consciousness. The family is a genuinely communitarian social organization. The family is also an ethical relationship because, after the philosopher recognizes the emergence of something new about the family after the tribal family, the individual recognizes strangers outside the family. I shall next expand upon the latter point and elaborate several further forms of an ethical ethos which, in each case, offers a differing role for the family.

CHAPTER EIGHT

The Laws of Civil Society

This is the point where the ethos of civil society (*Bürgerliche Gesellschaft*) enters into the development of legal consciousness. Hegel claims that civil society is not any ethos. It is an ethical ethos. We need to understand why civil society is considered ethical because the description of civil society as an ethical ethos seems counterintuitive in that the individualism of the arbitrary will dominates civil society. A formalism of rights and duties permeates civil society (PR 155).[1] The formalism of rights and duties reinforces the rupture between the self-conscious subject and the objectivity of consciousness.[2]

In order to understand why civil society exhibits ethicality, we need to gain a grasp of the identity of law in civil society. What is the character of civil society? Second, how does civil society manifest ethicality? an ethos? Third, how are intermediate organizations and the external state exhibited in civil society? Fourth, how is it legitimate? And finally, how does legal reasoning become mere formalism that is reified from the subjective freedom? In this chapter I shall address each of these issues in turn. Once the philosopher appreciates, however, how the civil society replicates the legal formalism described in Chapter 5, the philosopher will journey into the final domestic shape of domestic legal consciousness: the organic legal order.

I. THE CHARACTER OF CIVIL SOCIETY
AS A *SITTLICHKEIT*

The question that we must first address is, "what is the character of this ethos that emerges from a tribal legal order?" In particular, how is it possible that a legal order, which protects the arbitrary will of the individual, remains nested in the objectivity of consciousness? The basic thrust of Hegel's idea of a civil society is that the intersubjective social relationships are estranged from the presupposed objectivity of consciousness (PR 181–86). Given such social alienation, how could Hegel consider civil society an ethical ethos?

a) Subjectivity

As individual members leave the family for the greater objects of possession in civil society, the family slowly dissolves into "a multitude of separate atoms" (PS 476). The observed individual in civil society thereupon "proceeds atomistically and moves upward from the basis of individuality [*Einzelheit*]" to the shared universals of an organic legal order (PR 156A). Each atom is defined by posited rules in statutes (PR 184A). The rules posit rights and duties. This network of posited rules, though, is external to the atom. The family, which had offered a protective ethos for the family member, now becomes an obstacle to the "*self-sufficient individuals* [*Einzelnen*]" (PR 157).

At first sight, the emergent civil society marks the final subjective freedom of the individual. As Hegel describes civil society, "each individual is his own end, and all else means nothing to him" (PR 182A). The observed individual promotes her or his own self-interest without regard for the other. The guiding criterion of action is the subject's own personal standard of what counts as a good particularity (that is, a good desire or need) and what does not. My desires posit ends. My values struggle against your values. I act morally if I respect the inner freedom of all strangers to posit their arbitrary wills. Criminal codes, mental health acts, judicially created tort doctrines, and other posited rules protect my inner freedom. All other individuals—including one's family, spouse, children, friends, and colleagues—function as a means to my ends. Gans records Hegel's introductory lectures regarding civil society in this way: "the whole [of civil society] is the sphere [*Boden*] of mediation in which all individual characteristics [*Einzelheiten*], all aptitudes, and all accidents of birth and fortune are liberated, and where the waves of all passions surge forth, governed only by reason which shines through them. Particularity, limited by universality [of individual legal rights], is the only standard by which each particular [person] promotes his welfare" (PR 182A). And if a stranger transverses the legally delineated boundary of freedom—so well described by John Stuart Mill in *On Liberty*—the stranger harms my freedom of choice.[3] Hegel describes the court, as the guardian of such a boundary, as "the Third."

So, three principles characterize civil society: first, the monadic individual chooses her or his own ends; second, the monad depends upon others to satisfy her or his desires and needs (PR 182); third, a formalistic legal structure protects the first two principles. Bearing in mind Hegel's distinction between a person and a subject discussed in Chapter 1, the legal structure of civil society protects abstract empty persons, not intentional subjects.[4] The persons possess equal rights to property, not social equality. The three principles reinforce each other to inculcate a formal framework which protects the individual pursuit of economic self-interest.[5]

The subject is bonded to the institutional framework because it protects her or his arbitrary will. Despite the bonding of the subject to this framework, the structure fails to be reconciled with the subjective freedom of the individual. Each individual needs others to fulfill her or his own arbitrary will. Such intersubjective dependence is institutionalized in a contract. I recognize the other in the contract. But I do so as a self-absorbed subject with an arbitrary will. I use the stranger as a means to fulfill my ends, however idealistic her or his motives of action. If I think of myself as at home in a community, I am deceived. For I am recognized as having legal status in an institutionally constructed, but highly reified, institutional structure. Further, beneath the formalism of posited legal rights and duties, the stranger is my potential enemy. Distrust, deceit, and self-interest characterize such a social dependence. The formal laws, which protect such self-interest, remain estranged from my subjectivity. The posited rights and duties of legal formalism fail to access my private self-regarding actions.

b) Objectivity

Objectivity in civil society involves several universals. What are the universals of civil society? First, the universals include personhood, property, contract, and security of protection from public harm. Courts and public authorities enforce such universals even though the universals are alienated from the subject's self-consciousness in context-specific circumstances (PR 183). Second, the inner freedom of choice, which protects the arbitrary will, is a universal in the sense that this sense of negative freedom is shared amongst persons. The arbitrary will is internal to the individual's subjectivity. The concepts of personhood, property, contract, and public harm are external to such subjectivity. The effort to reconcile the two fails to address how each subject recognizes the other because only the arbitrary will counts as subjectivity. Third, the structure of consciousness includes the invisible hand of the market which, in turn, protects the atom's unlimited possessive self-interest. The arbitrary will dominates the marketplace. Fourth, another series of universals are intermediate between the observed individual and the institutional objectivity: charities, corporations, the public authorities, and international contracts. In sum, freedom of choice, the invisible arm of the market and the concepts of personhood, property, contract, public authorities, and crime constitute some of the shared universals of civil society.

The most important universal in civil society, though, is the state external to self-consciousness. Although private property gives emotional and economic security (PR 238), the success of civil society coincides with extreme poverty and disparities of wealth. Because of the disparity of wealth, the state must provide a minimum floor for social and economic security (PR 241). Further, the marketplace leaves the individual's future uncontrolled (PR 240). Accordingly, the external state is needed to supplement the objectivity of consciousness in civil society. The state needs to create institutions to adjudicate and arbitrate private disputes (civil wrongs) between the arbitrary wills. There must be further institutions to enforce and punish criminals who challenge the legitimacy of the legal order (public wrongs).

The critical issue is this: how is it possible that each monad can pursue its own self-interest and yet, that this be in the interest of the external state? This issue raises subsidiary questions. How does the state fulfill a social function in a cultural milieu of the acquisition of property interests in external things of nature? The gist of Hegel's response is that "[i]n furthering my end, I further the universal [the objective institutions and posited rules], and this in turn furthers my end" (PR 184A). Although Isaiah Berlin's negative freedom pictures the state as an external constraint upon one's ends,[6] Hegel insists that even the state of civil society is indispensably linked to subjective consciousness. This rational nexus concerns the individual's pursuit of private property and the individual's private conscience. The state is thereby related to subjectivity despite the separation of the arbitrary will from objectivity represented by the external state.

More specifically, first, the state posits institutions and rules that protect and secure the property and contracts that the atomistic individuals will (PR 249). The rights to property and contract reinforce the boundary of the inner sphere of life of the arbitrary will. Such rights thereby protect a particular class which thrives on the right to possess property: the bourgeoisie. Second, the state institutionalizes procedures to arbitrate and mediate disputes between property-holding individuals. The disputes are arbitrated with reference to the posited laws of the state. Third, the state functions to set a minimum economic baseline to prevent poverty-stricken individuals from becoming alienated from the ethos of civil society. The public authorities of the state and charitable institutions protect such a baseline. If the state could not redistribute wealth by taxation, the bourgeoisie would lack the universal needed to ensure the psychological security that has been lost with the dissolution of the tribal family (PR 184A). Chaos would erupt. Fourth, the external state institutionalizes schools and universities. Public education inculcates the universals into the future *bourgeoisie* of the civil society as well as the public servants who enforce the universals. In sum, there needs to be an external state even in a life-world or *Umwelt* dominated by the unlimited pursuit of the arbitrary will.

2. THE ETHICALITY OF CIVIL SOCIETY

Perhaps one can gain a better idea of Hegel's sense of ethicality in civil society by turning to two elements of ethicality: first, self-conscious action, and second, the relation of the individual's action to that of a stranger.

First, with respect to self-conscious action, the individual is an autonomous monad that pursues its own self-interest: "[i]n civil society, each individual is his own end, and all else means nothing to him" (PR 182A).[7] The subject is presupposed to be self-sufficient. Success is believed to be the consequence of the self's action rather than from luck, nature, or the virtuous action of oneself or of others.

Second, with respect to the relation of such an individual with others in civil society, "each has the other as its condition" (PR 184A). Each individual depends upon others to fulfill one's economic self-interest. Dependence does not cohere with self-determination, though. Freedom is supposed to be self-developing although the individual eventually recognizes her- or himself in the stranger and the stranger in her- or himself. The objectivity of consciousness incorporates institutions that play a role in mediating and adjudicating the dependency. The institutional mediation is shared between two arbitrary wills. Hegel explains that "through its reference to others," the particularities of one individual are shared with another: universals take form. Legislation, the state's courts, and public authorities constrain the unlimited pursuit of property. In addition to posited rules, there need to be institutions, such as courts, to arbitrate between private disputes (PR 157). In addition, *Verstand* is the form of reason that the courts use to adjudicate disputes since concepts (known today as rules, principles, and doctrines) constitute the units of legality (PR 182A). The concepts are units, not members, of the objectivity of consciousness. Judicial institutions, on behalf of the state, become a third party (what Hegel calls "the Third") with regards to disputes over property and contracts.

Social relationships are estranged, though, from the Third because the Third only defines differences amongst individuals as intellectual differences rather than as social differences in intersubjectivity. Further, the Third is established and appointed by the external state so that it is tilted in favor of one of the parties in criminal and constitutional issues before the Third.

More generally, the social estrangement from objectivity works to render the atomistic unit of civil society as forever unhappy. Emmanuel Levinas's insight about the ego's unlimited desire to colonize and totalize social relations would seem to be appropriate regarding the *Sittlichkeit* of civil society. The observed individual of the ethos of civil society is a monad who uses strangers to fulfill the arbitrary will: the monad "cannot accomplish the full extent of his ends without reference to others; these others are therefore means to the end of the particular [person]" (PR 182A). Because the individual acts as if all strangers are a means to one's arbitrary values, intersubjective *social* recognition with strangers is impossible. I cannot recognize the stranger as different from me. The monadic unit struggles against strangers much as Hobbes described the state of nature and as Hegel describes the master-slave relationships as I recounted in Chapter 4: "the private interest of each individual comes up against that of everyone else" (PR 289R). The externality of the state, its courts as the Third, and the state's conferral of personhood into beings by virtue of posited rights and duties—these elements of the objectivity of consciousness separate one monad from another. The courts are the guardian of this separation.

Thus, a tension permeates civil society. On the one side, the intentional subject feels at home in her or his estate, corporation, family, guild, university, and the like. On the other side, the universal rules and institutions of the state are external to such intermediate social relationships. As a consequence of the rupture between subject and object, self and stranger, inhabitant and state, social relations become alienated from the formalism of the objectivity of consciousness. Legality excludes consideration of the development of time-consciousness as subjective or an "ought" unrelated to binding laws. Legal forms define a fictitious reality.[8] Civil society is "lost in extremes" between particularity on the one hand and formalism on the other (PR 184A). Civil society "in the first instance [marks] the loss of ethical life" (PR 181).

3. WHY IS CIVIL SOCIETY AN ETHOS?

A question comes to the fore already. If the monad is so self-reliant and self-determinative of her or his own arbitrary will, how could Hegel possibly consider such a civil society as exhibiting an ethos? After all, the recognition of another human subject is as an empty legal person whom I can use to fulfill my arbitrary will.

One important factor in the ethos of civil society is Hegel's introduction of the role of intermediate organizations. Examples of intermediate organizations are the nuclear family, the corporation, the class, and charities. Religious organizations might be a further example. The monad works, socializes, and develops through such social groups. The individual becomes emotionally dependent upon other members in the association. The more bonded is the monad with strangers in an intermediate social organization, the deeper are one's duties to other members in the organization and, indirectly, to other strangers outside the organization to the extent that all share universal norms (PR 150). In contrast with the virtues about which Aristotle wrote, one's virtues in a civil society are drawn from one's station in the particular social organization.[9] Faith and trust enter into one's outlook when one reflects about the objectivity of consciousness as a member of such organizations.[10] When bonded with an intermediate social organization, one does not reflect as if one authored her or his ideas and outlook. Rather, one's reflections are drawn from shared assumptions and expectations in the intermediate social organizations. Indeed, individuals become so bonded with each other in intermediate social organizations that they share "a relationship which is immediate and closer to identity than even [a relationship of] *faith* or *trust*" (PR 147). For this very reason, Plato, in contrast, elaborated a theory of justice that prevented the rise of such intermediate organizations.

Such intermediate social associations of civil society do not override the subjectivity of the individual. To the contrary. The individual *chooses* to join an association, Hegel argues. The individual has a self-interest that requires that she or he participate in the universals of the estate. But the longer that one bonds with strangers in any intermediate association, "the *selfish* end which pursues its own particular interest comprehends [*faßt*] and expresses itself at the same time as a universal end" (PR 251). So, the civil society, driven by self-seeking atomistic individuals, is ameliorated by social organizations which such an individual joins. Social bonding with intermediate organizations compensates for the estrangement of the self-sufficient monad from the legal formalism of the objectivity of consciousness.

4. SHAPES OF INTERMEDIATE ORGANIZATIONS

a) The Family

In the previous chapter I identified several different senses of the family in the various structures of legal consciousness. The nuclear family in civil society has a very different content and role than the extended tribal family even though the shape, characterized by an unreflective immediacy, remains the same.[11] The tribal family exists without some higher state institution whereas the family in civil society plays an intermediary role between family member and the state. Indeed, Hegel claims that the nuclear family is the foremost intermediate social organization in civil society: "[t]he *family* is the first *ethical* root of the state; the *corporation* is second, and it is based in civil society" (PR 255). Again, "the family is the primary basis of the state, the estates [that is, social classes] are second" (PR 201A) and the family is "the inner roots of the state" (1817/18 122R). Despite its role with respect to the education of universals into the children, however, the family is an island in a sea of possessive individualism.

How does the family play a role in the ethicality of such a civil society dominated by possessive individualism? The family members care for each other. The family member accepts whatever the family gifts to her or him. The family contrasts with the unlimited acquisition of property in civil society. Feelings bond the family members together (PR 166, 203A). The direct bonding of child with the family and of parent with the family indirectly functions as a source of bonding with the social ethos of civil society. Parents inculcate the universals of personhood, property, contract, crimes, and the justice of the marketplace into the observed individual's consciousness of objectivity. The family compensates the estrangement of the monad from others in civil society. As a consequence of these factors, the family provides the environment, first, for the family member to feel secure against the struggle for economic worth, and second, for the individual to think about the external objectivity. Hegel's point is that the family is such an important part of the ethos of civil society that any effort to displace the family by the state would be artificial. Indeed, Renata Selecl describes how the Soviet state attempted to displace individual autonomy with legal formalism. The individual survived the alienation from the formalism with humor in intersubjective relations. Conversely, a literal application of the state's edicts would lead to madness.[12] Clearly, the family is a very special form of social organization.

b) Corporations (Korporationen)

The bonding that characterizes the family is imitated in other intermediate organizations. One such organization is the corporation (PR 252, 255R, 288). Hegel describes the corporation as a "second family" which constrains the unlimited desires of the individual (PR 253R). In one lecture, Hegel states that the corporation provides the common interest amongst self-seeking individuals (1817/18 121R).

Hegel's idea of a corporation is not ours today, though.[13] Far from it. Hegel has in mind the guild that was pronounced during the Hanseatic League of the late Middle Ages (thirteenth to seventeenth centuries) in northern Europe. Hegel understands a corporation as more like what we would today consider an industrial, trade, or professional association. Perhaps a contemporary professional society, such as the legal or the medical, comes closest to what Hegel intended by the "corporation." The association admits its own members, protects them, and trains prospective members (PR 252). Only members of the *Heimat* or village, for example, were nationals and thereby entitled to legal protection following World War I. Like the *Heimat* of Hegel's day, Hegel's corporation had a duty to protect unemployed members (PR 253).

The key idea here is that, as with the family, the corporation is the medium of bonding between individual and state: "[i]n short, it has the right to assume the role of a *second* family for its members" (PR 252).[14] The corporation supplements the otherwise "limited share" of the individual in the functioning of the state (PR 255A). The corporation is the second ethical root of the organic state, the *Sittlichkeit* (PR 255), which I shall examine in the next chapter. If a member challenges the assumptions and expectations of such a corporation, the member may well be expelled or shunned.[15] Conversely, without the bonding with social organizations, civil society leaves an observed individual "isolated." Further, the poor are left in contingent, unjust, and "humiliating" circumstances (PR 253R).

I shall take up one interesting element of the phenomenon of intermediate social organizations in the Conclusion chapter. Without doubt, Hegel claimed that such organizations are generated internally from the will's recognition of strangers. Further, the individual chooses which organizations to join. But once an organization exists socially, the external state confers legal status onto it: "[I]t is only through legal recognition that a community becomes a corporation" (PR 253R). This legal recognition remains important in civil society: "a community can *exist* in civil society only if it is legally constituted and recognized" (PR 253R). The corporation, in brief, becomes an instrument of the objectivity of consciousness, independent of subjectivity.

c) Economic Class ("Estate")

One's economic class, again a matter of choice according to Hegel, also bonds members into a social whole. Hegel identifies three classes: the peasantry and landholding class, the bourgeois class, and the universal class (PR 201–07). He calls them "estates."[16] Although a unit of the economic system, each individual chooses a class and becomes bonded with it over time. Each class has its own means of work, mode of satisfaction, and form of education (both theoretical and practical) (PR 201).

Hegel describes the first estate, the peasantry and landholding class, much as he describes, as we saw in the previous chapter, the woman in the family in civil society: both live close to nature (PR 204A). For the peasant, nature is the external thing to be exploited and known. Education, religion, and civil law hardly impact upon the peasant. Much like the person who wills property, the peasant reflects little about the relationship between the peasant and the objectivity. Passive intellectually, trust is important to the peasant (PR 203). As with family members, the peasant bonds with her or his estate as if the estate were also "a second nature." Satisfaction comes with work and "the tranquility of civil law." Unlike the barbarian, though, the peasant does share a certain level of development of self-consciousness. Further, in contrast with the lowest rank of barbarism (nomadism), the peasant lives in a fixed geographical location (PR 203R). The peasant class plays an important social role in the organic legal order which I shall address in the next chapter (PR 306–07).

The bourgeois estate, protected by the formal legal framework, is the second estate. Tradesmen, industrialists, and businessmen, in contrast with the peasant, reflect about the choices they have (PR 204A). Although the peasant considers nature as the object of possession, the bourgeois accepts money as the object of self-interest. *Verstand* is the bourgeois method of learning (PR 203A, 204). Learned objects are products to be used. Products, manufactured and processed, are represented by monetary signs. The signs become the shared universals of civil society. Even social needs, such as food, housing, and clothing, are signified by their exchange value. The signs represent the necessities as signified objects. The signified objects are concepts that mediate between the individual's self-interest and the exchange economy (PR 204). Bourgeois reasoning is instrumental in that it examines the means used to accomplish the objective posited by the arbitrary will.

The third class is a universal class that oversees and protects the universals of personhood, property, contract, public crimes, the invisible hand of the market, intermediate organizations, and state institutions. This class includes legislators and judges (PR 201–07). The member of the universal class acts from the spirit of universality rather than from the self-interest of a bourgeois. This is so because the universal class has been educated to comprehend the overall *telos* of the ethos (PR 205). Even law reform addresses how to codify the regulation and protection of the arbitrary will. Public servants mediate and arbitrate economic disputes amongst the self-serving bourgeois and peasants. Public servants need to persuade parents that the universal class joins with personal self-interests in the long run (PR 239). Public education aims to inculcate the universals of civil society.

Although the individual might have a natural affinity toward the estate, Hegel clearly writes that the individual chooses her or his own estate (PR 206R). Hegel wishes to depart from the determinism of *Moira,* nature, the polis, birth (the Indian culture), and tradition (the medieval feudal system). Even Oedipus was chosen king by luck, for example: namely, by his response to a riddle. Although birth and natural abilities do play a part in one's choice of a class in civil society, one will, for the most part, choose her or his estate, according to Hegel. Indeed, subjective choices become the "sole animating principle of civil society" (PR 206R).

The common feature of each estate is the member's bonding with others in the estate. On the one hand, at the subjective level, the member of the estate, by virtue of her or his choice of the estate, feels at home in the estate: "the subject, . . . as a *particular* entity in relation to the particularity of the objective realm, has its own particular content in its end, and this is the soul and determinate of the action" (PR 121). On the other hand, the members' choices are rooted in their particular arbitrary wills. Thus, the intermediate organizations mirror the arbitrary will of the member: the subjectivity is incorporated into the collective assumptions and expectations of the estate. The shared assumptions and expectations of the estate paradoxically provide a context of expression which constrains the arbitrary will at the same moment that the external state protects the arbitrary will in the inner sphere of life (PR 207).

d) Charitable Institutions

The fourth intermediate social organization in civil society is a charitable association (PR 245). The unlimited pursuit of property will lead to large-scale unemployment and economic poverty. Forced labor might be one "solution." But in a market economy, this would lead to overproduction as there will be an insufficient number of consumers to purchase products. Hegel turns to England and Scotland as examples of this (PR 245R). Voluntary charitable associations are a better solution than unemployment and poverty, Hegel says. Aside from bypassing the dynamics of the laissez-faire economy, a charity offers love (PR 242), something that the unlimited desire for property does not provide.

5. FUNCTION OF THE EXTERNAL STATE IN CIVIL SOCIETY

I have emphasized that the universals of civil society are personhood, property, contract, security of the person, the marketplace, the intermediate organizations, and the role of courts as a third party to private disputes. The external state is another such universal.[17] All universals are external to the self-consciousness of the individual. The state, along with the institutional structure, supplements the objectivity which conceals the arbitrary will. The four intermediate organizations mediate between the above-mentioned universals and the arbitrary will of the subject. The social organizations generate from their own social impetus at the same time that they are conferred legal status by state institutions. Only the charities are not so recognized. The question we must now face is, "what are the functions of this external state?"

a) Educational Institutions

The external state creates institutions of lower and higher learning (PR 239, 239A). Educational institutions socially function as intermediaries between the individual and the external state (and other institutions of objectivity) (PR 187, 239). Because the arbitrary will dominates the supplementary legal structure, there has to be a universal class (including judges, civil servants, teachers, and professors) to protect the institutionalized and implicit structure of consciousness (PR 205, 187, 187R). Instead of corrupting the immediacy of the family, as Rousseau complained (PR 187R), education inculcates the universals into the child so that the child will become a good citizen. Unless education succeeds in doing so, civil society will dissolve into the never-ending struggle of arbitrary wills.

It makes sense that, given the freedom of choice of the arbitrary will in civil society, the purpose of education is to tool the child with the "tasteless" *bourgeois* culture of the skilled knower (PR 187A). *Verstand* will help (PR 187R). Even the potential members of the universal class will learn how the market operates and how the individual and the state should acquire wealth in the marketplace. Rather than being considered the enemy of the monadic individual, the state will protect, guide, and enforce the market framework. Hegel describes the child/student of civil society much as he had described the barbarian: both are lazy, self-absorbed in a "dull and solitary brooding," preoccupied with learning skills in the consumer society, and living a vulgar life style (PR 197A). Only the potential member of the universal class is taught "true originality" (PR 187A), but this originality, again, is skills-oriented rather than *Bildung* (PR 182A, 187R).

b) Taxation and Welfare

The second function of the external state in civil society is to tax capital, to watch over the wealthy in order to prevent them from living in extravagance (PR 240, 240A), and to feed the economically depraved (PR 240A).[18] The market economy will inevitably produce widespread differences in wealth and poverty (PR 243, 244). Capital begets capital. Hegel lectured along the same lines in 1824/25 that "[t]he greater is one's capital, the greater are the undertakings one can support with it, and the lesser are the profits required to satisfy the possessor; all of this increases the capital yet more" (1824/25 W181). And again, he said, because many will work for minimal wages in civil society, the "lesser capitalists fall into poverty" (1824/25 W181). The rabble is created "by the disposition associated with poverty, by inward rebellion against the rich, against society, the government etc." (PR 244A). The objectivity of consciousness may become politically unstable because the masses, as autonomous beings who determine objectivity, may become conscious that they do not deserve their depravity and that the wealthy do not deserve their excessive wealth. This requires the minimum economic standard of the "the livelihood and welfare of individuals" (PR 230R). Further, luck combines with extreme poverty to reinforce the widespread lack of self-respect that accompanies the economic sinking of large masses of peoples (PR 224). Luck is arbitrary and, as such, anathema to the rational choices that one makes in the marketplace. Nature determines physical disabilities, for example, and this weakens one's ability to acquire wealth (PR 241).

c) International Legal Transactions

The domestic overproduction of consumer goods in civil society impacts internationally. In particular, the overproduction will lead to the need of civil society to colonize or to expand its markets to colonies (PR 246).[19] The monad will need strangers in other states. Trading links will be formed with colonies and other states: they are "the greatest educational asset [*Bildungsmittel*] and the source from which commerce derives its world-historical significance" (PR 247). Colonial expansion, like war, is inevitable for a civil society (PR 248, 248A). For colonialism depends upon international legal transactions for the marketing and supply of goods.

d) Public Authorities

The final function of the external state is to prevent widespread disparities of wealth and to ensure a minimal social security. To these ends, the external state creates public authorities.[20] The public authorities, for example, institutionalize the economic framework for subjective freedom (PR 232). They administer a minimum standard of welfare for the civil society (1817/18 p. 207, fn 45). In addition, they administer public utilities (such as street lighting), bridge building, the fixing of prices for necessities, and the provision of public health (PR 235, 236A). The public authorities also need to prevent fraud. Not unlike his view of crime, Hegel suggests that the extreme pursuit of self-interest may cause public harm to the legitimacy of objective freedom itself (PR 233). The role of public authorities thereby reinforces the legitimacy of the universals. The guarantee of a minimum welfare is one such universal (PR 231).

Contrary to the conservative-liberal ideology in North America today, the civil society's external state is not considered the enemy of the bourgeois after all. As Hegel puts it, the presupposed *Sittlichkeit* of civil society opposes the idea "that the police [public authorities] should have oversight over everything" (PR 236A). Instead, the external state ensures that the legal framework to pursue private property remains open to all. Minimum welfare ensures the stability and legitimacy of the pursuit of arbitrary will.

As a third party to private disputes, courts arbitrate and adjudicate the private disputes. Even universities are needed to train lawyers, engineers, doctors, teachers, and future public servants in the skills and instrumental rationality needed in the marketplace. Max Horkheimer and Theodor Adorno later pick up Hegel's focus upon the role of instrumental rationality in civil society.[21] The more complex and penetrating the culture of private enterprise, the greater the need for public authorities to constrain the arbitrary will of individuals. State agencies thereby ameliorate the number and intensity of economic conflicts as well as the risk of alienation by those who, through bad luck or disparity of capital, become conscious of economic injustice (PR 236R). To suggest that the role of public authorities in a civil society is to institutionalize a police state is absurd.

e) The Third

The courts also provide an important role in civil society.[22] The court, as an agent of the state, is external to subjective freedom. The judges need not examine the historical reasons why some legal rule arose (PR 119R). Nor need the judges relate the content of a rule to patriarchal hierarchy, coercion, or free choice. Nor does it matter that legal formalism, particularly as judicial reasoning, disguises violence. *Verstand* is the *modus operandi* of legal reasoning in civil society. In the spirit of *Verstand,* the court clarifies the boundary of the rules posited by the institutional objectivity, identifies the criteria that transcend the rules, analogizing from one rule to a revised rule, and then applies the criteria to concepts about the facts in phenomena. Since intellectualization determines the differences between one rule and another, the rule is self-standing in the sense of lacking any referent other than another rule. More than any other public authority in civil society, a judge does not exercise choice (PR 219R): "[t]his *cognition* and *actualisation* of right in the particular case, without the subjective feeling [*Empfindung*] of *particular* interest, is the responsibility of a public authority [*Macht*], namely the court of law" (PR 219). As Kant cautioned, according to Hegel, the judge must not inquire as to why posited rules are binding (PR 220, 222). The court is a guardian of the institutional objectivity of consciousness (PR 221). As such, the court adjudicates between private interests and thereby reinforces the framework whereby individuals pursue their own self-interest. Litigation helps to make the observed individual aware of the universals of such a framework (PR 96R, 218R, 218A, 218R). The objectivity of the institutional structure is accepted as a "given" (PR 218R).

6. THE LEGITIMACY OF THE LEGAL ORDER
IN CIVIL SOCIETY

The rupture between objectivity and subjectivity remains in civil society even though the civil society is a *Sittlichkeit*. The rupture separates the objectivity of universals such as property, contract, the marketplace, and external state from the subjectivity of the arbitrary will. This gulf requires that the philosopher addresses what renders a legitimacy to judicial reasoning in civil society (PR 216R).

First, the objectivity of civil society, in order to be legitimate, requires a closure to disputes between arbitrary wills. In a distinction which Raz develops,[23] Hegel explains that once a judicial decision is made, the official is excluded from deliberating about the content of the decision. The decision even excludes the incorporation of the judge's personal arbitrary will (PR 224R). A decision, to be a decision, ends the debate about the merits of its content. The judicial decision is legitimate by virtue of its institutional source in the state bureaucracy.

As a second factor of the legitimacy of the objectivity of civil society, it is important that rules be codified (PR 209, 211A). The codification must not just reenact a customary norm. That would reduce the flux of legality into indeterminacy, incompleteness, and an absence of systematicity. If the codification proceeds in an orderly and specific manner that is accessible to all inhabitants, an important attribute of justice is satisfied (PR 215R). "[L]ong and arduous work" is required to render "simple and adequate expression" of a rule (PR 217R). In order to intellectually distinguish one rule from another, the monad needs to know what are the two rules. Codification aids in this endeavor:

> the spirit . . . knows and wills itself as having *passed through the form of education*. The state therefore *knows* what it wills, and knows it in its *universality* as something thought. Consequently, it acts and functions in accordance with known ends and recognized principles, and with laws which are laws not only *in themselves* but also for the consciousness; and it likewise acts in determinate knowledge [*Kenntnis*] of existing circumstances and relations in so far as its actions have relevance to these. (PR 270)

Such was Napoleon's contribution to the European peoples, Hegel believes.[24]

There are several other points that Hegel makes about the need for a legislature or court to codify customs in civil society. First, customary norms reflect the "drives, customs [*Sitten*], and feelings" of uncivilized peoples (PR 211A). In contrast with the customs of the stateless condition, a code is authored by an institution such that deliberation and reflection about the content of the rules precede their enactment (PR 218A, 218R). Second, a custom is "obscure" and, as a consequence, only judges and lawyers, not the people, are privileged to know its content (PR 211R). Third, a custom is "subjective and contingent" in that it manifests the arbitrary wills of a people. A custom thereby undermines the need for a fixity and certainty in commercial contracts. Fourth, because of the indeterminacy and incompleteness of a custom, confusion results from customs as the English common law exhibited according to Hegel. What is a customary rule? The Emperor Justinian resolved this question by institutionalizing a college of jurists to posit customs as a code known as the "law of citations." He also burned all previous law books so that lawyers would have no dispute as to what were the customs.

A third factor making for the legitimacy of the objectivity of civil society is that legal reasoning depends on the capacity of inhabitants to access the institutions and rules of the state (PR 221A, 224). Legal knowledge is needed before one can prove one's legal claim (PR 222A). When the legal process is publicized, the citizenry will be "thereby convinced that justice [*Recht*] is actually being done" and the citizenry will more likely accept the decision (PR 224A).

A fourth factor of objectivity's legitimacy is that a lengthy and formal legal process undermines legitimacy (PR 216). The latter diverts attention from the harm caused. In order to overcome such a problem, there may be a need for a "simple court," such as a court of arbitration or a preliminary hearing, or for that matter, a court of equity. A court of equity reaches a decision on an individual case "without adhering to the formalities of the legal process and in particular to the objective evidence as the law may interest it" (PR 223R).

Finally, legitimacy in civil society requires that the public participate in the judicial process. The subject's mere presence at a trial "counts for little" (PR 228R). The subject needs to be present "in spirit and with their own knowledge." With participation in the judicial process, trust is inculcated in the objective institutions (1817/18 116.153). This is Hegel's ultimate justification for a jury trial (PR 228R). If judicial decisions are made without a jury, judges express a "foreign language" (PR 228R). Social alienation is the consequence: "[i]n this situation, members of civil society, who depend on their livelihood on *their activity, their own knowledge [Wissen] and volition*, remain *alienated* not only from their own personal interests but also from the substantial and rational basis of these, namely *right*, and they are reduced to a condition of *tutelage*, or even a kind of serfdom, in relation to the class [*Stand*] in question" (PR 228R).

The risk that the judiciary will become increasingly bureaucratized is real: "a distinct profession to which individuals must devote themselves completely" evolves with the consequence that knowledge of such laws "becomes all the more alien to the mass of the people" (1817/18 116R153).[25] When combined with the complex and foreign vocabulary and grammar of a code, the code will likely appear as "a closed, incomprehensible book for the great mass of the people" (1817/18 116.153).

In sum, Hegel identifies five criteria for the legitimacy of the legal process in civil society: a final judicial decision must bring closure to deliberation; the laws must be inscribed; rules, procedures, and reasoning must be accessible to the public; legal institutions need to be constructed to avoid the time-consuming complexities of courts; and the public needs to participate. The five criteria were missing from the "primitive institutions" of the tribe (PR 216R), the Roman legal process (PR 180R), and feudal legal systems (PR 216R). The five factors share this one principle: "right must be known in thought, it must be a system in itself, and only as such can it have any validity among civilized [*gebildeten*] nations" (PR 211A). The conditions work to encourage a bonding between the individual and the legal order. If fulfilled, the individual will think about the content of the legal rules. Such a self-consciousness is "the worthiest and most sacred possession of man" (PR 215A). Love, trust, and emotion will manifest the individual's relation with the legal process. The citizen will now recognize public harm to the legitimacy of the universals of the civil society (PR 218R).

7. THE REIFICATION OF LEGAL REASONING

In Chapter 3, I differentiated between two forms of legal reasoning: *Verstand* and *Vernunft*. *Verstand* takes a concept as the self-standing unit of legal knowledge. The knowers differentiate one concept from another. Because such knowledge is content independent, the concepts are "empty" and "dead" (PR 217R, 54, 103, 159).[26] Emotion, love, and trust are unimportant. The analysis of concepts lifts legality above the conscience, intentionality, arbitrary values, and feelings of subjectivity (PR 213A). This formal knowledge is critical to the rise and development of civil society.

a) The Concept as the Unit of Legal Reasoning

For one thing, because the unit of legal knowledge is separate from social phenomena, it is self-standing in that it does not need any referent other than another concept as I explained in Chapter 3. Legality thereby lacks a contingent social content (PR 207R). The sign, which represents a concept, is presumed to be transparent.[27] Today, the concept is often called a rule, sometimes a principle or a policy or a right.

b) The Enclosure of Particulars Inside the Concepts

Hegel explains, in addition, that concepts figure at two stages of legal reasoning in civil society. First, the official identifies the subjectivity of the parties in terms of "the details, circumstances, and objects of sensuous intuition and subjective certainty" (PR 227). Hegel naively believes that, ultimately, the oath guarantees the truthfulness of the litigant's intent (PR 227), although a jury trial is also said to preserve a respect for the intentionality of the parties (PR 227A). Second, legal reasoning categorizes the intent *under* and *inside* the boundaries of the self-standing concepts (PR 214, 225, 225R). The consequence is that "the facts of the case" are categorized in the "endlessly increasing diversity and complexity" of concepts (PR 213, 216A). Even the subjective feelings of "emotion, love and trust" are categorized insofar as such subjective phenomena "contain the aspect of abstract right" (PR 213). Concepts are applied to posited facts. Even facts are categorized in terms of which concept is relevant to the category of social facts (PR 211A). Such facts are brought under the concept and within its boundary. When the lawyer or judge speaks about social "needs," the needs are represented. The concept is the stuff of such representations. "Equal benefit of the law" or "substantive due process" exemplifies such representations.

As a consequence of the first and second stages of legal reasoning, the judicial decision subsumes subjective freedom *under* and *inside* the boundaries of legal categories (PR 228). The categories, being universals, "extend over the entire field of particularity" (PR 229A). What is categorized are "material of finitude and individuality [*Einzelheit*] whose extent is infinite" (PR 216R). Because of the remainder of actual social phenomena excluded from legal concepts, the completeness of a code is impossible to attain (PR 214A). An "empty ratiocination" proceeds. The more rigorous the analysis, the closer the jurist believes she or he is accessing legal truth. And yet, "[t]he greatest enemy of the good is the better."[28] The social phenomena are a remainder, a leftover that escapes legal analysis. Legal analysis represents the social world as if all that existed were representational thoughts [*Vorstellungen*] (PR 194).

c) Forgetting the Social Particulars in Legal Reasoning

This leads to the problem that legal reasoning in civil society reinforces legal formalism rather than the social relationships between individuals. Formalism leads to more and more micro concepts, the rise of a professional legal bureaucracy, and "an extensive apparatus of learned books and collections of verdicts based on divergent judgements, opinions, practices, etc., all expressed in a foreign language so that knowledge of the laws currently in force is accessible only to those who have made them an object of scholarly study" (PR 215R). Despite the excising of social phenomena from reasoning, the legal official "often regards this [knowledge] as its monopoly and no concern of those who are not among its members" (PR 215A).

Once we realize that the mediating concepts are imprisoned in the objectivity of consciousness in civil society, the legal analysis may become an instrument for domination and profit: "knowledge [*Kenntnis*] of right [hides] behind scholarship and a foreign language, and knowledge of the legal process [hides] behind complicated formalities" (PR297R). The official rigorously decomposes concepts as if she or he is accessing a practical world, yet such an enterprise takes the official into an ever more abstract world of the knowledge of concepts. Even one's arbitrary will is recognized as a concept (PR 192). What one associates with social need becomes an optical illusion. The more rigorous the method of the analysis of concepts, the more "absolutely astonished" will legal officials become when they are conscious that legal objectivity is really contingently structured. Any effort to relate the analysis of concepts to social phenomena is "beside the point" (PR 212R). Indeed, a machinelike character accompanies the technique of the analysis of concepts: the ratiocination, nested in abstractions that are taken as "real," "makes work increasingly *mechanical,* so that the human being is eventually able to step aside and let a *machine* take his place" (PR 198). Hegel explains in a Jena lecture that as machines replace nature through work, the work leaves the human being "machine-like, dull, spiritless."[29] This occurs at the cost of life in nature:

> the more he takes from nature, the more he subjugates it, the baser he becomes. By processing nature through a multitude of machines, he does not abolish the necessity of his own labor; he only pushes it further on, removes it from nature and ceases to relate to it in a living way . . . that work which is left to him becomes itself machine-like. The amount of labour decreases only for the whole, not for the individual; on the contrary, it is being increased, since the more mechanized labour increases, the less value it possesses, and the more the individual must toil.[30]

The work of legal reasoning replaces the natural biological being with the machinelike legal reasoning in a reified objectivity of consciousness.

The alienation of human experience from legal reasoning in the *Sittlichkeit* of civil society is reinforced by several factors that we have already considered in Chapters 3 and 5. First, legality is made determinate by the act of conferring formal legal status onto a human subject, not by the social relations presupposed in the content of the posited form (PR 219). Second, when one person recognizes another, a legal form institutionalizes such recognition. Third, the rights of civil society are reified abstractions themselves. Fourth, a person, not the intentional subject, owns the rights. Hegel does leave the structure of abstract right by turning to subjectivity. However, subjectivity is increasingly structured in an increasingly reified legal order as we proceed through Hegel's description of civil society. Public harm is understood, for example, in terms of the indeterminate concepts of personhood, property, contract, and individual rights, rather than in terms of intentionality (PR 220). Fifth, as noted above, a court particularizes concepts in concrete cases (PR 226). But a concept is "applied" to posited facts "without the subjective feeling [*Empfindung*] of *particular* interest" (PR 219). An untranslatable rupture remains between legal reasoning on the one hand and the social relations of reciprocal recognition on the other. "When right is posited and known [*gewußt*], all the contingencies of feeling [*Empfindung*] and opinion and the forms of revenge, compassion, and selfishness fall away" (PR 211A). The units (self-standing concepts) of legality are intellectually differentiated. Such intellectualization is believed to represent such subjectivity (PR 194R). Legal reasoning is stuck in a theoretical world.

To be sure, the existence of a court marks a substantial advance in the collective self-consciousness beyond the immediacy that had characterized the ethos of the undeveloped family or tribe (PR 229, 186). The ratiocination of *Verstand* remains a necessary step in the climb to a higher level of self-consciousness that can reconcile the objectivity with subjectivity. *Verstand,* though, is just one step in the development of self-consciousness. The problem is that the court and its formal method of ratiocination, like the state, are external to the social bonding needed to legitimize any judicial decision in a particular case.[31] As Hegel might put it, the court annuls the harm committed against a rule by canceling the particular contingent social phenomena that harm the rule. The court's annulment guarantees "the *undisturbed security* of *persons* and property" (PR 230). But it does so at the cost of forgetting social relationships. The individual (or the judge) can hardly be self-conscious of the interrecognition through social phenomena if the latter are excluded *ab initio* from legality. Even the judge's self-interest is excluded from legal ratiocination (PR 220). Legal philosophy must return to the relation of legality to subjectivity, but this begs a radically different structure of consciousness (PR 230). After all, legal reasoning, by virtue of its separation from social phenomena, reinforces, guides, and provides the framework necessary to protect the arbitrary will of the monadic individuals in civil society.

d) The Loss of Ethicality

Instrumental legal reasoning in civil society encourages state officials, such as judges and lawyers, to forget the importance of ethicality. The unlimited desire for things in the external objectivity of nature dissolves into an unremitting desire for rules (that is, for concepts). The desired things may seem concrete—the case name, the section of a statute, the doctrine. But what are desired are intellectually (not socially) produced concepts whose boundaries enclose context-specific experiences. The consequence is that legal reasoning reinforces the rupture between one observed individual and a stranger despite the economic and psychological dependence of the one subject upon the other. In civil society, "each individual is his own end, and all else means nothing for him" (PR 182A). And yet, one cannot fulfill one's own ends "without reference to others; these others are therefore means to the end of the particular [person]." Civil society becomes a forum of mediation amongst self-defining possessive individualists. Individuals become dependent upon the representing mediations. This dependence of the self-seeking individual upon the mediations constitutes a further shared universality of civil society.

Instead of closing the rupture between individuals and thereby institutionalizing ethicality, then, legal reasoning produces more abstract things that need to be consumed. Even signs (such as case names in today's legal education) become external things to be consumed. The "social needs" magnify in number and scope the more rigorously does the student or scholar intellectually decompose the concepts in the objectivity of consciousness (PR 195). There are no limits to needs in civil society, for needs are represented by concepts as accessed by *Vertstand*.

Hegel exemplifies his point by referring to the English use of the adjective *comfortable* to describe the inventions which, with such an elastic sense of need, lead to "infinite" and "endless" desires (PR 191, 191A). The individual's unlimited desires to possess external objects amount to a "boundless extravagance" and "false [*schlechte*] infinity" (PR 185A). Legal analysis of concepts "invents" concepts about social needs over and above the social relationships and the natural needs of clothing, shelter, and food (PR 109A). Legal formalism helps to induce such a false infinity of the consumption of knowledge.

In addition to the collapse of the family and the emergence of possessive individualism, the ethos of civil society loses the old-fashioned Kantian sense of morality in the day-to-day pursuit of material wealth and social status: "civil society affords a spectacle of extravagance and misery, as well as of the physical and ethical corruption common to both" (PR 185). And this leads to extreme poverty and depravity (PR 195A). Because social needs may well be forgotten as lawyers, students, and judges rigorously analyze concepts that represent the needs, the indeterminate multiplication of theoretical reasoning produces infinitely multiple external things to be consumed (PR 195A). Arbitrary wills, not rational choices, culminate as "the Law."

The consequence of all this juridification of social life is that if a self-conscious subject, despite her or his potential for personhood, is not conferred legal status by a legal institution or other public authority, she or he remains excluded from the institutional objectivity in civil society. This abstraction of social actuality creates the dependence of one individual upon another (PR 198). How so? Each atomistic unit, as a concept, needs the stranger to fulfill her or his infinitely demanding arbitrary will. But the stranger can only be imagined as a concept. Further, the stranger's desires are fulfilled when I categorize the stranger's acts under my concepts. By producing a category, I produce the means whereby I can satisfy the stranger (PR 192A)—or so I believe. Each observed individual plays into the hands of the other. A relation of abstract rights overtakes the human being who is paraded as a solipsistic unit. The invisible hand of legal reasoning links the one individual with the stranger through an act of intellectualization (PR 199). Professional law teachers and law students thereby play a critical role in the reification of legal reasoning. Peter Gabel especially exposed such a role some time ago.[32]

A still further consequence is the desperate separation of the individual from the objectivity of consciousness. There cannot be a unified bonding for an ethos as long as such a separation remains (PR 181A). Although there is a universality (represented by personhood, property, contract, crime, and the invisible hand of the market) that characterizes civil society, the individual becomes an abstract unit defined by legal status as posited by the state. The person, alone recognized as having legal status, is empty of content, isolated from others, and abstract. Indeed, the state itself is abstracted from the intentional subjects.[33] Needs are fulfilled by an "external organization" (PR 157). The individual becomes isolated, alone, and alienated from the objectivity of consciousness all the while that the latter posits abstract rights to protect the arbitrary will. Intermediate social associations help to alleviate such alienation. But the subject cannot feel at home with the objectivity in civil society, as constituted from posited concepts and formal institutional procedures that are reified from experiences. The legal formalism of civil society becomes preoccupied with the skills and technique of intellectual distinctions rather than with *Vernunft*. A "boundless extravagance" of the arbitrary wills of individuals has its heyday (PR 192A) without reconciling such arbitrary wills with the objectivity of consciousness. To escape from such a constraint upon freedom, Hegel urges that jurists turn to the religious practices, cultural assumptions, and social practices that contemporary Anglo American legal philosophers exclude from legality as "anthropological morality." This would address the possibility of an organic legal order, something which I shall explicate in the next chapter.

CONCLUSION

The state-centric *Sittlichkeit* of civil society has now displaced the stateless family. Despite the duty of the external state to provide a minimal economic welfare, taxation of capital, and public education—and despite the institutionalization of the individual's inner freedom of choice to posit her or his arbitrary will—the subject remains alienated from the institutional objectivity. The legal order is posited "out there" beyond the control of the observed individual. The most important element of *Recht*—ethicality—is denied, indeed forgotten. Hegel lectures in the year before he begins to write *Philosophy of Right* that the legal order of civil society is "a corpse, which in itself is dead, yet contains the life of worms" (1817/18 168R262). The legal formalism of civil society hides the "monstrous" arbitrary will that, though hidden, may deify itself as the god-emperor.

The formal categories, the enclosure of particularities under the categories, the peremptory exclusion of subjectivity from the forms of a judicial decision, and the function of the institutional structure as protector and guarantor of the freedom of choice posited by the arbitrary wills: these and other factors that I have highlighted lead Hegel to liken the objectivity of consciousness in the *Sittlichkeit* of civil society as a corpse plagued by the external life of worms. The ambition of observing how objectivity reconciles with subjective freedom remains problematic after this long journey from barbaric peoples to the modern, state-centric civil society. The observed individual still fails to feel "at home" with objectivity, although the reader might well do so. Conversely, the objectivity of the legal order needs to mirror the particularities of the individual (PR 141A). In the next two chapters, I shall identify what is necessary, at least in Hegel's view, to reconcile objectivity with subjectivity.

The pressing question is whether the latter two shapes of legal consciousness yet to be examined also exclude from legality the social actuality that Hegel has claimed as immanent in the development of self-consciousness. For example, does Hegel offer us a structure of legal consciousness where inhabitants can flourish through *Bildung*? After all, Hegel sets out early in his treatise (PR Preface, 3, 8) the need to relate *Bildung* with objectivity. Does Hegel finally access an institutional framework—an organic structure of consciousness—that ends the pursuit of self-consciousness, as most commentators of Hegel's legal philosophy believe (PR 265A, 260A, 287, 288)? I shall raise the possibility in Chapter 10 that such a state is situated in structures of international legal consciousness which, in turn, unfold as different shapes with different roles for the state.

CHAPTER NINE

Constitutional Shapes and the Organic Constitution

Generally, political commentators have read Hegel's works as elaborating two senses of a constitution. The one considers the constitution as external to the individual's consciousness. The second sense of a constitution locates the institutional objectivity of consciousness as implied in the social ethos. This dichotomy oversimplifies Hegel's understanding of constitutional law, however. For when Hegel addresses the nature of a constitution in *Philosophy of Right,* he identifies three very different forms of an external constitution (the original intent of the founding fathers, a constitution as a priori rights, and a constitution as a contract) as well as two different forms of an immanent constitution (historicist and organic). I shall examine each of these forms of a constitution.

Hegel's organic theory of constitutional law deserves special attention (PR 269). First, Hegel associates an organic constitution with a centralized organization. The organization appears as a rational, interconnected oneness. Second, Hegel subordinates the external state of civil society to the rule of law even when the state attempts to declare an exception. Third, the state has duties to protect the individual. These duties emanate from the social ethos. Drawing from Chapter 4, in particular, the state has duties to protect the individual's inner freedom to become self-conscious and to participate in governmentality. Further, the state owes duties to *Menshen* and not just to legally defined persons. Further, although the external constitution opposes the state to the individual's dignity, the organic constitution emulates the individual's dignity (PR 152). We shall come to appreciate that the duties of the state to the individual in an organic constitution require that legal reasoning be immersed in *Vernunft* rather than in *Verstand.* The latter method of legal reasoning, one may recall from Chapter 3, intellectually differentiates one concept from another. *Vernunft* relates such concepts to social-cultural practice. A public education that inculcates *Bildung* is important to the latter form of knowledge. Although the reflective ethical life may begin with subjective ends, interests, and considerations, along with historical and cultural presuppositions (PR 147R), the organic constitution will displace these with reciprocal recognition between individual subject and a stranger through shared concepts of the ethos.

I. THE EXTERNALITY OF A CONSTITUTION

Hegel faced two alternative views of a constitution in his day.[1] In the first, represented by the French and American revolutions, legitimacy is grounded in the original intent of the founding fathers of a basic text. Legal time begins with the posit of a basic text by the founding fathers. This time can be located on a calendar with days, months, and years. Time experienced before the birthdate of a constitution is excluded as prehistorical. In the second view of a constitution, instead of "hang[ing] in the air" (PR 265A), the constitution is embodied from unwritten customs whose origins cannot be known. There is no distinct and assignable founding father of a custom. Both forms of constitutional law exemplify the problematics of legal formalism which I addressed in Chapter 5.

a) The Original Intent Theory

Hegel raises two fundamental problems with the idea that a constitution is founded in the original intent of the founding fathers of a state (PR 273R, 274, PM 540).

First, this approach fails to address *why* the original framers possessed legitimacy to author the founding text in the first place. The silence with respect to such a question fails to consider why a legal norm posited pursuant the founding text is legitimate. Without such an inquiry, any relation of constitutional law with the self-conscious freedom of the individual would be fanciful. Hegel puts his concern this way in *Philosophy of Mind*:

> [t]he question—To whom (to what authority and how organized) belongs the power to make a constitution? is the same as the question, Who has to make the spirit of a nation? Separate our idea of a constitution from that of the collective spirit, as if the latter exists or has existed without a constitution, and your fancy only proves how superficially you have apprehended the nexus be-

tween the spirit in its self-consciousness and in its actuality. What is thus called "making" a "constitution," is—just because of this inseparability—a thing that has never happened in history, just as little as the making of a code of laws. A constitution only develops from the national spirit identically with that spirit's own development, and runs through at the same time with it the grades of formation and the alterations required by its concept. It is the indwelling spirit and the history of the nation (and, be it added, the history is only that spirit's history) by which constitutions have been and are made. (PM 540)

Whatever the rhetoric of the founding fathers or even of contemporary jurists about the wisdom of the fathers, the basic text does not necessarily represent the immanent development of a constitution. Although this may sound much like historical jurisprudence and open Hegel to the criticisms usually leveled at *Volksgeist* thinking, this is not so for reasons that I shall identify soon enough.

If the founding fathers do not posit a constitution, who does? Hegel responds in a lecture with "[n]o one, it makes itself. There is nothing easier than to formulate the general principles of a constitution, for in our day these concepts have become conventional abstractions" (1817/18 134R.190). Because of its isolation from the phenomenological movement of time shared before and after the posit of the founding text, the original intent may well become a figment of the wishful thinking of the contemporary jurist.

Second, the original intent theory lacks logic. For one thing, the original intent theory assumes that the territory within its jurisdiction lacks a constitution before the posit of the basic text. But we just cannot replace an earlier constitution with a later one by the mere expression of intent in writing. If no constitution previously existed, then no state previously existed. If the latter, the founding fathers would reflect the aggregate of the arbitrary wills of individuals (PR 273R). But the will manifests consciousness. Constitutional universals are not the mere aggregate of arbitrary wills. For Hegel, even a contract, such as Rousseau's, aggregates individual wills as parties to the contract. If a constitution does preexist the basic text of the founding fathers, then the founding fathers merely amend the constitution.

There is a third possibility. Hegel explains that the original intent manifests the violent founding of the legal order. However, whatever the constitutional rhetoric in domestic or foreign policies of some states today, no founding fathers, however brilliant, stand as godlike authors outside their culture. No basic text, posited by such founding fathers, can change the inward structure of an individual's consciousness overnight.

The basic problem of the original intent theory is that it reifies constitutionality from the social-cultural ethos of a particular society. For this reason, "it is at any rate utterly essential that the constitution should *not* be regarded as *something made,* even if it does have an origin in time" (PR 273R). In this respect Hegel sounds much like Chief Justice Edward Coke in the early seventeenth century.[2] Hegel notes, for example, that the Spaniards rejected an effort by Napoleon, despite its systematic and rational character, to posit "the constitution" as if it were alien to their heritage. The risk is that a written text posited as "the Constitution" fails to address the collective assumptions and expectations of inhabitants. New constitutional forms continually displace old ones as the cultural norms change. A constitution is "the work of centuries, the Idea and consciousness of the rational (in so far as consciousness has developed in a nation" (PR 274A). Without situating a text in its social-historical context, Hegel continues, "it will have no meaning or value, even if it is present in an external sense." Scholars of comparative law should heed Hegel's caution in one 1819/20 lecture that "[n]othing is more foolish" than to compare and evaluate different peoples by comparing the words in texts (1819/20 W214). The reason why social-cultural history is important is that subjectivity embodies (gives experiential body to) such history. If constitutionality were isolated from subjectivity, the laws would lack legitimacy. Constitutionality evolves immanently from within the quest for collective self-consciousness in objective spirit.

b) The Constitution as a priori Rights

This takes us to the idea that a constitution might be constituted from a priori rights (PR 273R, 274). Ronald Dworkin, in his earlier writings, emphasizes that constitutional rights trump the collective welfare.[3] If rights do not so trump the aggregate of private interests, constitutional law would differ little from an amalgam of ordinary statutes. Hegel critiques what becomes the gist of Dworkin's claim. The rights thesis ignores, Hegel explicates, the relation of constitutionality with a social-historical actuality. With the rights thesis, actuality becomes an utterly theoretical reality divorced from finite beings with particular desires and needs (PR 49). Indeed, as Ronald Dworkin has expressed in a representative essay about liberalism, "political decisions must be, as far as possible, independent of any particular conception of the good life, or of what gives value to life."[4] If a legal order elevates rights to the point of failing to account for the social content of the rights, the constitutional law lies external to the control of subjectivity. Even the right to equality becomes "vacuous and superficial." All that the lawyer can say is that persons ought to have equal property, property itself being an abstraction (PR 49A).

Social need, as I explained in the previous chapter, is thereby recoded as a concept. For a right, like a rule, is a concept. Since property is a form or concept conferred onto a seized thing, as I explained in Chapter 4, legal equality "*excludes* everything to do with possessions [of external things]" (PR 49R). Justice becomes "indifferent to particularity" (PR 49A) and empty of historical contingency (PR 36). Further, equality is only guaranteed to indeterminate persons (PR 49R) who lack concreteness in context-specific circumstances (PR 35). The moral imperative of the rights thesis is "Be a [empty] legal person and respect others as [empty] legal persons" rather than "Be a subject and respect others as subjects." The engine of modernity (the quest for subjective self-consciousness) lapses as legal formalism displaces actuality (PR 37). The subject remains autonomous and alienated from the objectivity of consciousness (PR 35).

And what does Hegel think about the diligent constitutional scholar who associates legal knowledge with the intellectual decomposition of rights as concepts? Such a view is for "uncultured people" (PR 37A). The "nobler mind" examines the social actuality behind legal formalism. This actuality relates the content of a right to a context-specific particularity. A right abstracts from the shared values in a socially and historically contingent circumstance. The problem is magnified because the rights lawyer believes she or he is actually protecting reality. Hegel summarizes his critique of the rights thesis in this way in *Philosophy of Mind*: the belief in the equality of rights substitutes "utter" and "superficial" "abstractness" in place of social actuality (PM 539). The "great truth" is that if people are equal, they are equal *outside* the rights constitution in the social-cultural ethos that the rights constitution ignores. As a consequence, "[t]he laws themselves, except in so far as they concern that narrow circle of personality, presuppose unequal conditions, and provide for the unequal legal duties and appurtenances therefrom" (PM 539).

Who is the person deserving of rights? An abstract person emptied of particularity. Who is accorded the right if the person so lacks social content? Whoever the judges say are deserving of legal status. So, the absence of particularity impacts upon the absence of rights for children, imbeciles, and lunatics who lack self-consciousness (PR 132R). Indeed, the rights of personhood may be consistent with the "non-existence of this or that individual people, family, etc., or the complete *absence of human life*" (PR 135R, his emphasis). The rights thesis thereby collapses into legal formalism. The worst atrocities that daily occur today will be possible at the same time that a state's officials continue to make intellectual distinctions about rights. Even the strategic use of rights rhetoric exists in thought alone.

Truth is pushed to the side (NL 123). The rights protect nothing since the rights "exist" as thought alone. And "where there is nothing, there can be no contradiction either" (PR 135A).

c) The Constitution as a Contract

Hegel offers a third sense of the externality of constitutional law: the constitution as a contract (PR 52, 75, 258R). The constitution as a contract characterized the feudal relations of German princes (1817/18 33.37) as well as the French Revolution. There are two types of contract, Hegel writes: a contract whose terms and conditions construct the state (that is, Hobbes's view), and one in which the state is a party to the contract (that is, Rousseau's view). Hegel raises several problems with both shapes of a constitution as a contract.

First, whichever sense of a contract pervades, the contractual approach assumes that the contract is the consequence of arbitrary wills. But, as I explained in earlier chapters, the arbitrary will represents an immediate identity of the individual with the willed object (PR 75). Such a will is arbitrary because it lacks the self-reflective character that Hegel offers as possible with a highly civilized society. Self-conscious choices are thereby lacking an arbitrary will. I just posit my values or feelings as a "given" without reflecting about the social relationships amongst individuals presupposed in the content of the values.

Second, the amalgam of arbitrary wills lacks the universality whereby one individual recognizes a stranger: that is, where there is ethicality. Such an amalgam of arbitrary wills is "superficial" for it covers over or ignores the universals which reflective wills share. Hegel desires a constitution that embodies "a *single* unity of different wills" (PR 75A). That is, the state will not be an amalgam of interest groups, the most powerful group dominating the others. Rather, the state will exist as greater than the sum of its parts. It will embody a legitimacy such that, as Socrates explains through the "Speech of the Laws" in *Crito* and as Hegel elaborates in his exposition of criminal law, the disobedience of one law will undermine the legitimacy of the objectivity of legal consciousness. The contractualist constitution, though, only entertains a common interest between contractees who, in turn, may withdraw from the contract since the arbitrary will had motivated them. The state may dissolve for the state, as the consequence of a contract, does not exist independent and greater than the amalgam of political interests. The universals represented by the state, though, mark a "great advance" of civilization, as we saw in Chapter 2 (PR 75A). Further, inhabitants just cannot break away from the state even if they so desire (PR 75A). The state even had to grant permission for an individual to enter or leave its territory. If an individual does not inhabit territory owned by a state, "reason requires that one [a state] be established" (PR 75A).

Third, the contractual constitution fosters social alienation. This is so, to begin with, because the contract may not necessarily recognize individuals who lack property: the contract only exists between property owners (PR 75R). This has to be so because the individual, who confers form onto seized external things, comes to realize that she or he cannot fulfill her or his needs without recognizing a stranger as a contractee. The exchange of property by a contract manifests such an interdependence. Once again, shared universals, existing *in itself,* are absent from the constitutional order based on a contract. For another thing, the contract abstracts from the social and historical contingency of particulars. The contract binds empty juridical persons who lack the intentionality of subjectivity (PR 258R). Further, the constitutional contract invites rebellion if officials fail to implement its terms. That is, the contract offers an either-or situation: either one fulfills the contract or one reneges upon its terms and rebels. Although it is unclear whether Hegel had Hobbes in mind, Hegel certainly represented Rousseau as grounding the social contract in atomistic arbitrary wills. As a consequence of the above three factors, the contractual constitutional regime might well institutionalize "the most terrible and drastic event." And what was that? Recalling my Introduction, the most terrible event was the French Terror. Hegel attributed the Terror to Rousseau's philosophy of the contractualist constitution.

Finally, *Verstand* is the appropriate form of legal reasoning for a contract. Little more need be said in the light of Hegel's sustained attack on *Verstand* as explicated in my earlier chapters. In sum, "talk of virtue *in general* can easily verge on empty declamation, because it refers only to something abstract and indeterminate" (PR 150R). *Verstand* reconciles one right with another. Rights are posited by a contract without locating the rights in the social ethos in which the rights are analyzed.[5] Even if the contract sets out hortatory assertions, we have observed above that such rights are empty of particular context-specific social content. As Hegel puts it, this "consists simply in disregarding and excluding particular interests as an inessential and even unworthy moment" (PR 261R). From Hegel's viewpoint, constitutional duties relate to one's role in an ethos, in "the duties of the circumstances [*Verhältnisse*] to which he belongs" (PR 150, 260). In contrast, *Verstand* produces "a *dead, cold letter* and a *shackle*" (PR Pref 17). For the anthropological character of the particularity of social relations is

excluded from the content of the contract. And, as with the legal formalism of the Roman jurists, all social differences are avoided in the name of
intellectually defined sameness (PR Pref. 19).

I shall explain in a moment the alternative which Hegel offers as a work-
able basis for the social bonding that constitutes the objectivity of consciousness. It must suffice at this moment to appreciate that when constitutionality is determined by the differences amongst concepts alone, constitutional
analysis becomes rights-oriented sophistry. This one-sidedness of constitutional law defines who is a person and what rights are attributed to the
person all the while that it necessarily creates a monstrous social spectacle
of exclusion, violence, and suffering (PR 258R). Hegel recounts how reason-
able lawyers and scholars, immersed in a rhetoric about the original intent of
the founding fathers, shudder when confronted with claims about "reason,"
"enlightenment," and "freedom" (PR 272R). They can believe in the wisdom
of the founding contract while that social monstrosity continues outside the
courthouse and lecture hall (PR 260A). This is a logical problem, rather than
a mere empirical probability, for all constitutions based on contract.

d) The Externality of Constitutional Legitimacy

The original intent, rights thesis, and contract theories of a constitution share the common denominator of legal formalism: the legitimacy of
constitutionality rests in an externality to self-consciousness. Three consequences flow from this external locus of constitutionality.

First, individual freedom involves a freedom *from* the state for the state,
being external to the individual subject, constrains the subject's freedom.
In this light, the constitution—whether as a basic text, a priori rights, or a
contract—protects individual rights from state interference (PR 38). "A basic prejudice" of the externality of the constitution is that the constitution
is grounded in a vast bureaucratic state-centric machine (GC 22). Because
of the exteriority of such constitutional sources, the rights and the state
duties rest in a reified rhetoric separate from social-cultural conditions of
particularity.

Second, the individual rights of the constitution are dependent upon
the de facto power (as opposed to legitimacy) of the external institutions.
The arbitrary will likewise displaces the rule of law (PR 295). The consequence, Hegel reasons in "The German Constitution," is that individual
rights become very "precarious" (GC 12). If the legal philosopher associates a constitution with individual rights, the constitution is like "a heap
of round stones which combine to form a pyramid. But since they are

completely round and must remain so without interlocking, as soon as the pyramid begins to approach the end for which it was constructed, they roll apart, or at least offer no resistance [to such movement]" (GC 40). The externality of the constitution vis-à-vis the alienated observed individual functions as if, like natural laws, the constitution controls and determines the actions of cattle as well as of the stars (PM 529).

Third, the externality of the constitution remains unrelated to the development of self-consciousness. An important element of the latter is the spirit of the nation that has evolved through the centuries. The external source of a constitution, though, freezes legal time at a specific time and place when the founding fathers posited the original intent, the a priori rights or the contract (PR 39). The external constitution exists outside of experiential time.

What is the nature of constitutionality if the state is external to self-consciousness, then? Why are rules, posited by the state's authorities, binding? Because legitimacy rests in the external source—external, that is, from the development of individual self-consciousness. Despite the good will and virtuous action of the rulers, constitutional law remains imprisoned in formalism beyond the social relationships of actuality. After all, the original intent of the founding fathers, the rights thesis, and the contract are external to the social-cultural life of a people. The Enlightenment's preoccupation with the autonomous individual is forgotten in the name of such formalities and externalities (PR 295R). The more rigorous the philosopher's intellectualized differences amongst concepts, the more binding does the external sense of constitutionality seem to be. Constitutional analysis pretends to describe reality all the while that politics remains untouched (PR 297R). Constitutional rights become a "foreign language" of "complicated formalities" (PR 297R). Even the day-to-day judicial appeal to individual rights as representative of the "people" is "superfluous and perhaps even insulting" (PR310R) since the rights rhetoric conceals the separated anthropological assumptions and expectations of particular human subjects or groups of human subjects. Hegel does believe, however, that a constitution, which I shall outline soon enough, can adequately express the latter assumptions and expectations.

2. THE HISTORICIST CONSTITUTION

Given the formalism that conceals the arbitrary will in the three types of external constitution, Hegel turns his attention to a constitution that emanates from customs of the *Volk*.[6] Both Savigny and seventeenth-century

English constitutional practice, as elaborated by Edward Coke, exemplified how constitutional obligation could be grounded in the habits of obedience of a populace towards the institutional structure of the state. Although Bentham and Austin recognized habits of obedience as the ultimate source of legal legitimacy,[7] they did not consider habits themselves as strictly legal—that is, as binding. Legality, as opposed to constitutional obligation (a distinction maintained in some jurisdictions),[8] rested in the texts expressed by a distinct and assignable author such as a legislature. Despite their source of constitutionality, the habits of obedience lacked the character of a legal obligation.

Hegel does not play down the importance of customs in a legal order. As he exemplifies, "it does not occur to someone who walks the streets at night that this might be otherwise, for this habit of [living in] safety has become a second nature, and we scarcely stop to think that it is solely the effect of particular institutions" (PR 268A). And as Oscar Schacter has argued, posited texts merely provide indicia for an internalized sense of legal obligation.[9] Customs bring "a living quality" to constitutionality. Justinian's three-volume *Corpus Iuris Civilis* (A.D. 529) exemplified such a living quality, according to Hegel, because the *Corpus* codified customary norms that were far more in tune with the Roman ethos than would the posit of some indeterminate text. Customary norms "always retain a certain particularity and association with history which people are reluctant to part with" (PR211A). A legal institution "evolve[s] in an apparently peaceful and imperceptible manner" "over a long period of time" (PR 298A). A constitutional order thereby "makes itself in history, through its own doing" (1817/18 134.191).

Despite the social actuality that customs might bring to laws, Hegel raises several problems with the historicist constitution. First, Hegel argues in "On the English Reform Bill" (1831) that customs grow haphazardly without a systematic character.[10] In this respect, the customary constitution, such as the English, Hegel continues, "lagged so conspicuously behind the other civilized states of Europe in institutions based on genuine right."[11] Further, only the lawyers and judges are privileged to know how to find and decipher what customs are binding (PR 272).

Second, a historicist constitution lacks self-conscious thinking. Without such a role for self-conscious action, the constitutional law becomes "pernicious" (PR 211A). Indeed, "habit blinds us to the basis of our entire existence [*Existenz*]" (PR 268A). Even the codification of customs is formless, indeterminate, and incomplete (PR 211R). Customary norms are ad hoc because they lack the self-conscious reflection about the content of the norms. Since Hegel associates freedom with just such self-conscious action, the subject must accept the posited custom, whatever its content (PR 211R). Not surprisingly, Hegel facetiously describes the unwritten constitution of the English in the "English Reform Bill" essay as arbitrary, rationally incoherent, and unscientific.[12] The content of an unwritten constitution, Hegel had written in the "German Constitution," need not be taken seriously if customs are taken seriously (GC 184). What are the binding customs depends upon an elite of expert knowers. Roman jurists, for example, adjusted to the ad hoc and arbitrary consequence of customs by establishing a college of "long-deceased lawyers" with a majority vote and a president (PR 211R).

3. THE CONSTITUTION AS AN ORGANISM

Against the problematics of a constitution grounded in an externality or the historical *Volk,* Hegel identifies a very different constitutional shape which, he initially believes, reconciles the institutional objectivity of consciousness with subjectivity.[13] He calls this constitutional shape, an organic constitution or "state proper" as Knox expresses the term. If the reflective will, which I described as *Vernunft* in Chapter 3, is incorporated into the forms of rules, principles, and institutions of legal formalism, the constitutional form becomes a living organism. I shall now set out Hegel's theory of an organic constitution. I shall do so by privileging five elements of the organic constitution: the metaphoric comparison of a constitution with an organism, the relation of a constitution to an individual's self-knowledge, intermediate associations, public education, and the organization as a social unity. In Sections 4, 5, and 6, I shall examine important facets of the organic constitution: the governmental structure, the rule of law, and the state of exception.

a) The Metaphor of an Organism

Hegel characterizes a constitution as an organism in several ways.[14]

First, like the organism of a plant, a constitution has branches and roots without which the constitution cannot live. Hegel's metaphor of an organism is likened to the fable, reported by Livy and Shakespeare, to the effect that in 503 B.C.E. a section of Rome, represented by plebeians, seceded from the city.[15] The Roman consul persuaded them to return by recounting the following story. All parts of a body rebel against the stomach, accusing the stomach of living from their labors. The stomach replies that the parts receive their food through the stomach. The consul likened the stomach to the Senate and the plebeians to the other parts of the body. Hegel privileges this bodily metaphor. Each organ needs other organs for the ultimate shape of a constitution (PR 286R). Hegel states the point in his 1817/18 lectures: "[t]he whole is an organic life, in which the universal element is maintained only by each organ being active in its particular function—equipping oneself for one's particular sphere and, by being thus equipped, promoting the universal" (1817/18 70R.85). Each organ of the constitution has a distinctive shape that is actual for itself (PR 279). Each organ is a member, not a unit, of the whole organism (PR 286R). If an organ is separated from the whole body, then the body would die (PR 276A). If the organ does not perform its proper function, then too the organism dissolves into dead matter. The legislature, executive, and judiciary are organs like the hand of a human body.[16] No one institution is self-sufficient. Nor does one part understand the other as a negative limitation (PR 272R). Nor is any one part a means to an end. The parts are members that make for an organism that lives a life of its own. If one of the institutions either dies or disproportionately outgrows the social ethos, the constitution becomes "a sick body" that lacks a "true reality" (PR 270A). If the social ethos is alienated from the constitution, such a constitution exists in form only, much like a hand cut from the body looks as if a hand but lacks a relation with the whole body.

Second, an organism, unlike a machine, is self-determining. An organism does not need some one external switch to turn it on: "the state is not a mechanism but the rational life of self-conscious freedom and the system of the ethical world" (PR 270R). A machine needs an external force to start it operating. An organism grows on its own into new shapes as time proceeds. So too, a constitution does not need external stimuli to live (PR 271). A constitution will be complete if it unifies the particulars of social contingency with institutional sources and posited laws. At that point, the constitution will institutionalize and mirror actuality (PR270A). The individual will bond with the objective institutions. The content of the constitutional organism will be closer to the individual's identity than is a relationship of faith or trust (PR 147). Faith and trust characterized the civil society, we saw in the last chapter.

Hegel's juxtaposition of an organism with a machine is picked up in the twentieth century by Jacob Johann von Uexkull (1864–1944) who argues in his important *Theoretical Biology* that a living being, in contrast with a machine, can self-generate.[17] This metaphoric contrast between an organism and a machine is emphasized by the legal philosophies worked out by Franz Kafka in *The Trial,* György Lukács (1885–1971), and Karel Kosik (1926–2003).[18] Francois Jacob (1920–) continues that a machine, unlike an organism, can only reproduce copies that wear out over time.[19] Léon Brillouin (1889–1969) describes an organism as having "some strange power of life."[20] Further, an organism can repair itself, unlike a machine.[21] Hegel's attribution of an organic character to the legal order contrasts with Gilles Deleuze's (1925–1995) description of the legal order as a machine with an indirect voice of a "murmur" without a living being as subject.[22]

Third, if a constitution reconciles the formal objectivity of consciousness with subjectivity, there may come a time when an emergency threatens the life of the organism. In such a case, all individuals and institutions must constrain their independent acts in favor of the legal (and, therefore, the social) whole as the arbitrary will of the state (PR 268R). This foreshadows Schmitt's and Agamben's theory of the state of exception.[23] According to Schmitt, the state alone decides what is an emergency (or "exception"), how to deal with the exception, and when the exception is lifted.[24] Lord Haldane (1856–1928), educated by the British idealists at Oxford, instituted and applied this notion when he constructed the emergency doctrine in common law countries.[25] Does the head of the state possess unlimited discretion to declare a state of exception in an organic constitution? I shall address this question in a moment.

b) The Relation of a Constitutional Organism to the Individual's Self-Consciousness

For Hegel, freedom lacks any further external constraint upon one's self-consciousness. This freedom exists when the subject is conscious of itself as the object of constraint. And this arises when the subject recognizes her- or himself in the stranger and the stranger in her- or himself. This reciprocal recognition constitutes actuality because each is free: "spirit is actual only as that which it knows itself to be" (PR 274). A bonded "we" or community finally exists. The organic constitution manifests such a freedom, according to Hegel (PR 258R, 266, 269, 274). The organic constitution grows "only to a small extent through habit and custom, but mainly through insight and reasoned argument" (PR 316A). The insight and argument of human subjects bond with objectivity (customs, codes, legal institutions, and doctrines). Hegel explains that "[a]n essential part of the fully developed state is consciousness or thought; the state accordingly knows what it wills and knows this as an object of thought [*ein Gedachtes*]"

(PR 270A). The organic constitution grows from within the consciousness of the individual. *Bildung* aids in this development (PR 270). The constitution, Hegel continues, sets out the institutional pillars which guard the development of self-consciousness "with known ends and recognized principles, and with laws which are laws not only *in themselves* but also for the consciousness." He adds that the state officials relate their knowledge to the "determinate knowledge [*Kenntnis*] of existing circumstances and [social] relations" (PR 270).

Ethicality is manifested in an organic constitution. For with ethicality, one recognizes the stranger in a social relationship. Such a social relation is embodied in the universals which individuals share. Such a sharing of universals binds the individual to the constitutional order, independent of the arbitrary will of any individual:

> [i]f the state is confused with civil society and its determination is equated with the security and protection of property and personal freedom, *the interest of individuals [der Einzelnen] as such* becomes the ultimate end for which they are united; it also follows from this that membership of the state is an optional matter. But the relationship of the state to the individual [*Individuum*] is of quite a different kind. Since the state is objective spirit, it is only through being a member of the state that the individual [*Individuum*] himself has objectivity, truth and ethical life. *Union* as such is itself the true content and end, and the destiny [*Bestimmung*] of individuals [*Individuen*] is to lead a universal life. (PR 258R)

The stranger is no longer an obstruction to one's freedom because both I and the stranger are reconciled through our shared universals. I am free because there is no longer a constraint external to my self-consciousness.

Because universals manifest self-consciousness, the universals are legitimate and therefore binding. A constitution is not "articulated and truly organized" until such a reconciliation occurs (PR 260A). Even moral duties link with the ethos (PR 161R). The constitution as an organism is situated through experience, not in Kant's noumena. The experience includes the content of religious practices, cultural assumptions, moral conscience, the bonding in intermediate associations, and rules posited by institutions of the state.

Further, the constitution, as an organism, can be brought under the rational control of the individual: "the subject bears *spiritual witness* to them [posited laws] as to its own essence" (PR 147). The individual is no longer separate from objectivity. The self-consciousness of the individual embodies the content of the constitution. What does this mean in practice? Instead of intellectually distinguishing doctrines and rules, as in *Verstand,* the individual identifies the boundaries of the structure of the social-cultural ethos in which she or he finds her- or himself, questions the relation of the doctrines to such boundaries, and elaborates the implications for the structure of such a relation. The social-cultural practice triggers issues about the geneology of the presupposed structure, the social and genderized classes that particulate in the enactment of legal norms, the extent of such participation, the exclusion of ethnic groups from the project, and other factors that enter into what Hegel calls "actuality" as elaborated in Chapter 1. Whatever the extent of Hegel's naiveté of the possibility of such individual participation in complex bureaucratic intermediate and state organizations, his point is that the individual will feel at home with such universals by virtue of her or his participation in them. Social alienation will dissipate.

Ethicality exudes from the organic constitution. When I recognize the binding character of any one such universal, I indirectly recognize the stranger because we share universals. The self-consciousness of each individual produces the shared universals and thereby recognizes the stranger as different and yet as a member of the ethical ethos. The individual overcomes social alienation without returning to the arbitrary will of subjectivist solipsism. The laws and institutions culminate in the individual's own development and self-consciousness. The laws become alive by virtue of being *Gesetze* in one's consciousness.

The individual's self-reflective will constructs the laws, and yet the individual's consciousness is objective because the individual has become a member of the ethos. I cannot feel "at home" in such a legal order, however, unless laws are posited in my consciousness. We enter into the state as members of social groups (PR 308R). So too, the state cannot break up into atomistic individuals and still maintain an identity as an organism: "[b]ut the state is essentially an organization whose members constitute *circles in their own right [für sich]*, and no moment within it should appear as an unorganized crowd" (PR 303R). Hegel continues that in the external state of civil society, the many live as an aggregate of individual arbitrary wills which unite into a "formless mass" that is "elemental, irrational, barbarous, and terrifying." Why terrifying? Because each individual, without an effort to become conscious of her or his relation with others (that is, without ethicality), will posit her or his arbitrary will. The arbitrary will reflects the lack of a thinking being. With civil society, there is the risk that the philosopher retrenches into the prelegal world of barbarism.

c) Intermediate Associations as Instruments of the Organism

Hegel has now reached an important point in his analysis of the legitimacy of a modern state-centric legal order. For he has come to appreciate that a law is binding because of the reconciliation of the objectivity of consciousness, manifested by posited standards and institutions, with the striving of an individual to become self-consciously free. If the individual becomes aware that the only external constraint on one's freedom is one's own self, then one has it within one's power and legitimacy to become free. This will happen if the individual feels "at home" with the objectivity of consciousness formerly manifested by the external state in civil society. Posited laws are binding if their content manifests the reciprocal recognition in social actuality. Returning to Chapter 1, "actuality" incorporates the self-consciousness of the individual as a member of an ethos. And this, in turn, addresses the extent of reciprocal recognition. Despite the very wide conception of what is "political" and "moral" for Ronald Dworkin, for example, Hegel's sense of the political and of morality incorporates the very ethos of what Hart and Dworkin exclude from legality as "anthropological morality." The Kantian "oughts" of the *noumena* are now the "is" immersed in actuality. Further, one's duties draw from one's role in intermediate associations and, in turn, from state institutions. Morality is now subordinate to ethical life. And ethical life, for Hegel, draws precisely from what Hart and Dworkin also exclude from legality: the phenomenology of time-consciousness of the ethos.

Hegel's organic constitution differs from the constitutional theory of his English predecessors such as Hobbes and Locke and his contemporary Jeremy Bentham. For the English tradition, the state of nature is characterized by individuals abstracted from their biographies, social relationships, and traditions.[26] The basic legal principles, the object of agreement in the state of nature, are transferred into civil society once the abstract persons gain a language and they can enter into agreements. The terms of the contract bind individuals in civil society. Bentham similarly draws the norm of the greatest happiness of the greatest number from nature and then uses it as the Archimedean point to evaluate the content of posited laws in civil society.[27] Each legal philosophy excludes the state of nature and its inhabitants as constituting prelegality. For Hegel, however, the difference between a stateless society and a state-centric society is not an all-or-nothing situation, as I explained in Chapter 2. A state, conversely, may deteriorate into a tyranny so as to become a state in name only.

Constitutional law includes social institutions, such as the family, the corporation, classes, and charities, which mediate between the individual and the state.[28] Such institutions socially integrate the individual with the legal order. One wills rules and rituals in the contingent context of loyalties and self-definition inside such intermediate associations. As a consequence, one plays a role that is conditioned by the ethicality of the ethos. Such an institutional role acculturates the individual member with the objectives of the intermediate association. The individual feels so bonded with intermediate organizations and with decisions and rules posited by the state that the organizations, decisions, and rules seem to be her or his own. This bonding with such intermediate organizations constitutes another manifestation of "actuality."

Institutional roles do not dictate the choices that an individual must make in day-to-day experiences nor in the electoral booth. If that were so, Hegel would be returning us to the customary constitutional order. Instead, Hegel maintains as I explained in Chapter 8, that the individual self-consciously chooses her or his intermediate social organizations in which to work and play. One grows intellectually and emotionally as one lives one's day-to-day life through such intermediate organizations.[29] Laws are considered binding only if their content recognizes the relation of the individual with the immanent organic universals shared in an ethos. If the content of a posited rule, for example, foments social conditions for the individual to be free in Hegel's sense of the development of self-consciousness, then it is binding. Only if posited laws succeed in doing so will the state, and its trappings, break from the sense of externality that characterizes civil society. Independent of objectivity, one's social participation in intermediate organizations induces the bonding that makes one feel at home with laws posited as a consequence of one's participation in the authorial process. The individual develops until the universals of the ethos mirror the self-conscious will of the observed individual. One has a morally developed personality when one has become a member of such a legal order. At that point, the autonomous and alienated individual is no longer separate from the objectivity. The objectivity of consciousness is ethical.

Hegel is trying to impress upon us how important it is for the philosopher to study legal phenomena in the context of the intermediate associations through which one lives from a day-to-day existence. This contrasts with the intellectual differentiations between concepts. Anthropological moral assumptions are not just a matter for politics as opposed to law. It is just not enough—indeed, it is misdirected—for a priori rights to be considered constitutive of constitutionality. It is also misdirected for jurists to believe that if there were a right to equality before the law, then there would be equality in "actuality." A written constitution does not guarantee universal rights. It is also misdirected for legal philosophers to entertain that the philosophy of law involves the mere clarification and classification of concepts. Instead, with an organic constitution, the philosopher must situate the observed individual in a social context; study the social roles she or he performs; and examine the distancing and, indeed, estrangement of both nonexpert and expert from *Versnunft*. Do the institutions recognize all inhabitants equally or are only citizens recognized as having legal standing? Is the human subject recognized as she or he plays a role in intermediate institutions? Is the subject recognized in the social relations with public officials, the enactment of legislation, the deliberations of lawyers and judges, the administration of unions, universities, churches, and the impact of the invisible hand of the market?

Let us closely examine one intermediate organization which figures highly in the organic constitution. The most important social institution in this respect is the family. Although we may tend to consider the family as separate from politics and law today, Hegel argues that the family helps to cement the social bonding needed to displace the alienation between the autonomous subjectivity and state institutions as in objectivity. The family succeeds in doing so to the extent that it inculcates universals into the child's consciousness. The child comes to appreciate and desire *Bildung*. With the aid of other intermediate social institutions, the individual no longer lives "long, disconnected experiences" (PS 451). The individual is no longer an atom in civil society where luck, a bureaucracy, widespread differences of wealth, and legal formalism set the conditions for the alienation of the subject from objectivity. At the same time that *Bildung* develops the capacity and conditions for the subject to become self-conscious, *Bildung* encourages the individual to recognize the stranger and, more generally, the social relationships amongst strangers as subjects. The state is no longer considered external from the individual. Rather, the individual comes to appreciate that she or he helps to construct the state and, further, that the former external state, which had posited rules as if the state were the authorizing source of the rules, is now situated in a larger social whole which incorporates religious, anthropological morality, deontological moral values, and *prejudicia* that the lawyers of the external state of civil society would have excluded from legality as nonlaw or "morality." Without legitimacy, legality now dissolves. Any effort of legal philosophers to separate legality from legitimacy now misses why legal units are binding.

Ethicality permeates the organic constitution. This ethicality is in-culcated through intermediate social organizations of which the family is the most important. When the observed individual recognizes a stranger through an intermediate institution, this fosters a shared self-worth. Just as important, the recognition helps to induce a feeling of identity with the associations—the family, the corporation, the union, the university, the business, and the civil society—so that the choices of the institution are *my* and *your* choices and that the institution is *mine* and *yours*. This iden-tity with one's institutions carries through to the enactment of statutes, the adjudication of disputes by courts, and the behavior of authorities. I become attached to the legal order just as I was attached to my family before I ventured into civil society from the tribal culture. The content of the constitutional order becomes a part of me and I become a part of the content of the constitutional order.

d) Public Education

Public education also plays an important role in an organic constitu-tion. Hegel distinguishes three forms of public education.[30] The first, which we might call the "entertainment" theory of education, privileges the arbitrary will of the student. The educational institution protects the student's arbitrary will, the courses taught, their content, and the method of teaching, with the student's arbitrary will as the standard.[31] Hegel de-scribes the entertainment theory in this way: it "represent[s] children, in the immature state which they feel they are in, as in fact mature, by en-deavouring to make them satisfied with the way they are" (PR 175R). To the entertainment theory of education, *Bildung* would appear to corrupt what, as parents and teachers, we ought to be doing (PR 187R). Rather, we ought to prepare our children and students for a civil society that struc-tures around the unlimited desires of the arbitrary will.

Not surprisingly, Hegel finds the entertainment theory suspect, as it

> distorts and obscures the true need of the children themselves for something better; it creates in them on the one hand an indifference towards, and imper-viousness to, the substantial relations of the spiritual world, and on the other a contempt for people inasmuch as they have presented themselves to them in a childish and contemptible light, and finally a vanity and self-importance which revels in its own existence. (PR 175R)

The entertainment theory remains stuck in solipsistic subjectivity. Ethi-cality is amiss. At best, the entertainment theory institutionalizes and fo-ments the first moment of self-consciousness: namely, of the natural being

who feels immediate with her or his arbitrary will as if there are no differences amongst strangers and their arbitrary wills. The entertainment theory plays to the arbitrary will of the monadic individual so important to
individualist civil society. The social-cultural ethos of the organic community, where reciprocal recognition bonds individuals together, is excluded
from the entertainment education (PR 187R).

The second theory of education is what we would call today a "skills
orientation." A government's department of education or even a university may explicitly or implicitly posit educational objectives in terms of
skills training. The skills are means to objectives. *Verstand* helps to induce
skills-oriented objectives. Hegel describes the skills approach in this way:
"needs, their satisfaction, the pleasures and comforts of individual [*par-
tikularen*] life, etc. are *absolute* ends" (PR 187R). The needs and objectives
may well go unspoken and unchallenged. Hegel's complaint, not surprisingly, is that "education will be regarded as merely a *means* to these ends"
(PR 187R). Education becomes instrumental rationality. The second form
of education, like the first, ignores the importance of the ethicality in the
development of self-consciousness (or spirit) and, therefore, of *Vernunft*.

Hegel situates the family and educational institutions of the state in
the context of a third approach to education. Here, the aim is to inculcate
Bildung (PR 197). It cannot be taught from books nor from punishment.
It incorporates a practical reason oriented towards ethicality. One has to
reflect about one's skills, intellectual analytic abilities, and arbitrary desires to strangers through shared universals of the context-specific circumstances in which one acts. The teacher must relate the first two forms of
education with the universals in action.

Bildung is a practical and a theoretical education (PR 197). First, it feeds
the capacity of the student/child's mind to be a self-starter as a thinking being (PR 187). Further, it helps the student/child to become conscious of
her or his ethical relations with others: "[e]ducation [*Pädagogik*] is the art
of making human beings ethical: it considers them as natural beings and
shows them how they can be reborn, and how their original nature can be
transformed into a second, spiritual nature so that this spirituality becomes
habitual to them . . . the resistance of the subject is broken" (PR 151A). Finally, *Bildung* inculcates the capacity of the child to recognize a stranger
in context-specific circumstances through shared universals of the ethos.
Hegel puts this final objective in this way: "[e]*ducation,* in its absolute determination, is therefore *liberation* and *work* towards a higher liberation"
(PR 187R). The education examines the social content and form of posited rules and institutional procedures. The student is thereby transformed

into a higher level of self-consciousness so that she or he feels at home with the universals shared in the community. With this third function of education, Hegel links the role of the family with the organic constitution. The objectivity of consciousness is reconciled with subjectivity through shared universals as represented in the content of rules, institutional procedures, tradition, religious and cultural practices, and the like. The arbitrary feelings and caprice of the subject are displaced in favor of the shared assumptions and expectations of the community. Education becomes a struggle to become self-conscious through the fostering of *Bildung*.

In the third theory of education, the parents/teachers attempt to instill two sets of conditions for *Bildung*. One, education needs "to eliminate *natural simplicity,* whether as passive selflessness [as in the family] or as barbarism of knowledge and volition [in the civil society]—i.e. to eliminate the *immediacy* and individuality [*Einzelheit*] in which spirit is immersed" (PR 187R). Two, education works to render the individual self-conscious of her or his role in the construction of the objectivity of consciousness: "[*e*]*ducation,* in its absolute determination, is therefore *liberation* and *work* towards a higher liberation; it is absolute transition to the infinitely subjective substantiality of ethical life, which is no longer immediate and natural [as in the family], but spiritual and at the same time raised to the shape of universality [which immanently transcends the particularities in civil society]" (PR 187R). The legal consciousness is thereby raised to the ever-changing structures of consciousness. The child/student fulfills her or his potential to become free. And all this is only possible, as Max Horkheimer later emphasizes,[32] if the student thinks critically about the presuppositions with which she or he begins the project of self-consciousness. The most important such presupposition concerns the act of thinking through time-consciousness as elaborated in Chapters 3 and 6.

e) The Organism as a Social Unity

Finally, the organic constitution is a unified, yet self-reflective, social ethos.[33] Although the state itself is said to embody the reconciliation of objectivity with subjectivity, Hegel's description of the ethos as a state is hardly recognizable as a state today. Perhaps we had better have Cicero's *de Republica* in mind. What we would consider today as the state—a centralized institutional structure whose Head claims absolute title over its territory—is only one member of the ethos. The constitution is rooted "in the unity" of the ethos as a whole (PR 278). The ethos, like the organism, exists *for* and *in itself*. Put briefly, the organism constitutes, Hegel writes in *Philosophy of Mind*, "the *self-conscious* ethical substance, the unification of the family principle with that of civil society" (PM 535). Intermediate organizations function to fulfill this unification because the self-conscious individual bonds with others. Such organizations are intermediate between the self-conscious individual and the shared universals of the ethos. Such an ethos embodies the organic constitution. The organism is generated from its own inward life force. It develops from within itself. And its posited rules are subjective by virtue of their shared character (PM 537). Such a self-sufficient ethos needs a symbol for its singularity.[34] The monarch fulfills such a symbol (PR 279R).

4. GOVERNMENTAL STRUCTURE

How does Hegel propose that the organic theory of a constitution be institutionalized? The key here lies in Hegel's etymological association of an organization with an organism.[35] Aside from this etymology, Hegel quite explicitly equates the organic unity of the state with a state-centric organization of public officials (PR 297A). Even the officials are said to be "organs" that function in an organic relation with other organs. The state itself "is essentially an organization whose members constitute *circles in their own right* [*für sich*], and no moment within it should appear as an unorganized crowd" (PR 303R). Indeed, without an organization where the mass attains its interests in "a legitimate and orderly fashion," the people function as "a destructive mass" opposed to the rule of law (PR 302A). So, Hegel elaborates how a state-centric organization will displace the chaos of arbitrary wills with order. Each official in the organization represents the universals at the same time that each official acts within the boundaries of its jurisdiction. The organization takes the shape of a pyramid. Hegel's description of the organization is a precursor to Max Weber's theory of a bureaucracy.[36]

The question that remains with us is whether such an organization ends the inquiry into the legitimacy of a modern legal order. Or does it continue the legal formalism that plagued civil society? Further, who is the author of the governmental organization? the monarch? the officials? And are some individuals strangers to the organization? For example, do officials of the organization have a duty to protect nonnationals? migrant workers? aboriginal peoples? other stateless peoples? Do the officials of the organization, that is, determine who has legal standing?

a) The Pyramid

Hegel is determined to explain and justify why the objectivity of consciousness is legitimate even though the individual is aware that she or he
is a thinking being autonomous of the objectivity. Part of his explanation
is the integration of the institution's organization into one pyramidal institutional whole. Michel Foucault expands upon Hegel's theory of the pyramidal form of governmentality in an important essay and in his lectures
on constitutionalism.[37] Hegel believes that a governmental organization
is a further step up the ladder of individual self-consciousness. Hegel does
not seem to conceive of the possibility of domestic conflict between one
pyramidal structure and another such as occurs today in a federal state.
Heavily influenced by Charles de Montesquieu (1689–1755),[38] Hegel sets
out the pyramidal structure in a nice clean and interconnected system of
lines: each subordinate structure is vertically and horizontally joined with
the next. Several branches of governmental organization lie on a horizontal line, each with equal status: the legislature, the executive, and the judiciary. The executive comprises subordinate authorities, including boards
and offices. The judiciary incorporates the administration of justice. The
vertical lines join each branch with the crown at the pinnacle of the pyramid. The three branches of the pyramid are subdivided into subordinate
sections. Each section is also organized in a pyramidal form. Each office
has its own jurisdiction, and each office has a head or director to oversee
the work of the underlings in the office. Because of the organizational interdependence of each office with the next, each office or official does not
act from an arbitrary will but from "*the end of the whole* (to which the indeterminate expression 'the *welfare of the state*' has in general been applied)"
(PR 278R). In the interdependent organizational structure, each official
acts within its own boundaries. This ensures the supremacy of forms over
the arbitrary will. Each official has freedom to act within the boundary of
its authority at the same time that she or he stands under the authority of
superior supervision (PM 543). The boundaries of jurisdiction add to the
objectivity of consciousness.

Hegel contrasts this pyramidal structure of governmentality with the
personalized despotic regimes of the eighteenth century, characterized as
they were by rebellion, arbitrariness and violent acts by rulers, civil wars,
and general devastation (PR 286R). Even the constitutional disputes of
feudal society were resolved by power rather than by legitimacy. Mindful
of the German principalities of Hegel's day, there was an absence of any

rationally coherent organizational structure that could embody the ethos. As a consequence, the arbitrary will, rather than law, characterized governmentality (GC 74). Chance and power, not shared universals, determined who and what decisions to make. The Enlightenment idea of the autonomous control of one's future had no place. Force reconciled conflicts of rights. The spheres of the legislature, courts, churches, and military overlapped and exhibited confusion. At best, there was a rogue state or what Hegel calls "a state in thought" (CG 43).

The pyramidal organization of an organic constitution, Hegel claims, ensures domestic peace. Rules of succession prevail so as to avoid the inevitable violence when a ruler dies or loses public support as in feudal regimes (PR 286R). The clamor of public opinion remains outside the universal interests of the governmental organization (PR 318). The officials are members, not parts, of an organic whole. By fulfilling its jurisdiction, each office maintains and protects other offices. Each official thereby represents the universal interest of the ethos as a whole, assuming that the governmental organization is synonymous with the constitutional organism. In contrast with the collective violence in the family, civil society, and even educational institutions,[39] peace prevails because the organization, including the state, grows immanently from the development of self-consciousness into the reciprocal recognition among strangers. The living organism preserves and embodies the governmental organization (PM 541). As Hegel puts it, the legal status and the juridification of social relationships in the governmental organization prevent subjective arbitrariness from interfering with the universal interests of the organism (PR 295). The more complex the organization, the more the intermediate organizations, such as the family, the guild or public authorities, decline as a threat to the objectivity of consciousness. When officials exceed the jurisdiction of their office, the head of state may intervene (PR 295R).

b) Separation of Powers

The separation of powers amongst the judiciary, the legislature, and the administrative arms of the organism adds to the organic character of a constitution as a living organism (PR 273). Each institution functions as an organ in the organism. The monarch as an organ, for example, reconciles subjectivity (as a living being) with objectivity (as the head of the institutional organization). The executive functions as particularity. The lower house legislates rules and, therefore, it represents universality. The upper house mediates between the universality and the particularity (PR 302). In order to unify government, it helps if the executive officials of the governmental organization are members of the legislature (PR 300A).

Intermediate social organizations (except for charities), being recognized with legal standing, delegate deputies to the upper house. Similarly, the estates gain a temperament and intellectual glimpse of the whole ethos. The executive, the *Volk* and the estates "embody in equal measure both the *sense* and *disposition* of the *state* and *government* and the *interests of particular* circles and *individuals [Einzelnen]*" (PR 302). The estates, being social and economic classes, ensure that individuals do not dominate as a disorganized crowd or as an aggregate of individuals who oppose the organic constitution. The democratic suffrage, if universal, invites arbitrary wills to dominate the decisions of state (PR 311R). The Estates Assemblies, as elements of the external state in civil society, now function as a forum for individual grievances, the enactment of legislation, and the taxation for the greater good. However, in the organic constitution, the Assemblies additionally function in the formation of *Bildung*: "[i]f the Estates hold their assemblies in public, they afford a great spectacle of outstanding educational value to the citizens, and it is from this above all that the people can learn the true nature of their interests" (PR 315A). Legislators develop the virtues, skills, and values that function as a model for the lives of ordinary citizens. Political parties do not exist in Hegel's scheme nor did they exist in European states as yet. The representatives of the estates are free-voting members of the legislature (PR 309).[40] Without a legislative assembly, the *Volk* is alienated from the state.

c) The Executive

The Executive is divided into administrative (or governmental) authorities and judicial offices (PM 541).[41] In both cases, the public servant is the product of a formal and informal education which has inculcated an appreciation for the universals in the consciousness of the public servant. Each section of a governmental department links with the social relationships in the ethos (PM 541). Each institutional office is linked with the next so as to sustain a political equilibrium (PM 541) and effective control from above (PR 290A). Without such interrelated offices in the Executive, the *Volk* is "a collection of scattered atoms" much as characterized civil society (PR 290A).

The subjective arbitrary wills of the members of the Estates Assemblies are thereby transformed into the objectivity of consciousness (PR 291). Together, the governmental organization, of which courts are an office, constitutes the "general legal order" (PM 528, 543). Since the governmental structure represents universality, fellow citizens and equals must have trust in the administrators (PR 288). For their part, the public servants must sacrifice their personal self-interests and arbitrary wills for the universals of the whole organization (PR 294R). The governmental departments, as a consequence, transcend particularity. However, unless a department of government fulfills its function with relation to the reciprocal recognition of individual with stranger, legal formalism returns.

d) The Legislature

The legislature, which plays such an important part in the enactment of laws, is a subordinate institution in the organic constitution (PR 198).[42] For the legislature embodies the "subjective formal freedom" of interest groups (PR 301, PM 544). In particular, the legislature or "estates-collegium" offers a forum where the arbitrary wills participate in governmentality (PM 544). Such participation is embodied in the legislative process.

That said, even the legislators must protect the universals rather than just the arbitrary wills of particular groups that she or he represents: the legislator must be a statesman rather than a politician (1824/25 W238). The legislative process adds to the bonding of the observed individual with the universals of the ethos. A statute, then, has two aspects. One is the universal aspect which joins the private interests pressuring for the statute with the interest of the organism as a whole. The second, more dominant element of a statute is the subjectivity reflected in interest group politics. Contingent and arbitrary wills dominate in the latter context of the legislative process. Political strength determines the legislative outcome. The legislation, like a written constitution, is external to consciousness. The jurist needs to be made aware of the arbitrariness and contingency of a statute (PM 529).

The political participation of the estates (or classes) in the legislation also helps to inculcate bonding amongst shared universals. Publicity of proceedings adds a consciousness of the universals and the role of subjectivity in creating the universals (PR 315). Conversely, the public deliberation educates individuals to become self-conscious as to how their particular interests dissolve in favor of shared universals with strangers. This, in turn, opens the individual to recognize the universal interests of the organism (PR 315A). The *Volk,* instead of representing the collective conscience, develops by manifesting the reciprocal recognition of members and strangers inside and outside the *Volk*. Rhetorical skills matter in the legislature. Politicians will only survive this public forum if they are "armed with wit and eloquence" in the legislature (PR 315A). The "virtues, abilities and skills" necessary for public deliberation function as a model for citizens generally (PR 315A). In addition to legal rhetoric, though, "insight and reasoned argument" "mainly" displace custom and collective violence as the source of recognition of particular interests (PR 316A).

In addition, legislators represent the universal interests of the organism (PR 311R). In one later lecture, Hegel says that since the self-conscious will is the qualification for voting, women should be allowed to vote (1824/25 W243). The legislature is based upon "the firm and recognized ground" of a constitution that has evolved over time (PR 298A). Although Karl Marx (1818–83) sees direct democracy as the alternative to monarchy,[43] Hegel asks whether a constitution would even exist if the content of laws were legitimate by virtue only of a majority will. Indeed, Hegel shudders at the thought of a direct democracy. In direct democracy, the *Volk* prevails because individuals do not reflect about their arbitrary wills (PR 301R). The will, after all, "is the fruit of profound cognition and insight, and this is the very thing [*Sache*] that the people lack" (PR 301R).

e) The Monarch

The monarch, as a subjectivity, particularizes the objectivity, as a governmental structure (PR 320A).[44] Without a human subject as head of state, the constitutional order would lack subjective freedom: it would be an anonymous machine "out there" no matter how organic the constitution is otherwise (PR 279, 292). The monarch does not author or enact laws.[45] The monarch is not necessarily a de facto ruler. The legitimacy of the monarch is not inherited. Nor does the legitimacy of the monarch depend upon particular popularity or meritorious traits of the monarch (PR 280A). The monarch is "the absolute apex of an organically developed state." The monarch is only one office in the pyramidal structure, though (PR 279R). As one office in the pyramidal structure, even the monarch is constrained by the rule of law that transcends the acts and decisions of the monarch. Many miss this, including Karl Marx.[46]

The monarch plays two roles. In the first role, the monarch signifies the objectivity of consciousness. This is so because the monarch inherits the Crown and, therefore, does not have to compete with others in the arena of arbitrary wills.[47] In addition, the monarch is only one institution in a complex of interrelated organizations (PR 279R). Further, the monarch remains subject to the preexisting governmental structure.[48] The monarch is situated at the pinnacle of the governmental organization of the organic constitution. The latter structure of jurisdiction, not some arbitrary whim of a monarch, characterizes the monarchical constitution. Further, the monarch's signature completes the governmental organization. The head of the state need only say "I shall" (PR 279A). The head need merely sign his or her name: "if the constitution is firmly established, he [the monarch] often has nothing more to do than to sign his name. But this *name* is important: it is ultimate instance and *non plus ultra* . . . an 'I will' must be pronounced by man himself on the issue to be decided" (PR 281A). In sum, the monarch symbolizes the personhood of the self-sufficient organism.

The monarch is subject to the rule of law because of a second role: the monarch, being a living being, signifies the subjectivity that is so indispensable to the legitimacy of a modern legal order. The monarch embodies the content of the objectivity with particularity.[49] The monarch, then, represents the objectivity of consciousness at the very moment that she or he represents the subjectivity of self-consciousness (PR 285).

Thus, the monarch joins objectivity with subjectivity. The monarch, as a symbol of this reconciliation, also has a signification. For there has to be a head of state to signify the relationship of subjectivity with objectivity in two contexts. Without such a head, first, the otherwise ad infinitum trace of one governmental office to the next "in the great edifice of the state" would lack termination. Second, without a head, how would one state know who represents the state in the international legal consciousness—more of the latter in the next chapter. Such symbolic and significatory unity was amiss during the feudal monarchies where there was no reconciliation of objectivity with subjectivity (PR 278).

5. THE RULE OF LAW OVER THE ARBITRARY WILL

The monarch and all other offices of the organic constitution are constrained, I have noted, by boundaries or the *vires* of their actions. This constraint marks an early development of the notion of the "rule of law" later developed by English constitutionalists.

a) The Subordination of State Institutions to Legality

Hegel explains the subordination of governmental offices to the rule of law in this manner: "[t]he protection of the state and the governed against the misuse of power on the part of the official bodies and their members is, on the one hand, the direct responsibility [*Verantwortlichkeit*] of their own hierarchy" (PR 295). The responsibility and answerability to officials higher in the pyramidal organization ensure that universals displace the arbitrary will of any one official. The individual is answerable to officials within the organizational hierarchy, not to the "people" or to social groups outside the hierarchy. The official plays a role within the institutional hierarchy. The role of the official is drawn from universal and objective elements in the structure as well as in the nonsubjective character of the official's decisions (PR 277). Merit, ability, skill, and character, rather than the salability or inheritance of offices as in medieval constitutions, determine the promotion and tenure of officials (PR 277A).

Several conditions work to subordinate the decisions and actions of the state's official to the rule of law.[50] For one thing, public officials act from impartiality. The judge acts as an agent of the organism (PM 532). The judge acts "in a third judgement which is disinterested" because she or he acts on behalf of the universals in the ethos as a whole. The judge lacks personal interest, for that would return the official to an ethos of the arbitrary will or of revenge (PM 500).

As another condition, the public official, like the citizen, is acculturated into the assumptions and expectations of the ethos (PR 295R). The third form of education, mentioned earlier in this chapter, helps form the official's mind-set towards context-specific problems. The "direct education in ethics and in thought" "provides a spiritual counterweight to the mechanical exercises and the like which are inherent in learning the so-called sciences appropriate to these [administrative] spheres" (PR 296). The official has been educated to reason in *Vernunft,* not just in *Verstand.*

As a third condition of constitutionality, intermediate organizations, such as the family, classes, and the corporation, are conferred legal status (except for charities). The arbitrary will of state officials may be institutionally constrained through such organizations (PR 295). Intermediate organizations also help to institutionalize the rule of law.[51]

As a final condition of constitutionality, the state is no longer external to the human subject. Rather, the state official is immersed in the time-consciousness of the inhabitants, all the intermediate organizations, and the complex governmental organization, all of which, when linked together, constitute an organic constitution. The organic legal order is very different from Marx's reading of the state as the "God-man" into Hegel's constitutionalism. The "God-man," unlike an organic state, posits its arbitrary will external to the ethos.[52] When Marx describes the state as the subject, he takes it, as we often do today, as the abstract liberal state that is externally separate from the human subject. So too does Carl Schmitt.[53] Because the state, as an organism, is a radically different phenomenon where anthropological social life constitutes the rule of law, Marx misses that, for Hegel, constitutionality is not an objectivity external to the never-ending development of self-consciousness. The resource material for legality includes assumptions and expectations, intermediate social organizations, and unwritten conventions among state institutions. The self-consciousness of the individual's role in such relationships constitutes constitutionality. The rule of law involves the binding character of such constitutionality over the individual's arbitrary will.

b) The Protection of Ethnic Minorities

The constitution is embodied from the social relationships represented by the content of universals in the ethos. But what of the Quakers who refused to defend the state against foreign enemies and who refused to recognize other duties towards the state? And what about the American slaves? Or the Jewish peoples against whom there was a public outcry between 1815–20 because of the xenophobia and nationalism following Napoleon's invasion and conquest of the Germanic principalities?

Hegel writes in a footnote that such excluded groups are an "anomaly" to the organic constitution (PR 270R).[54] However, in contrast with Fries' opinion in a pamphlet in 1816,[55] noted in the Preface of *Philosophy of Right*, the mature state needs to be tolerant of such religious and ethnic groups by relying upon "the power of custom and the inner rationality of its institutions to reduce and overcome the discrepancy." The ethicality of the organic constitution manifests the recognition that Jewish peoples, for example, are "human beings." Jewish peoples are "not just a neutral and abstract quality" that abstract personhood would confer upon them. The conferral of civil rights to the Jewish peoples protects and guarantees to them, Hegel continues in the above footnote, "a *self-awareness* as recognized *legal* [*rechtliche*] persons in civil society, and it is from this root, infinite and free from all other influences, that the desired assimilation in terms of attitude and disposition arises." The failure to recognize the Jewish peoples with legal standing reinforces the very alienation attributed to them and thereby results in the folly of governmental policy, according to Hegel.

c) State Duties to Inhabitants

In this context, the immanent universals of the organic constitution imply that certain state duties are owed to the stranger of the self-conscious individual (PR 261R). One set of duties protects freedom of conscience, freedom of thought, and the freedom of political participation (and this is not just the freedom to vote). Hegel also recognizes the need to respect the freedom of groups, such as the family, to educate group members, and to lead their own collective lives in certain directions that may depart from the social norms of the general community. That said, the need of an ethos requires that there be one compulsory educational system for all children. The legal order also needs to provide full information to the individual of what the government of the day is doing and why it is so acting. Further, legal officials have the duty to maintain a transparent political process. This is not just a matter of maintaining a noncorrupt and noncorruptible public service. Nor is it just a matter of ensuring the right to vote to all citizens. In addition, the legal order must set in motion institutional procedures to ensure that the citizen participates in the day-to-day deliberation about the content of posited laws, in the deliberation and decision about criminal trials in the form of juries, and in the scrutiny of the decisions of the Executive arm of the government.

Most importantly, the state has duties to protect the inner freedom of the individual to think, to will the world about her- or himself, and to act according to one's own reflective will with *Vernunft*. We saw in Chapter 4 that the freedom to develop self-consciousness is peremptory over the unlimited acquisition of property. To be recognized, each subject wishes to be consulted and to be given a hearing when her or his private interests are harmed (PR 317A). When one is granted such a hearing, the observed individual correspondingly widens her or his expectations of toleration of the legislature's actions. Hegel's sense of free speech calls for argument, rather than for the silence of opposition, to prevail. Since the assemblies "give expression to sound [*gediegene*] and educated insights concerning the interests of the state, leaving little of significance for others to say," and above all leaving little room for one to claim a distinctive importance to the content of their speech, free expression can be guaranteed without harm to the organic ethos (PR 319).

It is important for the family, corporations, religious organizations, and other social associations that laws posited by the external state encourage individual participation and freedom of speech. Legal institutions—the courts, the executive arm of the government and the legislature, and the public servants—have a duty to protect freedom of expression by positing rules. More, the state has the duty to inculcate a culture of respect towards the freedom of conscience and expression of the stranger. It is the duty of such state institutions to institutionalize procedures, social conditions, and a basic economic minimal standard for the social-cultural universals which manifest reciprocal recognition. This is required of the state in order that the subject and stranger can effectively feel "at home" with the objectivity of consciousness.

6. THE STATE OF EXCEPTION

Now, a serious problem might well undermine Hegel's organic constitution. Once the philosopher observes the reconciliation of objectivity with subjectivity in the institutionalization of the organic legal order, does this signify that the movement of time-consciousness has ended? Has the state become a subject? Is the state itself the embodiment of the *in itself* and the *for itself*? If so, has Hegel elaborated a philosophy of the subjectivity of the state as Schmitt suggests?[56] If so, is interstate war inevitable? And is any effort to observe how peremptory norms and humanitarianism constrain the state action a mere exercise in the nonpolitical as Schmitt puts it?

There is much to suggest that Hegel has done so. This is especially apparent when Hegel describes how all inhabitants must rally around the organism when the state is threatened (PR 278R). The observed individual has a duty to preserve the organism even if the individual's own life and property are threatened (PR 324). This is especially so in wartime (PR 234A). After all, the organic constitution manifests ethicality as well as a reflective bonding amongst the organism's members. Both subject and stranger feel at home with the objectivity of the institutions, such as the courts, legislature, executive, and monarch, as well as of the posited laws of the legislature and executive. Objectivity finally reconciles with subjectivity (at least until the reconciliation encounters other states in international legal consciousness). The organic constitution, which represents the reconciliation, is recognized by other organic constitutions as a legal person who "*knows* what it wills, and knows it in its *universality* as something *thought*. Consequently, it acts and functions in accordance with known ends and recognized principles, and with laws which are laws not only *in themselves* but also for the consciousness" (PR 270). There is no stranger possible if an ethos exists *for itself* and *in itself* and if the ethos recognizes itself in the stranger—that is, if the ethos is ethical. Indeed, at one point, Hegel suggests that the individual loses her or his capacity to reflect and to criticize the objectivity of consciousness as represented by the organic state:

> [i]n this way, *ethical substantiality* has attained its *right,* and the latter has attained *validity.* That is, the self-will of the individual [*des Einzelnen*], and his own conscience in its attempt to exist for itself and in opposition to the ethical

substantiality, have disappeared; for the ethical character knows that the end which moves it is the universal which, though itself unmoved, has developed through its determinations into actual rationality, and it recognizes that its own dignity and the whole continued existence [*Bestehen*] of its particular ends are based upon and actualized within this universal (PR 152).

So, the quest for self-consciousness seems to have "disappeared" once objectivity is reconciled with subjectivity in the domestic relations of individual within the territory of the state. The dissolution of the drive to become self-conscious especially closes the act of thinking. Has Hegel himself excluded the very freedom that generated the drive of the subject to become self-conscious? Has Hegel elaborated the philosophy of the state of exception?

There is substantial support for such a view in contemporary political philosophy. David Kolb takes this view, for example, when he writes in his *The Critique of Pure Modernity* that "[w]hen Hegel pulls everything into the transcendental realm, no longer does that realm face an empirical or external realm that it conditions. No structures based on ultimate opposition survive."[57] So too John Rawls accepts that the organic state ends Hegel's analysis about the nature of politics.[58] Rawls's *A Theory of Justice* constructs a theory of justice from an externally posited procedure that is purged from any ethos or any immediacy with which the subject can be identified.[59] E. Tugendhat claims that independent reflection is no longer needed.[60] Dudley Knowles also concludes that "Hegel's text does not read as though he is describing the mind-set of citizens with a lively sense of the publicly avowed credentials of authoritative institutions."[61] Indeed, Knowles asserts that one would be better off if one did not philosophize (in Hegel's speculative sense) if immersed in the organic constitution where objectivity (and the stranger) are reconciled with subjectivity. More, the *Sitten* of ethical ethos foreclose "the liberal self-awareness that continually holds the government to account in terms of public standards of justice."[62] Frederick Neuhouser, in his rich exegesis of Hegel's texts,[63] also attributes a loss of the individual conscience and social criticism in the organic constitution in that one will have already endorsed the content of legality once an organic constitution is institutionalized.[64] Jürgen Habermas suggests that one unifies with universals of the ethos "only in the framework of *monological* knowledge."[65] The organic state becomes the "ultimate self" which, when taken as an abstraction, is "simple and therefore an *immediate* individuality [*Einzelheit*]" (PR 280). And Schmitt claims that the dialectic ends with the arbitrary will of the state, not the never-ending quest for self-consciousness that Hegel holds out for philosophy.[66] The state becomes a higher-ordered subjectivity than is the subjective freedom of the individual. Hegel's organic structure of consciousness is the object of contemporary criticism precisely because it supposedly ends the project of self-consciousness.[67] But is this so?

a) The Arbitrary Will of the State

Both Anglo-American constitutional principles and multilateral treaties provide that when the life of the state is threatened internally or externally, the state may make an exception to the rule of law and impose its will over the domestic and international norms accepted in ordinary circumstances.[68] Article 4 of the *International Covenant of Civil and Political Rights,* for example, defers to the state of exception "[i]n times of public emergency which threatens the life of the nation and the existence of which is officially proclaimed."[69] It remains a moot issue in common law jurisdictions whether the declaration of an emergency authorizes the usurpation of the rule of law.[70] When we turn to leading legal philosophers of the legitimacy of a state of exception, such as Hart, Schmitt, and Agamben, we find a very different state than that which Hegel situates in the organic constitutional order. The method of legal reasoning held out by general jurisprudence, for example, remains imprisoned in *Verstand*. It is difficult for general jurisprudence to consider international law as binding upon the state which, after all, is founded on the rule of recognition.[71] Time-consciousness is missed in Hart's freezing of the experiential time in the rule of recognition. Schmitt, for his part, does locate a modern legal order in time-consciousness[72] but he ends such time-consciousness in the life and death struggle not unlike Hegel's master-slave struggle which I recounted in Chapter 4. Time-consciousness is fixed in one moment of the act of thinking. He thereby entirely misses the ethicality of an ethos.[73] For Schmitt, the sovereign state ends the movement of self-consciousness.[74] The state shares no universals with other states and, accordingly, the state has only enemies and friends. The state's arbitrary will dominates its relations with other states. And the presupposed social relations in the content of the laws posited by the state are immaterial to his legal philosophy. The state is an immediacy that competes with other immediacies without the particularity of reciprocal recognition in the act of self-consciousness.[75] The same holds for Agamben's claim that Hegel justifies a permanent state of exception since immediacy, according to Agamben's reading of Hegel, is the real. Language, which is said to incorporate immediacy into concepts, is a supplement of the real.[76]

The mere expression of the arbitrary will, however, is hardly what Hegel holds out for the organic objectivity of consciousness. State officials function in organs in the organism. A centrally organized structure constrains the acts of each organ in the legal organism. These boundaries even constrain the acts of the monarch, as we have seen. Further, any posit of the arbitrary will of the executive or of the executive on behalf of the state opens the state to the very critique which Hegel offers of legal formalism (as retrieved in Chapter 5) and of the externality and of the state in civil society (as retrieved in Chapter 8). Further, the arbitrary will of the state, as subject, counters the possibility of reciprocal recognition of subject and stranger. Certainly, any state of exception proclaimed from the arbitrary will of the executive or even of the public through the executive would lack legitimacy because, once again, Hegel has consistently maintained that legitimacy rests in the self-consciousness of the individual. The appeal to the immediacy of the state, no matter how passionately and seriously espoused by individual inhabitants, expresses the arbitrary will, not the reflective will of speculative philosophy that Hegel associates with *Vernunft*. The consequence is that "folly, outrage, and the destruction of all ethical relations" are produced (PR 270R).

b) Peremptory Norms Against the State's Arbitrary Will

The reading of a state of exception into Hegel's legal philosophy is also seriously problematic once one appreciates, as I argued in Chapter 4, that there are peremptory norms against state action, norms that render the state of exception void. Further, Hegel's very linkage of the identity of law with legitimacy begs that the imposition of an alleged state of exception by the state be examined in terms of the ethicality of the content of the declaration of the emergency. This opens the inquiry into any effort by the state, having embodied the reconciliation of objectivity with subjectivity, to repress the very presupposition of philosophy: namely, that there are only two elements of philosophy—immediacy and mediation. I shall now address this presupposition and the inability of any state to repress it.

In Chapter 4, I retrieved how immediacy draws from conscience, religious practices, thought, and belief, all of which are immune from state interference. When Hegel traces the movement of observed consciousness into mediation by thinking, here too he recognizes important elements of such thinking that are immune from any state of exception. Contracts may be void, for example, even if posited laws authorize contracts into slavery. Further, all human beings, however unconscious, have the potential to displace the violence of the arbitrary will (even of the state) with self-consciousness. Hegel is not just concerned with the extreme case of slavery although this is not to understate its importance today. Even the erasure by the state of the possibility of abstract personhood undermines the very mediation of thinking. Indeed, the will itself is the expression of *self*-consciousness. If the state denies the very possibility of the will by claiming the will of the state as the reconciliation of the objectivity of consciousness with subjectivity, the act of self-consciousness terminates. Indeed, Hegel's fundamental distinction between an animal and a human being rests upon the human propensity to think. The state as monologic subject, as held out by Habermas, Schmitt, and Agamben, is fit for animals, not humans.

c) *International Objectivity of Legal Consciousness*

What is critical to appreciate in this context is that even if the state were considered an organic legal order of which the state is only one organ, self-consciousness moves into the international objectivity of consciousness. The latter proceeds through several movements which I identify in the next chapter, just as Hegel described of the domestic legal order. This being so, the freedom of the state to impose its arbitrary will upon other states, as Schmitt claims, is the very early moment of immediacy with the objectivity of international legal consciousness. Schmitt, in particular, describes the inevitability of war in "the political" (that is, a situation of interstate struggle) as if the state cannot escape from the master-slave struggle for life that Hegel described of two immediacies that face each other without particularity.[77] Further, the arbitrary will of a sovereign state, so forcefully described by Schmitt and Agamben, is alien to the very spirit of self-conscious development that Hegel claims for the observed individual and for the philosophical consciousness.

d) *Closure of Development of Self-Consciousness*

The more serious problematic of the state as the subject with an arbitrary will is that such a state brings closure to the movement of self-consciousness. Once the interpreter reads closure into Hegel's legal philosophy, the logic of the reading leads to the very terror—only in this case a state terror—that cautioned Hegel in his own thinking about the nature and identity of law. The arbitrary will of the state excludes any public-spirited reflection and criticism about the content of laws and their institutions. So too, the state as arbitrary will excludes any consideration of the ethicality of the domestic and international ethos in which the state itself is situated. The organic constitutional order is not intrinsic in the sense of being self-sustaining and complete and, therefore, the ultimate source of freedom. The attribution of such an intrinsic character to the organic constitution closes philosophical inquiry just when the international objectivity of consciousness takes form. Turning to the passage with which I began this study, "as far as the individual is concerned, each individual is in any case a *child of his time*; thus philosophy, too, is *its own time comprehended in thoughts*" (PR 21). The readers of Hegel's legal philosophy would do well to recognize their own interpretations as contextualized in their own times. This is so of Carl Schmitt's reading of Hegel, immersed as he was in a world where hard sovereignty (a term that I shall develop in the next chapter) reigned supreme.

The organic constitution is not an end in itself but the institutionalization of the human quest for self-consciousness. This quest, one needs to recall, is generated from a spirit that Hegel likened to Socrates' *daimonic* voice and that he describes as divine by virtue of its invisibility or inaccessibility to human concepts. As Hegel explains in his *Vorlesungen über die Philosophie der Religion*:

> It is the organization of the state that the divine has broken through [*eingeschlagen*] into the sphere of actuality; the latter is permeated by the former, and the worldly realm is now justified in and for itself, for its foundation is the divine will, the law of right and freedom. The true reconciliation, whereby the divine realizes itself in the domain of actuality, consists in the ethical and juridical life of the state: this is the authentic discipline [*Subaktion*] of worldliness.[78]

The claim that the organic constitution ends the development of self-consciousness erroneously suggests a closure to time-consciousness. "Thinking is the absolute judge, before which the content must verify and attest its claims":[79] this is so for all the different forms of the objectivity of consciousness. Further, several elements of Hegel's legal philosophy exemplify the never-ending quest for self-awareness: the philosophic method of *Vernunft,* the continual movement of the philosopher's reflective will to recognize the relationship between the individual and the stranger, the place of the family in different structures of legal consciousness, the problematic of legal formalism, the problematic of the exterior state, and the various shapes of a constitution. Hegel's extraordinary insights about the unfreedom of each structure of reflective legal consciousness continues after the philosopher recognizes the reconciliation of objectivity with subjective self-conscious in an organic constitution. The next chapter will exemplify such a continual movement when the organic legal order finds itself as only one legal person in international legal consciousness.

CHAPTER TEN

Shapes of International Law

It is indeed tempting to end Hegel's journey with the organic constitution. Hegel seems to have reconciled objective institutions of the state with the internal subjectivity of the thinking being. However, in the final paragraphs of *Philosophy of Right*, in his *Introduction to the Philosophy of History*, and in part three of *Encyclopaedia* (*Philosophy of Mind*), Hegel situates the state in an international objectivity of consciousness, and he then continues to identify different shapes of such an international objectivity. Each shape of the international legal consciousness presupposes that the spirit of self-consciousness finds external constraints to its freedom. Only in this context, because the will has reached a domestic organic legal order, the will is now that of a sovereign state instead of an observed human being. Different shapes of an international *Sittlichkeit* gain momentum in the international consciousness. And ethicality continues to be the center of study in each international *Sittlichkeit*.[1] Socrates' commandment, "know thyself" (*Apology* 21d5, 23b5), does not stop at the territorial boundary of *Recht*, for Hegel. Each time that the observed state recognizes an emergent objectivity that constrains its freedom, Hegel explains in *Lectures on the Philosophy of History*, "[t]he Spirit, in its new inward determination, has new interests and ends beyond those which it formerly possessed" (PH 147). The rupture between subjectivity and objectivity continues into various *Sittlichkeit* of international law.

In short, the domestic reconciliation of objective institutions and laws with subjectivity generates the beginning of another series of movements of consciousness. On the one hand, the organic state, as the only recognized juridical person in international relations, is believed to reconcile objectivity with subjectivity domestically. On the other hand, in the context of international relations, the same organic state is a single person which posits its own arbitrary will unless that will causes harm to the universals of international legal consciousness. As with the individual legal person, ethicality exhibits the relations of one state with another (PR 279, 360). That said, Hegel is aware that "the welfare of a state has quite a different justification from the welfare of the individual [*des Einzelnen*]" (PR 337R).

Like the human subject, the interpersonal relations of the state, as the unit of the international legal order, are in continual flux. The organic state must develop vis-à-vis other states through the many "stages in the general development of mind in its actuality" (PM 536). As Hegel writes in the Preface to *Philosophy of Right*:

> since the rational, which is synonymous with the Idea, becomes actual by entering into external existence [*Existenz*], it emerges in an infinite wealth of forms, appearances, and shapes and surrounds its core with a brightly coloured covering in which consciousness at first resides but which only the concept can penetrate in order to find the inner pulse, and detect its continued beat even within the external shapes. (PR Pref. 21)

In this chapter, I shall exemplify such continual movement by identifying three shapes of international legal consciousness: international law as abstract right, international law as civil society, and an organic world history.

I shall begin by privileging Kant's legal formalism and Hegel's critique of the formalism. In the first shape of international legal consciousness—international abstract right—the state is not aware of its separation from shared international norms. In the second shape—the international civil society—such a monadic state recognizes that it is dependent upon other states to fulfill its arbitrary will. The treaty, like a contract, fulfills the state's arbitrary will. But still further external obstacles constrain state action in international civil society. This takes us to the third shape of international legal consciousness—world history. Shared peremptory norms void state action, even when that action is institutionalized in a treaty. I shall identify such peremptory norms. Hegel leaves us with the possibility that a state-centric international legal order may well dissolve, just as did the family, when the emergent peremptory universal norms displace international abstract right and civil society (PR 344).

I. KANT AND THE LEAGUE OF NATIONS

Our entry point into Hegel's philosophy of international law is Kant. In addition to Kant's "Perpetual Peace,"[2] Hegel cites other texts, particularly the works of Grotius, Pufendorf, and Christian Freiherr von Wolff

(1679–1754).[3] Once we understand Hegel's critique of Kant, I shall return to Hegel's analysis of the presupposed structures of international law.

a) Kant's Peace

There are several contexts where Hegel critiques the formalism of Kant's theory of international law. Kant begins "Perpetual Peace," for example, by setting out the now familiar principles of the freedom and equality of sovereign states inter se in an international legal order. No one state may acquire another by inheritance, exchange, purchase, or gift. No treaty of peace can have secret reservations. All states are considered equal juridical persons. A war of punishment (*bellum punitivism*) is "inconceivable" since such a war presupposes a hierarchy of regimes and therefore opposes the equality of states.

Kant's league involves a federation of states (a "league of nations") with a Third to resolve disputes between states. The Third is a suprastate permanent court. The federation of states, Kant believes, would bring peace because the interests of the federation would transcend the private interests of each member state. Refugees and displaced inhabitants would be protected by this federation. Standing armies of the sovereign states would be dismantled. War itself would be illegal for, "[a]fter all, war is only a regrettable expedient for asserting one's rights by force within a state of nature, where no court of justice is available to judge with legal authority."[4] Kant admits that since states would not consent to such a world government in his own day, he would have to be satisfied with a federation of states. Such a federation, he believed, would constrain the hostile acts of states although war would remain a possibility.

Kant identifies two structures of international legal consciousness, and each presupposes an objectivity that remains alienated from the subjectivity of the arbitrary will of the state. In the first, Kant falls back upon *ius gentium*, a concept first introduced by Cicero and the object of focus by Grotius.[5] The concept of *ius gentium* synthesizes the legal principles shared amongst civilized states. Kant's *ius civitas* (where the individual possesses civil rights against the state) and *ius gentium* share a fundamental problem: both recognize the freedom of the state to dominate internally within its territorial borders unless the state causes harm to another state.[6] The state, like the individual human subject, possesses negative freedom. That state is free if its inhabitants lack any legal obligation to another state.[7] Consent is the basis of international legal obligation.[8] State consent is so important to international law, according to Kant, that the laws of a state of nature, as claimed by Grotius and Pufendorf, "do not and cannot have the slightest *legal* force."[9]

The second structure of international law, according to Kant, is *ius cosmopoliticum* where both individual human beings and states are juridical persons with standing before the international court. This second structure, eventually institutionalized as the League of Nations following World War I, is "necessary" for there to be peace. What is needed is an "international state" (*civitas gentium*) which "would necessarily continue to grow until it embraced all the peoples of the earth."[10] Kant holds out the possibility of a "universal community" where "a violation of rights in *one* part of the world [is] felt *everywhere*."[11] The binding norms of such a universal community are, Kant says, an "unwritten code of political and international right" which can be transformed "into a universal right of humanity." Kant associates such universal norms with a "cosmopolitan state."[12] If a secular state harms the cosmopolitan legal structure, public harm is caused.

b) Hegel's Critique of Kant's League of Nations

The problem with Kant's league of nations, according to Hegel, is that the state is an abstract person, rather than an international subject, to use Hegel's vocabulary. As a consequence, Kant's theory of international law entertains the prospect of the alienation of intersubjective social relations between states vis-à-vis the formalism of interpersonal objectivity (PR 135R). Behind the legal formalism, the arbitrary wills of states dominate international relations. The league of nations amalgamates such arbitrary wills. The league's legitimacy might even be challenged by self-interested monadic states that are parties to the league. Thus, "even if a number of states join together as a family, this league, in its individuality, must generate opposition and create an enemy" (PR 324A). Philosophical consciousness observes how a league of states formally conceals such political struggle between states just as philosophical consciousness observed how legal formalism concealed the struggle of life and death between two immediate arbitrary wills. The league, that is, is reified from the power relations between states.

The league of nations risks collapse, according to Hegel, because the league represents an "*empty formalism*" or "empty rhetoric of '*duty for duty's sake*.'" As Hegel describes in the Preface to *Philosophy of Right,* this "philosophizing . . . could well have continued to spin itself into its own web of *scholastic wisdom* . . . [or] a *world beyond* which exists only God knows where" (PR Pref. 19–10).[13] Further, the league itself is an individual legal person which becomes aware of external constraints upon its own freedom. Nonmembers will be strangers to the league (PR 324A). As long as the international objectivity of consciousness is composed of abstract persons, whether as a state or a league of states, the objectivity is reified from the social relations between states.

This formalism of the league has serious ramifications, according to Hegel. For one thing, the formalism ignores that state parties to the league possess the potential to develop in self-consciousness. This potential for self-consciousness has a deceptive formality even for a domestically organic constitution. On the one hand, the domestic legal order may have institutionalized the *Sittlichkeit* of an organism since it may have reconciled objectivity with subjectivity. On the other hand, in its external relations with other states, the organic legal order associates the international objectivity of consciousness with its will. Immediacy characterizes the international objectivity of consciousness at the same time that ethicality characterizes the domestic consciousness. Hegel argues that the ethical ethos embodied in the organic constitution is only Objective *Sittlichkeit,* not Absolute *Sittlichkeit.*[14] Though organic domestically, the state only exists externally if other subjects of the international legal order recognize it as a person: "[w]ithout relations with other states, the state can no more be an actual individual [*Individuum*] than an individual [*der Einzelne*] can be an actual person without a relationship [*Relation*] with other persons" (PR 331A, 322). Drawing from Grotius, Hegel asserts that shared universals, such as customs and general principles, are critical elements to the interpersonal relations of sovereign states.[15] As the state emerges from the immediacy, its arbitrary will underlies the formalism of the contract or treaty with other states. The formalism is best represented by treaties (PR 270A, 333). Like the master/slave relationship recounted in Chapter 4, the struggle between arbitrary wills makes the stranger either a friend or an enemy.

2. THE BEGINNING OF LEGALITY

Hegel made a critical distinction in his understanding of the problematic of a modern legal order. This was his distinction between a stateless and a state-centric society. Nomadic peoples or "peoples at a low level of culture" (*vulgas*) can hardly be recognized as a state (PR 331R). The *vulgas* live in a "prelegal age."[16] Even if a tribe signed a treaty with a sovereign state, such as frequently took place between Amerindian tribes and the British during the sixteenth and seventeenth centuries, the treaty would not be considered binding upon states because the tribe lacked the legal status of statehood in the international legal order.[17] To the extent that the tribe or nation remains unrecognized in the objectivity, the objectivity is a mere empty shell that disguises the inward anthropological forces of a nation (PR 330R). The heroes of the prelegal peoples establish states (PR 350). "Civilization" has not yet arrived.

a) The Ethnic Nation

Now, in his discussion of international law at the end of *Philosophy of Right* and in his *Introduction to the Philosophy of History,* Hegel introduces the highest form of the noncivilized society: the ethnic nation.[18] As mentioned in Chapter 7, Hegel writes of the role of a family in international legal consciousness in two contexts.[19] In the first, he compares the ethnic nation to a family where individuals are immediate with the universals of the nation and, in the second, there is a family of nations (PR 340). Hegel explains that "in its initial stage, a nation [*Volk*] is not a state, and the transition of a family, tribe, kinship group, mass [o]f people], etc. to the condition of a state constitutes the *formal* realization of the Idea [Concept] in general within it" (PR 349). Immediacy characterizes the nation just as it did the family in the domestic ethos (PR 346). A nation, because it is a concrete actuality, experiences time (PM 548). The nation has no beginning on a certain calendar date. Rather, collective memories have been previously experienced by ancestors. This experiential element of a nation has a spiritual character. The nation becomes self-conscious in relation to its own immediacy (being).

Before the nation is a unified social entity, though, it is composed of individuals, much as Lucretius describes of creatures in the primitive condition without a language or laws.[20] The individual is not even aware of her or his separation from the nation's universals. Because of immediacy with the nation, the nation's members do not think. The nation lacks a form. Hegel describes such individual human beings as "*vulgas,* not *populus*" (PM 544, PR 279R). If the nation lacks the form of a state, it is "a condition of lawlessness, demoralization, brutishness: in it the nation would only be shapeless, wild, blind force, like that of the stormy, elemental sea, which, however, is not self-destructive as a nation—a spiritual element—would be" (PM 544). The members lack any self-consciousness of their membership in the nation.

The ethnic nation, like the individual of the family, becomes increasingly self-conscious of its identity and of its relation with other nations and states as the ethnic nation experiences time: the nation "lives at this point, and the deeds of that nation, achieve fulfilment, fortune and fame" (PR 345). When the masses become aware that they share a nation, they become members, rather than units, of the nation just as an individual increasingly becomes aware of her or his membership in the *Sittlichkeit* through time consciousness. Each nation, Hegel claims, possesses its own identity "in its *geographical* and *anthropological* existence [*Existenz*]." The nation is marked by physical conditions, especially geography and climate (PM 545, 548). That said, the nation remains unrecognized by strangers external to the nation.

b) The Beginning of History

Until statehood is recognized, as I have argued about Hegal in earlier chapters, we live in a "prehistoric" or a "prelegal" world: "[a] nation with no state formation (a *mere nation*), has, strictly speaking, no history—like the nations which existed before the rise of states and others which still exist in a condition of savagery" (PM 549). History begins, for Hegel, when a nation is recognized as a state: that is as a legal person in the objectivity of international consciousness (PR 349–51). Only the state, not the nation, is deserving of recognition.

To be externally recognized, the nation internally needs a centralized government (PR 349). Only when the nation becomes "organized" with "a governmental power" may private individual subjects participate in public affairs of the state (PM 544, 549). By inference, tribal members do not do so. The ethnic nation also needs courts of law, public authorities [*Obrig-keit*], and police to enforce the courts' decisions before it can be recognized as a legal person (PR 279R). Hegel explains the development of conscious-ness from the nation to the state in this manner: "in the existence of a *nation* the substantial aim is to be a state and preserve itself as such." Even the domestic organic legal order desires to be recognized as a subject by states in the interstate legal order. The nation exists domestically in actual-ity but not internationally (PM 549). The ethnic nation, though embod-ied in a self-conscious ethos, lacks the recognition until other sovereign states recognize it (PR 279R). Recognition of the nation as a state marks the development of the nation from *immediacy* to the mediation of formal personhood.[21] Like the leap from the prelegal immediacy of the tribe to the legality of thinking beings, the immediacy of the nation similarly leaps into civilization as a state (PM 544). The self-conscious nation becomes "a vehicle for the contemporary development of the collective spirit in its actual existence: it is the objective actuality in which that spirit for the time invests its will" (PM 550).

The *Volk* develops from a "natural" to the legal existence of statehood.

A nation, characterized by immediacy, acts from an arbitrary will without being aware of its separation from objectivity. When the ethnic nation recognizes itself as a nation ("geographically and anthropologically," using Hegel's criteria of a nation), and is then recognized as a sovereign state by other states, the nation gives bodily content to the form of the state. The state confers external form onto the nation as the content of the state (PM 552). The state becomes a self-determining author of the international objectivity of consciousness although the author is not yet conscious of its separation from the objectivity.

c) The State as the Mark of Civilization

Hegel is emphatic that the conferral of personhood upon an ethnic nation marks an advancement from prelegality to civilization.[22] Hegel's association of civilization with the state is probably the second most important assumption that Hegel makes in his legal philosophy.[23] When he discusses the nature of contract, for example, he asserts that the state, like an Enlightenment subject,

> is the rational destiny [*Bestimmung*] of human beings to live within a state, and even if no state is yet present, reason requires that one be established . . . The great advance made by the state in modern times is that it remains an end in itself, and that each individual may no longer base his relationship [*Beziehung*] to it on his own private stipulation, as was the case in the Middle Ages. (PR 75A)

As another example, Hegel insists that the inhabitant just cannot leave the state's territory even if the state has breached the terms of the alleged contract with the inhabitant: "[t]he state itself must give permission for individuals [*Einzelne*] to enter or leave it, so that this does not depend upon the arbitrary will of the individuals concerned" (PR 76A). The state has such legitimacy in the international objectivity that it may expel an individual even if the individual desires to live in the territory of the state. International law "entitled civilized nations [*Nationen*] to regard and treat as barbarians other nations which are less advanced than they are in the substantial moments of the state (as with pastoralists in relation to hunters, and agriculturalists in relation to both of these) in the consciousness that the rights of these other nations are not equal to theirs and that their independence is merely formal" (PR 351). In sum, the state is a "great advance" from barbarism to civilization.

3. INTERNATIONAL ABSTRACT RIGHT
AS HARD SOVEREIGNTY

The nation is the emerging, though unaware, subject in international legal consciousness. The nation struggles to recognize itself and to be recognized as a state (PR 351R). Once so recognized as a legal person, the spirit of the ethnic nation continues in the formal personhood of the state. How so? Because the nation constitutes the content of the legal form of a state (PH 100, PM 552). Thus, the philosopher arrives at a moment of international legal consciousness where the nation-state reconciles form (the legal person) with content (the nation) much as civil society reconciles the formalism of Abstract Right with the intentionality of *Moralität*. At this point, the nation-state leaps from the "barbarism and unjust arbitrariness" of the unaware nation (PR 360). Germany had the potential to do so.[24]

I pointed out in Chapter 2 that the problematic for the legal philosopher is to explain why the laws of a state are binding upon individuals in a culture where there are thinking beings autonomous of objectivity. I examined this problematic in the context of domestic social relations in Chapters 4 to 9. Hegel also explains this problematic in the context of public international law, however. Here, Hegel asks "why are international laws binding upon the state and, ultimately, the self-conscious individual when both state and individual are autonomous from the international objectivity?" When the state emerges from the ethnic nation, the state, like the abstract person of the domestic *Recht,* is unaware of its autonomy from international objectivity. Instead, the state immediately identifies with such objectivity.

In this early moment of international legal consciousness the state, for example, wills the possession, the conferral of form and the assignment of a sign to the territory. The seized territory is thereby transformed into the property owned by the state. Since immediacy characterizes the arbitrary will with such property, the state is unaware of other states. As Hegel quotes of Napoleon, "the French republic is no more in need of recognition than the sun is."[25] Or, as Hegel puts it elsewhere, "[t]he nation state is the spirit in its substantial rationality and immediate actuality, and is therefore the absolute power on *earth*; each state is consequently a sovereign and independent entity in relation to others" (PR 331). At this early shape of the development of international legal consciousness, the state is "completely abstract and without any inner development" (PR 322R). This abstract right of the international self-consciousness constitutes hard sovereignty.[26]

Like the abstract person in the formation of property, contract, and crime, a monadic state in the shape of international legal consciousness as abstract right exists *for* itself (PH 63-64). The state is unaware of its separation from the objectivity of international legal consciousness: the state exists "without relation [*Verhältnis*] with other states" (PR 331). Like the abstract person who emerges from immediacy of the tribe in the act of thinking about the objectivity of nature, the state is a unity "which can satisfy [its] own needs internally" (PR 332). The state considers itself self-sufficient economically, socially, and politically. This is so, internationally, whether or not the state is domestically external to self-consciousness or is an organism. And so, the state does not depend upon other states nor recognize other states. When the state relates externally to other states, it is considered "a *single* secular power . . . [with a] *single* people and army" (GC 21). Each state, like the person of domestic Abstract Right, feels immediate with the international legal consciousness so that international objectivity is whatever the state posits as objectivity. Other states are considered the same in content as the observed state: other states are assumed to have the same beliefs and national identity as the observed state.

The consequences for international relations are profound. The state is free within its own borders (PR 337). In terms of its external relations, all other states are mere things in the objectivity of nature. Because the abstract state is only constrained by unassimilated external objects, the state is forever unhappy unless and until it recognizes itself in such objects by assimilating, colonializing, and conquering them. As in the Abstract Right of domestic objective freedom, the state, as an empty abstraction unaware of other states as persons, may assimilate, annex, or conquer territory as its own (PR 322R). The state may even conquer other states and bring it into its own consciousness as a monadic abstract state-person. In this first moment of international self-consciousness, the state is the sole person (PM 539).

a) The Domaine Reservée

In its internal relations, many institutions and many individuals participate in the deliberation and enactment of laws in an organic constitution. And yet, in its external relations with other states, a single official, the head of the state, must represent the organic constitution (PR 329). The head of state possesses "direct and sole responsibility" for declaration of war and the making of peace, the commander-in-chief of the armed force, the diplomatic relations with other states by its ambassadors, and the negotiation of treaties on behalf of the state (PR 328, 329). Precisely be-cause the abstract state considers itself alone in international relations, the head of state is immune from criminal and civil wrong committed against another state.[27]

Legal formalism constitutes legal reality in this first moment of the international objectivity of consciousness. As a form, the state may never have happened in history (PM 540). Particularity (the ethnic nation) may well be sacrificed in the name of the maintenance of the formalism. Equal-ity before the international formalism is one element of the objectivity (PM 544). The international objectivity of consciousness, willed by the monadic state, conceals the arbitrary will of the state (PR336).

Schmitt best describes this early shape of the objectivity of international legal consciousness. The state, as Schmitt describes of his own historical period of the 1920s and 1930s, is "spatially self-contained impenetrable, unburdened with the problem of estate, ecclesiastical, and creedal civil wars."[28] The state acts solely from its own arbitrary will.[29] Since the state is the only person in the international objectivity, the enemy is another state, not the inhabitants of the latter state.[30] Because the state, like the person of domestic Abstract Right, is immediate with its own objectivity, there is no constraint upon its desire to possess and claim title to territory. The only constraint is another state which also acts from its arbitrary will. The stranger, at this point in international legal consciousness, is either an en-emy or a friend, as Schmitt puts it.[31] The state alone decides the exception to the rule of law.[32] And it is a state of affairs or preexisting structure (the objectivity of consciousness), not some external transcendent or justifica-tory source, that situates the state as the sole decision maker in interna-tional relations.[33]

Returning to Hegel, this early shape of international legal conscious-ness protects a negative *domaine reservée* with which no external state or other organization may interfere. One such element of the *domaine reservée* is the freedom of the state to confer nationality onto whomever it so de-sires. As yet another incident of the *domaine reservée,* the state possesses the right to life. If its life is threatened, the state may go to war. Another incident of the *domaine reservée* is that the state possesses ultimate title in its territorial possessions, a claim which plagues legal colonialism to this day (PM 545, PR 324).[34] The state must defend its claim to absolute title to property by force if necessary: a "mass of people can call itself a state only if it is united for the common defence of the totality of its property . . . this is in fact self-evident" (GC 15). This is so because each state retains plenary legitimacy over all inhabitants and all other objects within the boundary of its property: "over everything individual and particular, over life, property, and the latter's rights, and over the wider circles within it." This property-oriented legitimacy of a state in international legal consciousness is "the state's *own* highest moment" because the state is recognized as the only person in legal knowledge.

b) War

War is one of the two methods to resolve differences amongst states in the shape of international abstract right. Because the ethnic nation constitutes the social content of the person, "whole nations are often more prone to enthusiasms and subject to passion than their rulers are" (PR 329A). Further, although Hegel does not condone the annexation of smaller states by larger states, there is no obstacle to prevent such in the hard sovereignty of international abstract right.[35] This is so because of the immediacy of the individual state with the objectivity of consciousness in international *Recht*. War is inevitably the consequence of a struggle between arbitrary wills or "specific particularity" (PR 337). An unconditional peace between monadic states is just not possible. A state of war hovers behind all international relations.[36] The monadic state must protect itself against attack. "The *judgement* of politics" reigns supreme (GC 70). Like the domestic master-slave struggle, war may result in a "good" consequence: namely, the movement from immediacy (the ethnic nation) to the Abstract Right of the international structure of consciousness (the monadic abstract state). Given the presupposed structure of monadic equal states, "war should not be regarded as an absolute evil [*Übel*] and as a purely external contingency whose cause [*Grund*] is therefore itself contingent, whether this cause lies in the passions of rulers or nations [*Völker*], in injustices, etc., or in anything else which is not as it should be" (PR 324R). The shape of hard sovereignty, Hegel suggests, leaves an either-or choice before the abstract state: either the state must resolve disputes by a treaty-contract or it must go to war (PR 334).

Because of the freedom from interference in its *domaine reserveé* and because of the incapacity of the monadic abstract state's inability to recognize any other person (including a human being) as existing in the international objectivity of consciousness, the state may call upon an inhabitant to "rally to its [the state's] defence" (PR 326, 70A). And again, "[t]he true valour of civilised nations [*Völker*] is their readiness for sacrifice in the service of the state, so that the individual merely counts as one among many. Not personal courage but integration with the universal is the important factor here" (PR327A). So too, the state may sacrifice private economic interests to its own arbitrary will (PR 325). More strongly, "it is certainly the case that the individual [*einzelne*] person is a subordinate entity who must declare himself to the ethical whole. Consequently, if the state demands his life, the individual [*Individuum*] must surrender it" (PR 70A). Despite Hegel's claim that act of self-consciousness remains peremptory in a domestic *Sittlichkeit* as I pointed out in Chapter 4, self-consciousness is subordinate to the arbitrary will of the state in the abstract right of international legal consciousness.

In the time-consciousness of international abstract right, war has positive benefits which, in another shape of international objectivity, might be considered negative. War unifies a state. War thereby produces internal peace and strength to the state (PR 324R). With war, the state overcomes the domestic legal forms that otherwise protect possessive individuals (PR 321–40). The path of individual self-consciousness in a domestic *Sittlichkeit* may be ironically advanced because the inhabitants become conscious of their recognition of strangers and of themselves through strangers. Such a sense of the ethos might otherwise remain latent and unconscious in the domestic relations or in the interstate relations of international Abstract Right (PR 338). Accordingly, war ironically "entails" international law to the extent that the latter provides a framework for the pursuit of the state's arbitrary will.

c) The Legal Reasoning in International Abstract Right

There is another facet to the legal formalism of the hard sovereignty of Abstract Right. As with legal reasoning in civil society, the clarification and differentiation of concepts or *Verstand* become important in the international legal consciousness. The unit of law is a rule or principle (that is, a concept). Recalling the contrast between *Verstand* and *Vernunft* from Chapter 3, the problem with *Verstand* is that "ratiocination stops short at isolated determinations, and consequently knows only [individual] reasons [*Günde*], finite viewpoints, and *deduction* from such reasons" (PR 279R). The legal reasoning in the emergent international legal order of autonomous abstract state-persons "goes back and forth over the reasons in question" (PR 326R). Legal reasoning excludes the content of the objectivity of international consciousness—its values, religious practices, art, music and other cultural sources, collective memories, political assumptions, and economy (PR 326R). As a consequence, the philosopher fails to recognize any universals, except the empty indeterminate concepts of formalism (PR 337).

Hegel explains that social actuality, in the context of this emerging international legal consciousness, is represented at this point through unwritten customs (PM 547). A treaty represents the joint will of two abstract persons. Customary norms, in contrast, emanate from the social relations of such abstract persons (PM 547). What is taken as international legality disguises social actuality (PM 547). *Was bekannt, darum nicht erkannt* ["what we are acquainted with, we do not therefore know"]. If only states would become self-conscious of shared universals, each state would recognize the other state as a member of a community with shared universals through which each recognizes the other as a member of an international *Sittlichkeit*.

4. INTERNATIONAL *SITTLICHKEIT* AS CIVIL SOCIETY

The nation and the sovereign state develop through experiential time (PM 548). But the observed state in the international legal order needs to "attain knowledge of its own true nature, that it should objectivize this knowledge and transform it into a real world, and give itself an objective existence" (PH 64). This self-knowledge in the international context requires that the organism recognize itself through shared universals with other states (PM 377). Despite the binding character of laws domestically in an organic structure of legal consciousness, "it is equally essential that this legitimacy should be *supplemented* by recognition on the part of other states" (PR 331R). So, an important network of interstate relations overtakes the former system of monadic nation-states. One state exists if a second state recognizes it as a state and, further, if the first state recognizes the second state. Together, they share common interests as members of an international ethos. Accordingly, there is a twilight of legal legitimacy between the domestically organic state on the one hand and its external relations with other states on the other. The state may exist in content (that is, as a nation) but not in form: "accordingly, these other states cannot be indifferent to its internal affairs" (PR 331R).

Hegel identifies a movement in time into a second shape of international consciousness. I describe this as the international civil society. Soft sovereignty characterizes this shape of international consciousness. Each state/person recognizes its dependence upon other states and yet, each state remains driven by its arbitrary will. Because of the arbitrary will, each state is either hostile or a friend to other self-determining organic constitutions in the international legal consciousness (PR 328R). Each state recognizes the other as a legal person through mediating treaties. The mediation remains a matter of form because the parties to treaties are abstract persons. As with a contract, the treaties only become actual when they are enforced by the parties. The content of state party relations remains embodied by ethnic nations, families of nations, collective memories, shared expectations, and all the other *prejudicia* that embody the content of interstate relations in international legal consciousness (PR 341). The content crystallizes when the form, whether a league of nations or a treaty, is enforced. To that end, the philosopher must address the actualization of international legal forms (PR 341). Despite the absence of an objectivity that exists for and in itself, one state will recognize another and thereby recognize that there are rules that guide their relations with each other.[37]

a) The Civic Nation

Hegel appreciates that a state will not survive as a legal person if several ethnic nations provide the content of the legal form of one state: "if different nations constitute a single state, there remains within the state a certain weakness that is overcome only following the amalgamation of centuries" (1818/19 W249). What is needed, he believes, is a "civic nation."[38] Over time, however, the "ethos" of the state "along with the infection of universal rationality . . . lessens the disharmony" (1818/19 W249). The state becomes increasingly conscious of itself as a secularized nation.

b) The State's Consent to be Bound to International Law

The philosopher observes that this second shape of international law in modernity institutionalizes legal formalism much as Hegel describes of the domestic civil society. When one abstract state, which is party to a treaty, recognizes another state by virtue of the treaty-contract, the recognition is "purely formal, and the requirement that the state should be recognized simply because it is a state is abstract" (PR 331). Such a state, "even if it is completely abstract and without any inner development . . . makes its appearance in history" (PR 322R). The consequence is that objectivity of international legal consciousness is a mere shell which conceals the arbitrary will of the state-persons (PM 548). When two states recognize each other, each recognizes the arbitrary will of the other through the mediating concepts, contracts, institutions and treaties. These mediating forms ignore the internal ethos of states parties as well as their "present condition." The internal ethos includes the nation of the state. Despite the mediating concepts, there is no public *Recht* independent of the arbitrary wills of the state-persons. The treaty law is "so-called *inter-national* law" (PM 547). The treaty, like the contract in the domestic legal order, is a shell that preserves the potentially explosive arbitrary wills of states (PM 548).

The treaty becomes the important mediation of international civil society. The state as an observed immediacy in international abstract right comes to realize that its needs cannot be fulfilled on their own. So, the monadic state enters into contracts with other states.[39] A state now realizes that it will be free only when it recognizes other states through common interests. As Hegel explains early in his writing, treaties are "true contracts on which the reciprocal political rights of the powers are based" (GC 68). With the treaty, the one state recognizes the other state as an empty legal person. The treaty mediates between the state parties by assigning rights and duties to the contractees (PM 547). The treaty is like a contract between persons although treaties lack the diverse forms of private contracts (PR 332).

Consent provides an important element of this emerging international legal consciousness, as a consequence. First, if an international legal norm is binding on a state, this is so because the state has consented to the norm, not because there is a universal that is greater than the sum of the arbitrary wills of the state parties to the treaty. *Pacta sunt servanda*: a treaty binds parties to it. A treaty is binding because two abstract persons consent to the terms of the treaty by virtue of the self-interest of each state (PR 336). Hegel clearly has in mind here what we call today "bilateral" as opposed to "multilateral" treaties.

Second, as long as Hegel confines himself to the shape of international law as civil society, abstract persons confront each other as equal by virtue of their empty personhood left over from international abstract right. States are equal with each other despite their differences in strength, wealth, power, coercion, and the like (PM 539). Subject to the peremptory norms I identify in the next section, Hegel rightly offers little room for the rise and evolution of implicit obligations, better known today as customary legal norms, in this shape.

Third, the treaty, as a source of international legal objectivity, only relates to sovereign states as the institutionalized form of social relations. As a consequence, a nomadic tribe or "any people at a low level of culture" will not qualify for recognition as a juridical person: the nomad lacks "the abstract right to make whatever use he wills of his ownership in the land" (1817–18 21R.25). Treaties may constrain the possessive individualism of the state. In this vein, Hegel describes international civil society as "external state law." The particular person (the state) links with other particular persons (states) into an "outer" or international law (PM 536). As an elementary moment of the development of international law, "[t]he relationship of states to one another is a relationship between independent entities and hence between *particular* wills" (PR 336).

Finally, the international obligation in this emergent legal consciousness of international civil society, to the extent that it exists, cannot be enforced by some central international adjudicative body: "there is no praetor to adjudicate between states, but at most arbitrators and mediators, and even the presence of these will be contingent, i.e. determined by particular wills" (PR 333R). As Hegel puts the point, when a state recognizes other states, "the broadest view of these relations will encompass the ceaseless turmoil not just of external contingency, but also of passions, interests, ends, talents and virtues, violence [*Gewalt*], wrongdoing, and vices in their inner particularity" (PR 340). There cannot be international crimes at this moment of the international objectivity of consciousness.

c) The Recognition of the Dependence of One State upon Another

Ethicality begins to become important at this point.[40] The state becomes conscious of its separation from shared universals in the international objectivity. The state gains a will by virtue of this self-conscious separation. The state is also recognized as "the primary freedom and supreme dignity of the nation" (PR 322). Freedom develops as an *in itself* when the stranger is recognized as a stranger. But there is no *in itself* in an international civil society because its primary mediating institution, the treaty, merely manifests how states need each other to fulfill their own arbitrary wills. As Hegel affirms towards the end of *Philosophy of Right,* any one formerly abstract monadic state now recognizes that it is "the exception and will of the other state" (PR 331). That is, the state-persons become aware of their need for other states. However, such interdependence hardly coheres with freedom. Other states constrain its action.

So, the international civil society possesses two opposing tendencies. On the one hand, the philosopher observes that international civil society is initially a "latent childhood phase until it blossoms out in free ethical self-consciousness and makes its mark in universal history" (PR 347R). At this point, international civil society has a real existence or concrete spiritual principle in the "life of nations" (PH 30). On the other hand, as Hegel continues in the latter passage, this very structure of international civil society has built-in arbitrary wills that may die (PH 59).

Once again, as with the domestic development of self-consciousness, an immanent social actuality strives to be recognized as a new form:

> the [philosophical] spirit . . . knows how to bring the unreflected—i.e. the merely factual—to the point of reflecting on itself. It thereby becomes conscious of the limitation of such determinate things as belief, trust and custom, so that consciousness now has reasons for renouncing the latter and the laws which they impose . . . Spirit, in its new inward determination, has new interests and ends beyond those which it formerly possessed. (PH 146–47)

Put differently, international civil society is not concerned with the reconciliation of objectivity with subjectivity in the domestic *Recht*. Nor is international civil society concerned with individual instances of treaty relations between states (PH 51). Nor is the spirit of international civil society the spirit of a federation of states, as Kant had entertained. Instead, particularity in international legal consciousness grows immanently through the shared universals amongst states. The latter shared universals are the pillars of an emerging second international structure of objectivity.

The particularity is no longer the arbitrary will of the state as Schmitt claims but the reflective will that transpires from within the act of thinking by the state vis-à-vis universals shared with other states. This shared particularity, we shall see in a moment, subtly emerges into a worldwide objectivity that is reconciled with the subjectivity of the state and of the willing inhabitants of each state.[41] As this worldwide consciousness takes form, the state recognizes other states at a multilateral level. As an observed consciousness, the state believes that there is no further external obstacle posited in its self-consciousness (PH 53). The state finally becomes free as an organic legal order because its former separation from objectivity is reconciled with its subjectivity. The international objectivity of consciousness becomes *Recht* as *Recht*. When this moment of international legal consciousness develops, the observed consciousness has moved to a third moment beyond an international civil society.

5. THE *SITTLICHKEIT* OF WORLD HISTORY

The third shape of an international *Sittlichkeit* is "world history." As with the organic state domestically, world history emerges from several internal moments of international legal consciousness. As states become increasingly self-conscious of their universals shared with strangers (that is, other states) and of their roles in the objectivity of international consciousness, the beautiful life of the family of nations is displaced in favor of shared self-conscious universals.[42] The family of nations, a prelude to world history, is one shape of the content of the international consciousness (PR 347). Unlike the state as immediacy in domestic abstract right and unlike the external state in the international civil society, each state comes to accept shared norms that guide and even render void their own arbitrary wills. Unlike the less developed shapes of international consciousness, such shared universals protect the individual human subject from the state. The universals are peremptory because they constitute the pillars of the consciousness of world history. If the universals are challenged, the very legitimacy of the shape is challenged just as we found with Hegel's explanation of the nature of a crime.

Hegel introduces a person in this third moment of the international objectivity. I am referring to the human subject. World history returns us full circle to the individual's spirit of becoming self-conscious. In this third presupposed structure of international legal consciousness, the individual bonds with other individuals and with states because of the shared universals that draw immanently from self-consciousness: "[t]he fact that states reciprocally recognize each other as such remains, *even in war*—as the condition of rightlessness [*Rechtlosigkeit*], force, and contingency—a *bond* whereby they retain their validity for each other in their being in and for themselves, so that even in wartime, the determination of war is that of something which ought to come to an end" (PR 338).

Such a bond, which is manifested in the existence of war crimes and crimes against humanity (neither of which is, interestingly, of contemporary construction in public international law), does not bring closure to the quest for international self-consciousness though. There is no closure or fixed a priori phase of the international legal order even though, today, we may believe that "it is natural" that states go to war. Rather, the particulars (the ethnic nation, the state, the family of nations, the universal peremptory norms) are only experiential moments in the time-consciousness of the international objectivity. An ethnic nation may die just as it was born through time-consciousness. So too a sovereign state may be swept away (PR 340). As such, a "spirit of the world," where a state-centric legal order no longer exists, remains a possibility immanent in international self-consciousness. Indeed, Hegel explains towards the end of his lectures on the *Introduction to the Philosophy of History* that within, yet beyond, the organic constitution, there lies a "world-historical" nation (PH 82). This is not the ethnic nation that has developed from the clan or tribe. This is a reflective international *Sittlichkeit* which has returned full circle to the self-consciousness of the individual human subject.

a) The Content of World History

What exactly is the content of this form of international *Sittlichkeit*? World history is actual or existent in that the spirits of the ethnic nation, the family of nations, the hard sovereignty of the international abstract right, and the soft sovereignty of international civil society have become theoretical constructs or forms. As soon as the observed self-consciousness comprehends its own identity anew, spirit emerges as the content of a higher shape of international consciousness. As such, the earlier form becomes alien to the new stage of self-consciousness (PR 343). This occurs in external as well as domestic social relations.

If the philosopher remains imprisoned in the domestic organic *Sittlichkeit,* the philosopher would be overwhelmed with "empty words" and "a superficial play of contingent and allegedly 'merely human' aspirations and passions" (PR 343R). There would be no international objectivity of consciousness that was legitimate *in itself* and *for itself.* The arbitrary will of each state would dominate.[43] The state would posit its arbitrary will to fit its own utilitarian objectives. This shape of the international legal order as abstract right or even as international civil society does not close the development of self-consciousness, however. International abstract right is only one shape that develops into others and all movements through time-consciousness become mere shells in world history (PR 341). International Spirit is not a finite being (PM 549). Spirit is infinite in development (PM 548, 549).

b) The Subjective Life-Force of the Objectivity of International Consciousness

World history necessarily generates from the self-consciousness of the thinking being as do all presupposed structures of domestic and international consciousness. This is what authorizes the legitimacy of a modern state-centric objectivity of consciousness. And now we find Hegel suggesting that this very quest for self-consciousness legitimizes the laws of world history as the third moment of international legal consciousness. The elements of this form of reflective international *Sittlichkeit* are neither abstract nor irrational. Nor do they constitute the "blind fate" of a nation or *Volk* (PR 342). The engine of the emerging international structure is the very drive (of love) to recognize others, a drive that Hegel describes in the early pages of *Philosophy of Right* (PR 158, 158A, 147R) and confirms towards the end of the treatise (PR 342).

Justice, albeit an imperfect justice that has begun with the leap from the prelegal condition of statelessness, is meted out in this emerging international legal structure of world history. The philosopher of the early nineteenth century could not possibly have known what shape of international consciousness lay implicit in the social relations of observed states in our day. It is conceivable that the emergent international legal order tomorrow may well lack sovereign states as the primary persons of international *Recht*. Whatever shape the world spirit takes, the drive for self-consciousness is not terminated with a state-centric international legal consciousness. Nor does closure end with the rhetoric of universal human rights in a state-centric international legal order (PH 141). Further, the emergent universals of a presupposed international legal structure that reconciles objectivity with subjective freedom "falls outside" the points of view of "justice and virtue, wrongdoing, violence [*Gewalt*], and vice, talents and their [expression in] deeds, the small passions and the great, guilt and innocence, the splendour of individual and national life [*Volkslebens*], the independence, fortune, and misfortune of states and individuals [*der Einzelnen*]" (PR 345). The reconciliation of the objectivity of international consciousness with subjectivity emerges into the very statelessness with which Hegel began his philosophy of law. Hegel returns us to the very presupposition with which he began: namely, that philosophy concerns either immediacy or mediation.

The role of the lawyer/judge, as with the philosopher, is to recognize the emergence of such an international legal order, to identify the implicit peremptory presupposed pillars (what are called peremptory norms) of its structure, and to examine the content of the posited international legal rules and doctrines that hard and soft sovereignty have heretofore accepted as "givens." By studying the content in terms of how states recognize strangers, the philosopher examines the ethicality of international legal consciousness. Boundaries of thinking are revised. The scholar/philosopher becomes aware that the content of the shapes which she or he has taken for granted has outgrown its formal shapes. And that content is not drawn from rules posited by suprastate institutions nor from treaties/contracts but from the religious and cultural practices of individuals, their assumptions and expectations, their social organizations, images of art and literature, and the customs guiding and regulating the persons (the states) of existing structures of international legal consciousness. Hegel explains in his *Lectures on the Philosophy of History* that the spiritual self-consciousness of world history "is the sum total of all possible perspectives" (PH 30).

The world spirit emanates from the thinking being as a legal person recognized as a state. Such a spirit of the world is "the highest right of all" (PR 340). The universal spirit of the world is infinite in contrast with the finite spirits of particular states. The universal spirit is infinite because there is no object that stops or obstructs the development of world self-consciousness. Like the objective spirit (or organic constitution), so too the world spirit has a divine character: "[t]he ethical life is divine spirit indwelling in self-consciousness, as it is actually present in a nation and its individual members" (PM 552). Indeed, the spirit of self-consciousness that generated the various movements of self-consciousness constitutes world history. World history is what Hegel pronounces on several occasions as "the world's court of judgement" [*Weltgericht*] (PR 340)[44] or as "the higher praetor" of "universal spirit which has being in and for itself, i.e., the world spirit" (PR 339A). The court of world history, that is, is not an institutional court, such as Kant proposed, but a "court" of self-consciousness where states, as persons, are obligated to follow norms that are constituted from the shared universals in the emergent structure of world consciousness. Indeed, the state may not have explicitly consented to the norms (as in a treaty) nor implicitly done so (as in custom). It makes sense, then, that Hegel would not end his treatise, *Philosophy of Right,* with an excursus into the nature of the organic constitution as objective spirit. Rather, Hegel ends the treatise with an overview of a presupposed universal structure of international legal consciousness: that is, of absolute spirit.

c) The Legitimacy of the Objectivity of World History Consciousness

The thrust of Hegel's argument is that, like the human subject whose intentionality becomes an element of domestic legitimacy of the objectivity of consciousness, the state comes to realize that its intentional acts towards strangers bear upon the legitimacy of international objectivity. The intentionality, in turn, is also immersed in an ethos whose universals are historically contingent and separate from the state-party as a legal person. The universals become pillars of an emergent objectivity of consciousness within which and by virtue of which each state recognizes itself in the other states that heretofore had been considered enemies. The formerly monadic state of international abstract right and of the interpersonal relations of international civil society are slowly displaced in favor of a *Sittlichkeit* where the state is aware of its separation from the objectivity of international consciousness. In addition, the state becomes aware of other states/persons in the objectivity.

In addition, there is a reciprocal recognition of states (not a mere interdependence) in world history. This is manifested by the relation of "*another* to *another*" or as stranger to stranger as though the stranger were external to the state-person when in fact the stranger dwells inside the consciousness of the state-person (PR 323). The emergent international ethos gains ethicality. The state becomes bonded with the shared unwritten universals. The bond, the product of reflection this time, legitimizes the state's actions vis-à-vis strangers. Even war takes place within the boundaries of the universals of international humanitarian law [*Völkerrecht*] (PR 338).

As with my examination of harm in Chapter 4, harm in an international law context is private and public. In the international civil society, the monadic state, as a legal person, may be harmed by a breach of a treaty, for example, or by "an injury to the recognition and honour of the state" (PR 334). The harm is a private harm. In order to be an international criminal harm, we draw from Chapter 4, there has to be a public wrong where an act contravenes the very legitimacy of the international legal structure of consciousness as a whole (PR 335). This point arises with world history. International law now represents the "Idea [Concept] as a *concrete* whole" (PM 336). Hegel expresses this point when he says that public harms are directed against "the *idea* [*Vorstellung*] of such an injury as a *danger* threatening from another state" (PR 335). This concept of a public harm in the international objectivity of consciousness suggests that a state has legal duties to inhabitants of its own and other states as well as to other states.[45]

The domestic civil society and organic constitution of the *Philosophy of Right,* then, are only two steps in the progress towards a greater organism of the world community. This progress is never closed.[46] And so, the organic structure of actuality, represented by the sovereign state, is now displaced in favor of binding laws of an objectivity of international consciousness with norms that trump the arbitrary will of the state. The "present world" of equal sovereign states, as with international civil society, is but a "shell" whose "kernel" drives self-consciousness into a different presupposed structure of consciousness (PH 83). The emergent international legal structure "incorporate[s] a universal of a different order from that on which the continued existence of a nation or state is based" (PH 82). Once again, as with domestic intersubjective relations, a reflective *Sittlichkeit* takes hold of self-consciousness.

Consciousness has returned full circle to the very presupposition of a state-centric legal order: namely, the self-conscious thinking being. The basis of legal obligation is neither a treaty nor a customary norm. Instead, states share peremptory norms of the international structure of self-consciousness. These norms particularize the otherwise empty negativity of states as enemies or friends. The universals are greater than the sum of their parts, independent of the treaties to which a state had explicitly consented and independent of customary norms to which it had implicitly consented.

As an example, Hegel points out that one such peremptory norm is that the ambassador of a state be protected from prosecution or harm by the state of residence (PR 338). Further, peremptory norms ensure that states may not initiate or continue war for an unjust cause. One such unjust cause would occur if a state initiated war in order to preserve the arbitrary will of a ruler's family or the self-interest of a particular individual. Another unjust cause of war would occur if the particular arbitrary will of a state caused the war (PR 338).

Further, Hegel lectures that peremptory norms even guide the conduct of war. One such guiding norm is that war be conducted "in a humane manner" (PR 338A). Further, military officials owe duties to the officials of another army despite war and armed struggle. These humanitarian norms arise over time from an internal sense of obligation of the state towards foreign troops during wartime. The legal obligations of which Hegel writes and lectures proscribe and prescribe actions by a state, not the acts of individual citizens of the state: "[t]he current customs that war is waged only against the state as such, as a whole; it is waged against individual humans only insofar as they defend the state, so those who no longer attack or defend are protected" (1822/23 W257). The universal legal structure protects civilians as well as the officials of a state during war. Hegel lectures further that "[t]he rule is, then, to treat with hostility only those who act with hostility." Medics, priests, and physicians are exempted from harm by the enemy state. So too, prisoners are protected from harm by the enemy army (PR 339). Further, a conquering state owes duties to protect the citizens of the enemy state. One such duty is the freedom of a prisoner of war to contact family members and friends privately (PR 339).

General peremptory norms of the international consciousness of world history are not legally binding because some supranational institution has so enacted the norms (1824/25 W257, PR 339A). Rather, the general norms are binding because they manifest reciprocal recognition of strangers through shared universals represented by treaties, customary norms, and peremptory norms. Such universals emanate from within the states. Harm to individual human beings causes harm to the very legitimacy of the international legal order of which states are members as are individual human subjects (PR 339). When the state acts in its external relations in this third shape of international law, the state extends its particularities—including the social-cultural content of its nationhood—to the other states. The state recognizes itself in the stranger heretofore taken as an enemy or potential enemy. The stranger may well be another state or, more likely, an individual human subject, a foreigner or migrant worker, a stateless subject or an aboriginal of a state's territory. The stranger has become the very human being who always had the potential capacity to think. The project of self-consciousness began with the latter act of thinking. The general peremptory principles of civilized states evolve into the "spirit of nations."

d) Universal Peremptory Norms for the Protection of Subjectivity

Are there any hints in Hegel's works of a very different international legal structure than the hard and soft sovereignty inherited from the seventeenth century?

I shall end my retrieval of Hegel's philosophy of law by suggesting that Hegel, indeed, does address how the objectivity of international legal consciousness reconciles with individual self-consciousness. Central to the implicit structure in world history is the absence of state centrism. The most important element of world history rests upon peremptory norms that protect the self-consciousness of the thinking being in a presupposed structure of consciousness. Peremptory norms invalidate the posited domestic laws of the state as well as the treaties and customary norms that protect the traditional role of the state as the only legal person.[47] Hegel lectures that the *ius gentium* "gives the most advanced, more civilized peoples, who use the land better, a right to it—a right that does not, however, derive from personality" (1817/18 21R.25). The third moment of international legal consciousness derives from the peremptory norms of a presupposed structure that is independent of the arbitrary will of each state.

What are the arguments to suggest that the third shape of international law would privilege such peremptory pillars of the structure?

i) The Inalienability of Self-Consciousness

The first argument, recounted in Chapter 4, claims that some features of the human subject cannot be alienated to another person, including the arbitrary will of a state. The most important such feature is the very subjectivity of the human subject her- or himself. Elements of such subjectivity are "my universal freedom of will, ethical life, and religion" (PR 66). Hegel explains the sanctity of the subjective drive to become self-conscious in this way: "[t]he *comprehensive* totality of external activity, i.e. *life*, is not something external to subjectivity, which is itself this personality and *immediate*" (PR 70). This inner life cannot be alienated. The philosopher cannot retrieve how the individual recognizes others through the universals of a legal order without presupposing that the individual can become self-conscious. This, in turn, presupposes the source of self-consciousness, as I explained in Chapter 6, as love. Without the inalienability of the drive to become self-conscious, any structure of international legal self-consciousness that invalidates this drive would be illegitimate and therefore illegal. Although the state in the first two moments of international legal consciousness could expect the individual to sacrifice her or his life for the domestic organic legal order, this expectation has dissolved in an international consciousness that is no longer state-centric.

Hegel adds, in a lecture at the time of his writing *Philosophy of Right,* that property differs from those goods that are "not so much my possession as rather *constitute my very own person* [my emphasis]—my personality as such, freedom of the will, ethical life, religion—are accordingly *inalienable* [*univeräusserlich*] and *imprescriptible* [*unverjährbar*]" (1817/18 29.32). Hegel continues in his remarks in the lectures that there are some "inalienable and imprescriptible" things "of which, to the extent that I possess them, I cannot divest myself and of which, even to the extent that they are possessed by another, I am not prevented thereby from regaining possession should I so will" (1817/18 29R.32).

What is it that is inalienable and imprescriptible? Again, the subjectivity of the human being and, in particular, the inward self-conscious reciprocal recognition between two strangers through shared universals. Further, my subjectivity is even imprescriptible because the judge of the ethos in which I live is not a judge appointed by the state but my own self-consciousness. This, in turn, is inalienable with the rise of modernity (1817/18 29R.32–33). These inalienable elements of the human subject help to explain why a slave cannot freely agree to be a slave. They also help to explain why Hegel emphasized the importance of public education, of *Vernunft* in such an education and in the desirability of inculcating *Bildung* (1817/18 158.244), the concept with which I began this book about Hegel's philosophy of law.

Hegel offers examples of the return to individual self-consciousness in the objectivity of international consciousness. Although the slave is not aware of her or his inward freedom, the slave has the potential to become free (PR 66R). So too do barbarians and serfs possess the potential. The peremptory norms of life, personality, freedom to think, and the like even apply to barbarians: "[i]n fact, this is even recognised in reality in those situations where civilised nations come into contact with barbarian hordes" (PH 124). Peremptory norms that protect subjectivity include security of the person, the right to property and to contract, and freedom from slavery. Hegel considers a contract involving robbery, murder, or slavery as null and void: "anyone is entitled to revoke such a contract" (PR 66A). So too, no religious leader may dominate the beliefs of another since spirit lies immanent in the human subjectivity, not in some externally posited religious doctrine or text or self-proclaimed representative of spirit (PR 66A). There are also limits to the ownership of property.

ii) The Protection of Immediacy

In the emergence of the objectivity of consciousness that intercedes between individual human being and the objectivity of nature, the philosopher presupposes immediacy and mediation as the only sources of knowledge. This presupposition raises a second set of arguments as to why the international objectivity of consciousness protects individual self-consciousness from the arbitrary will of the state. When international objectivity emerges from international abstract right and civil society, the state itself is constrained from harming the potential for self-consciousness in the immediacy. Even heroes such as Hercules and Brutus lack a legitimacy to kill themselves. Life is immediate with the very subjectivity of the human being and, as such, the state may not kill or torture the individual just as in domestic society, the individual may not commit suicide (PR 70R). As Hegel explains, "[t]he disposal [*Entäußerung*] or sacrifice of life is, on the contrary, the opposite of the existence [*Dasein*] of *this* personality. I have, therefore, no *right* to dispose of my life" (PR 70, 70R). Hegel continues as follows:

> as *this* individual, I am not master of my life, for the comprehensive totality of activity, i.e. life, is not something external to subjectivity, which is itself immediately *this*. Thus, it is a contradiction to speak of a person's right over his life, for this would mean that a person had a right over himself. But he has no such right, for he does not stand above himself and cannot pass judgement on himself. (PR 70)

If the state could undermine or proscribe the very existence of immediacy, the very act of thinking would lack its beginning. The human being would lack a potential to develop.

This argument has a further prong for Hegel presupposes that if knowledge is not immediate, then it is mediated by concepts. In this vein, the rights and duties that the philosopher associated with *Moralität*, when extended to international law, presuppose the "*inalienable* [*unveräusserlich*] and *imprescriptible* [*unverjägrbar*]" human subject. Whatever the differences of particularity amongst individuals, "*all* [human beings] are identical. A *human being counts as such because he is a human being, not because he is a Jew, Catholic, Protestant, German, Italian, etc.*" (PR 209R). World spirit recognizes such an equality of human beings by recognizing the individual in the stranger through their shared universals immanent in the act of thinking. Individual rights and duties outweigh the structures of international abstract right, and the shape of international civil society. All the rights with which the contemporary constitutional lawyer is familiar "enter on the scene only with the consciousness of them." The international consciousness of objectivity crystallizes after the organic constitution recognizes itself in a former enemy, whether the enemy be another state or a "foreigner" living within or without its border. This, in turn, presupposes the inviolable inward kernel of subjectivity without which one cannot have constitutional rights in an organic constitution (PR 29R.33).

6. CONCLUSION

The philosopher's striving to observe the different implied structures of international legal consciousness must begin somewhere. And Hegel has it begin with the immediacy of the ethnic nation. If the philosopher observes the objectivity of international consciousness as if the latter were imprisoned with the immediacy of hard sovereignty, there would only be friends and enemies. The state would posit its arbitrary will with no recognition of difference in the international consciousness. Given the inward origin of the self-consciousness, there remains the possibility that the hard and soft sovereignty models of international objectivity contradict the very possibility of subjectivity. If such is the case, then the peremptory norms that protect subjectivity in world history may well invalidate state action. Such a *Sittlichkeit* will even be higher than an institutionalized religion since the world spirit is a higher form of self-consciousness than religious self-consciousness.[48] The universals of world history begin and end with the inward subjectivity of the human subject will. The universals emerge as pillars of the world historical legal structure of consciousness. Although there will invariably be movement implicit in the world historical structure, the drive to become self-conscious, grounded in unmoved love for the stranger, will invariably be nonalienable and imprescriptible.

The emergence of the legal consciousness of world history happens on its own. World historical individuals, without the joy of personal reward and happiness, transcend the immediacy (like Alexander), at the sacrifice of being murdered (like Caesar) or deported (like Napoleon) (PH 85). What distinguishes such world historical leaders is that in order to draw the latent social actuality from the shells of legal formalism, epitomized by hard sovereignty and even soft sovereignty, the world historical leaders may well contravene *Gesetze* in the sense of the posited laws of the state. Political and social struggle, conflict, and suffering may result. However, inhabitants will identify with the emerging boundaries of the world historical spirit. The possibility of a domestic or international *Sittlichkeit* lies latent in the earlier shapes of the objectivity of consciousness.

Philosophers, such as Savigny and Fries, Kant and Fichte, took the nation-state as the ultimate source of binding laws in Hegel's day. Even today, legal and political philosophers, such as Hart, Raz and Coleman, Schmitt, Derrida, and Agamben—all of whom have distinguished themselves from themes and arguments of Hegel's—assume that the state is the ultimate source of the legitimacy of international legal consciousness. But Hegel realized that a state-centric objectivity of international legal consciousness did not terminate the development of self-consciousness (PR 346, 347). Even the subjectivity of the state invariably becomes alienated from the objectivity of international consciousness. The forms protect and guide state action to the exclusion of the individual human being who remains a stranger to the international objectivity. A state-centric international legal consciousness becomes aware that it is unfree in the shapes of the international abstract right and international civil society.

Legitimacy, after all, rests in the development of self-consciousness in terms of the recognition of the subject with strangers inter se. If the state is the subject, the state remains unfree because of the external strangers to its territorial domain. Once the observed individual comprehends that the formalism of the objectivity of consciousness is contingent, constructed by human subjects, and estranged from subjective freedom, the implicit forces pierce the veil of the state-centric formalism which masks the reciprocal recognition of the stranger with the sovereign state in international legal consciousness (PR 347R).

The ethicality of a state-centric international law vis-à-vis the human subject becomes a possibility. And this possibility may be actualized when the will displaces nationalism, xenophobia, exclusionism, racism, and sexism, all apparent with the state-centric rupture between objectivity and subjectivity. The world history becomes "*another* nation," Hegel claims (PR 347R). Struggle, war, and interstate conflict now succumb to a social actuality that returns to Hegel's presupposition of the immediacy-mediation of knowledge. The human subject is no longer separate from international objectivity. In contrast with our own day, the possibility exists of an inalienable subjectivity that generates the ethicality of self-consciousness. Such a self-consciousness is Hegel's starting point in his journey to understand why the laws of a state are binding upon a thinking being.

Conclusion

Once the philosopher, like Hegel, begins to retrace the journey of self-consciousness through Western legal culture, it is very difficult to put the story aside. Hegel's legal philosophy is magnetic. Hegel's themes remain pressing in our own time. His issues and ours ask two questions. First, "what is the identity of a legal unit?" As to the identity of a legal unit, we ask whether there is more to legality than legal rules. Principles? Policies? Social interests? Fundamental values? The anthropological morality of an ethos? The content of rules, principles, and other concepts? Second, "why does a legal unit bind an individual in a culture which ascribes to a thinking being who is separate from objectivity as represented by institutions and legal units?" Hegel's legal philosophy suggests that the rule in a statute or *ratio* of a precedent is binding only if the lawyer or judge or philosopher is capable of relating the ethicality of its content—that is, the extent to which the content manifests the reciprocal recognition of strangers—to the presupposed objectivity of consciousness in an ethos. This concerns the ethicality of an ethos. The issues of the identity and binding character of legal units are alive and well today. For if the legal philosopher confines thinking to the identity of law without addressing the legitimacy (that is, the second) issue, the philosopher's project reinforces legal formalism. Indeed, the philosopher participates in the formalism.

The legitimacy of a legal unit is contextualized, for Hegel, in a presupposed structure of legal consciousness in an ethos. The philosopher becomes increasingly aware of its boundaries and of its content which subtly and eventually take form. The legal unit is situated in time-consciousness of the structure. Is a unit void if its content contradicts that imminent structure's pillars? Is the structure moving through experiential time to a different set of boundaries and assumptions? Does legal legitimacy depend upon the ethical relation of one individual with another as represented in the universals shared in an ethos? To what extent does legal reasoning address the rupture between the objectivity of legal institutions and the social relations between individuals? Does legal reasoning relate doctrines with social actuality? To what extent does the contemporary legal education institutionalize the reification of legality vis-à-vis social relations? In particular, if legality closes the rupture between self and stranger through shared universals, does legal education institutionalize the *Vernunft* needed for a competent lawyer to address issues about the rupture between subjectivity and objectivity? Does legal competence include the anthropological study of the rituals and customs of stateless peoples such as aboriginal peoples? the social history of different ways of organizing social relations? the relation of states to the peremptory norms of the objectivity of consciousness; and, most importantly, the modes and forms of exclusion of inhabitants from domestic and international structures of legal consciousness? Is the recognition of the stranger in Hegel's legal philosophy premised upon the stranger as located in territorial knowledge, a term I shall explicate in a moment? Is there any way to understand legal knowledge other than in terms of territorial space?

Today it might be tempting for the Anglo-American lawyer, judge, or philosopher to discard these issues as impractical, if not utopian. On the one hand, the elements of the domestic organic legal order, as elaborated by Hegel, have largely been institutionalized: the separation of powers, the independence of the courts as a third party to disputes, the codification of customs, statutory reforms, appellate courts, the public participation in adjudication through the jury, alternative forms of dispute resolution, the public financing of education, the hiring and promotion of public service on the basis of merit, a public service which represents the universals of the ethos, and the franchise. Even a higher education has been institutionalized where the rhetoric of the professional administrators may mimic the aspirations of *Vernunft,* despite the entry of professional schools, the entertainment praxis of education, the skills-objectives of higher education, and the cost-benefit basis of administrative decisions impacting upon the potentiality of self-consciousness.

On the other hand, despite such institutionalization of the elements and judicial rhetoric of an organic legal order, the characteristics of formalism and the arbitrary will remain in the domestic and international objectivities of consciousness. For one thing, we remain imprisoned in a structure of consciousness where the state is believed to be external to subjectivity and self-consciousness. Further, intermediate social organizations "exist" by virtue of the conferral of legal standing on them by the state authorities. As Hegel writes in this context, the institutional offices of governmentality are responsible to protect nongovernmental organizations. The state accords "legal recognition [*Berechtigung*]" to all such "communities and corporations" (PR 295). The state even confers legal standing to charitable or religious organizations. Both politics and adjudication proceed as if one arbitrary collective will were better than another. Instead of an active thinking subject who desires to become self-conscious, a media-infused entertaining culture plays to arbitrary wills of individuals and the arbitrary will of the aspiring organic state. The subject remains as disaffected and alienated from the objectivity of consciousness as she or he ever was in Hegel's day. Social actuality is characterized by, at best, soft sovereignty with interstate wars on the one hand and terror by the state officials against its inhabitants on the other despite the rhetoric of universal human rights. The media, politicians, inhabitants, and even legal philosophers seem to have lost the capacity to control their human constructions, including the state-centric international legal consciousness. With some universities excepted no doubt, Anglo-American institutions of higher education are rapidly losing any sense of *Bildung* as important to education and, instead, formalism, rhetoric, and *Verstand* are becoming the name of the game. Legal formalism permeates pedagogical materials of professional law schools as well as of the legal reasoning of judges. Indeed, the effort to relate the content of legal doctrines to social actuality is readily excluded from legal formalism as prelegal. *Vernunft* would require an ambitious educational program that related phenomenology with social history, the history of philosophy, Greek and Roman classics, literature, and the relation of these to the social relations of individuals presupposed in the substantive content of legal doctrines and institutional practices as experienced in *ethê*, including tribal *ethê*, through experiential time.

I. DOES HEGEL'S LEGAL PHILOSOPHY ESCAPE FROM LEGAL FORMALISM?

What we need to ask in light of the above events is whether Hegel's legal philosophy itself has escaped from the very legal formalism that he exposed of the legal philosophers of his own day. Does the idea of ethicality in an ethos, for example, exclude individuals who do not share the universals of the ethos? Does a domestic or international legal order, which claims to respect and institutionalize universal human rights, externalize the latter as merely hortatory? Are intermediate organizations indigenously generated immanent from self-consciousness, or do they exist by virtue of the legal status conferred by external state authorities? Has *Verstand* become entrenched in legal reasoning to the exclusion of *Vernunft*? Does the international legal consciousness protect the *domaine reservée* of the state with the consequence that private harm is caused in the name of public harm? Has the movement of self-consciousness been reduced to abstract concepts purged of self-consciousness by state officials as much as by passive subjects?

What motivated Hegel, more than anything, was his contempt for the legal formalism of his day and his fear of the consequential terror. His antipathy to legal formalism had its roots in the crises of Hegel's life: the alienation of the life experiences of the inhabitants of German principalities from the feudal objectivity, the social hierarchy that excluded meritorious public servants from the elite, the Treaty of Westphalia's failure to recognize Prussia or Germany as a state, the French Terror, the loss of his two school friends, his depressive personality, and the lack of recognition of his own philosophical potential until late in life. But did Hegel ever succeed in elaborating a legal philosophy that escaped from legal formalism?

a) Are Intermediate Organizations Intermediate?

To respond to this question, we might first examine Hegel's introduction of intermediate social organizations into his analyses of civil society and the organic constitution. Hegel explains that such organizations, generated independently from the state, play a critical role in the organic constitutional order that I retrieved in Chapter 9. The family, corporation, social classes, and public authorities exemplify such intermediate organizations. The individual is a member of the intermediate organization as well as a member of the state. Jürgen Habermas describes such intermediate social organizations as the "public sphere."[1] Habermas has directed our attention to the role of intermediate organizations in eighteenth-century England where private individuals, independent of the market and the feudal structure, deliberated in a common space about public issues. It is questionable, however, whether intermediate organizations infuse a uniform voice in the public space of an organic constitutional consciousness.[2] Scholars have also suggested that Habermas's historical claims about the decline of the public sphere in late-nineteenth-century England are suspect.[3] In addition, social changes did take place as a consequence of intermediate groups.[4]

I wish to suggest a different tack about the role of intermediate groups, at least with regard to Hegel's claim about their role in contributing to an organic constitutional structure of consciousness. From Hegel's standpoint, intermediate organizations take formation from their own indigenous generation. Further, inhabitants voluntarily choose whichever organizations are their own, although there is a "natural" proclivity to join one organization over another. Indeed, the most important intermediate social organization, the family, is generated from love.

Yet, once the intermediate organization has been formed, the state's institutions posit legal standing upon the organization as if the state were prior and external to the intermediate organizations themselves. Hegel is clear that this is so for every intermediate organization, except for a charity. As a consequence, the organization becomes a reified legal person in the objectivity of consciousness instead of functioning as the source of social bonding of the individual with strangers through shared universals. The latter universals mediate between the objective freedom of state institutions and posited laws on the one hand and subjective freedom of self-consciousness on the other (PR 302).[5] This is so of the family as much as it is of any other intermediate organization such as a corporation, union, or university. Accordingly, before an organic legal order is institutionalized where the inhabitant feels at home, governmental organizations confer legal status upon intermediate organizations and then assimilate them into the legal discourse about objectivity so that the organizations become important elements of the external state.

The consequence is that by Hegel's own terms, the social relationship, nested in intermediate organizations, becomes an untouchable remainder to the "organic" objectivity of consciousness. Further, the external state's conferral of legal status onto an intermediate organization, as a remainder, conceals the intentionality of the individual member. The intermediate organizations exist as instruments of the external state, not as manifestations of the individual's recognition of strangers (that is, ethicality). As with the universals of civil society, instead of institutionalizing the reflective will, the universals of the organic constitution appear to ignore social relationships in the intermediate organization.

b) The Problem of Institutionalizing Criminal Law

When Hegel examines the nature of criminal law, he introduces the notion of the legitimacy of the objectivity of consciousness. This legitimacy exists *in* and *for itself,* independent of private harm. Hegel believes that he has introduced an important advance over the contemporary criminal law of the European states as well as of Germany where crimes were considered private harms and were privately prosecuted. Hegel's challenge is to explain why a self-conscious individual would feel bound to laws that proscribed such public harms. Once he so establishes his claim, it would be legitimate for the state to possess a monopoly of violence within the border of its territorial title and to use violence to punish a criminal.

How would Hegel institutionalize the legitimacy of universals in the sentencing of a criminal, one might ask. In particular, would Hegel subscribe to a rational code of sentences for each crime? The last thing that Hegel would advocate, of course, is a sentencing code with a certain period of imprisonment for each type of crime committed. Instead, any particular sentence would be linked with the extent to which the criminal act challenges the very legitimacy of the legal order. But how is it possible to measure such a contradiction between the criminal act on the one hand and the legitimacy of the domestic or international legal order on the other if the criminal's harm is irrational? Further, are the criminal's intentional meanings even relevant? Must not the criminal internalize the universals of the legal order for retribution to be efficacious? And yet, Hegel would hardly think so since Hegel has given such weight to the self-conscious thinking of the observed individual independent of objectivity.

2. IS THE LEGAL ORDER LEGITIMATE INDEPENDENT OF THE ARBITRARY WILL?

This raises a further question concerning Hegel's legal philosophy. Hegel aspires to explain why a thinking being would feel bound to the state's centralized institutions and posited laws. Hegel believes that he can respond to this issue by elaborating how the subject would feel bound to the state by virtue of a reflective will. But has Hegel succeeded in this endeavor?

a) The Rule of Law and the Public Law

Hegel's notions of public (as opposed to private) harm and of the relation of public harm to the legitimacy of a legal order raise the possibility that Hegel himself has succumbed to legal formalism on a further account. The courts adjudicate disputes regarding private property and contracts. The public harm remains separate from the private realm. By accepting the private-public distinction, Hegel leaves it open for the state to dictate what is incorporated into the public realm. For, given the duality, the court may well consider the state's acts as political and therefore excluded from the scrutiny of the courts. The arbitrary will still posits the "law" of the all-important public realm. In addition, even if the enactment of a particular public harm were the consequence of public deliberation, the public harm, by virtue of its separation from private harm, would be left to politicians rather than to the rule of law adjudicated by the Third.[6] But this very separation of politics from legality, in turn, opens the risk that legality will be subordinated to the public realm. And this, in turn, raises the prospect that the arbitrary will of the state escapes from legislative and judicial scrutiny. Indeed, it raises the prospect of state terror. Hegel thereby restores the private rights, which he contextualizes in civil society, as a critical element of the reconciliation of objectivity with subjectivity in an organic constitution. And then, he does so at the same moment that he privileges the arbitrary will of the objective institutions as constitutive of public harm. Once again, Hegel fails in his effort to subordinate the arbitrary will to the reflective will.

b) The Displacement of Public Harm by Private Harm

There is a further consequence of Hegel's theory of legitimacy. When Hegel addresses the nature of a crime, he emphasizes that the criminal act challenges the very legitimacy of the legal order itself, of *Recht* as *Recht*. Hegel distinguishes public wrong from private wrongs in this regard. And yet, Hegel grounds the legitimacy of the emergent legal order, to a large extent, in terms of private economic and social relations.

In brief, the legitimacy of the objectivity of consciousness dissolves into the private disputes about property and contract because property, contract, and personhood constitute the universals of Abstract Right. The above-mentioned transformation of the subjectivity of intermediate organizations into the formalism of objectivity is just one further example of Hegel's reliance on private social relations. Indeed, Hegel's *Science of Logic* as well as his *Lesser Logic* are preoccupied with the interrelations of subject and object without the introduction of the objective spirit of institutions, posited human laws, unwritten customs, religious principles and practices, and the like. Hegel only begins to work the latter into a sense of objective spirit in section two of the *Philosophy of Mind* (1817), his lectures on legal philosophy beginning in 1817, and his *Philosophy of Right* (1821). When he does so, he retrenches legitimacy in the private subjectivity that emerges from tribal legal cultures. Even when Hegel addresses objective spirit in part III of *Encyclopaedia* (*Philosophy of Mind*) and in *Philosophy of Right,* the organic constitution—the ultimate domestic reconciliation of objectivity to subjectivity—depends upon the private relations of an individual *vis-à-vis* other individuals as strangers. The universals of the objectivity of consciousness do not exist independent of private harm. Public harm dissolves into private harm. Legality remains separate from legitimacy and the latter dissipates into the calculus of the individual arbitrary will as posited by the state officials.

c) Stateless Peoples

Hegel's effort to reconcile objectivity with subjectivity meets a further problem. Hegel distinguishes legal legitimacy from a premodern stateless society. This is the thrust of Hegel's problematic as retrieved in Chapter 2. Stateless peoples vary from the most violent (the Huns), because the Huns lacked centralized institutions and attachment to territory, to the more civilized barbarians (such as the Teutons). Now, Hegel claims that a philosopher's categorization of an ethos focuses upon the capacity of inhabitants to recognize strangers in their act of thinking. And thinking is advanced, Hegel postulates, if the inhabitants share common centralized institutions as well as assumptions and expectations that bond them with each other and with strangers in a stateless society. The highest form of civilization in this context is the emergence of a territorial state, in Hegel's view. For a state is a self-conscious author of written laws. Such laws are the inscription of deliberation and reflection by the state's officials. A tribal legal order lacks such self-conscious authorship. The tribal laws are unauthored. Hegel explains that such stateless societies therefore are best studied as "prehistorical" or "prelegal." The legal philosopher, Hegel claims, must "leap" from "the prelegal" to "the legal." For once human beings begin to think, they *re*-present the former identity of immediacy with unwritten customs. The immediacy is *re*-presented as concepts that mediate between the individual and the stranger. The quest for legitimacy hinges upon the extent to which the monad of civil society becomes a member of the objectivity of consciousness by feeling "at home" through just such mediation by concepts.

Hegel's hierarchy of societies, however, possesses an exclusionary as well as a bonding character. The leap into the philosophy of a state-centric legal consciousness excludes stateless societies by virtue of their immediacy between tribal members and the tribal custom. The leap also excludes stateless inhabitants who find themselves in a territory whose title is claimed by a territorial state. Not much territory under or above the territory of the globe, if any, remains *terra nullius,* if there ever were such. Even territory, which lacks any effective centralized governmental structure, is claimed by some states as their own entitlement. But if stateless, the inhabitant of a territory may lack diplomatic protection, be internally displaced, and be denied a public education, minimal social security, and the economic security of redistributive laws. These are precisely the sorts of protections that Hegel claims as peremptory over the arbitrary will of the state. And yet, formidable numbers of such groups appear exempt from protection in Western states today as well as from the organic constitution.

Aboriginal peoples in North and South America, for example, exemplify the enigma of statelessness in a state-centric international legal order. One might consider aboriginal organizations as intermediate vis-à-vis an organic constitution. However, unless the state has recognized the organization by virtue of a statute or a treaty, the aboriginal peoples remain stateless. As with the family, estates, corporations, and other intermediate organizations, the aboriginal peoples may well generate their own intermediacy, and yet, the state's conferral of legal standing upon aboriginal tribes incorporates the tribes as a reified legal form—the Aboriginal Peoples—into the presupposed objectivity of the legal consciousness. Thus, the universals of the ethos embody the recognition of the stranger at the risk that the individual stranger, as a member of a stateless aboriginal community, is a remainder exterior to the objectivity of consciousness.

Hegel's association of rationality with the self-consciousness of the individual, further, excludes the many groups today whose members feel immediate with the group. Hegel focuses upon intersubjective, not intergroup, relationships. The three moments of the will, the three domestic forms of the ethical ethos, and the two shapes (abstract right and civil society) of international law manifest highly reified legal orders to group identity. The notion of a collective memory especially underlines the exclusionary character of an ethical ethos.[7] Collective memories cannot be measured, discovered, or recovered as if elements in an objectivity of consciousness. The collective memories may be untrue in fact or may even be symbolic. They are experienced through a time-consciousness rather than posited as if a scientific fact. *Verstand* does not help the retrieval of collective memories precisely because they constitute the content of the differentiating concepts of *Verstand*.

Now, Hegel excludes such collective memories as prehistory and, therefore, as undeserving as elements of legal legitimacy. Further, his description of the three forms of the will in the early passages of *Philosophy of Right* describe how the objectivity of consciousness in Abstract Right "supersedes" (PR 21R), "penetrates" (PR 24), "overlaps" (PR 24), and "passes over" (PR 26A) the collective memories of a subject. All dependence upon any group identity is "eliminated" (PR 23). As a consequence, the excluded collective memories shared by individuals configure the group as a stranger to the ethicality of an organic constitution. This is so because only personal memories can be observed as elements of objectivity. Subjectivity remains constrained by collective memories. The latter have escaped observation as elements of objectivity. Strangers will remain vulnerable and even unprotected if their collective memories differ from the dominant collective memories of the ethical ethos.

The universals of the organic constitutional order, then, are not shared between subject and stranger despite Hegel's best effort to address the ethicality of a reflective ethos. The exclusionary character of Hegel's legal philosophy is especially exposed when Hegel raises the prospect that philosophers or even lawyers, judges, and legal scholars, in a civilized society, will officiate, teach, argue, adjudicate, decide, and enact laws with a "sense of an ethical ethos" in which they are immersed. Such officials must desire to play a role appropriate to the universals of the ethical ethos in which they find themselves.[8] The individual will desire to be self-conscious because that is just the way individuals behave in a civilized society. My point is not that this is just one more example of the never-ending character of the development of self-consciousness. For the individual may well become self-conscious of her or his place in the ethnic or racial hierarchy in the presupposed structure of law. Rather, my point is that the very core idea of spirit excludes important social phenomena that are not individualistically oriented. One self-conscious subject may well share a radically different collective memory than that of a self-conscious individual. Hegel's philosophy of law, in privileging the individual's self-consciousness over the group, has succumbed to the very legal formalism that he attributed to Fries, Savigny, Kant, Fichte, and Schelling.

d) Legitimacy and Violence

This raises a further element of the formalism of Hegel's organic constitution. For the individual's bonding with the universals of the organic constitution may well depend upon symbols, such as a flag in the case of the United States or a rock in the case of Scotland or the Crown in England, rather than upon signs that represent concepts.[9] Does a criminal's act contravene the objectivity of consciousness when the criminal's act offends universals that are symbolic rather than significatory? Does the symbolic bonding return the philosopher to the immediacy as experienced in an ethnic nation? Or is the bodily identity with a symbol the same reconciliation of objectivity with subjectivity that Hegel describes of a reflective *Sittlich-keit*? After all, the symbols are often the object of reflection by the Anglo-American philosopher and historian today. If legal legitimacy is associated with the symbolic universals of bonding with the organic constitution, how is it possible to quantify the harm caused to such symbols? Does the public harm meet a lesser standard in times of crisis than in times of peace, for example? Is the philosopher left with Hegel's theory of punishment grounded in shades of legitimacy? Of shades of barbarism and of modernity?

If this is so, how can there really be crimes against international universals *in* and *for* themselves without an inquiry into the ethicality of the presupposed international objectivity of consciousness? Can the state even conduct war against another state if its own legitimacy is dependent upon the historically contingent shape of the objectivity of international consciousness? If the content of the objectivity outgrows the form that privileges the arbitrary will of the state, does war remain legitimate? Can the state officials enforce state terror in the name of the organic whole if the shape of the development of international consciousness that had protected the arbitrary will of the state has dissolved in favor of an international civil society or, better, a world history? Can war ever be legitimate if the legitimacy itself of a state's laws is up for grabs?

Hegel has enormous faith that the secular organic state represents and constitutes the self-reflective will. Indeed, the critical distinction between barbarity and modernity is the extent to which social relations are organized in a centralized state that other states recognize as a state. The reason why he gives such "enormous strength and depth" to the modern organic state is that it allows for the development of self-conscious subjectivity at the same time that the state is reconciled with such subjectivity (PR 260). The state, Hegel explains, does more than embody the particular experiences of its citizens: the state's officials think about the objects of consciousness. The state officials know the state's will, and they know this will as an object of the state's consciousness (PR 270A). Indeed, Hegel suggests that the inhabitant just cannot escape from the territory owned by the state. Without a state, Hegel assumes, inhabitants would return to Fate, nature, customs, or the arbitrary will to determine legality.

The serious issue, for us today, is whether such a state possesses a *domaine reservée* free from scrutiny and external interference. May the state posit its own arbitrary will against its own inhabitants if the inhabitants are alleged to have questioned the very legitimacy of the state? May such a state, for example, indefinitely intern, torture, expel or participate in the disappearance of inhabitants whom state officials deem enemies of the universals shared in the organic objectivity of consciousness? May the *domaine reservée* of external sovereignty justify the state's decision to enter into war? May the state officials presuppose that the state's arbitrary will is legitimate without addressing the identity of the shape of international objectivity?

The international legal order never gets off the ground as long as organic states act as if they have unlimited internal and external freedom to posit an arbitrary will. Conversely, if the structure of international consciousness presupposes a world history that institutionalizes peremptory norms and the reconciliation of objectivity with individual self-consciousness, is a state of exception even possible? For issues of legality invariably collapse into issues of legitimacy if we have learned anything from Hegel, and the state of exception presupposes that the state is nested in the abstract right, not the civil society or world history, of the international objectivity of consciousness.

Chapter 9 suggests that Hegel assumes the importance of the framework of the rule of law in the domestic interrelations of individuals and governmental authorities. We saw in my Introduction that Hegel personally reacted against the violence of revolutionary terror, civil war, feudalism, and the revenge of tribal heroes. Hegel distinguished the modern legal order from the stateless society precisely because of the priority of the thinking over immediacy. The organic legal order clearly subordinated the monarch, all public authorities, and the populace to the rule of law by which Hegel signified the conferral of form over the arbitrary will. But is Hegel consistent in this respect? Does he not maintain a role for violence in the day-to-day interpretative acts of the state's officials?

The issue is important because it remains with us today. Hegel reminds the philosopher, as do Hart, Stanley Fish,[10] and Derrida[11] more recently, that the modern legal order, not unlike a tribal one, is constituted from violence. And Hart has admitted that "nothing succeeds like success."[12] But one must ask whether Hegel succeeds in excluding a role for violence in even the very constitutive acts of the organic legal order or of world history. For, if we return to the initial moments of a self-conscious individual in a stateless society, the violent possession of an external thing generates the basic legal concepts of property and contract. So too, a state's claim of title to territory follows the physical seizure of land. Further, violence is the main pillar by which Hegel stands in his explanation of the theory of retributive punishment. And, in his description of the nuclear family of civil society, he asserts that parents may coercively break the arbitrary will of the child in an effort to inculcate universals into the consciousness of the child. Violence is manifested through the inculcation of universals in public education: the violence will involve a "pedagogical coercion or coercion directed against savagery and barbarism [*Wildheit und Rohheit*]" (PR 93R). More generally, the development of self-consciousness in a society may be subtly violent, Hegel admits. This subtle violence permeates the displacement of a stateless society by a state. Why is the organic legal order legitimate and the stateless tribal order illegitimate if both are constituted from violence? Why does Hegel's philosophy require a leap from the prelegal tribe to the legality associated with a state if all shapes of self-consciousness are explicitly or implicitly infused with violence upon the stranger?

e) The Third

Hegel makes a serious effort to explain the dissipation of violence in terms of the role of an impartial judiciary. As mentioned before, Hegel calls such a judiciary "the Third." Such a judiciary, appointed by merit, transcends private and public disputes. The court adjudicates disputes between arbitrary wills with reference to the spirit of the universals of the objectivity of consciousness. For one thing, the Third acts in a disinterested and impersonal manner between the parties. Further, the Third treats them equally before the objectivity of legal units. Further, the Third institutionalizes the anonymity of a rule or of an impartial judicial entity to any dispute. The court guards the boundary between private and public. The court also guards the jurisdictional boundaries of officials and offices in the governmental organization. The governmental organization, in turn, offers an opportunity for subjects to access objectivity through a court representative and the jury. Without a Third of some sort, Hegel's subject would have duties towards the stranger out of fear that she or he might be colonized, or massacred, or excluded from the territory of habitation by the arbitrary will of the state. Or, she or he might be deprived from the minimal economic and social security that Hegel describes of the domestic civil society.[13] Hegel's Third renders a judgment with the ethicality of the reciprocal recognition in the social ethos in mind. So too, the state, in turn, acts as the Third on behalf of the organic legal order in external relations with other states. The Third acts independently of the state when the state is a party to a dispute.

Or does it? Is the Third really impartial and independent of the arbitrary wills of disputants? Is the Third not tilted towards one of the parties in both private and public disputes?

The problem is particularly obvious in light of the problematic that Hegel poses as recounted in Chapter 2. For the reflective *Sittlichkeit* is state-centric in civil society, or in an organic legal order, or in the first two shapes of international law. The state is directly or indirectly a party to disputes in the context of both domestic and international law. This is so not just with respect to public harms against *Recht* as *Recht*. The tilting towards the state occurs in commerce, international trade, the *ultra vires* acts of officials, the absence of state action to prevent public harm, and the state's exclusion of groups from the minimal economic and social conditions for the development of self-consciousness. The state is the dominant element of the actuality of the ethical ethos. The Third represents the point of view of the actuality. But since actuality is state-centric, the Third tilts in favor of one of the parties—the state—against the peremptory norms that manifest and protect individual self-consciousness. The judge's language and consciousness represent and enforce universals that presuppose the state as the most important element of the reflective *Sittlichkeit*. More generally, when all is said and done, the Third perpetuates the problematic of nonstate intermediate organizations and of stateless tribal structures in a state-centric *Sittlichkeit*.[14]

Once again, the rupture between objectivity and subjectivity is maintained. The individual remains unfree because of the rupture. Only, in this case, the Third acts as if the rupture does not exist or, perhaps better, that the rupture between subjectivity and objectivity could be reconciled by the judge and the judge's appeal to the universals posited by the state's institutions. The alienation of social relationships remains problematic in this important effort to institutionalize the Third in a formalistic objectivity. This alienation is doubled when one becomes aware that the social relationships of ethicality are the very sorts of issues that are excluded from legality by the intellectual differentiation between concepts, better known by Hegel as *Verstand*.

If the radical distinction between the stateless prelegality and state-centric legality undermines the universality that Hegel holds for the modern legal order, how can the manner and form of adjudication by the Third replace the loss of universality? Does not naked violence underlie punishment because of the Third's deference to the major organ in the organic objectivity of consciousness? Is not judicially sanctioned punishment a disguised form of revenge—a revenge from harm to the Third's organization—characteristic of the barbaric legal order? The parent represents the Third in the family. But the parent may inculcate a subtle violence over the education of a child. In civil society, universals include the rights to property, contract and the invisible hand of the market, and the external state. The Third protects such universals against harm. But the Third, once again, guides, protects, and arbitrates the struggle of private interests. Further, the social actuality only comes on the scene when the universals are enforced. The enforcement of criminal law, in particular, tests the legitimacy of the legal order, Hegel argues. But the enforcement of criminal law is assigned to the public authorities of the executive arm of the state. As a consequence, the role of the Third remains tilted away from the social actuality.

Perhaps most importantly in a state-centric domestic or international legal order, it is difficult to imagine the court as the Third in a dispute which addresses the ethicality of a reflective *Sittlichkeit* impartially when one of the disputants manifests a tribal consciousness of immediacy. For such a party would remain in the prelegal realm, according to Hegel. But Hegel excludes from examination the prelegal as "barbaric" or "savage." As noted earlier in Chapter 2, Hegel begins the lectures on the philosophy of history by excluding "this prehistorical period" from the present investigation (PH 134).[15] Indeed, the latter lectures also admit that the constitution of a legal order is violent in that the state-centric legal order is forced upon the territory inhabited by stateless peoples. And yet, against a background of mass statelessness of indigenous peoples in the twentieth century, just such violence arises in Anglo-American general jurisprudence and constitutional regimes.

3. HEGEL'S ASSUMPTIONS

Hegel's legal philosophy proceeds as if it lacks any presuppositions except one: that philosophy is either constituted from immediacy or from mediation. The legitimacy of a legal order depends upon the social-cultural contingencies of a particular epoch and ethos in which the individual finds her- or himself. The role of the philosopher is to look backward at dusk to see how a contingent ethos has evolved through experiential time-consciousness. I now wish to question whether Hegel's legal philosophy is so presuppositionless as he claims for it. Indeed, it may well be that Hegel shares with the contemporary Anglo-American general jurisprudence certain assumptions that need to be addressed if ethicality is relevant to legitimacy and if, contrary to general jurisprudence, legality cannot be addressed without an examination of legitimacy.

a) The Human-Animal Duality

First, the movement of philosophical consciousness, as much as of the observed individual, presupposes that each human being is driven by a desire to become self-conscious: self-conscious individuals "knowingly and willingly acknowledge [a] universal interest even as their own substantial spirit, and actively pursue it as their ultimate end" (PR 260). This desire to think distinguishes the human being from an animal, according to Hegel.

But does a human being think if she or he is happy as a passive recipient of television entertainment? A passive subject may have the capacity to think but lack the desire to do so. Why would an individual, content as a couch potato watching the Saturday night hockey and Monday night football games, desire to think about concepts that mediate between the individual and the objective world, including strangers? Indeed, why would an employee in an institution, such as a corporation or university already overladen with bureaucracy, feel at home with the shared universals of such an organization when communication is by e-mail or when all face-to-face social relations are left to the annual seasonal fête? Further, for Hegel, the legitimacy of the organic legal order depends upon the participation of the individual in the political and judicial process. But is a legal order legitimate on Hegel's own terms if the passive subject participates little and knows less about the history, social assumptions, languages, political expectations, and political and legal institutions in which one lives? How would voters or even elected representatives "direct their will to a universal end" (PR 260) if they did not participate in the enactment and adjudication of the universals? If they did not even desire to attain *Bildung*? If the public education did not fulfill the conditions of or even aspire to inculcate *Bildung*? Why would an uninformed individual lacking in *Bildung* desire to bond with the laws, authorities, and institutions of the external state so as to feel that the state's posited laws and institutions were no longer alienated from her or his consciousness? Or why would the individual even desire to question the state authorities that take her or him into war?

Indeed, the very idea that human beings are rational and that animals lack reason presupposes a speciesism that fixes objectivity and subjectivity against the progressive character of Hegel's immanent method. There are some fish and mammals that possess a language, for example.[16] More serious is the question whether the criterion of a species is an objective criterion of nature rather than culturally induced ideas of what it means to be a human being. Indeed, is it not ironic that Hegel builds his philosophy of law upon the very nature that he is so determined to differentiate from human experience and the objectivity of consciousness—the biological distinction between animals and humans? Further, even if Hegel were correct to accept such a clear-cut distinction between an animal and a human being, is there a possibility for progressive self-knowledge if one human subject has the propensity, particularly in the *Sittlichkeit* of the hard sovereignty of international abstract right or of the soft sovereignty of civil society in international law, to drown the stranger with her or his own insatiable individualism? This is especially problematic if we do not know who qualifies as possessing the capacity for self-consciousness. For in the latter circumstance, one cannot distinguish human beings from the external nature that is the object of "insatiably greed" and the "drown[ing of] everything" (PR 26).

b) The Organism as an Organization

This raises a further assumption. Hegel assumes that an institutional organization represents the organic character of a legal order. To this end, we have observed in Chapter 9, Hegel postulates that the pyramidal governmental structure vertically and horizontally links complex offices with each other. Such a pyramidal structure represents unity or singleness (PR 321). As such, in contrast with the shared customs of the tribal family, the institutional organization is believed to represent the universals (PR 289). Such a governmental structure renders the self-conscious, rational will possible in social relations because, as a unit, it authors the expression that signifies the legal concepts (PR 279, 280).

But does it? Like an organism, the governmental structure is self-determining. But that is just the problem. As a self-determining organismlike institutional network, the institutional structure may remain self-determining without a reciprocal relation from the inhabitants' subjectivity. Does a bureaucracy perform such a reconstruction? Do not the governmental offices take on their own self-interests? Does not the bureaucracy add to the very anonymous estrangement from objectivity that Hegel found problematic with the Roman and feudal legal institutions? If the nonexpert does not know (or even cannot know) the universals of an ethos or if representatives are elected from numerically unequal constituencies (PR 308), does Hegel leave it to the impartial public service to know the "shared" universals of the ethos? Does he leave it to political inertia to decide what intermediate organizations will be conferred legal standing (PR 308) or what are universals shared amongst all individuals?

c) The Hierarchy of Civilizations

This takes us to a further assumption in Hegel's philosophy of law. This assumption pervades the constitutional structures of many contemporary states as it does of the shapes of international hard sovereignty of abstract right and the soft sovereignty of international civil society. We have learned that Hegel postulates levels of civilization and of barbarism. This hierarchy of barbarian and civilized societies is built into his differentiation between an animal and a human being, his notion of the barbarian, the levels of barbaric societies, the levels of civilized societies and, finally, progress. Indeed, the barbarian is someone who lacks *Bildung* and that, in turn, involves a lack of a centralized state as the primary reflective author of the objectivity of consciousness. In his lectures on the philosophy of history Hegel rules out from the start any effort to explain the importance of "prehistorical" societies. For any such society "precedes culture and development" (PH 216). When the individual has sought knowledge, she or he has usurped territorial spaces that belong to the stateless person by the violent possession and claim of title to territory. This has had the consequence of massacring, assimilating, enslaving, and expelling the stranger. This has happened despite the conscious and intentional innocence of the motives of the territorial subject: "the white man's burden" and all that. Given such an exclusion of tribal and nonstate-centric societies, how can Hegel claim that the organic constitution reconciles universals with subjectivism or that such a constitution even manifests shared universals? Indeed, can one even define a particular without a universal and, if not, how can the organic legal order be anything but nominalism if it fails to explain or account for the social actuality and social universals of non-state-centric societies?

d) The Abstract Individual

However, by focusing upon the individual's relations with strangers, Hegel abstracts from the unconscious actions and collective memories of groups. This individual is not the abstract empty person of Abstract Right. I have recounted how the abstract person is unable to be self-identical. This very inability led to *Moralität* and then to *Sittlichkeit*. But Hegel has another abstract person in his legal philosophy. This is the very subject who seeks knowledge. For this subject, despite Hegel's assumption that she or he is a concrete, finite, context-specific being, is abstracted from the prelegal, prehistorical social bonding of nonstate societies. Hegel tries to reconcile the stranger as an object of consciousness with the thinking subject through knowledge—that is, through the mediation of concepts. But can the thinking subject know the stranger by concepts alone when the languages of the subject and of the stranger are ignored? Can the subject reconcile with the stranger if recognition occurs through the knowledge of concepts and the shared act of thinking to the exclusion of the opaque signs that represent the concepts? Can one recognize the stranger if the signs which represent the immediacy as a group phenomenon are untranslatable? Indeed, if the reflective will lops off the experiential body of the arbitrary will, is not the experience of the stranger, to the extent that the experience is bodily, excluded from recognition in social relationships? After all, the experiential body represents the arbitrary will against which Hegel condemns his contemporary philosophies of law. As such, the embodied individual hardly fits Hegel's description of the reflective will.

In sum, when Hegel lectures and writes about the self-conscious individual, he too privileges a human being abstracted from a biography, collective memories, and context-specific experiences as a member of a group. For the subject and the structure of consciousness are *concepts* about concrete human beings. Such an abstracted individual is not unique—that is, she or he is not a particularity—because Hegel insists on a reductionist exclusion of prehistorical and prelegal experiential time from legitimacy and therefore from legality. Hegel's anonymous philosopher, also abstracted from particularity, excludes the unique intentional and social member of a stateless society. Hegel's effort to access an organic legal order masks the embodied unique individual despite his attempt to do otherwise. Hegel's thinking being—and philosophy, law, and justice begin with such a thinking being—is an anonymous disembodied abstraction.

e) Ethicality as the Individual-to-Individual Relation

Now, the point I wish to emphasize is something more serious. The enigma of social relationships in Hegel's legal philosophy takes the individual, rather than the group, as the subject of freedom. When we consider contemporary humanitarian law and refugee law, claims are entertained by individuals as members of ethnic, religious, and national groups. To the extent that the international human rights treaties offer institutional procedures for remedies for stateless individuals and groups, the treaties are considered weak because they offer remedies to individuals to show harm done to the individual despite the fact that the harm to the individual is by virtue of membership in an ethnic, linguistic, religious, or racial group.

Hegel's legal philosophy, then, presupposes that ethicality concerns the relation of one individual with another individual to the very exclusion of the group of which the individual is a member. We need not fault Hegel for such a presupposition in light of the strongly individualist sense of morality of his predecessors such as Kant, Rousseau, Locke, Hobbes, Pufendorf, and Grotius. Further, in his preoccupation with distinguishing the immediacy of the tribal legal order from civilization, the thinking individual separates her or his will from the objectivity of consciousness. At that point, the individual gains a will. Legal consciousness progresses if the nonthinking individuals intellectually and socially "leap" into the centralized institutional structure of thinking individuals. But Hegel is preoccupied with the recognition of one individual towards another and of one immediacy towards another.

The pivotal source of consciousness, for Hegel, is the individual. It is the individual's consciousness whose concepts transform external things of nature into property. *Moralität* is constituted from the intentionality of the individual. And ethicality involves the extent to which one individual recognizes another individual. Although Hegel emphasizes the relation of an individual with intermediate organizations—the genesis of the relation itself being problematic—and although Hegel understands ethicality in terms of the ethos of a community, he remains preoccupied with the individual in the organization and in the ethos. This individual is abstracted from collective memories and reduced to a thinking individual. The abstraction and reduction thereby lift the concrete being into the "subject" as a presupposed universal. Although Hegel appeals to love as the life force behind the experiencing of time, much as Plato describes Diotima's eros in *Symposium,* Hegel continually frames his arguments in terms of the individual in a prelegal nonthinking contingency and the individual in the reflective *Sittlichkeit.*

The point is that Hegel offers a dyadic character to ethicality. For Hegel, it is the *individual* who has a will, and the relation of the individual to universals is by virtue of universals as exemplars of one individual's sharing them with other individuals. Eventually, of course, the universals become greater than the sum of the individuals. But the initial ethical relation lies between individuals and the recognition of the stranger as an individual. When we address such individualism in terms of territorial knowledge, a concept which I shall explicate in a moment, one's duties are owed by one individual to another inside the border of a territory whose title is claimed by a state. If the stranger to whom ethical duties are owed were a group, the group would suggest shared experienced universals in Hegel's sense of a universal. But that, in turn, would contradict the social dyadic relation of one individual with another. There is little in Hegel's legal philosophy to suggest that the individual is self-conscious by virtue of being a member of a group other than an intermediate group to whom the state confers legal status. The problematic of the indigenous generation of group identity is excluded as prehistorical and prelegal.

e) The Invisible Origin of Legal Legitimacy

This leaves us with the most important presupposition in Hegel's own philosophy of law: the invisible origin of the legitimacy of a modern legal order. Hegel warrants great weight to the governmental organization as a self-determining organism. But there has to be an end to the continual deference to higher and higher rungs in governmentality. I have explained why Hegel found that the traditional sources of the legitimacy of a legal order—historicism, the original intent of the founding fathers of a written constitution, the a priori character of legality and the social contract—were problematic because they ended reasoning in a presupposed externality to the act of thinking before ever addressing the act of thinking itself. The traditional approaches of legal philosophy had deferred to an external source or foundation to legality in order to bring the disparate, lawless particularities into a unity (PR 278R). Some scholars claim that Hegel attributes the finality of the objectivity of consciousness with the monarch who is situated at the pinnacle of the governmental institutional structure. And yet, the monarch too is constrained by the boundaries of action as just one more organ in the interconnected offices of the governmental organization. More, the attribution of closure, as represented by the monarch in the pyramidal institutional structure, flies in the face of the infinite development of shapes of self-consciousness.

Hegel considers the legitimacy of a modern legal order as a self-determining circle where the mediation of the objectivity of consciousness eventually returns to the self-conscious subjectivity of the individual. The legitimacy of any one shape of legality rests with this self-consciousness in the epoch of any particular ethos. But what drives the individual to become self-conscious? Why is the individual dissatisfied with each shape of the objectivity of consciousness? Put differently, what could be more idyllic than a couch potato who happily lives from day-to-day with the basic economic and social security guaranteed by the external state? Why does a being desire to be logical or even to think? Taking Hegel's argument through several moments of experience, why would the being desire to break from immediacy to recognize strangers through shared universals in the act of thinking?

Hegel's response is that there is something inaccessible to the mediation of concepts that generates this desire to know. This "something" is invisible or divine in that it is inaccessible to the knowledge of concepts. He attributes the spirit to the "something." As Hegel lectures as early as 1806:

> [t]hrough consciousness, spirit intervenes in the way the world is ruled. This is its infinite tool—then there are bayonets, cannon, bodies. But the banner [of philosophy] and the soul of its commander is spirit. Neither bayonets, nor money, neither this trick nor that, are the ruler. They are necessary like the cogs and wheels in a clock, but their soul is time and spirit that subordinates matter to its laws. An *Illiad* is not thrown together at random, neither is a great deed composed of bayonets and cannon: it is spirit that is the composer.[17]

This spirit, though, Hegel admits, has a divine character much as did Socrates' description of the *daimonic* voice that generates his desire for self-knowledge (PR 279R, 279A).[18] Despite the influence of the Enlightenment upon Hegel as a young man, Hegel continually accepts the *daimonic* origin of reciprocal recognition.[19] Hegel describes it as divine on many occasions in his works. The desire to be ethical is "unmoved" and "ungrounded" (PR 281). Hegel describes the will itself as "the ultimate ungrounded self" (PR 281). Even the legal "is" is "ungrounded." The arbitrary will does not produce the Concept—that is, the development of all shapes of consciousness. "Something unmoved" is said to generate the Concept. Even the majesty of the monarch cannot generate the Concept. The monarch acts through spirit on earth (PR 282A). The monarch's majesty is "entirely self-originating" (PR 279R).

In sum, an invisible life force immanent in the being—invisible in the sense of being inaccessible to knowledge or language—drives the human being to become self-conscious. As Hegel explains in his *Introductory Lectures on the Philosophy of History,* "[m]an is an end in himself only by virtue of that divine principle within him which we have all along referred to as Reason (or, in so far as it is internally active and self-determining, as freedom)" (PH 91). Even the domestic organic constitution, because it finally reconciles objectivity with subjectivity, should be regarded "as divine and enduring, and as exalted above the sphere of all manufactured things" (PR 273R). Hegel continues in the latter paragraph that the *polis* also shared such a divinity. But only in modernity, Hegel advises, is the human subject conscious of her- or himself as separate from the universals of an ethos. And yet, this drive to reach self-consciousness, not the state, is effectively the "march of God on earth." The state merely represents or signifies the "march of God on earth" (PR 258A). Hegel explains in his *Lectures on the Philosophy of Religion* 1827, for example, that legal institutions of the state are divine because they embody ethicality, not because the state is some invisible author external to self-consciousness.[20] Spirit, not the state, moves the inward *daimonic* or invisible voice that forever leaves self-consciousness open to development. Since the legitimacy of a modern legal order rests in the very reciprocal recognition whose generation Hegel attributes to an invisible life force, Hegel's legal philosophy, like that of others, marks something that is presubjective and preobjective.

The invisible life force behind the legitimacy of the state-centric domestic or international legal order is critical to Hegel's legal philosophy for several reasons.[21] First, this invisibility saves the objectivity of consciousness "from being dragged down into the sphere of particularity with its arbitrariness, ends, and attitudes, from the strife of factions round the throne, and from the enervation and destruction of the power of the state" (PR 281). Second, if the ultimate legitimacy were left to a popular or elected source—such as the referendum of the peoples, or the intent of the founding fathers of an institution, or the parties to a social contract—legitimacy would defer to the arbitrariness of the external foundation or grounding of legitimacy. The consequence is that the legitimacy of the state would be transformed into the private property of the external source. The sovereignty of the state would thereby be "weakened and lost, and the state is dissolved from within and destroyed from without" (PR 281R).

Hegel falls back upon an invisible *arche* immanent in the act of thinking in order to maintain the legitimacy and stability of *Recht*. But at what price? Has Hegel not lost the very Enlightenment autonomous subject who acts rationally and freely of objective constraints? How can the universals of the domestic legal order constitute legitimacy to punish a criminal if the universals are constituted from and by an immanent invisibility? And does the organic state embody the reconciliation of objectivity with subjectivity if the state itself depends upon legitimacy that is inaccessible to human knowledge? Most importantly for our own day, there is the question whether peace and, indeed, ethicality are possible if the legitimacy of a modern legal order is rooted in an invisibility to the mediation of concepts.

4. THE RUPTURE BETWEEN TWO FORMS OF LEGAL KNOWLEDGE

This leaves us with a very important paradox in Hegel's legal philosophy. This paradox permeates contemporary constitutional law of Western state-centric legal orders today as it also does of contemporary international law. Hegel postulates, as I argued in Chapter 2, that the thinking being, in contrast with animals, is driven to know what is external to the consciousness of the being. This desire to know, as I argued in Chapter 6, is generated from an intellectually inaccessible presubjective and preobjective life force, love, immanent in the consciousness of the human being. And yet, this thinking being never accesses this presubjective and preobjective life force. I suspect that it is the same thing to say that the thinking being never returns to the immediacy that begins the process of thinking. This inaccessibility to a presubjective love through language explains why Hegel quite rightly attributes divinity to it. And yet, the *daimonic* generated love drives the individual on and on to know the objects of nature and the concepts of the stranger's consciousness. In the movement of time-consciousness, the human being comes to recognize the stranger as different and yet, as sharing the act of thinking. This reciprocal recognition gives cause for the philosopher, lawyer, judge, and law student to become conscious of different structures of legal consciousness as experienced over time. Hegel's project is to identify how individuals socially relate with each other in different ethê and different epochs. The inquiry continues into international law and from there to the peremptory norms that protect the spirit of self-consciousness from the state itself, even the organic state. This *daimonic* drive to recognize the stranger, though, never succeeds.

Why it never succeeds presents the paradox of Hegel's legal philosophy. When philosophical and observed consciousnesses move through identifiable structures of legal consciousness, they live through experiential time. And yet, the knowledge that is acquired by consciousness is a territorial knowledge.[22]

a) Time and Space

On the one hand, the time that Hegel describes is not measurable on a clock. It is experienced. Love is interpreted by Hegel as an experience between strangers through time (PR 152R). Immediacy is a presence of experience in time (PR 64). The moments of experience emanate through time (PR 32A). I have argued that Hegel's sense of time in an organic constitution is experiential. So too, Hegel associates international law with experiential time-consciousness: "world history as a whole is the expression of the spirit in time, just as nature is the expression of the Idea in space" (PH 128). Indeed, the philosopher observes how the individual experiences objectivity through time as a constraint upon her or his self-determination. Hegel also understands progress in terms of experiential time (PH 128–31). Time has the "corrosive aspect" of "dissolving every determinate content it encounters" (PH 147). The observed individual moves through time-consciousness in the context of ethicality. This time-consciousness takes several shapes: the various ethê of the family, the legal formalism of civil society, the organic legal order, the hard sovereignty of abstract international law, the civil society of international law, and the world history.[23]

On the other hand, the recognition of the stranger by a knowing being takes the character of the stranger as if the stranger were located as a physical spot on a map. Hegel's *Philosophy of Right* attempts to contextualize the logic of intersubjective relations in territorial space. Because of their concern with humanly posited laws (rather than laws of nature as in *Science of Logic* and *Lesser Logic*) and because of their focus on objectivity as institutional and posited laws, Hegel's lectures on the philosophy of law from 1817, his *Philosophy of Right* and lectures on the philosophy of history make sustained references to just such a territorial sense of knowledge. A state—the mark of civilization—claims title to territory. The title follows the seizure, possession, and control of the territory. So too, property follows the seizure, possession, and control of external things of situated in nature. The stranger as a foreigner to the state is located "external" to the self-consciousness of the territorial state just as is the stranger located external to the self-consciousness of the individual. More generally, the very emergence of a modern legal order from statelessness is marked by a territorial-like centralized organization with organs of the organization defined in terms of a territorial-like jurisdictional boundary that separates the one organ from another in the organization. The modern state-centric legal order possesses a plenary of authority and monopoly of violence over all inhabitants and all objects in the territory. All inhabitants, after all, are objects in the shapes of the international objectivity of consciousness. Indeed, the legitimacy of the objectivity of consciousness exists in terms of territorial space. This is so both domestically and in the international legal order of hard and soft sovereignty.

b) Territorial Knowledge

Permit me to privilege how knowledge presupposes territorial space a moment longer. Hegel begins the journey from statelessness by distinguishing between various levels of barbarism and of civilization, as I argued in Chapter 2. His analysis presupposes that progress develops from the lowest form of society, that of a nomadic tribe, to a territorially controlled state. Hegel's survey of society after society in *Introduction to the Philosophy of History* and in the concluding paragraphs of *Philosophy of Right*—Roman, Old World, New World, Africa, Asia, and Europe—takes territorial control as the critical element in the philosophical observation about the level of self-conscious will and, therefore, of civilization. The nomadic tribe lacks any control over territory. A treaty is not binding against a tribe because a tribe lacks the centralized territorial state. As such, the tribe cannot claim title over the territory it inhabits even if it has inhabited the territory for a thousand years. Again, nomadic peoples such as the Mongols, who lack any centralized institutions or attachment to territory, are described by Hegel as the most barbaric. The objectivity of nature and even the objectivity of consciousness both locate the individual and external things on territorial space. Objects of such territorial space constrain the freedom of the will. Hegel's philosophical consciousness observes the constraints on the observed subject's freedom in terms of territorial space.

The constraint of freedom in each moment of Abstract Right and of *Moralität,* as I argued in Chapters 4 and 5, is also imagined in terms of a territorial boundary. In Chapter 4, for example, I explained how, in the first moment of self-consciousness in modernity, the subject confers forms onto seized things of nature without knowing that she or he is autonomous of the forms with which she or he feels immediate. Property is conceptualized as the conferral of a form onto seized external things of nature, including the *terra nullius* of nature (1817/18, 20R.22; PH 168).[24] The contract represents the shared mutual interests of two monads with arbitrary wills which desire external things of nature. When Hegel introduces crime, he understands the criminal act in terms of the legitimacy of the newly emerging universals. But these universals of property, contract, and crime presuppose territorial knowledge. Property is generated from the physical seizure of territory or of a thing in a territory. A contract represents the common interest of two arbitrary wills as they try to control a territory or a thing in a territory. A crime represents an act against the universals shared in a territory. The legal order has a plenary control over all human acts within a bordered territory. The legal order has a monopoly of violence within its territorial jurisdiction. The constraints to the individual's freedom are territorially external to the subject's self-consciousness. In an effort to overcome the constraints of territorial knowledge, Hegel has the philosophical consciousness return to the time-consciousness of *Moralität.* But the intentionality of subjectivity also overcomes the unfreedom of legal formalism only by turning to the territorial knowledge of various shapes of bonding in the territorial *ethê* that control territory.

When the philosopher recognizes that the observed subject is located in an ethos, the *ethê*—the family, the civil society, the organic state, the hard sovereignty of international abstract right, the ethnic nation, the family of nations, and the soft sovereignty of international civil society—are all located as political entities that claim title to territory. Even the family is a territorial unit with a head at the pinnacle of the territory represented by the family (PR 171). The whole effort of the subject to feel "at home" with universals in objectivity of consciousness presupposes that "home" has a territorial locus. The objectivity represented by the state's posited statutes, precedents, and institutional structure is territorially configured. The subject feels at home with the latter, and yet there remains a rupture between the subject located in the territory and the objectivity that controls the territory. Even the pyramidal structure of governmentality, I showed in Chapter 9, is imagined in territorial terms with vertical and horizontal lines of nexus in governmentality. The offices on these lines are measurable precisely because they are modeled on territorial knowledge. The family, the external state in civil society, and the organic constitution are all modeled on a territorial pyramid with a head at the pinnacle. Even the state of exception, so important today in contemporary legal theory and public international law as well as the day-to-day life inside the territorial borders of states, presupposes that the legitimacy of the state and the state of exception are known in terms of territorial knowledge. Indeed, the very domestic reconciliation of objectivity and subjectivity is located in an international legal consciousness that associates the state with the title to territory. So too, the hard sovereignty of international abstract right and soft sovereignty of international civil society presuppose the primary legal person as the territorial state.[25]

Even the Third is the guardian of the territorial knowledge. The Third is held out as disinterested in the subjectivity of the litigant and yet, at the same time, the Third is the guardian of the universals of the territorial space. The Third privileges one of the parties (the external and organic territorial states) to any dispute. Further, the territorial knowledge disembodies the experiential time that lies at the core of self-consciousness. The human being is considered a mere physical mass locatable on a map. More importantly, the Third guards and adjudicates the very territorial boundary that separates the one individual from a stranger, particularly if the stranger lacks the desire to be self-conscious or if the other lacks membership in a state. In consequence, the experiential time once again is excluded from territorial knowledge. The subject knows concepts imbued with territoriality.

c) The Rupture of Two forms of Knowledge

The conclusion is warranted that the rupture between subjectivity and objectivity, the thinker and the stranger, the legal and the prelegal separates two radically different forms of legal knowledge. The two forms of knowledge render freedom problematic. Hegel recognizes the two different forms of knowledge at the very beginning of his argument in *Philosophy of Right*: "Finitude, according to this determination, consists in the fact that what something is *in itself* or in accordance with its concept is different in its existence [*Existenz*] or appearance from what it is *for itself*; thus, for example, *in itself* the abstract mutual externality of nature is space, but *for itself* it is time" (PR 10R). The thinker's knowledge of objectivity presupposes that the objectivity constrains freedom because of its territorial character. And yet, despite the projection of constraints to self-consciousness in territorial knowledge, the philosophical consciousness observes how the individual subject experiences such constraints through time. Hegel's philosophical journey configures the subject in experiential time. This association of objectivity with territorial space and subjectivity with experiential time is a fundamental and consistent presupposition in Hegel's works. Hegel would want today's philosopher to question this very presupposition.

The most important element of his distinction between experiential time and territorial space, then, is Hegel's claim that knowledge begins for the philosopher and the observed consciousness with the "leap" from the prelegal experiential time in statelessness to the mediation of concepts framed in territorial knowledge. This leap proceeds through movement after movement of self-consciousness. This begins with the conferment of a concept upon seized things. The constraint upon the will's freedom is a territorial knowledge. But the peremptory norms that protect the subjectivity—norms that I identified and argued in Chapters 4 and above—draw from the time-consciousness of the subject who becomes self-conscious. The peremptory norms, though, are constrained by the territorial context in which the norms are situated. As another example and only as an example, Hegel continues this deep contradiction in *Science of Logic*. A subject is free when the subject recognizes that the object is its own act of thinking through time-consciousness. The movement from immediacy to mediation of concepts to the particularity of the act of thinking shared between the two—this movement experiences the becoming of immediacy through time.

But when Hegel extends this logic to objective freedom, the latter object of consciousness is quantifiable in a territorial sense of space. Each constraint to the subject's freedom is territorially identified. The site of universals is quantifiable and known territorially. The consequence of the rupture between two very different senses of knowledge is that the rupture can never be closed. Nor can the stranger ever be recognized within Hegel's paradigm of philosophical knowledge. The rupture between subject and stranger is a rupture between experiential time and measurable territorial knowledge.

The clash between the two forms of legal knowledge presents a further ramification. Although Hegel situates the form of the mediating concepts between strangers in territorial knowledge, the content of such concepts is—including the relationship between strangers—observable through a language experienced in time. The subject cannot respond to a stranger through territorial knowledge except through the subject's own language or perhaps the subject's territorial recodification of the stranger's language. The recodification, though, is territorial recodification. The experiential time of the stranger remains unrepresented and unrepresentable in this territorial knowledge of self-consciousness. Indeed, one is pressed to ask, "how is it possible for an unrepresented and unrepresentable individual in territorial knowledge to respond to the objectivity of consciousness that is known as territorial?" The individual must accept the Third's decision. Further deliberation about the individual's experiences through time-consciousness is foreclosed. The individual cannot respond through her or his own language. The shared universals are of territorial space rather than of experienced time. The rule of law Third thereby utters a monologue through territorial knowledge that cannot access the experiential time of the stranger. The contemporary effort to incorporate human rights norms into public international law exemplifies how problematic is Hegel's faith in the Third as a respondent to the stranger. The consciousness of experiential time becomes an instance of the Third's territorial knowledge.

The institutions in an organic constitutional order have to make a decision which impacts upon human beings. This finality of a decision is often said to distinguish law from morality. What is more to the point is that the universal categories of the constitutional and international legal orders identified by Hegel privilege territorial knowledge which, in turn, reinforces the very formalist and exclusionary consciousness that Hegel finds problematic in Abstract Right, the very first moment of legal consciousness.[26] This is especially obvious during alleged emergencies where the state officials claim that the life of the territorial structure is at stake. These are the very states of exception when the state de jure or de facto denationalizes nationals, or when the state's officials torture or are complicit in sexual slavery, indefinite internment, internal displacement, mass expulsion, or the disappearance of strangers from the state's territory. The very impartiality and neutrality of the Third distances the lawyer/judge from the collective biography of a respondent whose experiential time lacks legal status. Peremptory norms, universally shared amongst all human beings on the territory of the Earth, thereby become a circulating totality all in the name of the universals of territorial knowledge. Indeed, the universals stand for everyone, yet the instance of the felt experience of the subject dissolves into the totalizing territorial knowledge despite the historical and social contingency of the knowledge.

d) The Stranger as a Remainder to the Modern Legal Order

In sum, the universalizing discourses of the organic constitutional structure of consciousness and of the various shapes of international legal consciousness reconstitute the consciousness of the subject to the point that the subject's face is *masked outside of time*. The mask hides the collective memories and meaning-constituting acts—acts of time-consciousness—which remain nested inside the reconstituting of the subject in a territorial space. In the name of ethicality, the official discourse of the state perpetuates the territorial decision of the subject-state to expel strangers under the Third's color of neutrality, objectivity, and detachment. Further, the organic legal order reclaims legitimacy to oppose justificatory acts onto the concealed time-consciousness of human subjects. The same holds for the hard and soft sovereignty of international law. Philosophical consciousness takes a point of view that reinforces the apparent neutrality and objectivity of the international legal structure as a whole at the same moment that the constraining factors to the freedom of the subject cannot hear or respond to the stranger. The stranger is projected as an object excluded from the presupposed territorial knowledge of the philosopher despite the experienced time-consciousness of observed subject and stranger alike. The experiences of the stranger become a remainder to Hegel's legal philosophy.

Thus, Hegel's appeal to the universal and impartial Third, "rule of law," and judicial institutions displaces legal formalism with a rationally and rhetorically disguised violence. The rupture between objectivity and subjectivity poses an untranslatable gap between territorial knowledge and experiential time. The subjectivity still moves in a different direction from the institutional objectivity. Because the totalizing state-centric discourse assumes the territorial border that separates the territorial space of a state from the "rightful" locus of the subject defined in terms of the border, even a universalist claim, such as one finds in multilateral and regional human rights treaties today, need not access and cannot access the intentional acts of the stranger. Experiential time is externalized to the prelegal, prehistorical unknowable and unknown. Experiential time remains a mysterious "phantom" that "haunts" legal analysis, as Hart would put it.[27] As a consequence, the time-consciousness of the stranger escapes the structure of legal consciousness which territorializes the knowledge about objectivity.

But because territoriality is the basis of Hegel's sense of the objectivity of consciousness, the subject, as a bodily mass on the map, reminds the philosopher that there is an unassimilated remainder to the freedom of territorial knowledge. This remainder is embodied through experiential time. Territorial knowledge must either insist or pretend that the mass does not exist or assimilate its consciousness into territorial legal knowledge. And this, the territorial knowledge accomplishes by excluding time-consciousness from legality and thereby excluding legality from legitimacy on Hegel's own terms. The body of experiential time is terminated in either case. Peace remains formidably problematic. Indeed, so does justice if justice addresses the recognition of the stranger through a shared time-consciousness as Hegel postulates for the ethical ethos.

Notes

Notes

INTRODUCTION: HEGEL'S CRISES

1. According to Allen W. Wood, Rudolf Haym's *Hegel und seine Zeit* (Berlin: Rudolf Gaertner, 1857) is considered the chief source of the reading of Hegel's legal philosophy as an apology for the Prussian reactionary laws of 1820. See Allan W. Wood, *Hegel's Ethical Thought* (Cambridge: Cambridge University Press, 1990), 257–58. I discuss the context of the Decrees below.

2. See esp. Karl Popper, *The Open Society and Its Enemies* vol. 2, *The High Tide of Prophecy: Hegel, Marx and the Aftermath* (London: Routledge [1945] 1991, 5 ed. rev'd.); John Dewey, *German Philosophy and Politics* (Freeport, NY: Books for Libraries Press, [1915] 1970).

3. See D. P. Verene, "Hegel's Account of War" in *Hegel's Political Philosophy: Problems and Perspectives,* ed. by Z.A. Pelczynski (Cambridge: Cambridge University Press, 1971), 168–80; Errol E. Harris, "Hegel's Theory of Sovereignty, International Relations, and War" in *Hegel's Social and Political Thought: The Philosophy of Objective* Spirit, ed. by Donald Phillip Verene (Atlantic Highlands, NJ: Humanities Press, 1980), 137–50.

4. Carl Schmitt, *The Concept of the Political,* trans. with intro. by George Schwab; fwd. by Tracey B. Strong & Notes by Leo Strauss (Chicago: University of Chicago Press, 2007 [1932]), 25.

5. Schmitt, *Concept of Political, ibid.* 44.

6. Schmitt, *Concept of Political, ibid.* 24.

7. Z. A. Pelczynski, "The Hegelian Conception of the State" in Pelczynski, *Hegel's Political Philosophy, supra* note 3, 1–29; Shlomo Avineri, *Hegel's Theory of the Modern State* (Cambridge: Cambridge University Press, 1972).

8. Frederick Neuhouser, *Foundations of Hegel's Social Theory: Actualizing Freedom* (Cambridge, MA: Harvard University Press, 2000); Paul Franco, *Hegel's Philosophy of Freedom* (New Haven: Yale University Press, 1999); Allen W. Wood, *Hegel's Ethical Thought* (Cambridge: Cambridge University Press, 1990); and *Cambridge*

Companion to German Idealism, ed. by Karl Ameriks (Cambridge: Cambridge University Press, 2000).

9. See, e.g., Joseph Raz, "The Nature of Law" in *Ethics in the Public Domain* (Oxford: Clarendon, 1994), 195–209; "Legitimacy, Law and Morality" in Raz, *Ethics, ibid.* 210–37; Carl Schmitt, *Legality and Legitimacy,* trans. & ed. by Jeffrey Seitzer, intro. by John P. McCormick (Durham, NC: Duke University Press, 2004).

10. See, e.g., John Gardner, "The Legality of Law" in *Associations: J for Legal and Social Theory* 7 (2003), 89–101; "The Virtue of Justice and the Character of Law" in *Current Legal Problems* 53 (2000), 1–30.

11. Robert Stern, "Introduction" in *G.W.F. Hegel: Critical Assessments,* ed. by Robert Stern, 4 vols. (London: Routledge, 1993), vol. 1, 21–31.

12. Plato, *Laws,* VIII, 838d. Also see Aristotle, *Politics,* II, 5, 126b 36–7; V, 9, 1310a 14–7. This immediacy disguised the coercive character of a custom, according to Aristotle. *Ethics* X, 9, 1179b 33–4.

13. Harris, *Hegel's Development: Night Thoughts (Jena* 1801–1806), 2 vols. (Oxford: Clarendon, 1983), vol. 1, 152. [*Hegel's Development*]. However, this view of the Athenian social and political life has been recently disputed. See Edward E. Cohen, *The Athenian Nation* (Princeton, NJ: Princeton University Press, 2000).

14. Harris, *Hegel's Development, ibid.* vol. 2, 62.

15. Harris, *Hegel's Development, ibid.* vol. 1, 66.

16. Terry Pinkard, *Hegel: A Biography* (Cambridge: Cambridge University Press, 2000), 80.

17. Harris, *Hegel's Development, supra* note 13, vol. 1, 125.

18. *Hegel: The Letters,* trans. by Clark Butler with Christiane Seiler & with commentary by Butler (Bloomington: Indiana University Press, 1984), 8 [Hegel, *Letters*]; Pinkard, *Hegel, supra* note 16, 133–36.

19. Commentators and biographers describe Hegel as depressed throughout his career. I use the same term although one should be aware of the niceties of the clinical sense of depression. It is doubtful that Hegel ever was clinically depressed in the sense of having a psychosis.

20. Pinkard, *Hegel, supra* note 16, 86.

21. By this time Schelling had published the following: *The Unconditional in Human Knowledge: Four Early Essays* (1794–1796), trans. by Fritz Marti (Lewisburg: Bucknell University Press, 1980); *Einleitung an dem Entwurf eines Systems der Natruphilosophie oder über den Begriff der speculativen Physik und die innere Organisation eines Systems der Philosophie* (1799) in Schelling, *Ausgewählte Schriften,* ed. by Manfred Frank (Frankfurt am Main: Suhrkamp, 1985).

22. Pinkard, *Hegel, supra* note 16, 225.

23. Hegel, *The Difference between Fichte's and Schelling's Systems of Philosophy,* trans. by H. S. Harris & Walter Cerf (Albany: State University of New York, 1977).

24. *Natural Law,* trans. by T. M. Knox with intro. by H. B. Acton (Philadelphia: University of Pennsylvania Press, 1975). [NL]. Also in abbreviated form in Hegel, *Political Writings,* ed. by Laurence Dickey & H. B. Nisbet (Cambridge: Cambridge University Press, 1999), 102–80. [Hegel, *Political Writings*].

25. Harris, *Hegel's Development, supra* note 13, vol. 1, 274.

26. Hegel, "The German Constitution" (1798–1802) in Hegel, *Political Writings, supra* note 24, 6–101.

27. For a full examination of the shift in Hegel's view of the state in the Jena period see esp. Z. A. Pelczynski, "The Hegelian Conception of the State" in Pelczynski ed., *Hegel's Political Philosophy, supra* note 3, 1–29. Also see Pinkard, *Hegel, supra* note 16, 145–53.

28. See generally, Hegel, *Letters, supra* note 18, 31–44. Schelling considered God as free, absolute, and infinite. Only God was free because God lacked any object to constrain its freedom. Human beings endlessly strove to access God in order to be free. But they could never be free because they invariably experienced external constraints upon their freedom. Thus, God possessed a nonhuman character.

29. Pinkard, *Hegel, supra* note 16, 115.

30. See Harris, *Hegel's Development, supra* note 13, vol. 1, 109, 155, 269–70; Pinkard, *Hegel, supra* note 16, 55.

31. Hegel, *Logic,* as cited in Wood's Notes to *PR*, p. 384, fn 10.

32. Hegel wrote to Niethammer that Fries had "gone beyond the Kantian philosophy by interpreting it in the most superficial manner, by earnestly watering it down ever more, making it ever more superficial." Hegel continued by describing Fries' *Logic* as "spiritless, completely superficial, threadbare, trivial, devoid of the least intimation of scientific coherence." Fries' explanations were "slovenly disconnected, explanatory lecture-hall twaddle, such as only a truly empty-headed individual in his hour of digestion could come up with." See *Letters, supra* note 18, 257.

33. Harris, *Hegel's Development, supra* note 13, vol. 2, p. xxi; Pinkard, *Hegel, supra* note 16, 117.

34. Pinkard, *Hegel, supra* note 16, 235. To show his knowledge of botany, Hegel even recounted to Goethe (who was influential at Heidelberg) a report conveyed from Schelling to Hegel of a diviner who located underground water by feeling the "pull" on a stick he held. The scientist was later found to be a fraud.

35. Pinkard, *Hegel, supra* note 16, 221–23.

36. As Hegel wrote to Niethammer on 18 October 1806, "[b]ut one request I cannot avoid: to send me money; I am in urgent distress . . ." as translated and printed in Walter Kaufman, *Hegel: A Reinterpretation* (Notre Dame, IN: University of Notre Dame Press, 1978 [1965]), 319. Like the younger Kant, Hegel's income varied with the number of students attending. Kant had taught twenty-nine hours per week at one point. This was normal in Germany even until the 1930s. Today, the dependence upon the number of one's students for payment may be more disguised in Anglo-American universities. Napoleon's march into Jena likely left few students to attend Hegel's lectures.

37. Harris, *Hegel's Development, supra* note 13, vol. 1, lxix.

38. They had been friends at the *Stift,* Hegel had regularly written to Schelling from Berne in 1794 and from Jena until 1807, and Schelling had "hired" Hegel as a *Privatdozent* in 1801. It did not help their friendship that Hegel strongly disliked Schelling's mistress and future wife, Caroline Schlegel, who had been married to one of the Schlegel brothers.

39. Hegel would not support Ludwig in any effort to attend university. Instead, Ludwig became a military officer and was eventually accepted into Hegel's household. Ludwig died in the same year as Hegel.

40. As quoted from correspondence by Hegel to Mrs. Frommann, in Pinkard, *Hegel, supra* note 16, 301.

41. Harris, *Hegel's Development, supra* note 13, vol 1, lxiii. Hegel's earlier sense of obligation to Ms. Burkhardt had "dropped by the wayside" by the time he proposed to Marie von Tucker. Pinkard, *Hegel, supra* note 16, 301.

42. What Hegel understands by philosophy, especially legal philosophy, is elaborated in text *infra* Chapter 1.1, 3.7, and 9.3.

43. *Letters, supra* note 18, 243–44.

44. See Hegel, *Lectures on Natural Right and Political Science: the First Philosophy of Right.* Heidelberg, 1817–1818 with Additions from the Lectures of 1818/1819. Trans. by J. Michael Stewart & Peter C. Hodgson; ed. by Staff of Hegel Archives with intro. by Otto Pöggeler (Berkeley: University of California Press, 1995). [Hereafter cited as 1817/18]. An Appendix to Stewart & Hodgson incorporates the lectures during 1818/19. His 1819/20 lectures, based on students' transcriptions by Gans, are included in part as Supplements in the Alan White translation of the *Philosophy of Right* (Newburyport, MA: Focus Philosophical Library, 2002).

45. *Science of Logic* was first translated into English by William Wallace in 1873 and then as *Hegel's Logic,* trans. by William Wallace with fwd. by J. N. Findlay (Oxford: Oxford University Press, 1975; 3rd ed.). G.W.F. Hegel, *Hegel's Science of Logic,* trans. by A. V. Miller (Oxford: Oxford University Press, 1969). [SL]. The SL is the object of an exhaustive commentary by David Gray Carlson. See Carlson, *A Commentary to Hegel's* Science of Logic (New York: Palsgrave Macmillan, 2007).

46. *Lesser Logic* has been recently translated as *The Encyclopaedia Logic* [EL] in 1991. G.W.F. Hegel, *The Encyclopaedia Logic: Part* 1 of the Encyclopaedica Sciences with the Zuzätze, trans. by T. F. Geraets, W. A. Suchting, & H. A. Harris (Indianapolis: Hackett, 1991 [1817]). *Lesser Logic* added chapters to *Science of Logic* and omitted important elements concerning the act of thinking that one finds in the *Science of Logic.*

47. For the purpose of addressing Hegel's philosophy of law, I have not differentiated between *Science of Logic* and *Lesser Logic,* choosing passages from both to exemplify Hegel's argument.

48. "Inaugural Address," delivered at University of Berlin, October 22, 1818, reprinted in Hegel, *Political Writings, supra* note 24, 181–85.

49. "Inaugural Address" *ibid.,* 181.

50. See Manfred Riedel, "Nature and Freedom in Hegel's 'Philosophy of Right'" in Pelczynski, *Hegel's Political Philosophy, supra* note 3, 136–50, at 136 for an elaboration of this distinction.

51. See Joachim Ritter, *Hegel and the French Revolution: Essays on the Philosophy of Right* (Cambridge, MA: MIT Press, 1982 [1969]), 44.

52. Hegel did not explicitly refer to Savigny in the Preface to the PR. However, Hegel certainly had Savigny in mind at Preface 10–11. The dominant tradition of German law by this time was the historical school as elaborated in *infra.* chap. 3. The historicist school was the object of Hegel's attack in PR 211R, 212R.

53. Rousseau left an especially important mark on Hegel's theory of law. For a different interpretation of Rousseau's legal philosophy see William E. Conklin, *The Invisible Origins of Legal Positivism* (Dordrecht: Kluwer, 2001), 123–36.

54. As quoted in Paul Franco, *Hegel's Philosophy of Freedom* (New Haven: Yale University Press, 1999), 121.

55. *Letters, supra* note 18. Also see Z. A. Pelcyznski, "Introduction" in Hegel, *Political Writings,* trans. by T. M. Knox with intro. by Z. A. Pelczynski (Oxford: Oxford University Press, 1964), 5–137, at 122–23. [Pelcyznski, *Writings*]. Also see Hegel, "Proceedings of the Estates Assembly in the Kingdom of Württemberg, 1815–16" [1815–16] in *ibid*. 246–94.

56. Hugo Grotius, *Law of war and peace, including the law of nature and of nations,* trans. with notes and illustrations from political and legal writers by A. C. Campbell, with intro. by David J. Hill (Washington & London: M. W. Dunne, 1901 [1609]).

57. Christopher Clark, "Germany 1815–1848: Restoration or pre-March?" in *German History since* 1800, ed. by Mary Fulbrook (London: Arnold, 1997), 38–60, 39.

58. See generally, Joachim Whaley, "The German lands before 1815" in Fulbrook, *German History ibid*. 15–37, at 22–27.

59. The Treaty of Westphalia, he complains, prevented Germany from becoming a sovereign state with a political power [*Staatsmacht*]. "The Constitution of Germany" (CG) in Hegel, *Political Writings, supra* note 24, 73. Hegel claims that "[i]n the Peace of Westphalia, Germany's statelessness became organised," 74. It is unclear—indeed mystifying—that Hegel begins this essay with "Germany is no longer a state," inferring that it had been a state at some point in time.

60. "On the recent internal affairs of Württemberg, in particular the inadequacies of the municipal constitution" in Hegel, *Political Writings, supra* note 24, 1–5.

61. "The German Constitution" in Hegel, *Political Writings, supra* note 24, 6–101. [GC].

62. For the translations into English of excerpts from these lectures see the Key to Abbreviations in the front matter of this book.

63. Hegel, "Proceedings" *supra* note 55.

64. Even Hegel's patron, Niethammer, implicitly sided with Fries. Pinkard, *Hegel, supra* note 16, 307.

65. In his pamphlet in 1816, Fries wrote amongst other things as follows: "Jews can be *subjects* of our government, but as Jews they can never become *citizens* of our people, for as Jews they want to be a distinct people, and so they necessarily separate themselves from our German national community. Indeed, they form not merely a people, but at the same time they form a state." As quoted in Wood PR p 458, fn 7.

66. When Hegel criticized this speech, Fries claimed that he had some Jewish friends and that his speech had not been anti-Semitic because there was a distinction between attacking "Jewishness" and attacking "Jews."

67. Kotzebue criticized the French Revolution, the Enlightenment, democracy, Napoleon, academic freedom, and freedom of the press. See Pinkard, *Hegel, supra* note 16, 444ff.

68. As quoted from Wood's Note in *PR*, p 389, fn 18. Karlsbad is in the present-day Czech Republic, although it was part of the Austro-Hungarian monarchy in Hegel's time. This law continued in force until 1848.

69. Hegel offered three months' wages for bail for Asverus. Eventually, Asverus was tried and convicted, with the king releasing him on a pardon.

338 Notes to Chapter 1

70. Hegel supported several students who were subsequently imprisoned.

71. This particular struggle pitted Hegel against Schleiermacher.

72. Other students whom he supported were Friedrich Christoph Förster (1791–1868) and Leopold von Henning (1791–1866).

73. However, the authenticity of this dissociation has sometimes been questioned. See, e.g., *Letters, supra* note 18, 461–65. Hegel was one of the official professorial sponsors of the *Burschenschaften,* several of his own students were present at Wartburg, Hegel withheld criticism in his Preface of the burning of Haller's books, he condemned Fries even though Hegel shared the importance of the idea of an ethos with Fries, and he had maintained his friendship over the years with F. H. Jacobi (1743–1819). Jocobi had condemned the French Revolution and the German Romantic movement.

74. Hegel used the term *concrete. PR* 290. For other similarities between Fries and Hegel see Wood's notes in *Philosophy of Right,* pp. 384–87, fns 11–12.

75. Hegel, *Letters, supra* note 18, 457–61.

76. Harris, *Hegel's Development, supra* note 13, vol. 1, 324.

77. For a similar nexus, though between the aesthetic and religion, see John Walker, "The Concept of Revelation and Hegel's Historical Realism" in *Hegel-Studien,* Band 24 (1989), 79–96; and "Philosophy, Religion and the End of Hegel" in the *Bulletin of Hegel Studies of Great Britain* 47/48 (2003), 61–72.

78. Hans-Georg Gadamer, *Truth and Method,* trans. by Garrett Barden & John Cumming (New York: Crossroad Publishing, 1985), 238–40.

1. HEGEL'S VOCABULARY

1. Aristotle, *Ethics* 1142a30–1143b15.

2. With a personal unconscious, I have experienced events which I can, with the aid of therapy, retrieve into my consciousness. With a collective unconscious, I am born into a language and culture whose members share collective prejudgments which I cannot retrieve through therapy because I have not personally experienced them. The narratives about some great battle, a war, an exodus of refugees, the heroes of a war, or the founding fathers and their independence from the mother state exemplify elements that enter into a collective unconscious. Karl Jung and Northrop Frye distinguish between personal and a collective memory in Jung, "The Concept of the Collective Unconscious" in *Literature in Critical Perspective,* ed. by Walter K. Gordon (New York: Appleton-Crofts, 1968), 504–08; and Northrop Frye, *Anatomy of Criticism* (Princeton: Princeton University Press, 1957) as reprinted in *The Language of Poetry,* ed. by Allen Tate (New York: Russell & Russell, 1960), 3–33.

3. As quoted from the 1822–23 lectures in Wood's notes in PR, p. 397.

4. Joseph Raz, "On the Autonomy of Legal Reasoning" in *Ethics in the Public Domain* (Oxford: Clarendon, 1995), 326–40, at 335, 338–39. [Raz, *Ethics*].

5. Raz, "Authority, Law and Morality" in Raz, *Ethics, ibid.* 231–35, 237.

6. H.L.A. Hart frequently uses the term, *officials,* to connote judges who, by reference to the rule of recognition, take an internal viewpoint towards primary rules. *Concept of Law,* with postscript by Penelope A. Bullock & Joseph Raz, 2nd ed. (Oxford: Clarendon Press, 1994, [1961]). Contemporary Anglo-American jurisprudence frequently takes the term for granted. See, *Oxford Handbook of Juris-*

prudence and Philosophy of Law, ed. by Jules Coleman & Scott Shapiro (Oxford: Oxford University Press, 2002), *A Companion to Philosophy of Law and Legal Theory,* ed. by Dennis Patterson (Oxford: Blackwell, 1999).

7. I include as "officials" the legal scholars, law students, lawyers, and paralegals of the contemporary state-centric legal order. I do so because they are expert knowers of the concepts (that is, of rules, principles, and procedures).

8. This second view of unfreedom and Hegel's critique of it is best reconstructed in M. J. Inwood, *Hegel* (London: Routledge & Kegan Paul, 1983), 473–82.

9. See, e.g., PR 3, 3R, 40R, 43R, 75R; PH 203–05, NL 102.

10. John Rawls, *Lectures on the History of Moral Philosophy,* ed. by Barbara Herman (Cambridge: Harvard University Press, 2000), 329–71, at 331.

11. This is explained in detail in Stephen Houlgate, "The Unity of Theoretical and Practical Spirit in Hegel's Concept of Freedom" in *Review of Metaphysics* 48 (1995), 859–81.

12. A sign represents an object. The object, called a *signified* by de Saussure, may be an idea or a perceived object. See Ferdinand de Saussure, *Course in General Linguistics,* ed. by C. Bally et al. & trans. by W. Baskin (New York: McGraw-Hill, 1959). See Conklin, *Phenomenology of Modern Legal Discourse* (Aldershot: Dartmouth, 1998), 13–21. [Conklin, *Phenomenology*]. Hegel's point is a logical one: one cannot assert the existence of X by asserting the improbability or impossibility of its negation. The principle is called "proof by contradiction." One cannot prove that someone caused a London bombing by proving that the person was a member of the same mosque as other bombers.

13. For the difference between the two forms see Gadamer, "Hegel's Inverted World" in *Hegel's Dialectic: Five Hermeneutic Studies,* trans. by P. Christopher Smith (New Haven: Yale University Press, 1976), 35–53, at 36–37. The essay is also translated by John F. Donovan in *Review of Metaphysics* 28 (1974–75), 401–09.

14. This idea of philosophical progress is elaborated in Hegel, *On the History of Philosophy,* in Hegel, *On Art, Religion, and the History of Philosophy,* ed. by J. Glenn Gray & intro. by Tom Rockmore (Indianapolis: Hackett, 1997), 207–317, at 228–31.

15. As translated by C.D.C. Reeve, *The Trials of Socrates* (Indianapolis: Hackett, 2002). Thomas G. West and Grace Starry West translate the passage as "something divine and daemonic comes to me, a voice . . . it always turns me away from whatever I am about to do, but never turns me forward" *Texts on Socrates* (Ithaca, NY: Cornell University Press, 1998, rev. ed.).

16. See generally *The Socratic Enigma: a Collection of Testimonies through Twenty-Four Centuries,* ed. by Herbert Spiegelberg in collaboration with Bayard Quincy Morgan (Indianapolis: Bobbs-Merrill, 1964), 235–36, quoting from Hegel, *Vorlesungen über die Geschichte der Philosophie* in *Wekem XIVm,* 102 ff. For an exhaustive study of the Socratic tragedy (and some relevant comparisons with the common law process), see David Lamb, *Hegel—from Foundation to System* (The Hague: Martinus Nijhoff, 1980), 45–71.

17. For the movements of universality see EL 169–78.

18. A legislative or judicial rule is such a concept as are doctrines, principles, policies, and other standards of adjudication. Even a constitutional value, so described by judges, may be considered by officials as a concept. Hart describes the intellectualization as the rule of recognition.

19. Gadamer, "Hegel's Inverted World", *supra* note 13, 41.

20. John Stuart Mill, *On Liberty,* ed. by Mary Warnock (Glasgow: William Collins, 1962 [1869]).

21. 999 U.N.T.S. 171, [1980] ATS 23, Ca. T.S. 1976 No. 47.

22. For these and other distinctions and concepts of Hegel's see esp. Michael Inwood, *A Hegel Dictionary* (Oxford: Blackwell, 1992).

23. Of course, this is not entirely correct as we speak about signs that represent the concepts.

24. Hans-Georg Gadamer, *Truth and Method,* trans. by Garrett Barden and John Cumming (New York: Crossroad Publishing, 1985), 230–34.

25. Gadamer calls this, *noeton eidos.* See esp. Gadamer's discussion of this in his "Hegel's Inverted World,", *supra* note 13, 40.

26. See Hart, *Concept of Law, supra* note 6, 94.

27. This idea is best explained by Michel Foucault in "What is an author?" in *The Foucault Reader,* ed. by Paul Rabinow (New York: Pantheon, 1984), 101–20.

28. William E. Conklin, "Lon Fuller's Phenomenology of Language" in *International J. for the Semiotics of Law* 16 (2006), 93–125.

29. Raz, "Authority, Law and Morality" in Raz, *Ethics, supra* note 4, 231–35. Raz also describes the thesis as the claim that social facts are binding "under its naturalistic rather than under its moral description" at 235.

30. In a famous debate between Lord Devlin and H.L.A. Hart during the 1950s, Devlin claimed that morality was constituted from the *custos morum* or underlying social-cultural assumptions of a community. Legality incorporated such unwritten assumptions. Accordingly, homosexuality, since it contradicted such values in British society at the time, should be considered illegal. Hart claimed that morality required justifications for action. The mere anthropological morality of a community had to remain separate from a justificatory act. The former addressed "being obliged" and the latter, "having an obligation." See Lord Devlin, *The Enforcement of Morals* (Oxford: Oxford University Press, 1959); H.L.A. Hart, *Law, Liberty and Morality* (London: Oxford University Press, 1963); *The Morality of Criminal Law: Two Lectures* (London: Oxford University Press, 1965); "Immorality and Treason" in *Morality and Law,* ed. by Richard Wasserstrom (Belmont, CA: Wadsworth, 1971), 49–54; Ronald Dworkin, "Lord Devlin and the Enforcement of Morals" in *Yale Law Journal* 75 (1965–66), 986–1005; reprinted in "Liberty and Moralism," in *Taking Rights Seriously* (Cambridge, MA: Harvard University Press, 1977), 240–58.

31. See Ronald Dworkin, *Taking Rights Seriously, ibid.*; "Rights as Trumps" in *Theories of Rights,* ed. by Jeremy Waldron (Oxford: Oxford University Press, 1984), 153–67.

32. After the slave revolt in 73 B.C.E., legislation protected how a slave was treated.

33. The slave could use the *peculium* as a source of capital income and, over time, could amass sufficient funds. See Andrew Borkowski and Paul du Plessis, *Textbook on Roman Law* 3d. ed. (Oxford: Oxford University Press, 2005), 96–97.

34. This was abandoned during the late Republic (133 B.C.E.–31/30 B.C.E.) only to be resumed under Constantine.

35. In addition, legal status was also conferred onto nonhuman entities such as *collegia, municipia,* churches, charities, and the state.

36. *Justinian's Digest,* trans. with intro. by Peter Birks and Grant McLeod (London: Duckworth, 2001), 1.5.

37. This point is explained in Bruce W. Frier and Thomas A. J. McGinn, *A Casebook on Roman Family Law* (Oxford: Oxford University Press, 2004), 11–15.

38. *Institutes of Gaius,* trans. with intro. by W. M. Gordon & O. F. Robinson (London: Duckworth, 2001); *Justinian's Digest, supra* note 36. The *Codex* updated imperial legislation, the Fifty Decisions (530 C.E.), and the *Digest* (533 C.E.).

39. Alan Watson, *Spirit of Roman Law* (Athens: University of Georgia Press, 1995), 66.

40. A citizen could not be crucified. Crucifixion involved suffering for a long period and, therefore, was the punishment for subjects who lacked legal status. The legal person could own property, exchange property in a contract, inherit property, and devolve property by will.

41. This point is developed by Robert Bernasconi in "Persons and Masks: The *Phenomenology of Spirit* and its Laws" in *Hegel and Legal Theory,* ed. by Drucilla Cornell et al. (New York: Routledge, 1991), 78–93, at 82–6.

42. Ronald Dworkin, *Law's Empire* (Cambridge, MA.: Harvard University Press, 1986), 400–13.

43. See generally, A. S. Walton, "Hegel, Utilitarianism and the Common Law" in *Ethics* 93 (1983), 753–71.

44. Alasdair McIntyre, *After Virtue* 2 ed. (Notre Dame, IN: University of Notre Dame Press, 1997 [1981]).

45. Michael Sandel, *Liberalism and the Limits of Justice* (Cambridge: Cambridge University Press, 1982).

46. Raz, "On the Autonomy of Legal Reasoning" in Raz, *Ethics, supra* note 4, 333; "Duties of Well-Being" in *ibid.* 3–28, at 25–27; "Liberating Duties" *ibid.,* 29–43; "Rights and Individual Well-being," *ibid.* 44–59.

47. Raz, "Right-based Moralities" in Waldron, *Theories, supra* note 31, 182–200; "The Relevance of Coherence" in Raz, *Ethics, supra* note 4, 277–325, at 289.

48. This focus upon time consciousness departs from Anglo-American general jurisprudence and appellate legal reasoning, both of which freeze concepts as if time were a measurable unit of legality not unlike the measurement of time on a clock or calendar. See generally Conklin, *Phenomenology, supra* note 12, esp. 69–101, 135–68 for discussion and examples.

2. HEGEL'S PROBLEMATIC

1. Hart, *Concept of Law* 2 ed. (Oxford: Clarendon, 1994, [1961]), 92. [Hart, *Concept of Law*].

2. Hart, *Concept of Law, ibid.,* 91.

3. Gadamer, "Hegel's Inverted World" in *Hegel's Dialectic: Five Hermeneutic Studies,* trans. by P. Christopher Smith (New Haven: Yale University Press, 1976), 35–53, at 41.

4. Hegel distinguishes the two, for example, in PR 347, 349.

5. For an example of the Epicurean view, see Lucretius, *De Rerum Natura,* trans. by W.H.D. Rouse (Cambridge, MA: Harvard University Press, 1959), Book 5, esp. lines 1446, 1157. For an example of the Stoic view see Seneca, *Epistulae Morales,* trans. by Richard M. Gummere, 3 vols. (Cambridge, MA: Harvard University Press, 1953), vol. 2, letter 76.9–10; vol. 3, letter 124.13–14.

6. See generally, PR 102, 197A, 211A, 359, 360, PH.

7. Hart, *Concept of Law, supra* note 1; Giorgio Agamben, *Homo Sacer: Sovereign Power and Bare Life,* trans. by Daniel Heller-Roazen (Stanford: Stanford University Press, 1998 [1995]), 19, quoting affirmatively from Carl Schmitt.

8. See generally, William E. Conklin, "Legal Modernity and Early Amerindian Laws" in Loon, ed., 60 maal recht en 1 maal wijn: Rechtssociologie, Sociale Problemen en Justitieel Beleid (Leuven: Acco, 1999), 115–28; Conklin, *The Invisible Origins of Legal Positivism* (Dordrecht: Kluwer, 2001), 26–34, 44–47 [Conklin, *Invisible Origins*]; "Hegel, the Author and Authority in Sophocles' *Antigone* in *Justice v. Law in Greek Political Thought,* ed. by Leslie G. Rubin (Lanham, Md.: Rowman and Littlefield, 1997), 129–51.

9. The "exception" is the creation and definition of territorial space of the sovereign legal order. According to Agamben, it is not something which, like a tribal legal order, precedes order but something that "results from its suspension by the state." See, e.g., Agamben, *Homo Sacer, supra* note 7, 18. Also see *ibid.* 17, 19, 106, 109. Agamben cannot distinguish between the rule and the exception (*ibid.* 65) because he presupposes that all legal orders are state centric. How can the state suspend law (this being Agamben's understanding of the state of exception) if the law cannot be suspended by virtue of its being constituted from experiential time and space as in a tribal legal culture? For the role of bodily experience in a state-centric legal order see, Samuel Weber, "The Limits of Professionalism" in his *Institution and Interpretation,* fwd. by Wlad Godzich (Minneapolis: University of Minnesota Press, 1987; Theory and History of Literature, vol. 31), 18–32; J. Huizinga, *Homo Ludens: A Study of the Play-Element in Culture* (Boston: Beacon Press, 1955), 76–88 ("Play and Law"); 89–104 ("Play and War"); Murray Edelman, "The Political Language of the Helping Professions" in *Politics and Society* 4 (1964), 295–310. Also see Conklin, *Phenomenology of Modern Legal Discourse* (Aldershot: Dartmouth, 1998), 136–68. [Conklin, *Phenomenology*].

10. Benedict Spinoza, *Ethics* in the *Collected Works of Spinoza,* ed. & trans. by Edwin Curley (Princeton: Princeton University Press, 1985), vol. 1, 408–617, Pt. iii, D2. See generally, Conklin, *Phenomenology, ibid.* 201, 222–24.

11. See esp. Luce Irigaray, "The Necessity for Sexate Rights" in *The Irigaray Reader,* ed. by Margaret Whitfrid (Oxford: Blackwell, 1991), 198–203.

12. Hegel distinguishes between savages and civilized persons throughout *Philosophy of Right* (PR 75A, 78-79, 107A, 330, 349–360) and his *Lectures on the Philosophy of History.* Kant offered a geographical explanation (in terms of climate, for example) and race to explain the inferiority of non-Europeans. See generally, David Harvey, "Cosmopolitanism and the Banality of Geographical Evils" in *Public Culture* 12 (2000), 529–64, at 532–36.

13. PH 216, an excerpt added to Hegel's lectures in 1826–27.

14. See, e.g., H. S. Harris, "Hegel's System of Ethical Life: an Interpretation" in G.W.H. Hegel, *System of Ethical Life* and *First Philosophy of Spirit* (part III of the

System of Speculative Philosophy 1803/04), ed. & trans. by H. S. Harris & T. M. Knox (Albany: State University of New York Press, 1979), 48–49.

15. Huizinga, *Homo Ludens, supra* note 9, 76–88. The Roman legal practice was draped with play. See esp. *ibid.* 85–87.

16. See generally, A. C. Bradley, "Hegel's Theory of Tragedy" in *Hegel on Tragedy,* ed. by Anne Paolucci & Henry Paolucci (Garden City, N.Y.: Doubleday, 1962), 367–88.

17. Hegel especially contrasts the legitimacy of the legal order of the tribe with that of the polis in Chapter VI of *Phenomenology of Spirit.* The lack of a *nomos-physis* dichotomy in early Greek tribes is discussed in Conklin, *Invisible Origins, supra* note 8, 13–35.

18. Conklin, *Invisible Origins, supra* note 8, 19-20, 26–34.

19. Francis Macdonald Cornford, *From Religion to Philosophy* (New York: Harper, 1957), 93, 103.

20. In Hobbes's case, the beings in the state of nature resemble human beings but lack conventions associated with signs with which to understand and communicate with each other. See Hobbes, *Leviathan,* ed. with intro. C. B. Macpherson (London: Penguin, 1968 [1651]), chap. 17, 226. Savagery, solitude, and habitation in caves conditioned life. Hobbes even abstracted from the life of Amerindians by describing the latter as lacking a language without reflection, agreements, and peace. *Leviathan,* chap. 13, 187, chap. 30, 378. John Locke also abstracted from social relationships in his description of the state of nature. Each individual lived in a state of war (para. 16–21) and subdued inhabitants in other territories in an "unjust war" (para. 178, 180). The state of war created the condition of slavery (para. 24). Each also had the right to punish another for private harm (para. 7). See John Locke, *Second Treatise of Government,* ed. by C. B. Macpherson (Indianapolis: Hackett, 1980 [1690]). Rousseau claimed that there is no prelegal world, this being composed of "savages." A "vast distance" exists between such savages and civilized beings, *On the Origin and Foundation of the Inequality of Mankind* in *The Social Contract and Discourses,* trans. with Intro. by G.D.H. Cole (Dutton, N.Y.: Everyman's Library, 1913 [1755]), 119–229, at 161, 219.

21. Sometimes, Hegel's stateless society has been erroneously associated with the philosophic tradition of a state of nature. See, e.g., Manfried Riedel, *Between Tradition and Revolution* (Cambridge: Cambridge University Press, 1984), 67.

22. When the individual acquires a language, the conventions of language open up the possibility of entering into agreements, according to Hobbes. With such shared conventions concerning the signification of sounds, individuals enter into a social contract. With this contract, the contractees leap into civil society. See Conklin, *Invisible Origins, supra* note 8, 80–90.

23. In Book V of his *De rerum natura,* Lucretius (99–55 B.C.E.) identifies three stages in the development of human beings. His second stage is characterized by violence and the third by the rule of law, centralized governmental institutions, and the state. The first stage emerges from creatures who live a monadic existence of survival to a pastoral community centered about a village. See Lucretius, *De Rerum Natura, supra* note 5, Book 5. 1011–13. Some scholars have considered Lucretius's theory of justice as emanating from such a pastoral stage of civilization. See, e.g., John M. Armstrong, "Epicurean Justice," *Phronesis* 92 (3) (1997), 324–34.

24. Jean-Jacques Rousseau, *The Social Contract,* trans. by Christopher Betts (Oxford: Oxford University Press, 1994), 45.

25. Hegel also uses the term to describe the "people" in a Rousseau populace.

26. See, e.g., CG 77.

27. Hegel, "Lectures on the Philosophy of History" in Hegel, *Political Writings,* ed. by Laurence Dickey and H. B. Nisbet (Cambridge: Cambridge University Press, 1999), 221.

28. See, e.g., *Campbell v. Hall* (1774) 1 Cowp. 204, 98 E.R. 1045; (1774) Lofft 655; 98 ER 848; *Johnson and Graham's Lease v. M'Intosh,* (1823), 8 Wheaton 543, 21 US 240 per Marshall, C.J. at 573–74, 588. As Marshall, C. J. stated, "it may be doubted whether those tribes which reside within the acknowledged boundaries of the Ununited States can, with strict accuracy, be denominated foreign nations. They may, more correctly, perhaps, be denominated domestic dependent nations. They occupy a territory to which we assert a title independent of their will, which must take effect in point of possession when their right of possession ceases [by sale, war, or other means]. Meanwhile, they are in a state of pupillage. Their relation to the United States resembles that of a ward to his guardian . . . [P]eople so low in the grade of organized society as the Cherokee could not be considered a nation." *Cherokee Nation v. State of Georgia* (1831) 30 US 1 at 17. This perspective continues into the late nineteenth and early twentieth centuries, e.g., in *St. Catherine's Milling and Lumber Co. v. The Queen* (1888), 14 App. Cas. 46, at 55, 58 per Lord Watson; and *Amodu Tijani v. Secretary, Southern Nigeria,* [1921] 2 AC 399, at 403 per Lord Haldane.

29. Kant also accepted the inferiority of the tribal legal order. See David Harvey, "Cosmopolitanism and the Banality of Geographical Evils" in *Public Culture* 12 (2000), 529–64, at 532–36.

30. I take the notion of a symbol and its juxtaposition with a sign from Paul Ricoeur in *The Conflict of Interpretations* (Evanston: Northwestern University Press, 1974 [1969]), 12–13, 58–61. A directness or immediacy characterizes a symbol. A sign represents and therefore mediates between the speaker and an object. A structure of signs that interrelate with each other cannot explain what is a particular symbol in an ethos nor what the symbol signifies. Also see Kenneth Burke, *On Symbols and Society* (Chicago: University of Chicago Press, 1989).

31. Henry Jones suggests that Cromwell, Luther, and Mohammed were heroes because "their *ideal self* was co-extensive with the larger self of their world." Jones, "Social Organism" in *The British Idealists,* ed. by David Boucher (Cambridge: Cambridge University Press, 1997), 3–29, at 16.

32. Derrida, "Force of Law: The "Mystical Foundation of Authority," trans. by Mary Quaintance *Cardozo Law Review* 11 (1990), 919–1045.

33. And this is the point where Derrida and Stanley Fish depart from Hegel. See Derrida, *ibid.* and Fish, "Force" in *Doing What Comes Naturally: Change, Rhetoric and the Practice of Theory in Literary and Legal Studies* (Durham, NC: Duke University Press, 1989), 503–24.

34. The association of the state with civilization is a thread through Hegel's works. If a people lack the form of a state, they lie at a lower level of civilization. See, e.g., PR 249R, 257R, 310, 349, 349R, & 351.

35. Sophocles, *Antigone,* trans. by Paul Woodruff (Indianapolis: Hackett, 2001).

36. It is possible that Hart had this story in mind when he raised the scenario of Rex I in the *Concept of Law, supra* note 1, at 58–61.

37. I have in mind Michel Foucault's "What is an Author?" in *The Foucault Reader,* ed. by Paul Rabinow (New York: Pantheon, 1984), 101–20.

38. Hart too accepts this and, to this end, the rule of recognition is really a rule of misrecognition as explained in Conklin, *Invisible Origins, supra* note 8, at 227–28.

39. Hart puts it this way: officials in a modern legal order must "step" from the prelegal tribal community to the intelligible rules of a modern state. See Hart, *Concept of Law, supra* note 1, 94. This step is a matter of "faith."

40. Hegel, *Philosophy of Fine Art,* trans. by F.B.P. Osmaston, 4 vols. (New York: Hacker, 1975), vol. 1, p. 250.

41. See esp. Hart, *Concept of Law, supra* note 1, 85–99.

42. Hart, *Concept of Law, supra* note 1, 87.

43. After an enormous effort to understand Lon Fuller's internal morality of law, e.g., Hart defers to the radically different unstated and unwritten meanings that differentiate Hart's from Fuller's theories of law: "I am haunted by the fear that our starting-points and interests in jurisprudence are so different that the author and I are fated never to understand each other's work." Hart, "Lon L. Fuller: *The Morality of Law*" in Hart, *Essays in Jurisprudence and Philosophy* (Oxford: Clarendon, 1983), 343–64, 343.

44. Hart, *Concept of Law, supra* note 1, at 53, 170. Both Hart and Hegel describe the moment of immediacy as "prelegal." See my text, *supra* accompanying note 3.

45. See, e.g., *R. v. Mitchell* [2001] 1 SCR 911 per McLaughlin, C. J.; *Delhamuuk v. British Columbia,* [1997] 3 SCR 1010; 153 DLR (4th) 193 per Lamer, C.J.C; *R. V. Marshall,* [1999] 3 SCR 533, (1999), 179 DLR (4th) 193; *R. V. Van fer Peet* [1996] 2 SCR 507, 137 DLR (4th) 289. Also see Peter Fitzpatrick, *Modernism and the Grounds of Law* (Cambridge: Cambridge University Press, 2001), 98–99; *The Mythology of Modern Law* (London: Routledge, 1992), 192–97.

46. CG in Hegel, *Political Writings, supra* note 27, 6–101, at p. 273, fn 2.

47. Although Hegel refers to Grotius on several occasions in the "Constitution of Germany," Grotius argued that the state's *domaine reserveé* was subject to the *ius gentium* represented in the international legal order. Hugo Grotius, *Law of war and peace, including the law of nature and of nations,* trans. with notes and illustrations from political and legal writers by A. C. Campbell, with intro. by David J. Hill (Washington & London: M. W. Dunne, 1901 [1609]). Vattel has been known to have ignored the latter and, like Kant, to have claimed that international law was an "ought" except to the extent that a state consented to a constraining norm through a treaty. Vattel, *The Law of Nations or the Principles of Natural Law,* trans. Charles G. Fenwick with Intro. Albert de Lapradelle, 3 vols. (Washington: Carnegie Institution, 1916 [1756]; Classics of International Law), vol. 3.

48. Johann Gottlieb Fichte, *The Science of Knowledge* [*Wissenschaftslehre,* 1794] with the two introductions of 1797, trans. by P. Heath and J. Lachs (New York: Appleton, 1970).

49. This point is also suggested in Laurence Dickey, *Hegel: Religion, Economics and the Politics of Spirit, 1770–1807* (Cambridge: Cambridge University Press, 1987), 236–37.

50. Antigone lacks such an inward conscience, Hegel explains in PR 144A, PS 437, PH 38–39.

51. This is best set out in PR Pref., 2–10, 71, 279R.

3. LEGAL REASONING

1. Raz, "On the Autonomy of Legal Reasoning" in *Ethics in Public Domain: Essays in the Morality of Law and Politics.* (Oxford: Clarendon Press, 1994), 326–40, at 335, 338–39. [Raz, *Ethics*].

2. The possibility of experiential space and time in legal reasoning is developed in Conklin, "A Phenomenological Theory of the Human Rights of the Alien" in *Ethical Perspectives* 13 (2006), 245–301. I examine this possibility more closely in the Conlusion.

3. In this essay Hegel advises that the world of philosophy is inverted. The essay was written as the Introduction for the short-lived journal, *Critical Journal of Philosophy,* edited by Hegel and Schelling, of which there were three issues for each of 1802–04. It is reprinted in part in *Hegel: a Reinterpretation,* ed. by Walter Kaufmann (Notre Dame, IN: University of Notre Dame Press, 1978 [1965]), 56.

4. Hegel elaborates the metaphor in PS 143–65. The metaphor is not Hegel's. We learn from Donald Verene that the inverted world is the title and object of plays by Ludwig Tiech in 1799 (eight years before Hegel published *Phenomenology of Spirit,* where the inverted world first appears), Christian Weise (1683), Johann Ulrich von König (1725), and in German literature generally in the Middle Ages. See Donald Phillip Verene, *Hegel's Recollection: a Study of Images in the* Phenomenology of Spirit (Albany: State University of New York, 1985), 50–55. In addition, Shakespeare's fool in *King Lear* inverts the world of legitimacy.

5. *Philosophy of Fine Art,* trans. by F.B.P. Osmaston, 4 vols. (New York: Hacker, 1975), vol. 1, p. 250 as quoted in text, *supra* chapter 2 at fn 40.

6. Hart, *Concept of Law,* ed. with Postscript by Penelope A. Bulloch & Joseph Raz, 2d. (Oxford: Clarendon Press, 1994 [1961]), 94.

7. Coleman and Simchen, "Law" in *Legal Theory* 9 (2003), 1–41, 41.

8. See generally, e.g., *Windsor Yearbook of Access to Justice,* vols. 10 (1991) & 19 (2001). For a review of how access to justice scholarship is stuck in the first supersensible world see William E. Conklin, "Whither Justice? The Common Problematic of Five Models of 'Access to Justice'" in *Windsor Yearbook of Access to Justice* 19 (2001), 297–316.

9. The inverted world here is described in PS 143–65. See esp. Gadamer's discussion of this in his "Hegel's Inverted World" in Gadamer, *Hegel's Dialectic: Five Hermeneutic Studies,* trans. by P. Christopher Smith (New Haven & London: Yale University Press, 1976), 35–53, at 40. Gadamer's essay is also translated by John F. Donovan in *Review of Metaphysics* 28 (1974–75), 401–22. Hegel's inverted world analysis is discussed in general in Joseph C. Flay, "Hegel's 'Inverted World'" in *Rev of Metaphysics* 23 (1969–70), 662–78. Also see Murray Greene, "Hegel's No-

tion of Inversion" in *International Journal for Philosophy of Religion* 1 (1970), 161–75; Donald Phillip Verene, "The Topsy-Turvy World" in *Hegel's Recollection, supra* note 4, 39–58; Joseph Flay, "Hegel's Inverted World" in *Review of Metaphysics* 23 (1970), 662–78; and Robert Solomon, *In the Spirit of Hegel* (New York: Oxford University Press, 1983), 376–85.

10. The reason why the institutional source of a state-posited law is important to Raz is that he claims that the analysis of concept can only go so far, at which point a value has to be posited. Raz claims that this ultimate posit of a value renders the judicial decision a political decision. Raz, "On the Autonomy of Legal Reasoning" in Raz, *Ethics, supra* note 1, 339. Raz accepts that the positing of a personal value would be illegitimate. But the positing of the same value by an institution of the state is legitimate. *Ibid.* 335, 338–39. The institutional posit of a value is thereby a "moral fact." See Raz, *Practical Reason and Norms* (Princeton: Princeton University Press, 1990; 2d.), 12. All rules that derive their authority from the posited value are also binding. See Raz, *Authority of Law* (Oxford: Clarendon Press, 1979), 22–25, 234–37. Raz, of course, believes that he saves the decision from naked violence because the value is posited by objectivity as represented by an official of the institutional structure of the state. Raz, *Practical Reason and Norms* 2d. (Princeton, NJ: Princeton University Press, 1990), 12. This is what Raz calls the "sources thesis," best explained in Raz, *Authority of Law.* The institutional structure of the state, though, is presupposed before Raz examines the act of legal reasoning despite his claim to the contrary. The state is external to the act of thinking by an official.

11. Hart, *Concept of Law, supra* note 6, 100–10.

12. Hans Kelsen, *Pure Theory of Law,* trans. by Max Knight (Berkeley: University of California Press, 1970), 194.

13. Ronald Dworkin, *Law's Empire* (Cambridge, MA: Harvard University Press, 1986), 400–13. Although it may seem counterintuitive for Dworkin to claim that there can be a transcendent pure "law beyond law" implicit in an imperfectly coherent narrative structure, one is encouraged to return to Dworkin's final chapter, a chapter that has been ignored in the prolific rereadings of Dworkin's works.

14. The best explanation of this, though addressing human experience generally rather than legal experience, is H. S. Harris, *Hegel: Phenomenology and System* (Indianapolis: Hackett, 1995), esp.17–21.

15. Hart distinguishes between an external and internal point of view. The observer takes an external viewpoint when she or he observes and describes a social practice as existing despite the fact that the observer may personally object to the practice. The external statement recognizes that others accept the internal statement as binding. The external statement recognizes a legal obligation; an internal statement expresses the feeling of being obliged. Hart, *Concept of Law, supra* note 6, 57–61. Although Raz interprets Hart as supporting the idea of a "committed" viewpoint to the legal order as a whole, William Twining quite rightly points out that although officials may be so committed, this may not be so for the outside non-expert or the outside observer who takes account of the internal point of view of others. See generally, William Twining, "Other People's Power" in *Globalisation and Legal Theory* (London: Butterworths, 2000), 108–35, at 132–33. Indeed,

Hart very clearly states that the internal standpoint is that of the official, not that of the nonexpert.

Raz adds a third form of external point of view: the scientific. Raz, *Authority of Law, supra* note 10, 137–39. With an internal viewpoint, according to Raz, the official may well subscribe to the content of a rule as just or unjust. The official may be committed or internally bonded with the standards that the statement recognizes. This commitment may incorporate experiential factors into legal reasoning. Instead, the official should take the viewpoint of the legal system as a whole. Raz suggests that with the scientific viewpoint, the official may "endorse" the content of a standard without being personally committed to it.

16. Gadamer, *Truth and Method* (New York: Crossroad, 1985).

17. Gadamer draws on Paul Graf Yorck von Wartenburg, *Briefwechsel zwischen Wilhelm Dilthey und dem Grafen Paul Yorck von Wartenburg 1877–1897,* (1923; Reprint Hildesheim, 1995).

18. The best explanation of this point is J. Glenn Gray, *Hegel and Greek Thought* (New York: Harper & Row, 1941), 53–67. Also see *Hegel on Tragedy,* ed. by Anne Paolucci & Henry Paolucci (Garden City, New York: Anchor, 1962), 165–236 (Dramatic Motivation and Language); and A. C. Bradley, "Hegel's Theory of Tragedy" in *ibid.* 367–88.

19. The contrast between the two different ethical lives is discussed in M. J. Inwood, "Hegel, Plato and Greek 'Sittlichkeit'" in *The State and Civil Society: Studies in Hegel's Political Philosophy,* ed. by Z. Pelczynski (Cambridge: Cambridge University Press, 1989), 40–54.

20. Of the contemporary jurists of general jurisprudence, Jules Coleman best describes the self-standing character of concepts. See generally, Coleman, "Methodology" in *Oxford Handbook of Jurisprudence,* ed. by Jules Coleman and Scott Shapiro (Oxford: Clarendon, 2002), 311–51, at 314, 345, fn 43.

21. Hart, *Concept of Law, supra* note 6, 90. There remains a remainder which a concept cannot incorporate within its boundary. A concept is a fixed thing that brings meant objects within its boundary as if the boundary had a territorial character. Hart also realizes that "buried" in a concept there is a multiplicity of experiential meanings. The buried meanings constitute the "prelegal" world for, being bodily, they characterize the customs that Hart attributes to tribes. See generally, Conklin, *Invisible Origins of Legal Positivism* (Dordrecht: Kluwer, 2001), 209–11, 214–31. I use the term *meaning* as the embodiment of a signification. The latter relates a sign to the signified object. The former incorporates the experiential body. See Conklin, *Phenomenology of Modern Legal Discourse* (Aldershot: Dartmouth, 1998), 37, 90, 161–62.

22. Hart, *Concept of Law, supra* note 6, 13–17.

23. See generally, Coleman, "Methodology", *supra* note 20. Also see Bernard Williams & Alan Montefiore, "Introduction" to *British Analytical Philosophy* (London: Routledge & Kegan Paul, 1966); Thomas Baldwin, "Analytic Philosophy" in *Routledge Encyclopaedia of Philosophy* (London: Routledge, 1998), 223–29; and Donald C. Galloway, "The Axiology of Analytical Jurisprudence: A Study of the Underlying Sociological Assumptions and Ideological Predictions" in *Law in a Social Context: Liber Amicorum Honouring Professor Lon L. Fuller,* ed. by Thomas W. Bechtler (Netherlands: Kluwer, 1978), 49–97.

24. The classic statement along these lines is Hart, "Definition and Theory in Jurisprudence: An Inaugural Lecture." Delivered before the University of Oxford on May 30, 1953 (Oxford: Clarendon Press), 1–28. Reprinted in *Law Quarterly Review* 70 (1954): 37–60, and in Hart, *Essays in Jurisprudence and Philosophy* (Oxford: Clarendon Press, 1983), 21–48. Also see Hart, *Concept of Law, supra* note 6, 13–17, 239–44.

25. Hart, *Concept of Law, supra* note 6, 117–23.

26. Hart, *Concept of Law, supra* note 6, 101.

27. Jules Coleman, *Practice of Principle* (Oxford: Oxford University Press, 2001), 179.

28. As Coleman and Simchen write, for example, "[o]ur understanding of what law is would be greatly diminished if we failed to appreciate law as providing content-independent reasons for action." Coleman and Simchen, "Law"*, supra* note 7, at 41.

29. Coleman and Leiter, "Legal Positivism" in *A Companion to Philosophy of Law and Legal Theory,* ed. by Dennis Patterson (Oxford: Blackwell, 1999 [1996]), 241–60, at 244. Raz and Hart recognize the importance of the immediate bonding of an individual with state institutions as the ultimate grounding of legitimacy. Raz, "Government by Consent" (1987) in *Ethics, supra* note 1, 355–69, at 366–69. For examples of Hart's reliance upon social bonding as the ultimate source of legitimacy, see Conklin, *Invisible Origins of Legal Positivism, supra* note 21, 215–22. However, once the leap into the modern centralized institutions has been made, legal units are considered content independent. See, e.g., Coleman and Leiter, "Legal Positivism" *ibid.,* 259; Coleman, "Constraints on the Criteria of Legality" in *Legal Theory* 6 (2000), 171–83, at 181.

30. See, e.g., Glanville Williams, *Learning the Law* (London: Sweet and Maxwell, 2002); Stephen Waddams, *An Introduction to the Study of Law* (Scarborough: Carswell, 2004).

31. Kant, *Critique of Practical Reason,* trans. by Lewis White Black (New York: Macmillan, 1956 [1788]).

32. Kant, *Grounding for the Metaphysics of Morals,* trans. by James W. Ellington, 3d. (Indianapolis: Hackett Publishing, 1993 [1785]).

33. H.G.W. Hegel, *Faith and Knowledge,* trans. by Walter Cerf and H. S. Harris (Albany: State University of New York Press, 1977 [1802]), 63–66.

34. This is the suggestion of Adriaan T. Peperzak, *Modern Freedom: Hegel's Legal, Moral, and Political Philosophy* (Dordrecht: Kluwer, 2001), at 34, fn 43 and 56–60.

35. Hart, *Concept of Law,* note 6, 13–17. See text, *supra* corresponding to note 24.

36. Joseph Raz does accept that there is room for the interpretation of a concept although "[l]egal philosophy merely explains the concept that exists independently of it." Raz, "Two Views of the Nature of the Theory of Law," *Ethics, supra* note 1, 280. Raz continues that "having a concept can fall well short of a thorough knowledge of *the nature of the thing* it is a concept of . . . [A] philosophical explanation . . . aims at improving [people's] understanding of *the concept* in one respect or another." Emphasis added but italics on first three words removed. There is a truth in the legal philosopher's project, according to Jules Coleman, but such a truth stands "at a greater distance or remove from experience than do other beliefs" such as synthetic claims. Coleman, "Methodology"*, supra* note 20, 344.

37.   Hart, *Concept of Law, supra* note 6, 15–17, 78–81.

38.   Also see, *supra* note 24. For Raz's adoption of this method, see how he approaches social and moral issues in his *Ethics in the Public Domain, supra* note 1. Also see Matthew H. Kramer, N. E. Simmonds, & Hillel Steiner, *A Debate over Rights: Philosophical Enquiries* (Oxford: Oxford University Press, 1998).

39.   See Raz, "On the Autonomy of Legal Reasoning" in *Ethics, supra* note 1.

40.   See Hegel, *The Jena System, 1804–5: Logic and Metaphysics,* trans. by John W. Burbidge & George di Giovanni (Kingston: McGill-Queens, 1986 [1804–05]), 53.

41.   Georg Hans Gadamer, *Truth and Method, supra* note 16.

42.   Max Horkheimer & Theodor Adorno, *Dialectic of Enlightenment,* trans. by John Cumming (New York: Continuum, 1972 [1944]). Also see Horkheimer, *Critique of Instrumental Reason,* trans. by Matthew J. O'Connell (New York: Seabury Press, 1974); Horkheimer, *Critical Theory: Selected Essays,* trans. by Matthew J. O'Connell (New York: Continuum, 1982 [1968]. Also see William E. Conklin, "The Legal Theory of Horkheimer and Adorno", *supra* note 8.

43.   This can best be located in PR 31–33.

44.   In his studies of the constitutions of Sparta, Crete, Carthage, and Athens in *The Constitution of Athens* (New York: Hafner, 1974 [1950]), Aristotle examines social practices, political practices, the distribution of wealth, the relations between the sexes, economic obstacles to access to office, the de facto relationship of one institution to another, the consequences and, finally, the objectives of legislation. These are just indicia of the unwritten constitution of each city-state. Aristotle evaluates the social practices in terms of who is a flourishing or complete person (*eudaimonia*]. The flourishing person in a particular city-state informs one of the end or *telos* of the persons in the society. That constitution is best where each citizen participates as a flourishing person.

45.   This social understanding of a constitution is best elaborated in Michael Salter & Julie J. A. Shaw, "Towards a Critical Theory of Constitutional Law: Hegel's Contribution" in *Journal of Law and Society* 21 (1994), 464–86.

46.   H.L.A. Hart takes this view in the "step" from the prelegal to the legal reality in *Concept of Law, supra* note 6, 94. For this interpretation of Hegel's climb up the ladder of civilization, see Howard P. Kainz, Hegel's *Philosophy of Right with Marx's Commentary: a Handbook for Students* (Hague: Martinus Nijhoff, 1974), 42.

47.   Alan Brudner, *Constitutional Facts* (Oxford: Oxford University Press, 2004), 302–09.

48.   Frederick Copleston, *A History of Philosophy* 9 vols. (New York: Doubleday, 1985), vol. 7, at 211.

49.   See, e.g., Leo Rauch, "Hegel, spirit and politics," in *The Age of German Idealism,* ed. by Robert C. Solomon and Kathleen M. Higgens (London: Routledge, 1993), 281; Jürgen Habermas, *The Philosophical Discourse of Modernity,* Frederick Lawrence trans. (Cambridge, MA: MIT Press, 1987), 39–41. Also see Habermas, *Theory and Practice* (Boston: Beacon Press, 1973).

50.   Joseph Raz for one has recognized this. See, e.g., Raz, "The Autonomy of Legal Reasoning" (1993) in Raz, *Ethics, supra* note 1, 335, 338–39.

51.   Raz, "Authority, Law and Morality" in *Ethics, supra* note 1, 210–37, at 237.

52.   See, e.g., Cicero, *De Republica* 5.5; *De Legibus* 1.17.

4. PERSONS, PROPERTY, CONTRACT, AND CRIME

1. Hegel expresses this generally in PR 41, 70.

2. As a consequence, Hegel begins *Philosophy of Right* where he had left off in *Phenomenology of Spirit*. Some commentators of Hegel's *Philosophy of Right* have missed this. See, e.g., Michel Rosenfeld, "Hegel and the Dialectics of Contract" in *Hegel and Legal Theory,* ed. by Drucilla Cornell, Michael Rosenfeld, David Gray Carlson (New York: Routledge, 1991), 228–57 at 236–39. [Cornell, *Hegel and Legal Theory*]. In *Phenomenology,* the philosopher begins with subjectivity and slowly becomes conscious of the objectivity of consciousness. The *Philosophy of Right* begins with the latter objectivity and eventually turns to subjectivity.

3. John Rawls, *A Theory of Justice* (Cambridge, Mass.: Harvard University Press, 1975 [1971]), 118–23.

4. Kant considered that a person, such as a slave, could become a thing. Accordingly, he introduced a third form of law, a *rem in personam* where, by virtue of legal status posited by the state such as occurred in classical Roman law, one had a right over another person (such as the master over the slave, the husband over the wife, the father over the child) against the world. The principle of noninterference intellectually encloaked such a relationship.

5. This idea goes hand in hand with the constitutional doctrine, recognized by *Campbell v. Hall* (1774) 1 Cowp. 204, 98 E.R. 1045, to the effect that the Crown gains title to lands of aboriginal peoples when the Crown takes possession of the land and implants a sign, such as the flag, into the land and then establishes outposts with soldiers to signify control of the territory. The seizure may be peaceful (as when the land is vacant or terra nullius) or openly violent (as when the territory is conquered by an army).

6. Gaius, *Institutes* 2.66, trans. with intro. by W. M. Gordon & O. F. Robinson with the Latin text by Seckel & Kuebler (London: Duckworth, 1988).

7. See, e.g., *Guerin v. The Queen,* [1984] 2 SCR 335. SCC. However, see *R. v. van der Peet* [1996] 2 SCR 507; 137 DLR (4th) 289 per Lamer CJC, para. 30. This principle has a deep constitutional heritage. See *Campbell v. Hall* (1774) 1 Cowp. 204, 98 E.R. 1045; (1774) Lofft 655; 98 ER 848; *Johnson and Graham's Lease v. M'Intosh,* (1823), 8 Wheaton 543, 21 US 240 per Marshall CJ at 573–74, 588; *St. Catherine's Milling and Lumber Co. v. The Queen* (1888), 14 App. Cas. 46, per Lord Watson at 55, 58; *Amodu Tijani v. Secretary, Southern Nigeria,* [1821] 2 AC 399, at 403 per Lord Haldane. Also see Francisco Vitoria, "On the American Indians" in Francisco de Vitoria, *Political Writings,* ed. by Anthony Pagden & Jeremy Lawrence (Cambridge: Cambridge University Press, 1991), 239–92 and Carl Schmitt, *The* Nomos *of the Earth,* trans. & annotated by G. L. Ulmen (New York: Telos, 2003), 130–38.

8. Walter Benjamin, "Critique of Violence" in Benjamin, *Reflections,* ed. with intro. by Peter Demetz (New York: Schocken, 1978), 277–300; Jacques Derrida, "Force of Law: 'The Mystical Foundation of Authority,'" trans. by Mary Quaintance, *Cardozo Law Review* 11 (1990), 919–1045. Also see text, *supra* Chapter 2 corresponding to fn 32.

9. Derrida, "Force of Law" *ibid.*; Fish, "Force" in *Doing what comes Naturally: Change, Rhetoric and the Practice of Theory in Literary and Legal Studies* (Durham, NC: Duke University Press, 1989), 503–24.

10. *Guerin v. The Queen* [1984] 2 SCR 335; 13 DLR (4th) 321.

11. See esp. Wood, in PR, 410–11, fn 3, 4.

12. Hegel explains how rights take form in *Phenomenology of Mind,* PM 488–502.

13. I especially draw this possibility from PR 35R, 57R, and 66R.

14. Also see PM 424–37; PS 178–119.

15. See generally, Adriaan T. Peperzak, *Modern Freedom* (Dordrecht: Kluwer, 2001), 260–63.

16. Edmund Husserl, *Logical Investigations* 2 vols. (New York: Humanities Press, 1970), vol. 2, Investigation VI, 711–12, 727.

17. That said, Hegel frames the concept of respect for persons in the context of time-consciousness.

18. Jürgen Habermas, *Theory and Practice* (Cambridge, MA: MIT Press, 1973), 126-27, 147–48; cf. Alan Brudner, "Hegel and the Crisis of Private Law" in Cornell, *Hegel and Legal Theory, supra* note 2, 127–73 at 140.

19. Cf. Alan Brudner, *The Unity of the Common Law* (Berkeley: University of California Press, 1995), 78.

20. Plato's claim of the need for communal property amongst the guardians and auxiliaries in *Republic* misses the relation of property with the intentional subject, according to Hegel. Plato could not come to terms with the free will that Socrates exhibited in his trial (PR 46R). In the *Laws,* 739b–c, Plato precludes the right to private property from other classes as well.

21. The aboriginal peoples of North America did not have property in their lands because they had no sense of private ownership or exclusivity that comes with property. This absence of personhood and private property may explain, in part, why Hegel considered them barbarians, although the central factor was that they did not have a centralized state, recognized by other states as such.

22. Frederick Neuhouser, "Introduction" in J. G. Fichte, *Foundations of Natural Right: According to the Principles of the* Wissenschaftslehre (Cambridge: Cambridge University Press, 2000), xxvi.

23. Hegel explains the nature of a contract best in PR 71–81.

24. This reading of Hegel differs from the general view offered by Jeremy Waldron in *The Right to Private Property* (Oxford: Clarendon, 1988), 267 that property relations exist between persons and other persons rather than between the appropriator and the object. Also see John Plamenatz in "History as the Realization of Freedom" in *Hegel's Political Philosophy: Problems and Perspectives,* ed. by Z. A. Pelczynski (Cambridge: Cambridge University Press, 1971), 30–51, at 41; and Shlomo Avineri, *Hegel's Theory of the State* (Cambridge: Cambridge University Press, 1972), 88–89. Renato Cristi's reading of Hegel's theory of property as a subjective possessive individualism erroneously reads possessive individualism into property relations at this stage of Abstract Right. However, possessive individualism requires the struggle of arbitrary wills of subjects, and this does not arise until Hegel's analysis of interpersonal relations in civil society. See Christi, *Hegel on Freedom and Authority* (Cardiff: University of Wales Press, 2005), 76–90.

25. An excessive damage involved a thing sold for less than half its true value. A stipulation was a formal promise to perform a contract, much as we might call

a letter of intent today. A consensual contract had a tacit sign of agreement such as the taking of possession or the planting of rocks for a boundary.

26. This is explained in detail in H. S. Harris, "Hegel's System of Ethical Life: an Interpretation" in G.W.H. Hegel, *System of Ethical Life* and *First Philosophy of Spirit* (part III of the System of Speculative Philosophy 1803/04), ed. & intro. by H. S. Harris & T. M. Knox (Albany: State University of New York Press, 1979), 38–41.

27. It is unclear whether a form of tort existed in Hegel's principality.

28. Fuller's phenomenological theory of contract is examined in Conklin, "The Phenomenology of Lon Fuller's Theory of Language" in *International J. for Semiotics of Law* 19 (2006), 93–125.

29. See generally, *Gaius Institutes, supra* note 6, 3.182.

30. Kant, *Metaphysical Elements of Justice,* trans. by John Ladd (New York: Macmillan Publishing Co., 1985 [1797]), 318, 229. [Kant, *Justice*].

31. Kant, *Justice, ibid.* line 318. Kant even raises this "strange and unexpected pattern in human affairs" in "What Is Enlightenment?" in *Kant's Political Writings,* trans. by Hans Reiss (Cambridge: Cambridge University Press, 1970 [1784]), 54–60, at 59.

32. Kant, *Justice, supra* line 323.

33. Kant, *Justice, supra* note 30, line 320.

34. "Now it is an essential *principle* for every use of reason to push its knowledge to the point where we are conscious of its *necessity* . . . It is an equally essential *limitation* of the same reason that it cannot have insight into the *necessity* either of what is or what happens, of what ought to happen, except on the basis of a *condition* under which it is or happens or ought to happen. In this way, however, the satisfaction of reason is merely postponed again and again by continual enquiry after a condition. Hence reason unrestingly seeks the unconditionally necessary and sees itself compelled to assume this without any means of making it comprehensible—happy enough if only it can find a concept compatible with this presupposition." Kant, *Groundwork of the Metaphysic of Morals,* trans. & analyzed by J. J. Paton (New York: Harper, 1964), line 463.

35. The subject may only complain of, not challenge, a sovereign's actions. To critique the head, one undermines the faith in the possibility of the foundation of metaphysics of law. The civil constitution represents a legitimacy that is "so holy and inviolable that it is a crime even to doubt it or suspend it for an instant." Kant, *Justice, supra* note 31, "General Remarks," line 319, p. 84. Judges and other legal officials must protect the external authorizing origin of legal legitimacy. As Kant states, "[t]he origin of supreme authority is, from the practical point of view, not open to scrutiny by the people who are subject to it; that is, the subject should not be overly curious about its origin as though the right of obedience due it were open to doubt (*jus controversum*)." Kant, *ibid.,* "General Remarks," line 318, p. 84. Humanly posited laws may punish, execute, or exile individuals if the latter "ruminate" about the origins of the legitimacy of a modern legal order. *Ibid.* line 319, pp. 84–85. The subject must passively accept the legitimacy of the posited legal norms. *Ibid.* line 317, pp. 82–83.

36. Hegel certainly urges the declining use of the death penalty (PR 101A).

37. I take the idea of rights as trumps from Ronald Dworkin in *Taking Rights Seriously* (Cambridge, MA: Harvard University Press, 1977), 205; and "Rights as Trumps" in *Theories of Rights,* ed. by Jeremy Waldron (Oxford: Oxford University Press, 1984), 153–67.

38. I take *Einzelheit* as "singularity" to better understand the term. The difference between *der Einzelne* and *das Individuum* is elaborated in Section 6 of Chapter 1.

5. LEGAL FORMALISM

1. Kant published the *Critique of Practical Reason* in 1781, *Metaphysical Elements of Justice* in 1797, and *Religion within the Limits of Reason Alone,* in 1793.

2. The critical passages in the PR are Pref., 3, 15A, 122–125, 136–141, & 211R.

3. See text, *supra* Chapter 1, Section 2 & chapter 3 fn 1.

4. See text, *supra* Section 6 of Chapter 3. Also see Raz, "On the Autonomy of Legal Reasoning" (1993) in Raz, *Ethics in the Public Domain* (Oxford: Clarendon Press, 1995), 326–40, at 339, 340.

5. The paragraphs in the PR with regards to this theme are Pref., 15, 29–30, 37–38, 40, 132–135, 141–157, 175R, 211R.

6. Hans Kelsen eventually takes up this notion of the "imputation" of a legal act. Hans Kelsen, *The Pure Theory of Law,* trans. M. Knight (Berkeley: University of California Press, 1967 [1st ed. in German, 1934]), 91, 26–27. See generally Conklin, "Kelsen on Norms and Language" in *Ratio Juris* 19 (2006), 101–26.

7. Kant, *Religion within the Limits of Reason Alone* (New York: Harper, 1960 [1794 2d. ed., 1793]), 88.

8. See Theodore M. Greene, "The Historical Context and Religious Significance of Kant's *Religion*" in Kant, *Religion, ibid.* p cxxx, fn 122.

9. Kant, *Metaphysical Elements of Justice,* trans. by John Ladd (New York: Macmillan, 1985), 223–25. [Kant, *Justice*].

10. Kant, *Justice, ibid.,* 330.

11. J. G. Fichte, *Foundations of Natural Right,* ed. by Frederick Neuhouser, trans. by Michael Baur (Cambridge: Cambridge University Press, 2000 [1796–97]); *The Vocation of Man,* trans. by William Smith with intro. by E. R. Ritchie (Indianapolis: Bobbs-Merrill, 1956 [1800]).

12. Kant, *Critique of Pure Reason,* trans. by Norman Kemp Smith (London: Macmillan Education, 1989), A327, B383.

13. Ronald Dworkin, *Law's Empire* (Cambridge, MA: Harvard University Press, 1986), 400–13.

14. Kant, *Critique of Pure Reason, supra* note 12, A 316–17, B 373–74.

15. Kant, *Justice, supra* note 9, 340.

16. Ronald Dworkin follows a similar avenue by positing a "law beyond law" or "pure narrative coherence" that can only be symbolized by a star and the like. See Dworkin, *Law's Empire, supra* note 13.

17. Kant, *Justice, supra* note 9, line 237.

18. Peter Gabel, "The Phenomenology of Rights-Consciousness and the Pact of the Withdrawn Selves" in *Texas Law Review* 62 (1984), 1563–99; "Reification in Legal Reasoning" in *Research in Law and Sociology* 3 (1980), 25–51; "Intention and Structure in Contractual Conditions: Outline of a Method for Critical Legal Theory" in *Minnesota Law Review* 61 (1977), 601–93.

19. David Harvey, "Cosmopolitanism and then Banality of Geographical Evils" in *Public Culture* 12 (2000), 529–64, at 532–36.

6. THE ETHICALITY OF AN ETHOS

1. Alan Brudner, *Constitutional Goods* (Oxford: Oxford University Press, 2004), 299.

2. Allen W. Wood is also of this opinion in *Hegel's Ethical Thought* (Cambridge: Cambridge University Press, 1990), 203. For his excellent explanation of Hegel's sense of "ethical life" in general (though without a legal context), see *ibid.* esp. 195–236.

3. Henry Jones, "Social Organism" in *The British Idealists,* ed. by David Boucher (Cambridge: Cambridge University Press, 1997), 3–29, at 9.

4. Aristotle, *Ethics* 1177a7–1178a5.

5. The key paragraphs where Hegel explains this are PR 104–114.

6. The key paragraphs related to blameworthiness are PR 115–28.

7. The theme of ethicality is best set out in PR 142–56.

8. See Emmanuel Levinas, *Otherwise than Being or Beyond Essence,* trans. by Alphonso Lingis (Dordrecht: Kluwer, 1974); "The Rights of the Other Man" in *Alterity and Transcendence,* trans. by Michael B. Smith (New York: Columbia University Press, 1999), 145–49; "Peace and Proximity" in *Alterity and Transcendence,* trans. by Michael B. Smith (New York: Columbia University Press, 1999), 131–44; "The Trace of the Other" in *Deconstruction in Context: Literature and Philosophy,* ed. by Mark C. Taylor (Chicago: University of Chicago Press, 1986), 345–59; "Humanism and An-archy" in E. Levinas, *Collected Philosophical Papers,* trans. by Alphonso Lingis (Dordrecht: Martinus Nijhoff, 1987), 127–39; "No Identity" in *Collected Philosophical Papers, ibid.,* 141–51.

9. Emmanuel Levinas, *God, Death and Time,* trans. by Bettina Bergo (Stanford: Stanford University Press, 1993 [1991]), 72, 133. Also see *Totality and Infinity,* trans. by Alphonso Lingis (Pittsburgh: Duquesne University Press, 1969), 102; "Franz Eisenzweig: A Modern Jewish Thinker" in Levinas, *Outside the Subject,* trans. by Michael B. Smith (Stanford; Stanford University Press, 1993), 49–66.

10. Emmanuel Levinas, "Ethics as First Philosophy" in *The Levinas Reader,* ed. by Seán Hand (Oxford: Blackwell, 1989), 74–87, at 76.

11. Emmanuel Levinas, *Otherwise than Being, supra* note 8, 83.

12. Emmanuel Levinas, "Ethics as First Philosophy" *supra* note 10, 77.

13. Emmanuel Levinas, "Being and the World" in *God, Death, and Time, supra* note 9, 131–35, at 133.

14. Emmanuel Levinas, "Infinity" in *Alterity and Transcendence, supra* note 8, 53–76, at 70.

15. Levinas, "The Prohibition against Representation and 'The Rights of Man'" in *Alterity and Transcendence, supra* note 8, 121–30, at 122–23.

16. Levinas, "Infinity" in *Alterity and Transcendence, supra* note 8, at 70.

17. As cited in Michael B. Smith, "Introduction" to Levinas, *Outside the Subject, supra* note 9, xxii, quoting from Malka, *Lire Levinas* 2 ed. (Paris: Les Editions du Cerf, 1989), 105. Also see Levinas, "Franz Eisenzweig" *supra* note 9, 49–66.

18. Levinas, "Franz Rosenzwig" *supra* note 9, 50, 64.

19. Meinecke also publicly supported the Third Reich, especially its antisemitic laws, although he became unpopular with the Nazis in 1935.

20. Dworkin describes the elements of the ethos excluded from legality in "Lord Devlin and the Enforcement of Morals" in *Yale Law Journal* 75 (1965–66): 986–1005; reprinted in *Morality and the Law,* ed. by Richard Wasserstrom (Belmont, Calif.: Wadsworth, 1971), 55–72. For Hart's exclusion of the ethos see "Immorality and Treason" in Wasserstrom, *Morality and the Law, ibid.,* 49–54, 51; "Positivism and the Separation of Law and Morals" in *Harvard Law Review* 91 (1958): 593–629, 629 and reprinted in *Society, Law and Morality,* ed. by Frederick A. Olafson (Englewood Cliffs, NJ: Prentice-Hall, 1961), 439–70, 469; *Concept of Law* 2nd ed. (Oxford: Clarendon Press, 1994), 57. Both Dworkin and Hart describe the ethos as "anthropological morality."

Lon Fuller attended to the importance of the prelegal as do Peter Fitzpatrick and Brian Z. Tamanaha. See generally, Peter Fitzpatrick, *Modernism and the Grounds of Law* (Cambridge: Cambridge University Press, 2001) [Fitzpatrick *Modernism*]; Fitzpatrick *Mythology of Modern Law* (London: Routledge, 1992) [Fitzpatrick, *Mythology*]; Brian Z. Tamanaha, *A General Jurisprudence of Law and Society* (Oxford: Oxford University Press, 2001); and Tamanaha, *Realist Socio-Legal Theory* (Oxford: Oxford University Press, 2001). Also see Conklin, "Lon Fuller's Phenomenology of Language" in *International J. for the Semiotics of Law* 19 (2006): 93–125;

21. Kant, *Grounding for the Metaphysics of Morals,* James W. Ellington trans., 3rd. ed. (Indianapolis: Hackett, 1993), 414, 439.

22. Jules Coleman, more than anyone today, has elaborated how legal "existence" is constituted from concepts and how the justification of the concepts draws one into an evaluation of the particular content of concepts. The latter evaluative inquiry, he claims, addresses "oughts." Coleman, "Methodology" in Jules Coleman and Scott Shapiro's *Oxford Handbook of Jurisprudence and Philosophy of Law* (Oxford: Oxford University Press, 2002), 311–51; and Coleman, *Practice of Principle* (Oxford: Oxford University Press, 2001).

23. Kant, "What is Enlightenment?" in *Kant's Political Writings,* trans. by H. B. Nisbet, ed. with intro. & Notes by Hans Reiss (Cambridge: Cambridge University Press, 1970 [1784]), 54–60, at 59.

24. Although Kant's view of the separation of law from morality permeates *Metaphysical Elements of Justice,* trans. by John Ladd (New York: Macmillan, 1985), perhaps a clearer exposition is in Kant, "On the Common Saying: 'This may be True in Theory, but it does not Apply in Practice'" in *Kant's Political Writings, ibid.,* 61–92, at 81–86.

25. This leads, in turn, to a particular shape of an international legal order which I shall retrieve in Chapter 10. In *Phenomenology of Spirit,* in contrast, Hegel

describes the culmination of self-consciousness in religion. The explanation for the two different movements from conscience is that Hegel focuses upon freedom in *Philosophy of Right*. In *Phenomenology of Spirit,* however, he aims to determine what kind of knowing could qualify as knowledge. See PR, White, p 121, fn 78.

26. Edmund Husserl, *Cartesian Meditations,* trans. by Dorion Cairns (Den Hague: Martinus Nijhoff, 1960); Emmanuel Levinas, *Totality and Infinity, supra* note 9; Bernhard Waldenfels, *Topographie des Fremden.* 4 vols. *Studien zur Phänomenologie des Fremden,* 2nd ed. (Frankfurt am Main: Suhrkamp Verlag, [1990] 1997) vol. 1.

27. See generally, PR 147, 158–68, 212A.

28. Raz implicitly raises love in the context of his remarks about social bonding as the basis of legitimacy, albeit a conception of legitimacy externally separate from legality as I explained in Chapter 3, fn 10. He exemplifies this with friendship. See Raz, "Government by Consent" in *Ethics in the Public Domain* (Oxford: Clarendon Press, 1995), 355–69, at 366–69 [Raz, *Ethics*]; *Authority of Law* (Oxford: Clarendon Press, 1979), 255. Also see Zen Bankowski, *Living Lawfully* (Dordrecht: Kluwer, 2001).

29. For the view that love, for Hegel, remains at the level of feeling, see Susan Moller Okin, "Women and the Making of the Sentimental Family" in *Philosophy and Public Affairs* 11 (1981), 65–88.

30. Duncan Kennedy and Peter Gabel, "Roll-over Beethoven" in *Stanford Law Review* 34 (1984), 1–55.

31. Hegel built his theological work on such a view of love as reconciling the beauty of Greek religion and the morality of Kant to produce a beauty of the heart. See Richard Kroner, "Introduction" in Hegel, *On Christianity: Early Theological Writings,* trans. by T. M. Knox (New York: Harper, 1948), 1–66, 9. Also see Andrew Priori, *Revolution & Philosophy: The Significance of the French Revolution for Hegel and Marx* (Cape Town: David Philip, 1972), 32–44.

32. The nexus of recognition with communication at this moment is best explained in Jürgen Habermas, *Theory and Practice* (Boston: Beacon Press, 1973), 146.

33. Jules Coleman argues that this sort of trust inculcates legal reasoning. Coleman carries this idea further when he suggests that legal reasoning presupposes a faith that reasons count in a deliberative process. Jules Coleman, "Authority and Reason" in *Natural Law,* ed. by Robert P. George. (Oxford: Clarendon Press, 1992), 287–319. Joseph Raz picks up this idea of loyalty, trust, and friendship as an analogy to explain the ultimate bonding needed for the legitimacy of laws. Joseph Raz, "The Obligation to Obey: Revision and Tradition" in *Ethics, supra* note 28, 341–54; "Government by Consent" in *Ethics, ibid.,* 355–69; "The Politics of the Rule of Law" in *Ethics, ibid.,* 370–78.

34. See esp. Alice Ormiston, *Love and Politics: Re-interpreting Hegel* (Albany: State University of New York, 2004), 78–80.

35. See generally, PR 142–155.

36. See, e.g., Michael Sandel, *Liberalism and the Limits of Justice* 2d. (Cambridge: Cambridge University Press, 1997 [1982]; Charles Taylor, *Philosophical Arguments* (Cambridge, Mass.: Harvard University Press, 1995), 249–56. See esp. Peter Fitzpatrick, *Mythology, supra* note 20, 192–97 and *Modernism, supra* note 20, 98–99.

37. Hart, *Concept of Law, supra* note 20, 94–95.

38. See generally, William E. Conklin, *The Invisible Origins of Legal Positivism* (Dordrecht: Kluwer, 2001), 248–69.

39. This is the view of both Habermas in *The Philosophical Discourse of Modernity* (Cambridge, MA: MIT Press, 1987), 36 and Emmanuel Levinas, *Alterity and Transcendence, supra* note 8, 70; "Ideology and Idealism" in Levinas, *Levinas Reader, supra* note 10, 235–48, at 245. I shall further address some such criticisms in the Conclusion chapter.

7. THE SHAPES OF FAMILY LAWS

1. Martin Heidegger develops the distinction esp. in *An Introduction to Metaphysics,* trans. by Ralph Manheim (New Haven, CT: Yale University Press, 1959), 14; "Modern Science, Metaphysics and Mathematics" in Heidegger, *Basic Writings,* ed. by David Farrell Krell (New York: Harper & Row, 1977), 243–82, esp. at 250. The idea that time and space are measurable dominated early Renaissance science. See Alexandre Koyre, "Plato and Galileo" in *Galileo Studies,* ed. by John Mepham (Hassocks: Harvester Press, 1978), 404; and "Galileo and the Scientific Revolution of the Seventeen Century" in *Philosophical Review* 52 (1943), 333–48. The measurable sense of time in the modern legal discourse is explained and described in William E. Conklin, *The Phenomenology of Modern Legal Discourse* (Aldershot: Dartmouth, 1998), esp. 103–33. [Conklin, *Phenomenology*].

Julia Kristeva especially describes the unmeasured and unmeasurable experienced time in a dialogic relation in "Word, Dialogue and Novel" in *The Kristeva Reader,* ed. by Toril Moi (Oxford: Basil Blackwell, 1986), 34–61, at 36–37. The possibility of experiential time in legal reasoning is developed in Conklin, "A Phenomenological Theory of the Human Rights of the Alien" in *Ethical Perspectives* 13 (2006), 245–301; and Conklin, *Phenomenology, ibid.* 135–68.

2. Hegel explains this notion in PR 157–162, PS 438–476.

3. See generally, Patricia Jagentowics Mills, "Hegel's *Antigone*" in *Owl of Minerva* 17 (1986), 131–52.

4. It would be consistent with the pyramidal structure of the state that only a male could be a monarch. For the pyramidal organization represents the patriarchal family as described, e.g., by Luce Irigaray in "The Eternal Irony of the Community" in *Speculum of the Other Woman* (Ithaca: Cornell University Press, 1985), 214–26. H. S. Harris is of the view that Hegel's use of the pronoun *him* is generic in intent.

5. This is expanded upon by Hegel in PS 457. See, e.g., Seyla Benhabib, "On Hegel, Women and Irony" in *Feminist Interpretations and Political Theory,* ed. by Mary Lynden Shanley and Carole Pateman (Cambridge: Polity Press, 1991), 129–45 [Shanley, *Feminist Interpretations*]; Valerie Kerruish, "Persons and Available Identities: Gender in Hegel's Philosophy of Law" in *Law and Critique* 7 (1996), 153–72.

6. The passages from Aristotle that support such a determinative sense of natural law are examined in Conklin, *Invisible Origins of Legal Positivism* (Dordrecht: Kluwer, 2001), 19–20. [Conklin, *Invisible Origins*].

7. See, e.g., Kerruish, "Persons and Available Identities", *supra* note 5, at 160–64.

8. Luce Irigaray, *Speculum of the Other Woman* (Ithaca: Cornell University Press, 1985), esp. 218: "she becomes the voice, the accomplice of the people, the slaves, those who only whisper their revolt against their masters secretly." The woman lacks a voice to articulate her case in the ethical life. As a consequence, women have no development as a self-conscious will. Also see John N. Findlay, *Hegel: A Reexamination* (London: Allen and Unwin, 1958), 553.

9. For the former, see Carole Pateman, "Hegel, Marriage, and the Standpoint of Contract" in Shanley, *Feminist Interpretations, supra* note 5, 209–23. For the latter, see Jacques Derrida, *Glas,* trans. by John P. Leavey Jr. and Richard Rand (Lincoln: University of Nebraska Press, 1986), 113.

10. See, e.g., Heidi M. Ravven, "Has Hegel Anything to Say to Feminists?" in Mills, *Feminist Interpretations, supra* note 5, 225–52, at 230–32; Frances Olsen, "Comments on 'Lucinde's Shame'" in Shanley, *Feminist Interpretations, supra* note 5, 109–17, at 116, fn 13; Mills, "Hegel's *Antigone*", *supra* note 3; Seyla Benhabib, "On Hegel, Women and Irony" in Shanley, *Feminist Interpretations, supra* note 5, 129–45.

11. See Luce Irigaray, "The Necessity of Sexuate Rights" in *The Irigaray Reader,* ed. by Margaret Whitford (Oxford: Blackwell, 1991), 198–203. Also see, Irigaray, "Sexual Difference" in *French Feminist Thought,* ed. by Toril Moi (Oxford: Basil Blackwell, 1995; 1987), 118–30.

12. See, e.g., H.L.A. Hart, *Concept of Law,* 2nd ed. (Oxford: Clarendon, 1994, [1961]), 58–61, 91–92, 94–95,140.

13. *Ibid.* 58–61, 91–92.

14. This claim is argued in Conklin, *Invisible Origins, supra* note 6, 21–26. Aristotle, following Plato in the *Laws,* writes of natural justice as a second nature when he says that natural justice is "everywhere having the same force" (*Ethics* 1134b 24–25) and as contingent (it "does not exist by people's thinking this or that" *Politics* VII, 7, 1334b 18–19). Without such an immediacy between an individual and the state, inculcated by education, the state will not be sustained as a community (*Politics* II, 5, 1263b 36–37).

15. See generally, Martin Heidegger, *Early Greek Thinking: The Dawn of Western Philosophy,* trans. by David Farell Krell & Frank A. Capuzzi (Cambridge: Harper and Row, 1984; 1975), 79–101. Also see, Erwin Schrödinger, *Nature and the Greeks* (Cambridge: Cambridge University Press, 1954), 1–31. Commentators often miss this difference between such a presence or immediacy on the one hand and the representative character of the written laws of the city on the other. See, e.g., Gilbert Murray who argues that the gods are cognitive creations of divine worshippers. Murray, *Five Stages of Greek Religion,* 3rd ed. (New York: Doubleday Anchor Books, 1951), 29. Also see Roland Barthes, who argues in "Myth Today" in *Mythologies* (Paris: Edition du Seuil, 1957) that myths are connotative stories that represent the experiences of the figures without honoring the lived experience of the listener who brings meaning into the story.

16. The archaic family is examined at PR 144A, 166R, PS 440–443, 450, 464. I describe the tribal family archaic even though the term *archaic* is associated with the Greek polis in contemporary exhibitions of Greek art.

17. H. and H. A. Frankfort, "Myth and Reality" in Frankfort, John A. Wilson, & Thorkild Jacobsen, *Before Philosophy: The Intellectual Adventures of Ancient Man* (Harmondsworth: Penguin, 1949), 29–36.

18. See A. C. Bradley, "Hegel's Theory of Tragedy" in *Hegel on Tragedy,* ed. by Anne Paolucci and Henry Paolucci (Garden City, New York: Doubleday, 1962), 367–88; Jean-Pierre Vernant, *Myth and Society in Ancient Greece,* trans. by Janet Lloyd (Atlantic Highlands, N.J.: Humanities Press, 1974), 12. Also see R. P. Winnington-Ingram, *Sophocles: An Interpretation* (Cambridge: Cambridge University Press, 1980), 150–55.

19. The family in civil society is examined in PR 169–77, 262–63.

20. See generally, Bruce W. Frier & Thomas A. J. McGinn, *A Casebook on Roman Family Law* (Oxford: Oxford University Press, 2004), 18.

21. This contrasts with the Roman law which did not allow the son to become a legal person. As a consequence, according to Hegel, the son could be sold (PR 180A) or killed (PR 180A) at the hands of the father. Daughters were excluded from inheritance. Hegel did not distinguish the presently accepted different periods of Roman law as identified by present-day scholars of Roman law.

22. This image of the family is elaborated in PR 262–65.

23. Hegel best describes the ethnic nation in PR 181R, 274, 279R, 336–37, 344–51.

24. Laurence Dickey and H. B. Nisbet, "Editorial Notes" in Hegel, *Political Writings,* ed. by Dickey & Nisbet (Cambridge: Cambridge University Press, 1999), fn 99 at p. 295.

25. H. S. Harris, "Hegel's System of Ethical Life: An Interpretation" in Harris, *Hegel's System of Ethical Life* (Albany, N.Y.: State University of New York Press, 1979), 3–96, at 48.

26. Charles Taylor, "Nationalism and Modernity" in *The State of the Nation: Ernest Gellner and the Theory of Nationalism,* ed. by John A. Hall (Cambridge: Cambridge University Press, 1998), 191–218. For a critique of the civic nation see Bernard Yack, "The Myth of the Civic Nation" in *Critical Review* 10 (1996), 193–211.

27. See text, *supra* Chapter 2, sect. 2(b).

28. Lucretius, *De rerum natura,* trans. by R. E. Latham, rev'd with intro. by John Godwin (London: Penguin, 1994), Bk V.

29. William E. Conklin, *Invisible Origins of Legal Positivism, supra* note 6, 80–82.

30. See, e.g., John Locke, *The Second Treatise of Government* ed. by C. B. Macpherson (Indianapolis: Hackett, 1980 [1690]), para. 52, 79, 80, 86. Rousseau claims that the family is the first political society after human beings develop from savagery. *Social Contract* in *Social Contract and Discourses,* trans. with intro. by G.D.H. Cole (New York: Evertyman's Library, 1913), Bk 1, ch 2, p. 8.

31. Hart, *Concept of Law, supra* note 12, 88.

32. Hart, *Concept of Law, supra* note 12, 87. Emphasis added.

8. THE LAWS OF CIVIL SOCIETY

1. Contemporary general jurisprudence remains preoccupied with the relationships of rights and duties. See, e.g., Matthew Kramer, N.E. Simmonds, and Hillel Steiner, *A Debate Over Rights* (Oxford: Oxford University Press, 1998).

2. Wesley Newcombe Hohfeld, "A Vital School of Jurisprudence" in *Fundamental Legal Conceptions,* ed. by Walter Wheeler Cook (Westport: Greenwood, 1978 [1919]).

3. John Stuart Mill, *On Liberty,* ed. by Mary Warnock (Glasgow: William Collins, 1962 [1869]); *Principles of Political Economy,* ed. by Donald Winch (London: Penguin, 1970 [1848].

4. Adriaan Peperzak suggests that this is not so. He describes the subject of civil society as a *Mensch* (human being) whom he contrasts with the abstract person of Abstract Right of property, contract, and crime and with the intentional subject of morality in Part II of the *Philosophy of Right.* Peperzak, *Modern Freedom* (Dordrecht: Kluwer, 2001), 435. Civil society, I submit, marks the continued separation of abstract persons as holders of legal rights on the one hand and subjects as intentional moral actors on the other. Persons are only equal by virtue of their emptiness. We cannot speak of human beings as equal human beings until the third domestic form (the organic legal order) of *Sittlichkeit.*

5. Hegel distinguishes the bourgeois from the citizen in his lectures (1817/18 72R.89, 89R.113; 1822/24 W147). The *bourgeois* is an inhabitant of a market town (*bourg*). To have trading privileges, the bourgeois has to be a member of an association. The member seeks his self-interest in the association. A citizen, in contrast, is a member of the state.

6. Isaiah Berlin, "Two Concepts of Liberty" in *Four Essays on Liberty* (Oxford: Oxford University Press, 1969), 118–72.

7. I describe the human being here as an "it" because the being is purged of all intentionality and exists only as a legal person as defined by rights and duties posited in the objectivity of consciousness.

8. See generally, Andrew Arato, "A Reconstruction of Hegel's Theory of Civil Society" in *Hegel and Legal Theory,* ed. by Drucilla Cornell et al. (New York: Routledge, 1991), 301–20, at 303–07.

9. See generally, Francis Herbert Bradley, "My Station and its Duties" in *Ethical Theories: A Book of Readings,* ed. by A. I. Melden, 2nd ed. (Englewood Cliffs: Prentice-Hall, 1967 [1876]), 393–424.

10. One has to have faith, as Raz points out, to cement the essential sense of belonging. Raz, "Government by Consent" (1987) in *Ethics in the Public Domain* (Oxford: Clarendon Press, 1995), 355–69, at 366–69. Raz writes that he draws the importance of trust from Hart's claim that individuals bond with institutions in internal statements. See Raz, *ibid.* 368, fn 10.

11. Hegel's exposition of the nuclear family in civil society is best gleaned from PR 238–40, 262–63.

12. Renata Selecl, *The Spoils of Freedom: Psychoanalysis and Feminism after the Fall of Socialism* (London/New York: Routledge, 1994).

13. See generally, PR 188, 250–55.

14. Hegel suggests elsewhere that the estate is second in importance to the family. PR 201A.

15. I have in mind the reaction of law deans and law faculty members in North America to the Critical Legal Studies Movement during the late 1970s and early 1980s. See generally, Paul D. Carrington, "Of Law and River" in *J. Legal Educ.* 34 (1984), 22–228. Correspondence by Peter W. Martin, Robert W. Gordon, Paul

Brest, Philip E. Johnson, Louis B. Schwartz, William van Alstyne, Guido Cala-
bresi, & Owin M. Fiss re Carrington, "'Of Law and River,' and of Nihilism and
Academic Freedom" in *J. Legal Educ.* 35 (1985), 1–26. The issues are placed in a
fictitious, yet realistic, context at the time and eventually published in Conklin,
"The Trap" in *Law and Critique* 13 (2002), 1–28.

16. See generally, PR 199–207.

17. The externality of the state in civil society is best set out in PR 256, 258, 262.

18. The taxation and welfare function of the external state is examined in PR
241–45.

19. International contracts are discussed at PR 247–48.

20. I use the term *public authorities* rather than *police* (Hegel uses the term
Polizei) because the *Polizei* performed far more activities than what we associate
with the police today. Hegel understands the "police" as entertained in the *Prussian General Legal Code* of 1794: that is, as an administrative authority in a market
economy. See Allen W. Wood, *PR*, p. 450.

21. Max Horkheimer and Theodor W. Adorno, *Dialectic of Enlightenment,*
trans. by John Cumming (New York: Continuum, 1982 [1944]); Horkheimer,
"The End of Reason" in *The Essential Frankfurt Reader,* ed. by Andrew Arato &
Eike Gebhardt with Intro. by Paul Piccone, (New York: Continuum, 1982), 26–
48; Horkeimer, "On the Problem of Truth" in *Reader, ibid.,* 407–43; Horkheimer,
Critical Theory, trans. by Matthew J. O'Connell (New York: Seabury, 1972).

22. See generally, PR 208–29.

23. See Raz, *Authority of Law* (Oxford: Clarendon, 1977), 22–25, 234–37; *Practical Reason and Norms,* 2nd ed. (Princeton: Princeton University Press, 1990),
141–46; "Reasons for Action, Decisions and Norms" in Raz ed., *Practical Reasoning* (Oxford: Oxford University Press, 1978), 128–43.

24. As noted by Wood from Hegel's 1819–20 lectures in PR p. 447, note 2.

25. Max Weber takes up this point. See generally, Anthony T. Kronman, *Max
Weber* (Stanford: Stanford University Press, 1983), 182–88.

26. See generally, PR 211–29.

27. Cf. Jacques Derrida, "Sending: On Representation," trans. by Peter and
Mary Ann Caws in *Social Research* 49 (1982), 295–326. See Conklin, "The Trace of
Legal Idealism in Derrida's Grammatology" in *Philosophy and Social Criticism* 22
(1996), 129–73.

28. PR 216R, "Le plus grand ennemi du bien c'est le mieux."

29. *Hegel and the Human Spirit,* trans. by Leo Rauch (Detroit: Wayne State
University Press, 1983), 232, 237.

30. As translated and quoted by H. B. Nisbet in PR p. 444, fn 1 of PR para. 198.

31. The most perceptive source in this respect is Georg Lukács, "Reification
and the Consciousness of the Proletariat" in *History and Class Consciousness,* trans.
by Rodney Livingston (Cambridge, MA: MIT Press, 1968), 83–222.

32. Peter Gabel, "The Phenomenology of Rights-Consciousness and the Pact
of the Withdrawn Selves" in *Texas Law Review* 62 (1984), 1563–99; "Reification in
Legal Reasoning" in *Research in Law and Sociology* 3 (1980), 25–51. Also see, Isaac
D. Balbus, "Commodity Form and Legal Form: An Essay on the 'Relative Autonomy of Law'" in *Law & Society* Rev. 11 (1977), 571–88.

33. For an understanding of how the state could be considered abstract, see Alexandro Passerin d'Entrèves, *The Notion of the State* (Oxford: Clarendon, 1967).

9. CONSTITUTIONAL SHAPES AND THE ORGANIC CONSTITUTION

1. See generally, PR 258, 273, 279–81.

2. Coke was Chief Justice of the Common Pleas from 1606–13 and of the King's Bench from 1613–16. Early-seventeenth-century English constitutionalism was marked by the rise of (or perhaps undermining of the former) judicial independence. With some reconstruction, and indeed creation, of English case law, Coke retrieved the constitution from the unwritten conventions of centuries past. See e.g., *Prohibitions del Roy* (1608), 12 Co. Rep. 63, 77 E.R. 1342 (K.B.); *Case of the Lords President of Wales and York* (1609), 12 Co. Rep. 50, 77 E.R. 1331 (K.B.); *Case of Proclamations* (1610), 12 Co. Rep. 74, 77 E.R. 1352 (K.B.); *Dr. Bonham's Case* (1610), 8 Co. Rep. 113b, 77 E.R. 638 (K.B.). Also see 1 *Coke Inst.* 282b; 2 *Coke Inst.* 51, 74; 3 *Coke Inst.* 111; 4 *Coke Inst.* 41. Thomas Hobbes summarizes the judicial appeal to the fundamental laws at the time in *A Dialogue between a Philosopher and a Student of the Common Laws of England,* ed. by & with intro. by Joseph Cropsey (Chicago: University of Chicago Press, 1971).

3. Ronald Dworkin, *Taking Rights Seriously* (Cambridge, MA: Harvard University Press, 1978); "Rights as Trumps" in *Theories of Rights,* ed. by Jeremy Waldron (Oxford: Oxford University Press, 1984), 153–67.

4. Ronald Dworkin, "Liberalism" in *Public and Private Morality,* ed. by Stuart Hampshire (Cambridge: Cambridge University Press, 1978), 113–43, at 127.

5. Cf. Joel Feinberg, *Social Philosophy* (Englewood Cliffs, NJ: Prentice-Hall, 1973), 55–97.

6. Hegel addresses this form of a constitution throughout his *Philosophy of Right*, See, e.g., PR Pref., 31–32, 211, 212R, 258R, 258 fn, 316.

7. In *Bentham and the Common Law* (Oxford: Clarendon Press, 1986), 240, Gerald Postema quotes from an unpublished manuscript from Bentham as stating that "[t]he obedience paid to any particular law rests ultimately on a circumstance extrinsic to all Laws, a *general habit of obedience*" (Bentham's emphasis). For problems arising from John Austin's reliance upon the indeterminacy of habits of obedience as the source of legitimacy of laws properly so-called, see W. L. Morrison, *John Austin* (Stanford: Stanford University Press, 1982), 82–83. Also see William E. Conklin, *Invisible Origins of Legal Positivism* (Dordrecht: Kluwer, 2001), 142–70.

8. See, e.g., *Patriation Reference* (*Reference re Amendment of the Constitution, Nos.* 1, 2, 3), [1981] 2 SCR 793; 140 DLR (3d) 385. Interestingly, the Supreme Court of Canada, in *Reference re Secession of Quebec* [1998] 2 S.C.R. 217, dissolves the distinction and holds that what it formerly considered "moral" or unwritten principles were now binding.

9. Oscar Schachter, *International Law in Theory and Practice* (Hague: Martinus Nijhoff, 1991).

10. Hegel, "On the English Reform Bill" in Hegel, *Political Writings*, ed. by Laurence Dickey & H. B. Nisbet (Cambridge: Cambridge University Press, 1999), 234–70, 239.

11. *Ibid.*

12. *Ibid.* 238–40.

13. Hegel's view of an organic constitution can best be drawn from PR 257–261, 269–273, 301–303.

14. Hegel especially works out the idea of an organic constitution in PR 12R, 259, 271, 302.

15. As described by Wood at p. 458, fn 1 of para 269.

16. This reminds one of Durkheim's organic metaphor of the state as the thinking brain of society. See Roger Cotterrell, *Émile Durkheim* (Edinburgh: Edinburgh University Press, 1999), 28, 222–27.

17. Jacob von Uexkull, *Theoretical Biology*, trans. by D. L Mackinnon (London: Kegan Paul, 1926); "A Theory of Meaning" in *Semiotica* 92 (1982), 25–82.

18. Georg Lukács, "Reification and the Consciousness of the Proletariat" in *History and Class Consciousness*, trans. by Rodney Livingstone (Cambridge, MA: MIT Press, 1968), 83–222; Karel Kosik, *Dialectics of the Concrete* (Dordrecht: D. Reidel, 1976; Boston Studies in the Philosophy of Science v. 52).

19. Francois Jacob, *The Logic of Life; A History of Heredity*, trans. by Betty E. Spillman (New York: Vintage, 1982 [1973]), 9.

20. Léon Brillouin, "Life, Thermodynamics and Cybernetics" in *American Scientist* 37 (1949), 554–68.

21. See Erwin Schrodinger, *What is Life? Mind and Matter* (Cambridge: Cambridge University Press, 1967).

22. "There is no such thing as either man or nature now, only a process that produces the one within the other and couples the machines together." Gilles Deleuze, & Felix Guattari, *Anti Oedipus: Capitalism and schizophrenia,* trans. by Robert Hurley, Mark Seem, & Helen R. Lane with Pref. by Michel Foucault (Minneapolis: University of Minnesota Press, 1983), 2; *A Thousand Plateaus: Capitalism and Schizophrenia,* trans. & fwd. by Brian Massumi (Minneapolis: University of Minnesota Press, 1987).

23. Carl Schmitt, *The Crisis of Parliamentary Democracy* trans. by Ellen Kennedy (Cambridge, MA: MIT Press, 1988 [1923, 1926]); *The Concept of the Political,* trans. with intro. by George Schwab, fwd. by Tracey B. Strong & notes by Leo Strauss (Chicago: University of Chicago Press, 2007 [1932]); *Political Theology,* trans. by George Schwab with fwd. by Tracy B. Strong (Chicago: University of Chicago Press, 1985 [1922]); *Legality and Legitimacy,* trans. & ed. by John R. McCormick (Durham: Duke University Press, 2004 [1932]). Giorgio Agamben, *State of Exception,* trans. by Kevin Attell (University of Chicago Press, 2004).

24. See Schmitt, *Political Theology, ibid.* 3, 13, 15, 19–22. Schmitt notes that this contrasts with Kelsen's objectivism in *Political Theology, ibid.* 29.

25. See generally, *In re Board of Commerce Act, 1919 and the Combines and Fair Practices Act, 1919* [1922] 1 AC 191, 60 DLR 513 (PC), aff'g (1920), 60 SCR 456, 54 DLR 354; *Fort Francis Pulp and Paper Company v. Manitoba Free Press Company* [1923] AC 695, [1923] 3 DLR 629 (PC); *Toronto Electric Commissioner v. Snider* [1925] AC 396, [1925] 2 DLR 5 (PC), reversing [1924] 2 DLR 761 (CA). Haldane had been heavily influenced by Hegelians at Oxford when he was a student. See generally, Stephen Wexler, "The Urge to Idealize: Viscount Haldane and the Constitution

of Canada" in *McGill, L. J.* 29 (1970), 55–69; Jonathan Robinson, "Lord Haldane and the British North America Act" in *University of Toronto L. J.* 20 (1970), 55–69; Conklin, *Phenomenology of Modern Legal Discourse* (Aldershot: Dartmouth, 1998), 125–31, 136–40. [Conklin, *Phenomenology*].

26. See text chap. 2, *supra* at fn. 20.

27. See Philip Schofield, "Jeremy Bentham, The Principle of Utility, and Legal Positivism" in *Current Legal Problems* 56 (2003), 1–39.

28. Hegel's theory of the intermediate organizations is best gleaned from PR 270, 270A, 276, 303–309.

29. Jürgen Habermas picks up on this idea in his well-known idea of the public sphere in eighteenth-century England where private persons, unaffiliated with the feudal state and the market, gathered together to discuss issues of common concern. The state had to be accountable to such a public body as well as committed to the deliberative process of the public sphere, infused as it was with intermediate social organizations that Hegel describes as important elements of an organic legal order. See Habermas, *Between Facts and Norms: Contributions to a Discourse Theory of Law and Democracy,* trans. by William Tehg (Cambridge, MA: MIT Press, 1996), 150; *The Structural Transformation of the Public Sphere* (Cambridge, Mass.: MIT Press, 1991).

30. Hegel, *On the Philosophy of History* in Hegel, *On Art, Religion, and the History of Philosophy,* ed. by J. Glenn Gray & intro. by Tom Rockmore (Indianapolis: Hackett, 1997), 207–317, at 262–66.

31. Even course offerings these days may be a response to opinion polls, sometimes more subtly called "teacher evaluations," which represent the arbitrary wills of students. The absence of the history of legal thought in the curriculum of most Anglo-American law schools reinforces the entertainment theory of legal education.

32. See esp. Max Horkheimer and Theodor W. Adorno, *Dialectic of Enlightenment,* trans. by John Cumming (New York: Continuum, 1982 [1944]); Horkheimer, *Critical Theory,* trans. by Matthew J. O'Connell (New York: Seabury, 1972); Horkheimer, *Critique of Instrumental Reason,* trans. by Matthew J. O'Connell (New York: Seabury Press, 1974).

33. See generally, PR 269, 271, 278, 280.

34. I use the term *symbol* differently from a *sign*. A sign represents an object. The individual is immediately bonded with a symbol.

35. T. M. Knox raises the importance of the association of the two concepts in Knox, p. 364, fn 9.

36. Hegel's theory of the bureaucracy resembles the later exposition by Max Weber. See, e.g., Max Weber, "Bureaucracy" in *From Max Weber: Essays in Sociology* (London: Routledge & Kegan Paul, 1970); J.E.T. Eldridge, ed. & intro. *Max Weber: The Interpretation of Social Reality* (New York: Scribners, 1971), 53–70; David Beetham, *Max Weber and the Theory of Modern Politics* (London: Polity, 1985), 63–94.

37. Michel Foucault, "Governmentality" in *The Foucault Effect: Studies in Governmentality,* ed. by Graham Burchell, Colin Gordon, & Peter Miller (Chicago: University of Chicago Press, 1991), 87–104. Also see his "Two Lectures" in *Power/*

Knowledge: Selected Interviews & Other Writings, 1972–1977, ed. by Colin Gordon (New York: Pantheon, 1980), 91–97.

38. Hegel frequently cites Montesquieu. See generally, Charles de Montesquieu, *The Spirit of the Laws,* ed. by Anne M. Cohler et al. (Cambridge: Cambridge University Press, 1989 [1748]). Federalism appears to enter the history of legal philosophy in the 1830s with John Austin's lectures.

39. Hegel writes that "one of the chief moments in a child's upbringing is discipline, the purpose of which is to break the child's self-will in order to eradicate the merely sensuous and natural. One should not imagine that kindness alone is sufficient for this purpose" (PR 174A).

40. The best study of the separation of powers and the role of the estates and the peoples in government is Z. A. Pelczynski, "Introduction" in *Hegel's Political Writings,* trans. by T. M. Knox (Oxford: Oxford University Press, 1964), 122–27.

41. For Hegel's theory of the Executive arm of the state see generally, PR 273, 287–93, 296–97.

42. See generally, PR 298–314.

43. Marx, "Critique of Hegel's Philosophy of the State" (1843) in *Writings of the Young Marx on Philosophy and Society,* ed. & trans. by Lloyd D. Easton & Kurt H. Guddat (Garden City, NY: Doubleday/Anchor Books, 1967), 151–202, at 172–74. [*Writings of the Young Marx*]; "Contribution to the Critique of Hegel's *Philosophy of Right*" in *The Marx-Engels Reader,* ed. by Robert C. Tucker, 2nd ed. (New York: Norton, 1978), 16–25, 19–21.

44. Hegel's view of the monarch is best gleaned from PR 265–67, 272–74, 275–86.

45. Renato Cristi seems to miss this symbolic function of the monarch. The symbolic function contrasts with the idea of the monarch as a de facto author of posited laws. See Christi, *Hegel on Freedom and Authority* (Cardiff: University of Wales Press, 2005).

46. See generally, Marx, "Critique of the Philosophy of the State" in *Writings of the Young Marx, supra* note 43, at 166–67.

47. Knox, "Introduction" in *Hegel's Political Writings, supra* note 10, 127.

48. Karl Marx thinks that the de facto ruler is the monarch. Marx, "Critique of Hegel's Philosophy of the State", *supra* note 43, 172; "Contribution to the Critique", *supra* note 43, 19.

49. See generally, Alan Brudner, "Constitutional Monarchy as the Divine Regime: Hegel's Theory of the Just State" in *History of Political Thought* 2 (1981), 119–40.

50. See generally, PR 279R, 293, 295.

51. See generally PR 303–14.

52. Marx, *The German Ideology* in Tucker, *Marx-Engels Reader, supra* note 43, 147–200, at 166, 167.

53. The state competes with intermediate social organizations, according to Schmitt. See Carl Schmitt, *Concept of the Political, supra* note 23, 44. The state exists above the social. See *ibid.* 24. The state is presupposed to have external social relationships below it. See *ibid.* 25. The state, not subjectivity, decides. See *ibid.* 52.

54. Hegel associates slavery with such an anomaly. It is unclear that the anomaly is the refusal to recognize the legitimacy of the state or that the state tolerates excluded groups such as slaves and Quakers.

55. As noted earlier, Fries claimed that the Jewish people formed a state, not a mere nation. But, as shared by many today, only a nation with a monologic ethnicity could be institutionalized as a state. "Jews can be *subjects* of our government, but as Jews they can never become *citizens* of our people, for as Jews they want to be a distinct people, and so they necessarily separate themselves from our German national community."

56. Schmitt, *The Crisis of Parliamentary Democracy, supra* note 23, 56–8; *The Concept of the Political, supra* note 23, 63; *Political Theology, supra* note 23, 29.

57. David Kolb, *The Critique of Pure Modernity* (Chicago & London: University of Chicago Press, 1986), 238.

58. John Rawls, for example, assumes that the reconciliation of objectivity with subjective freedom in the organic constitution, which he takes to end the movement of self-consciousness, differs from liberalism. See John Rawls, *Lectures on the History of Moral Philosophy,* ed. by Barbara Herman (Cambridge, Mass.: Harvard University Press, 2000), 360. Also see Errol E. Harris in "Hegel's Theory of Sovereignty, International Relations, and War" in *Hegel's Social Thought: The Philosophy of Objective Spirit,* ed. by Donald Phillip Verene (Atlantic Highlands, NJ: Humanities Press, 1980), 137–49; and see Henry Paolucci, "Hegel and the Nation-State System of International Relations" in *Hegel's Social Thought, ibid.,* 151–66. Cf. J. N. Findley, *Hegel: A Re-examination* (London: George Allen & Unwin; New York: Humanities Press, 1958), 333, where Findley erroneously complains that Hegel did not account for other forms of international law. I shall argue otherwise in my next chapter.

59. John Rawls, *A Theory of Justice* (Cambridge, MA: Harvard University Press, 1973).

60. E. Tugendhat, *Self-consciousness and Self-Determination,* trans. P. Stern (Cambridge, MA: MIT Press, 1986), 315.

61. Knowles, "Hegel's Citizen" in *Bulletin of Hegel Soc. Grt Br.* (2004) no. 49–50, 41–53, at 49.

62. *Ibid.* 50.

63. Frederick Neuhouser, *Foundations of Hegel's Social Theory* (Cambridge: Cambridge University Press, 2000), 240–80.

64. *Ibid.* 240.

65. Jürgen Habermas, "Hegel's Concept of Modernity" in Habermas, *The Philosophical Discourse of Modernity,* trans. by Frederick Lawrence (Cambridge, MA: MIT Press, 1987), 23–44, at 39–40. Emphasis added.

66. Schmitt, *Crisis of Parliamentary Democracy, supra* note 23, 56–58.

67. Karl Popper, Open Society and its Enemies 2 vols. (London: Routledge, 1962).

68. For the U.S.A. state of exception doctrine see Conklin, *Phenomenology, supra* note 25, 76–83, 146–55. For the Canadian adoption of the state of exception see Conklin, "The Transformation of Meaning: Legal Discourse and Canadian

Internment Camps" in the *International J. for Semiotics of Law* 9 (1996), 227–56.; Conklin *Phenomenology, supra* note 25, 138–40. Also see citations, *supra* fn 25. Also see *Reference re Anti-Inflation Act,* [1976] 2 SCR 373; 68 DLR (3d) 452 per Laskin C.J.C.

69. 999 U.N.T.S. 171, [1980] ATS 23, Ca. T.S. 1976 No. 47.

70. The executive decision remains reviewable in the courts. The state's executive must "show" evidence that there is an emergency and that the emergency is tantamount to war or insurrection or a plague. In ordinary circumstances, the rights to property and contract are preserved as the dominant universals as is the invisible hand of the market. So too, the division of the state into federal units may remain protected.

71. See, e.g., Hart, *Concept of Law,* ed. with Postscript by Penelope A. Bulloch & Joseph Raz, 2d. (Oxford: Clarendon Press, 1994 [1961]), 213–37. It is remarkable, though consistent with the externalization of the foundation of legitimacy in the arbitrary will of the state, that contemporary general jurisprudence warrants so little commentary about the nature of international law.

72. Schmitt, *The* Nomos *of the Earth in the International Law of the* Jus Publicum Europaeum, trans. & annotated by G. L. Ulmen (New York: Telos, 2006).

73. See Schmitt, *Concept of the Political, supra* note 23, 63; *Crisis of Parliamentary Democracy, supra* note 23, 56.

74. See esp. Schmitt, *Concept of the Political, supra* note 23, 25, 34–5, 62–63; *Political Theology, supra* note 23, 29.

75. Schmitt, *Concept of the Political, supra* note 23, 63, 24–25

76. Giorgio Agamben, *Homo Sacer: Sovereign Power and Bare Life,* trans. by Daniel Heller-Roazen (Stanford: Stanford University Press, 1998 [1995]), 21; *State of Exception, supra* note 23, 36–37.

77. See esp. Schmitt, *Concept of the Political, supra* note 23, 63.

78. Hegel, 1831 addition to lectures in *Vorlesungen über die Philosophie der Religion,* ed. by Georg Lasson (reprint Hamburg 1966 [Leipzig 1925–29]), as quoted in Hegel, *Lectures on the Philosophy of Religion, One Volume Edition: The Lectures of 1827,* ed. by Peter C. Hodgson; trans. by R. F. Brown, P. C. Hodgson, & J. M. Stewart with assistance of H. S. Harris (Berkeley: University of California Press, 1988), at 484, fn 250.

79. *Ibid.* at 488, fn 265.

10. SHAPES OF INTERNATIONAL LAW

1. The key texts are PR 330–340, 279, 360; and PH.

2. Kant, "Perpetual Peace" in *Kant's Political Writings,* ed. with intro. and notes by Hans Reiss (Cambridge: Cambridge University Press, 1970), 93–130.

3. Hugo Grotius, *Law of war and peace, including the law of nature and of nations,* trans. with notes and illustrations from political and legal writers by A. C. Campbell, with intro. by David J. Hill (Washington & London: M. W. Dunne, 1901 [1609]). Vattel has been known to have ignored the latter and, like Kant, to have claimed that international law is an "ought" except to the extent that a state consents to a constraining norm through a treaty. Vattel, *The Law of Nations or the*

Principles of Natural Law, 3 vols. Trans. Charles G. Fenwick with intro. by Albert de Lapradelle (Washington: Carnegie Institution, 1916 [1756]); Classics of International Law) vol. 3. Also see, Samuel Pufendorf, *On the Law of Nature and of Nations in Eight Books* in *The Political Writings of Samuel Pufendorf,* ed. by Craig L. Carr, trans. by Michael J. Seidler (New York: Oxford University Press, 1994); *Elements of Universal Jurisprudence in Two Books* (1658), Book 1 in *Political Writings ibid.,* Bk 1; *De Jure Naturae et Gentium Libri Octo* (1688), ed. by C. H. Oldfather & W. A. Oldfather (Oxford: Clarendon, 1934), Bk 1–8. Also see, Christian Freiherr von Wolff, *The Law of Nations treated according to a scientific method,* intro. & trans. by Francis J. Hemett; text trans. by Joseph H. Drake (Oxford: Oxford University Press, 1934 [1738–39]; Classics of International Law no. 13).

4. Kant, "Perpetual Peace,", *supra* note 2, 96.

5. See, e.g., Cicero, *De Officiis* 3.69, 3.23.

6. Kant, "Perpetual Peace", *supra* note 2, 99 fn. John Stuart Mill later takes up this idea. It remains with us today to the suffering of displaced and stateless inhabitants. Mill argues that a state is free unless it causes harm to another state. See Mill, "A Few Words on Non Intervention" in *Essays on Equality, Law and Education,* with intro. by Stephan Collini in *Collected Works of J. S. Mill,* ed. by John Robson, 33 vols. (Toronto: University of Toronto Press, 1984), vol. 2, 111–24.

7. Kant, "Perpetual Peace," *supra* note 2, 99 fn.

8. Kant, "Perpetual Peace," *supra* note 2, 99, fn.

9. Kant, "Perpetual Peace," *supra* note 2, 103.

10. Kant, "Perpetual Peace," *supra* note 2, 105.

11. Kant, "Perpetual Peace," *supra* note 2, 108.

12. Kant, "Perpetual Peace," *supra* note 2, 108.

13. Schmitt makes the same point regarding the League and humanitarianism more generally. See, e.g., *The Concept of the Political,* trans. with intro. by George Schwab, fwd. by Tracey B. Strong & notes by Leo Strauss (Chicago: University of Chicago Press, 2007 [1932]), 53–58.

14. Adriaan Peperzak emphasizes this distinction at several points in his *Modern Freedom* (Dordrecht: Kluwer, 2001), 601–03, although I disagree with his association of Absolute Spirit and the Christian God.

15. See Grotius, *Law of War and Peace, supra* note 3.

16. Hegel, *Philosophy of Fine Art,* trans by F.B.P. Osmaston, 4 vols. (New York: Hacker, 1975), vol 1, p. 250. Interestingly, as I noted in Chapter 2, H.L.A. Hart picks up this terminology to artificially differentiate a modern from a premodern legal order.

17. This restates Hegel's postulate that self-consciousness must leap from the prelegal to the legal world of thinking beings. Until relatively recently at least, treaties entered into by the British state with aboriginal tribes in North America were not binding for this very reason. See, e.g., *Cherokee Nation v. State of Georgia* (1831) 30 US 1; *R. v. Marshall* [1999] 3 SCR 456; 177 DLR (4th) 513, para. 47, 48.

18. See generally, PR 181R, 274, 279R, 336–337, 344–351.

19. Hegel best describes the family in this second context in PR 339A, 340.

20. Lucretius, *De Rerum Natura,* trans. by W.H.D. Rouse (Cambridge, MA: Harvard University Press, 1949), Book 5. 1011–13.

21. Hegel likens ethical life to a plant whose organic elements are individuals in a whole. Hegel, *System of Ethical Life,* ed. and trans. by H. S. Harris & T. M. Knox (Albany: State University of New York, 1979), 108–09 [422–28].

22. It is not a coincidence that Article 38(1)(c) of the Statute of the International Court of Justice recognizes an important source of international law as "the general principles of civilised nations."

23. It is apparent from my earlier chapters that Hegel's most important assumption is his acceptance that the desire to become self-conscious is imminent in each human being.

24. Indeed, in *On Art, Religion and the History of Philosophy: Introductory Lectures,* ed. by J. Glenn Gray; intro. by Tom Rockmore (Indianapolis: Hackett, 1997), at 303–04, Hegel claims that there had only been two epochs with such a monologic nation: the Greek and the Teutonic.

25. As cited in PR 331A.

26. Hard sovereignty is best described in PR 320–29.

27. The head, as representative of the state-person in international law, offers an added reason why a constitutional monarch or some semblance of such a monarch, such as the president of the United States or the governor-general of Canada, is needed in a domestic organic constitutional order.

28. Carl Schmitt, *The* Nomos *of the Earth: in the International Law of the* Jus Publicum Europaeum, trans. with annotations by G. L. Ulmen (New York: Telos, 2006 [1974]), 129.

29. Schmitt, *Concept of the Political, supra* note 13, 51.

30. Schmitt, *Concept of the Political, supra* note 13, 29 fn 9.

31. Schmitt, *Concept of the Political, supra* note 13, 28–35.

32. Carl Schmitt, *Political Theology,* trans. by George Schwab with fwd. by Tracy B. Strong (Chicago: University of Chicago Press, 1985 [1922]), 12–3.

33. Schmitt, *Political Theology, ibid.* 1, 12. It is not a coincidence in this respect that Haldane's and Schmitt's idea of the state of exception was formed during the post–World War I period when the arbitrary will of the state had reached its pinnacle in public international law. This was evidenced, e.g., by the lack of enforcement of the Minorities Treaties after World War I by the European states.

34. See, e.g., *Johnson v. M'Intosh* (18230, 8 Wheaton 543, 21 US 240, at 573–74, 588 of Wheaton, per Marshall, C. J. Also see *Worcester v. State of Georgia* (1832), 6 Peters 515, 31 US 530, per Marshall, C. J.

35. *Vorlesungen über Rechtsphilosophie,* ed. K.-H. Ilting (Stuttgart: Frommann Verlag, 1974), vol. 4, 732 as quoted in PR p. 473.

36. Schmitt elaborates this as the norm of international legal consciousness in *Concept of the Political, supra* note 13, 33. Hans Morgenthau and Henry Kissinger were influenced by Schmitt's theory of the monadic state. Morgenthau, *Politics among Nations: The Struggle of Power and Peace* (New York: Knopf, 1948); Kissinger, *The Necessity for Choice* (New York: Harper, 1961). See Tracey B. Strong, "Foreword: Dimensions of the New Debate around Carl Schmitt" in *Concept of the Political, supra* note 13, ix–xxxi, xxiii, fn 42.

37. This shape of the international legal order is best elaborated in PR 181R, 274, 279R, 336–37, 344–51.

38. Bernard Yack, "The Myth of the Civic Nation" in *Critical Review* 10 (1996), 193–211; Charles Tilly, "The State of Nationalism" in *Critical Review* 10 (1996), 299–306; Benedict Anderson, *Imagined Communities: Reflections on the Origins and Spread of Nationalism* (London: Verson, 1991).

39. Hegel best describes the relation of a treaty to this form of international law in PR 330–37.

40. This shape of international law is best described in PR 338–40.

41. However, Adriaan Peperzak suggests otherwise in *Modern Freedom, supra* note 14, 583, 588. However, nationalism is not the highest dimension of *Sittlichkeit*. To the contrary.

42. See generally PR 341–60.

43. Carl Schmitt best represents this particular shape of the international legal consciousness. See, e.g., Schmitt, *Concept of the Political, supra* note 13, 51, 63.

44. "World history is the world's court of judgement" comes from Schiller's poem "Resignation." White, PR, p. 257, fn 93.

45. Henry Jones, "The Coming of Socialism" in *British Idealists,* ed. by David Boucher et al. (Cambridge: Cambridge University Press, 1997), 195–213, at 212.

46. Also see T. H. Green, "The Right of the State over the Individual in War" in *British Idealists, ibid.* 217–36, at 236. However, another British Hegelian argued that the conflagration of World War I was due to the failure of the state to fulfill its duties to inhabitants rather than to some absence of an explicit federation of states in an international organization. See Bernard Bosanquet, "The Function of the State in Promoting the Unity of Mankind" in *British Idealists, ibid.* 270–95, at 289.

47. See generally, PR 35R, 57R, 66A, 66R, 67, 261R.

48. Hegel, "Lectures on the Philosophy of History (1827–1831), part IV, section 3: The New Age" in Hegel, *Political Writings,* ed. by Laurence Dickey & H. B. Nisbet; trans. by H. B. Nisbet (Cambridge: Cambridge University Press, 1999), 197–224, at 198.

CONCLUSION

1. Jürgen Habermas, *Between Facts and Norms: Contributions to a Discourse Theory of Law and Democracy,* trans. by William Tehg (Cambridge, MA: MIT Press, 1996), 150. Also see Habermas, *The Structural Transformation of the Public Space* (Cambridge, MA: MIT Press, 1991).

2. Such problems are generally raised in James Bohman, *Public Deliberation, Complexity and Democracy* (Cambridge, MA: MIT Press, 1996).

3. For a critique of Habermas's historical analysis see Nancy Fraser, "Rethinking the Public Sphere: A Contribution to the Critique of Actually Existing Democracy" in *Habermas and the Public Sphere,* ed. by Craig Calhoun (Cambridge, MA: MIT Press, 1999), 109–42, at 116. [Calhoun, *Habermas*].

4. The public sphere offered societal transformation. See Geoff Eley, "Nations, Publics and Political Cultures: Placing Habermas in the Nineteenth Century" in Calhoun, *Habermas, ibid.* 289–339, at 291. Habermas now accepts that many intermediate publics existed concurrently in the public space of the time. See Habermas, "Further Reflections on the Public Sphere" in Calhoun, *Habermas, ibid.,* 422–61.

5. Indeed, Shlomo Avineri is of the opinion that the intermediate organizations possess no universal interests. See Avineri, *Hegel's Theory of the Modern State* (Cambridge: Cambridge University Press, 1972), 18.

6. Hans Kelsen explains that the public-private duality privileges the state to be above the law. The state looms as an externality over the rules that address private matters. As an externality, the state can become absolute as if it were "political" and, therefore, immune from judicial scrutiny. See Kelsen, "God and the State" in *Essays in Legal and Moral Philosophy* (Dordrecht: Reidel, 1973), 61–82.

7. See text *supra* Chapter 1 at fn 2.

8. Hegel is not alone here. One can find a similar sense of justice presupposed in John Rawls's *A Theory of Justice* (Cambridge, MA: Harvard University Press, 1999 [1971]); in Ronald Dworkin's "sense of integrity" in *Law's Empire* (Cambridge, MA: Harvard University Press, 1986), and in "The Original Position" in *Reading Rawls: Critical Studies on Rawls'* A Theory of Justice, ed. by Norman Daniels (Oxford: Basil Blackwell, 1975), 16–53; and in Kant's admission that his theory of morality only concerns those who desire to be moral. See Kant, *Grounding of the Metaphysics of Morals,* trans. by James W. Ellington, 3rd ed. (Indianapolis: Hackett Publishing, 1993), at line 463.

9. As noted in Chapter 2, fn 30, one identifies immediately with a symbol. A symbol has a presence which affects the experiential body. A sign represents an object, including other signs.

10. Stanley Fish, *Is There a Text in this Class? The Authority of Interpretative Communities* (Cambridge, MA: Harvard University Press, 1980); *Doing What Comes Naturally: Change, Rhetoric and the Practice of Theory in Literary and Legal Studies* (Durham, NC: Duke University Press, 1989).

11. Jacques Derrida, for example, distinguishes between the constitution of law and the interpretation of law. Derrida, "Force of Law: The 'Mystical Foundation of Authority,'" trans. by Mary Quaintance in *Cardozo Law Review* 11 (1990), 919–1045. Contrary to Hegel, Derrida argues that, once constituted violently, legal interpretation continues to be violent.

12. In explaining the retrospective character of legitimacy as well as in the interpretation of particular rules of a legal order, Hart writes that "[t]he truth may be that, when courts settle previously un-envisaged questions concerning the most fundamental rules, they *get* [his emphasis] their authority to decide them accepted *after* [my emphasis] the questions have arisen and the decision has been given. Here all that succeeds is success." H.L.A. Hart, *Concept of Law* 2nd ed. (Oxford: Clarendon Press, 1994), 153.

13. Levinas, "Ethics as First Philosophy" in *The Levinas Reader,* ed. by Sean Hand (Oxford: Blackwell, 1989), 75–87, at 82.

14. See generally, Conklin, "Statelessness and Bernhard Waldenfels' Phenomenology of the Alien" in *British J. Phenomenology* 38 (2007), 280–96.

15. See generally, text, *supra,* chap. 2 at fn 39.

16. See generally, Peter Singer, *Expanding Circle: Ethics and Socio-biology* (New York: Farrar, Straus & Giroux, 1981); Singer, *One World: The Ethics of Globalization* (New Haven: Yale University Press, 2002); *Great Ape Project: Equality Beyond Hu-*

manity, ed. by Paola Cavalier & Peter Singer (New York: St. Martin's Press, 1994); Singer, *In Defence of Animals: The Second Wave* (Malden, MA: Blackwell, 2006).

17. As quoted in Avineri, *Hegel's Theory, supra* note 5, 64, quoting from a fragment in the Jena period from *Hegel-Studien* vol. 4, p. 14.

18. So too, it is like Ronald Dworkin's "law beyond law" nested as it is internal to the rationality of the legal narrative. For Dworkin, the "law beyond law" cannot be accessed through knowledge or language. Ronald Dworkin, *Law's Empire* (Cambridge, MA: Harvard University Press, 1986).

19. Anglo-American legal thought is less open into an inquiry concerning the legitimacy of binding laws. For each of Rousseau, Hobbes, H.L.A. Hart, Hans Kelsen, and Joseph Raz takes for granted the invisible character of the legitimacy of binding laws. See generally, Conklin, *Invisible Origins of Legal Positivism* (Dordrecht: Kluwer, 2001). Also see, Conklin, "The Invisible Author of Legal Authority" in *Law and Critique* 7 (1996), 173–92; and "The Secret Foundation of Sovereignty in Legal Positivism" in *Rechtstheorie Beiheft* 17 (1998), 83–92.

20. [1827]. *Lectures on the Philosophy of Religion, One-Volume Edition, The Lectures of* 1827, ed. by Peter C. Hodgson, trans. by R. F. Brown, P. C. Hodgson, & J. M. Stewart, with the assistance of H. S. Harris (Berkeley: University of California Press, 1988), p. 484, lines 264–65.

21. The term *invisibility* is examined in Conklin, *Invisible Origins, supra* note 19, 37–55.

22. I develop this notion of territorial knowledge in Conklin, "A Phenomenological Theory of the Human Rights of the Alien" in *Ethical Perspectives* 13 (2006), 245–301.

23. Lon Fuller shares such a sense of experiential time. See generally, Conklin, "Lon Fuller's Phenomenology of Language" in *International J. for Semiotics of Law* 19 (2006), 93–125.

24. There were about eleven million human beings living in the alleged "prelegal" North American territory categorized by British lawyers as *terra nullius* when the thinking beings arrived in North America. Incidentally, this is one more example of how Hegel's thinking being is abstracted from the experiential being of the prelegal world.

25. Indeed, Carl Schmitt has traced the very idea of territoriality in public international law through European legal philosophy from the Greeks until the interwar period. Schmitt, *The* Nomos *of the Earth: In the International Law of the* Jus Publicum Europaeum, trans. with annotations by G. L. Ulmen (New York: Telos, 2006 [1974]). Giorgio Agamben also presupposes that legal knowledge is territorial and that the state is situated in territorial space. See, e.g., Agamben, *Homo Sacer,* trans. by Daniel Heller-Roazen (Stanford, CA: Stanford University Press, 1998 [1995]), 19, 36–37.

26. Bernhard Waldenfels, *Topographie des Fremden.* 4 vols. *Studien zur Phänomenologie des Fremden* 2nd ed. (Frankfurt am Main: Suhrkamp Verlag, [1990] 1997) vol. 1, at 123.

27. Hart, *Concept of Law, supra* note 12, 87.

Further Reading

Further reading concerning Hegel's legal philosophy needs to begin with the historical and intellectual currents before and during Hegel's lifetime. The best English-language exhaustive studies, with excellent primary sources, are Terry Pinkard's *Hegel: A Biography* (Cambridge: Cambridge University Press, 2000) supplemented with his *German Philosophy, 1760–1860: The Legacy of Idealism* (Cambridge: Cambridge University Press, 2002). More general introductory essays are helpful in Karl Americks's *Cambridge Companion to German Idealism* (Cambridge: Cambridge University Press, 2000). More detailed overviews are Frederick C. Beiser's *Enlightenment, Revolution and Romanticism: The Genesis of Modern German Political Thought, 1790–1800* (Cambridge: Cambridge University Press, 1992) and *Fate of Reason: German Philosophy from Kant to Fichte* (Cambridge: Cambridge University Press, 1993). Important background contributions are also Joachim Ritter's *Hegel and the French Revolution: Essays on the Philosophy of Right* (Cambridge, MA: MIT Press, 1982) and Manfried Riedel's *Between Tradition and Revolution* (Cambridge: Cambridge University Press, 1984).

Three further background sources are suggested. Hegel's vocabulary can best be gleaned from Michael Inwood's *A Hegel Dictionary* (Oxford: Blackwell, 1992). H.S. Harris offers the best short overview of the *Phenomenology of Spirit* in *Hegel: Phenomenology and System* (Indianapolis: Hackett, 1995). Duncan Forbes's "Introduction" to Hegel, *Lectures on the Philosophy of World History: Introduction: Reason in History*, trans. by H. B. Nisbet (Cambridge: Cambridge University Press, 1975) offers an excellent overview of Hegel's philosophy of history.

The main source of further reading about Hegel's legal philosophy concerns commentaries about Hegel's *Philosophy of Right*. Merold Westphal's *Hegel, Freedom and Modernity* (Albany: State University of New York, 1992) provides a general overview of key themes in Hegel's text. Dudley Knowles's *Hegel and the* Philosophy of Right (London: Routledge, 2002) offers an exegetical introduction. The themes of freedom, the family, civil society, the state, and Hegel's very idea of political philosophy are retrieved and analyzed in Paul Franco's *Hegel's Philosophy of Freedom* (New Haven & London: Yale University Press, 1999). Renato Christi criticizes Hegel's possessive individualism and monarchal constitutionalism in

Hegel on Freedom and Authority (Cardiff: University of Wales Press, 2005). Commentaries about Hegel's ethical and social philosophy are important for Hegel's theory of ethicality, the family, civil society, and the organic legal order. See, especially, Allen W. Wood's *Hegel's Ethical Thought* (Cambridge: Cambridge University Press, 1990), Robert P. Williams's *Hegel's Ethics of Recognition* (Berkeley: University of California Press, 1997); Frederick Neuhouser's *Foundations of Hegel's Social Theory* (Cambridge, MA, & London: Yale University Press, 2000); and Michael O. Hardimon's *Hegel's Social Philosophy: The Project of Reconciliation* (Cambridge: Cambridge University Press, 1994). Neuhouser examines the subjective and objective elements of freedom. Hardimon explains how reconciliation, rather than conflict, leads to Hegel's view of the state. Continental secondary sources can be found in Adriaan T. Peperzak's excellent exegesis in *Modern Freedom: Hegel's Legal, Moral, and Political Philosophy* (Dordrecht: Kluwer, 2001), and Alan Brudner compares and contrasts Hegel's legal philosophy with Anglo-American political and legal theory in *Constitutional Goods* (Oxford: Oxford University Press, 2004).

The above readings need to be supplemented by commentaries about Hegel's philosophy of logic. In this regard, Richard Dien Winfield's *Reason and Justice* (Albany: State University of New York, 1988) offers the best accessible overview. David Gray Carlson's *A Commentary to Hegel's* Science of Logic (New York: Palsgrave Macmillan, 2007), with the aid of diagrams and excellent secondary sources, offers a clause-by-clause analysis of Hegel's major logic text.

Hegel's privileging of the family can best be gleaned from a series of essays in *Feminist Interpretations and Political Theory*, ed. by Mary Lyndon Shanley and Carole Pateman (Cambridge: Polity Press, 1991) as well as in the Salter and Lamb anthologies noted below. Essays by Selya Benhabib and Patricia Mills are required reading. Alice Ormiston's *Love and Politics: Re-interpreting Hegel* (Albany: State University of New York Press, 2004) connects Hegel's theory of the family to Hegel's sense of ethicality.

Against the above readings, one can turn to more technical analyses of the many diverse themes from Hegel's works. These are reprinted in a series of anthologies, the most important of which are edited by Michael Salter in *Hegel and Law* (Aldershot: Dartmouth Publishing, 2003) and by Drucilla Cornell, Michel Rosenfeld, and David Gray Carlson in *Hegel and Legal Theory* (New York: Routledge, 1991). The latter includes important contributions to private law as well as classic essays by Theunissen, Bernasconi, Weinrib, and Brudner. Further essays on Hegel's views on crime, the family, women, and other themes are reprinted in David Lamb's *Hegel*, 2 vols. (Aldershot: Ashgate, 1998). Contemporary contributions about Hegel's legal and political philosophy take for granted important earlier anthologies edited by Alasdair MacIntyre in *Hegel: A Collection of Critical Essays* (Notre Dame, IN: Notre Dame University Press, 1976), by Donald Phillip Verene in *Hegel's Social and Political Philosophy* (Atlantic Highlands, NJ: Humanities, 1980), and by A. A. Pelczynski in *The State and Civil Society: Studies in Hegel's Political Philosophy* (Cambridge: Cambridge University Press, 1989) and in *Hegel's Political Philosophy: Problems and Perspectives: A Collection of New Essays* (Cambridge: Cambridge University Press, 1971). Further diverse essays on political, social, and moral philosophy are reprinted in Robert Stern's four-volume *G. W. F. Hegel: Critical Assessments* (London: Routledge, 1993). Stern's two excellent Introductions in volume one offer important overviews of the contemporary literature.

Index

Abstract right, 113–14; actuality 151; arbitrary will 231; contract 131; crime 144; ethicality 178; first moment 170; intentionality 137; international 271, 278–83, 285–89; Kant 155–56; nature 164; objectivity 125, 138, 144; property 114, 123; reasoning 230. *See also* World history

Actuality, 29–33, 52–56; inverted world, 86–90; organic, 244, 269, 287; performance, 135–37; reasoning, 91–94; rights, 236–38; *Vernunft,* 107; *Verstand,* 95–99

Agamben, Giorgio, 62, 245, 266, 342n9

Animal-human dichotomy, 30, 58–61, 146, 313–15; freedom, 152–53; hierarchy, 64–65; natural being, 71, 191–93; nature, 120; property, 126. *See also* Barbarian, Master-slave

Anthropological: morality, 47, 172, 231, 248, 299, 340n30; knowledge, 9, 38, 57, 108–10, 155, 241, 262. *See also* Ethnic nation

Antigone, 71–74, 189, 192–97

Antiquity, 29, 57, 108, 175

Apology, 36–37, 80, 150, 270

Barbarian, 61–64; legal order, 65–66; levels, 64–65; progress, 66–70

Being. *See* Immediacy

Bentham, Jeremy, 242, 248, 363n7

Blameworthiness, 62, 137, 165–67

Bildung, 14, 27–29, 35, 81; bonding 185; constitution 246; education, 27–29, 234, 250–53, 257, 295; formalism 152;

international 204, 221; *Vernunft* 104, 119; women 191. *See also* Education

Bureaucracy, 68, 92–93, 106, 254, 314; formalism, 227, 250; legitimacy, 223; problematic, 314, 315

Cicero, 111, 253, 272

Civic nation, 202–3, 206, 275–77, 284, 288, 297, 324

Civil society, 178–79, 195, 231–32; ethicality, 212–13; ethos, 214–15; family, 189–90, 196–201, 215–16; intermediate organizations, 215–18; international law, 283–87; legal reasoning, 225–31; legitimacy, 223–25; objectivity, 207; 210–12; progress into, 66, 109–10; state, 194, 219; subjectivity, 209–10; women, 191. *See also* Legitimacy

Coke, Edward, 236, 242, 363n2

Coleman, Jules, 349n36, 356n22. *See* General jurisprudence

Concept, 54

Concepts: difference, 98; interaction of, 97; representation 97–98; self-standing, 94–97.

Constitutional law: a priori rights, 236–38; contract, 238–40; externality, 234–41; historicist, 241–43; intermediate associations, 248–51; legitimacy, 240–41; organism, 243–54; original intent, 234–36; public education, 251–53; social

Jurists: Profiles in Legal History

GENERAL EDITOR

William Twining

Lightning Source UK Ltd.
Milton Keynes UK
UKHW012050281220
375546UK00022B/266/J